Praise for *Head First Learn to Code*

"This is one of the most surprising, entertaining and brilliantly-planned software books [...] It's more interesting and better thought-out than all other beginning programming boo[...] together. I run into people all the time who need to learn programming and want to know what course to take; I plan to tell them to forget about courses and get this book instead."

— **David Gelernter, Professor of Computer Science, Yale** [...]

"*Head First Learn to Code* has humor, emotions, and step by step instructions. [...] brain, makes you laugh and teaches you to be a code master—it's a ke[...]"

— **Smore Magazine, a science magazine to know more a[...]**

"The book is a great read, even for an experienced programmer, with new pe[...] difficult concepts we take for granted. Whether your just starting out or trying to figure out ways to bring more people to code, this book will serve you well. Eric has made learning to code accessible and approachable without dumbing anything down and setting the expectations of effort and difficulty that actually exist."

— **Avi Flombaum, Dean and Chief Product Officer of the Flatiron School**

"As a high school computer science teacher, *Head First Learn to Code* is my new primary resource for introducing topics to students. It has an immensely personal touch and its conversational nature, humor, and general style make it feel as if you are learning from another human rather than merely reading a piece of text."

— **Brandon Shufflebarger, Regents School of Austin**

"This is the book I wish would have been around when I first started learning to code. Unlike other beginner's programming books, Freeman strikes a perfect balance of humor, concise tutorials, and helpful background information—without sounding condescending or overly technical. *Head First Learn to Code* will certainly be a valuable resource for beginning coders at our school fablab."

— **Patrick Benfield, Innovation Director, The Magellan International School**

"It takes talent and creativity to write in such an accessible manner. I am looking forward to using the book next school year in an introductory course. I became enthralled with the relevant and accessible examples that were substantive rather than the typical irrelevant and superficial examples presented to the reader of a typical text on the subject."

— **Josh Sharfman, Teacher, Shalhevet Advanced Studies, Computer Science**

"In keeping with a book about a language named for Monty Python, there's a lot of meta-humor here about the software industry, about programmer culture, and about tutorial books themselves. It's nice to be reminded that coding takes place in the (sometimes illogical) world of humans."

— **Adjunct Professor of Music Technology at NYU and Montclair State University**

"As a National Champion Rock Band Coach, I understand that students must feel inspired by a subject in order to consistently practice and enjoy themselves in the process. Without inspiration and joy, people eventually lose focus and enthusiasm. That's why good teachers are so valuable to our society. They can break a potentially boring complex subject, like learning code, down into easily digestible, delicious nuggets of fun. As and educator, Eric Freeman is masterful. He shows us how learning can be simple, enjoyable and easily retainable."

— **James Mays, Director, Band Aid School of Music**

"HFL2C is a pleasurable, entertaining and effective way to learn computational thinking and python basics. The book has strong pedagogical underpinnings, an exciting array of learning activities and is well written in a fun and conversational tone that is approachable and breaks down complex computational concepts in an easy, digestible way."

— **Troy Welch, Coordinator, Innovations, Thompson Rivers University**

Praise for other books by Eric Freeman

"I feel like a thousand pounds of books have just been lifted off of my head."

— **Ward Cunningham, inventor of the Wiki**

"The admirable clarity, humor and substantial doses of clever make it the sort of book that helps even non-programmers think well about problem-solving."

— **Cory Doctorow, co-editor of Boing Boing, Science Fiction author**

"Freeman continues to use innovative teaching methods for communicating complex concepts to basic principles."

— **Mark Arana, Strategy & Innovation, The Walt Disney Studios**

"I can think of no better tour guide than Eric."

— **Miko Matsumura, VP of Marketing and Developer Relations at Hazelcast Former Chief Java Evangelist, Sun Microsystems**

"The definitive book on HTML5 for everyone from beginners to experienced developers."

— **Aaron LaBerge, CTO, ESPN**

"The highly graphic and incremental approach precisely mimics the best way to learn this stuff..."

— **Danny Goodman, author of *Dynamic HTML: The Definitive Guide***

"Eric clearly knows his stuff. As the Internet becomes more complex, inspired construction of web pages becomes increasingly critical. Elegant design is at the core of every chapter here, each concept conveyed with equal doses of pragmatism and wit."

— **Ken Goldstein, former CEO of Shop.com and author of *This is Rage: A Novel of Silicon Valley and Other Madness***

Other O'Reilly books by Eric Freeman

Head First HTML and CSS

Head First JavaScript Programming

Head First HTML5 Programming

Head First Design Patterns

Other books in O'Reilly's *Head First* series

Head First HTML and CSS

Head First JavaScript Programming

Head First HTML5 Programming

Head First Design Patterns

Head First Servlets and JSP

Head First Java

Head First Python

Head First
Learn to Code

Wouldn't it be dreamy if there was a book for learning to code that was more fun than going to the dentist and more revealing than an IRS form? It's probably just a fantasy...

Eric Freeman

Beijing · Boston · Farnham · Sebastopol · Tokyo    O'REILLY®

Head First Learn to Code

by Eric Freeman

Printed in the United States of America.

Published by O'Reilly Media, Inc., 1005 Gravenstein Highway North, Sebastopol, CA 95472.

O'Reilly Media books may be purchased for educational, business, or sales promotional use. Online editions are also available for most titles (*http://oreilly.com/safari*). For more information, contact our corporate/institutional sales department: (800) 998-9938 or *corporate@oreilly.com*.

Editors:	Jeff Bleiel, Dawn Schanafelt, Meghan Blanchette
Cover Designer:	Randy Comer
Production Editor:	Melanie Yarbrough
Indexer:	Lucie Haskins
Proofreader:	Rachel Monaghan

Printing History:

January 2018: First Edition.

ISBN: 978-1-491-95886-5

[M]

Before KISS I had zero experience playing in a rock band
that wears makeup. —Gene Simmons

Eric Freeman

Eric is described by Head First series co-creator Kathy Sierra as "one of those rare individuals fluent in the language, practice, and culture of multiple domains from hipster hacker, corporate VP, engineer, think tank." And his background matches that description well. By training, Eric is a computer scientist, having studied with industry luminary David Gelernter during his Ph.D. work at Yale University. Professionally, Eric is a former media company executive—having held the position of CTO of Disney.com at The Walt Disney Company. Eric has also held positions at O'Reilly Media, NASA, and several startups, and his IP is licensed and in use on every Mac and PC. Over the last 15 years Eric has been one of the top-selling technical authors on topics from beginning web development to high-level software design.

Eric is currently is a Principal at WickedlySmart, LLC, and lives with his wife and young daughter in Austin, Texas.

Write to Eric at *eric@wickedlysmart.com* or visit *http://wickedlysmart.com*.

Table of Contents (summary)

Table of Contents (the real thing)

Intro

Your brain on coding. Here *you* are trying to *learn* something, while here your *brain* is doing you a favor by making sure the learning doesn't *stick*. Your brain's thinking, "Better leave room for more important things, like which wild animals to avoid and whether naked snowboarding is a bad idea." So how *do* you trick your brain into thinking that your life depends on knowing how to code?

thinking computationally

Getting Started

Knowing how to think computationally puts you in control. It's no secret the world around you is becoming more connected, more configurable, more programmable, and more, well, **computational**. You can remain a passive participant, or you can *learn to code*. When you can code, you're the director, the creator—you're telling all those computers what they should be doing *for you*. When you can code, you control your own destiny (or at least you'll be able to program your internet-connected lawn sprinker system). But how do you learn to code? First, learn to **think computationally**. Next, you grab a **programming language** so you can speak the same lingo as your computer, mobile device, or anything with a CPU. What's in it for you? More time, more power, and more creative possibilities to do the things you really want to do.

simple values, variables, and types

2 Know Your Value

Computers really only do two things well: store values and perform operations on those values. You might think they're doing a whole lot more, as you send texts, shop online, use Photoshop, or rely on your phone to navigate in your car; however, everything computers do can be broken down into **simple operations** that are performed on **simple values**. Now, part of **computational thinking** is learning to use these operations and values to build something that is much more sophisticated, complex, and meaningful—and we're going to get to that. First, though, we're going to take a look at what these values are, the operations you can perform on them, and just what role **variables** play in all this.

booleans, decisions, and loops

3 Decisive Code

Have you noticed how, so far, our programs aren't very, well, interesting? That is, all our code has strictly been a set of statements the interpreter evaluates from **top to bottom**—no twists in the plot, no sudden turns, no surprises, no independent thinking. For code to be more interesting, it needs to **make decisions**, to **control its own destiny**, and to do things **more than once** straight through. And in this chapter that's exactly what we're going to learn to do. Along the way we'll learn about the mysterious game called shoushiling, meet a character named Boole, and see how a data type with only two values could be worth our time. We're even going to learn how to deal with the dreaded **infinite loop**.

lists and iteration

4 *Providing Some Structure*

There's more to data types than numbers, strings, and Booleans.

So far you've been writing Python code using **primitive types**—those floats, integers, strings, and of course Booleans—with values like `3.14`, `42`, `"hey, it's my turn"`, and `True`. And you can do a lot with primitives, but at some point you'll want to write code that deals with lots of data—say, all the items in a shopping cart, the names of all the notable stars, or an entire product catalog. For that we need a little more *ummph*. In this chapter we're going to look at a new type, called a **list,** which can hold a collection of values. With lists, you'll be able to provide some **structure** for your data, rather than just having a zillion variables floating around your code holding values. You're also going to learn how to treat all those values as a whole as well as how to **iterate** over each item in a list using that *for* loop we mentioned in the last chapter. After this chapter, your ability to deal with data is going to grow and expand.

functions and abstraction

5 Getting Functional

You already know a lot. Variables and data types and conditionals and iteration—that's enough to **write** basically **any program** you'd ever want to. In fact, a computer scientist would tell you it's enough to write any program that anyone could ever conceive of. But you don't want to stop now, because your next step in computational thinking is learning how to **create abstractions** in your code. That may sound complex, but it's actually going to make your coding life simpler. Creating abstractions gives you leverage; with abstraction, you can more easily create programs of increasing complexity and power. You can put your code in neat little packages that you can reuse over and over. And you can forget all the nitty-gritty details of your code and to start thinking at a higher level.

sorting and nested iteration

4
Putting Some Order in Your Data

part 2

Sometimes the default ordering of your data doesn't cut it.

You've got that list of high scores on 80s arcade games, but you really need it sorted alphabetically by game name. Then there's that list of the number of times your coworkers have stabbed you in the back—it would be nice to know who's at the top of that list. To do that, though, we need to learn how to sort data, and to do that we'll need to explore some algorithms that are a little more involved than the ones we've seen so far. We're also going to have to explore how nested loops work as well as think a little about the efficiency of the code we're writing.

text, strings, and heuristics

6 Putting It All Together

You've already got a lot of superpowers. Now it's time to use them. In this chapter we're going to integrate what we've learned so far, bringing it all together to build some **increasingy cool code**. We're also going to keep adding to your knowledge and coding skills. More specifically, in this chapter we'll explore how to write code that **grabs some text**, slices it, dices it, and then does a little **data analysis** on it. We're going to find out what a **heuristic** is too, and implement one. Get ready—this is an all-out, heads-down, pedal-to-the-metal, serious coding chapter!

Definitely some sophisticated writing in this book.

modules, methods, classes, and objects

7 *Getting Modular*

Your code is growing in size and complexity. As that happens you need better ways to abstract, to modularize, to organize your code. You've seen that functions can be used to group lines of code together into bundles you can reuse over and over. And you've also seen that collections of functions and variables can be placed into modules so that they can be more easily shared and reused. In this chaper we'll revisit modules and learn how to use them even more effectively (so you're all ready to share your code with others) and then we're going to look at the ultimate in code reuse: *objects*. You're going to see that Python objects are all around you, just waiting to be used.

Nice job, I was quickly able to use the analyze module, especially with the help of the great documentation!

CRIME SCENE DO NOT ENTER   CRIME SCENE DO NOT ENTER   CRIME SCENE DO NOT ENT

recursion and dictionaries

8 Beyond Iteration and Indices

It's time to take your computational thinking up a notch. And this is the chapter to do it: we've been happily coding along with an iterative style of programming—we've created data structures like lists and strings and ranges of numbers, and we've written code to compute by iterating over them. In this chapter we're going to look at the world differently, first in terms of computation, and then in terms of data structures. Computationally we'll look at a style of computing that involves writing code that *recurs*, or calls itself. We'll expand the kinds of data structures we can work with by looking at a dictionary-like data type that is more like an *associative map* than a list. We'll then put them together and cause all kinds of trouble. Be forewarned: these topics take a while to settle into your brain, but the effort is going to pay off in spades.

saving and retrieving files

9 *Persistence*

You know you can save values in variables, but once your program ends poof!—they're gone forever. That's where *persistent* storage comes in—storage that allows your values and data to stick around a while. Most of the devices you're going to run Python on also have persisistent storage, like hard drives and flash cards, or they may have access to storage in the cloud as well. In this chapter you'll see how to write code to store and retrieve data from files. What good is that? Oh, anytime you want to save a user's configuration, store the results of your big analysis for the boss, read an image into your code to process it, write some code to search a decade's worth of email messages, reformat some data to be used in your spreadsheet app—we could go on and on.

using web apis

10 You Really Should Get Out More

You've been writing some great code, but you really need to get out more. There's a whole world of **data** just waiting for you on the web: Need weather data? Or how about access to a huge database of recipes? Or are sports scores more your thing? Maybe a music database of artists, albums, and songs? They're all out there for the taking from **Web APIs**. To use them all you need is to learn a bit more about how the web works, how to speak the local web lingo, and how to use a couple of new Python modules: `requests` and `json`. In this chapter we're going to explore Web APIs and take your Python skills to new heights; in fact, we're going to take them all the way to outer space and back.

widgets, events, and emergent behavior

11 *Getting Interactive*

You've certainly written some graphical applications, but you haven't created a real user interface yet. That is, you haven't written anything that lets the user interact with a graphical user interface (otherwise known as a GUI). To do that you need to adopt a new way of thinking about how a program executes, one that is more **reactive**. Wait, did the user just click on that button? Your code better know how to react and what to do next. Coding for interfaces is quite different from the typical procedural method we've been using, and it requires a different way of thinking about the problem. In this chapter you're going to write your first real GUI, and no, we're not going to write a simple to-do list manager or height/weight calculator, we're going to do something far more interesting. We're going to write an artificial life simulator with emergent behavior.

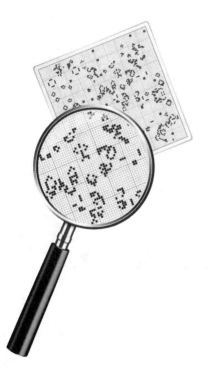

object-oriented programming

12 A Trip to Objectville

In this book you've used functions to abstract your code. And you've approached coding in a **procedural manner** using simple statements, conditionals, and `for`/`while` loops with functions—none of this is exactly **object-oriented**. In fact, it's not object-oriented *at all!* We have looked at objects and how to use them in our code, but you haven't created any objects of your own yet, and you haven't really approached designing your code in an object-oriented way. So, the time has come to leave this boring procedural town behind. In this chapter, you're going to find out why using objects is going to make your life so much better—well, better in a **programming sense** (we can't really help you with other areas of your life *and* your coding skills, all in one book).

appendix: leftovers

The Top Ten Topics (We Didn't Cover)

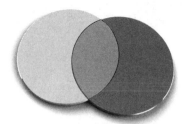

We've covered a lot of ground, and you're almost finished with this book.

We'll miss you, but before we let you go, we wouldn't feel right about sending you out into the world without a little more preparation. We can't possibly fit everything you'll need to know into this relatively small chapter. Actually, we *did* originally include everything you need to know about Python programming (not already covered by the other chapters), by reducing the type point size to .00004. It all fit, but nobody could read it. So we threw most of it away, and kept the best bits for this Top Ten appendix.

Server-side code executes on a server on the internet.

request

Client-side code executes on the client—that is, on your computer.

Intro

In this section, we answer the burning question: "So, why DID they put that in a book on learning to code?"

Who is this book for?

If you can answer "yes" to all of these:

(1) Do you want to **learn, understand,** and **remember** how to **program?**

(2) Do you prefer **stimulating dinner party conversation** to **dry, dull, academic lectures?**

this book is for you.

[Note from marketing: this book is for anyone with a credit card.]

> **This is NOT a reference book.** *Head First Learn to Code* **is a book designed for *learning* to code. It's not an encyclopedia of programming facts (you have Google for that, right?).**

Who should probably back away from this book?

If you can answer "yes" to any one of these:

(1) **Are you <u>completely</u> new to computers?**

If you don't know your way around your computer, how to manage files and folders, how to install apps, or how to use a word processor, you should probably learn those first.

(2) Are you a kick-butt programmer looking for a *reference* book?

(3) Are you **afraid to try something different?** Would you rather have a root canal than mix stripes with plaid? Do you believe that a technical book can't be serious if we have fun learning to code?

this book is not for you.

We know what you're thinking.

"How can this be a serious book?"

"What's with all the graphics?"

"Can I actually learn it this way?"

And we know what your brain is thinking.

Your brain craves novelty. It's always searching, scanning, *waiting* for something unusual. It was built that way, and it helps you stay alive.

Today, you're less likely to be a tiger snack. But your brain's still looking. You just never know.

So what does your brain do with all the routine, ordinary, normal things you encounter? Everything it *can* to stop them from interfering with the brain's *real* job—recording things that *matter*. It doesn't bother saving the boring things; they never make it past the "this is obviously not important" filter.

How does your brain *know* what's important? Suppose you're out for a day hike and a tiger jumps in front of you. What happens inside your head and body?

Neurons fire. Emotions crank up. *Chemicals surge.*

And that's how your brain knows…

This must be important! Don't forget it!

But imagine you're at home, or in a library. It's a safe, warm, tiger-free zone. You're studying. Getting ready for an exam. Or trying to learn some tough technical topic your boss thinks will take a week, 10 days at the most.

Just one problem. Your brain's trying to do you a big favor. It's trying to make sure that this *obviously* non-important content doesn't clutter up scarce resources. Resources that are better spent storing the really *big* things. Like tigers. Like the danger of fire. Like how you should never again snowboard in shorts.

And there's no simple way to tell your brain, "Hey brain, thank you very much, but no matter how dull this book is, and how little I'm registering on the emotional Richter scale right now, I really *do* want you to keep this stuff around."

We think of a "Head First" reader as a <u>learner</u>.

So what does it take to *learn* something? First, you have to *get* it, then make sure you don't *forget* it. It's not about pushing facts into your head. Based on the latest research in cognitive science, neurobiology, and educational psychology, *learning* takes a lot more than text on a page. We know what turns your brain on.

Some of the Head First learning principles:

Make it visual. Images are far more memorable than words alone, and make learning much more effective (up to 89% improvement in recall and transfer studies). It also makes things more understandable.
Put the words within or near the graphics they relate to, rather than on the bottom or on another page, and learners will be up to twice as likely to solve problems related to the content.

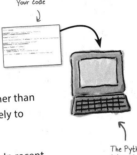

Your code

The Python Intepreter

Use a conversational and personalized style. In recent studies, students performed up to 40% better on post-learning tests if the content spoke directly to the reader, using a first-person, conversational style rather than taking a formal tone. Tell stories instead of lecturing. Use casual language. Don't take yourself too seriously. Which would you pay more attention to: a stimulating dinner party companion, or a lecture?

I really think you'll want to abstract that code into a function.

Now that I have your attention, you should be more careful using global variables.

Get the learner to think more deeply. In other words, unless you actively flex your neurons, nothing much happens in your head. A reader has to be motivated, engaged, curious, and inspired to solve problems, draw conclusions, and generate new knowledge. And for that, you need challenges, exercises and thought-provoking questions, and activities that involve both sides of the brain and multiple senses.

<u>Don't</u> just learn to code—learn to think computationally.

Get—and keep—the reader's attention. We've all had the "I really want to learn this, but I can't stay awake past page one" experience. Your brain pays attention to things that are out of the ordinary, interesting, strange, eye-catching, unexpected. Learning a new, tough, technical topic doesn't have to be boring. Your brain will learn much more quickly if it's not.

Touch their emotions. We now know that your ability to remember something is largely dependent on its emotional content. You remember what you care about. You remember when you *feel* something. No, we're not talking heart-wrenching stories about a boy and his dog. We're talking emotions like surprise, curiosity, fun, "what the...?" , and the feeling of "I rule!" that comes when you solve a puzzle, learn something everybody else thinks is hard, or realize you know something that "I'm more technical than thou" Bob from Engineering *doesn't*.

Metacognition: thinking about thinking

If you really want to learn, and you want to learn more quickly and more deeply, pay attention to how you pay attention. Think about how you think. Learn how you learn.

Most of us did not take courses on metacognition or learning theory when we were growing up. We were *expected* to learn, but rarely *taught* how to learn.

But we assume that if you're holding this book, you really want to learn how to code to create programs and apps. And you probably don't want to spend a lot of time. And you want to *remember* what you read, and be able to apply it. And for that, you've got to *understand* it. To get the most from this book, or *any* book or learning experience, take responsibility for your brain.

The trick is to get your brain to see the new material you're learning as Really Important. Crucial to your well-being. As important as a tiger. Otherwise, you're in for a constant battle, with your brain doing its best to keep the new content from sticking.

I wonder how I can trick my brain into remembering this stuff...

So how *DO* you get your brain to think coding is as important as a tiger?

There's the slow, tedious way, or the faster, more effective way. The slow way is about sheer repetition. You obviously know that you *are* able to learn and remember even the dullest of topics, if you keep pounding on the same thing. With enough repetition, your brain says, "This doesn't *feel* important to him, but he keeps looking at the same thing *over* and *over* and *over*, so I suppose it must be."

The faster way is to do ***anything that increases brain activity,*** especially different *types* of brain activity. The things on the previous page are a big part of the solution, and they're all things that have been proven to help your brain work in your favor. For example, studies show that putting words *within* the pictures they describe (as opposed to somewhere else in the page, like a caption or in the body text) causes your brain to try to make sense of how the words and picture relate, and this causes more neurons to fire. More neurons firing = more chances for your brain to *get* that this is something worth paying attention to, and possibly recording.

A conversational style helps because people tend to pay more attention when they perceive that they're in a conversation, since they're expected to follow along and hold up their end. The amazing thing is, your brain doesn't necessarily *care* that the "conversation" is between you and a book! On the other hand, if the writing style is formal and dry, your brain perceives it the same way you experience being lectured to while sitting in a roomful of passive attendees. No need to stay awake.

But pictures and conversational style are just the beginning.

Here's what WE did:

We used **pictures**, because your brain is tuned for visuals, not text. As far as your brain's concerned, a picture really *is* worth 1,024 words. And when text and pictures work together, we embedded the text *in* the pictures because your brain works more effectively when the text is *within* the thing the text refers to, as opposed to in a caption or buried in the text somewhere.

We used **redundancy**, saying the same thing in *different* ways and with different media types, and *multiple senses*, to increase the chance that the content gets coded into more than one area of your brain.

We used concepts and pictures in **unexpected** ways because your brain is tuned for novelty, and we used pictures and ideas with at least *some* **emotional** *content*, because your brain is tuned to pay attention to the biochemistry of emotions. That which causes you to *feel* something is more likely to be remembered, even if that feeling is nothing more than a little **humor**, **surprise,** or **interest.**

We used a personalized, **conversational style**, because your brain is tuned to pay more attention when it believes you're in a conversation than if it thinks you're passively listening to a presentation. Your brain does this even when you're *reading*.

Be the Python interpreter

We included more than 120 **activities**, because your brain is tuned to learn and remember more when you **do** things than when you *read* about things. And we made the exercises challenging-yet-doable, because that's what most *people* prefer.

BULLET POINTS

We used **multiple learning styles**, because *you* might prefer step-by-step procedures, while someone else wants to understand the big picture first, while someone else just wants to see a code example. But regardless of your own learning preference, *everyone* benefits from seeing the same content represented in multiple ways.

Puzzles

We include content for **both sides of your brain**, because the more of your brain you engage, the more likely you are to learn and remember, and the longer you can stay focused. Since working one side of the brain often means giving the other side a chance to rest, you can be more productive at learning for a longer period of time.

And we included **stories** and exercises that present **more than one point of view,** because your brain is tuned to learn more deeply when it's forced to make evaluations and judgments.

They're coming along with us.
↓

We included **challenges**, by providing exercises and by asking **questions** that don't always have a straight answer, because your brain is tuned to learn and remember when it has to *work* at something. Think about it—you can't get your *body* in shape just by *watching* people at the gym. But we did our best to make sure that when you're working hard, it's on the *right* things. That **you're not spending one extra dendrite** processing a hard-to-understand example, or parsing difficult, jargon-laden, or overly terse text.

We used **people**. In stories, examples, pictures, and so on, because, well, *you're* a person. And your brain pays more attention to *people* than it does to *things*.

We used an **80/20** approach. We assume that if you're going to be a kick-butt programmer, this won't be your only book. So we don't talk about *everything*. Just the stuff you'll actually *need*.

Here's what YOU can do to bend your brain into submission

So, we did our part. The rest is up to you. These tips are a starting point; listen to your brain and figure out what works for you and what doesn't. Try new things.

Cut this out and stick it on your refrigerator.

(1) Slow down. The more you understand, the less you have to memorize.

Don't just *read*. Stop and think. When the book asks you a question, don't just skip to the answer. Imagine that someone really *is* asking the question. The more deeply you force your brain to think, the better chance you have of learning and remembering.

(2) Do the exercises. Write your own notes.

We put them in, but if we did them for you, that would be like having someone else do your workouts for you. And don't just *look* at the exercises. **Use a pencil.** There's plenty of evidence that physical activity *while* learning can increase the learning.

(3) Read the "There Are No Dumb Questions"

That means all of them. They're not optional sidebars—*they're part of the core content!* Don't skip them.

(4) Make this the last thing you read before bed. Or at least the last *challenging* thing.

Part of the learning (especially the transfer to long-term memory) happens *after* you put the book down. Your brain needs time on its own, to do more processing. If you put in something new during that processing time, some of what you just learned will be lost.

(5) Drink water. Lots of it.

Your brain works best in a nice bath of fluid. Dehydration (which can happen before you ever feel thirsty) decreases cognitive function.

(6) Talk about it. Out loud.

Speaking activates a different part of the brain. If you're trying to understand something, or increase your chance of remembering it later, say it out loud. Better still, try to explain it out loud to someone else. You'll learn more quickly, and you might uncover ideas you hadn't known were there when you were reading about it.

(7) Listen to your brain.

Pay attention to whether your brain is getting overloaded. If you find yourself starting to skim the surface or forget what you just read, it's time for a break. Once you go past a certain point, you won't learn faster by trying to shove more in, and you might even hurt the process.

(8) *Feel* something!

Your brain needs to know that this *matters*. Get involved with the stories. Make up your own captions for the photos. Groaning over a bad joke is *still* better than feeling nothing at all.

(9) *Create* something!

Apply this to something new you're designing, or rework an older project. Just do *something* to get some experience beyond the exercises and activities in this book. All you need is a pencil and a problem to solve…a problem that might benefit from programming.

(10) *Get sleep.*

You've got to create a lot of new brain connections to learn to program. Sleep often; it helps.

Read Me

This is a learning experience, not a reference book. We deliberately stripped out everything that might get in the way of learning whatever it is we're working on at that point in the book. And the first time through, you need to begin at the beginning, because the book makes assumptions about what you've already seen and learned.

We want you to learn the thinking process behind programming.

Some might call that computer science, but here's a little secret: computer science isn't a science and it's not even all that much about computers (any more than astronomy is about telescopes). It's a way of thinking, otherwise known these days as computational thinking, and once you learn to think computationally, you'll be in a good position to apply that to any problem, environment, or programming language.

In this book we use Python.

Learning to drive without a vehicle is a little academic. And learning to think computationally without a programming language is more of a thought experiment than a marketable skill. So, in this book we use the very popular Python language. We'll tell you more about its accolades in Chapter 1, but whether you're a hobbyist or hoping to land a six-figure software development position, Python is a good place to start (and maybe end).

We don't exhaustively cover every aspect of the Python language.

Not even close. There's a lot you can learn about Python. This book is not a reference book, it's a learning book, so it doesn't cover everything there is to know about Python. Our goal is to teach you the fundamentals of coding and computational thinking so that you can pick up a book on *any programming language* and not feel totally lost.

You can use a Mac or PC, or Linux for that matter.

As Python is our primary vehicle used in this book and it is cross-platform, you can use whatever operating system you're used to. Most of the screenshots in this book are from a Mac, but they should look similar on your PC or Linux box.

This book advocates well-structured and readable code based on best practices.

You want to write code that you and other people can read and understand, code that will still work in next year's version of Python. In this book we're going to teach you to write clear, well-organized code from the get-go—code you can be proud of, code you'll want to frame and put on the wall (just take it down before you bring your date over). The only thing that differs from what we'd write as professional code is that this book uses handwritten annotations next to code to explain what the code is doing. We found this works better in a learning book than traditional comments in code (if you have no idea what we're talking about, you will; just give it a few chapters). But don't worry because we'll teach you how to document your code and we'll show you examples of how we'd document our own code. All that said, we're interested in teaching you to write code in the most straight-forward way so you can get the job done and move on to better things.

Annotations like this

Programming is serious business. You're going to have to work, sometimes hard. A programmer has a different mindset, a different way of thinking about the world. At times you're going to find coding very logical, while at other times it can be very abstract, if not downright mind bending. Some programming concepts take time to sink into your brain—you actually do have to sleep on them before you'll get it. But no worries; we're going to do all that in a brain-friendly way. Just take your time, give the concepts time to sink in, and go over the material multiple times if needed.

The activities are NOT optional.

The exercises and activities in this book are *not* add-ons; they're part of the core content of the book. Some of them are to help with memory, some are for understanding, and some will help you apply what you've learned. If you skip them you will be missing large parts of the book (and you'll probably be very confused). The crossword puzzles are the only things you don't have to do, but they're good for giving your brain a chance to think about the words in a different context.

The redundancy is intentional and important.

One distinct difference in a Head First book is that we want you to really get it. And we want you to finish the book remembering what you've learned. Most reference books don't have retention and recall as a goal, but this book is about learning, so you'll see some of the same concepts come up more than once.

The examples are as lean as possible.

Our readers tell us that it's frustrating to wade through 200 lines of an example looking for the two lines they need to understand. Most examples in this book are shown within the smallest possible context, so that the part you're trying to learn is clear and simple. Don't expect all of the examples to be robust—they are written specifically for learning, and aren't always fully functional. That said, for the larger examples we also try to make them fun, fascinating, and downright cool—something you'd want to show your friends and family.

We've placed all the example files on the web so you can download them. You'll find them at *http://wickedlysmart.com/hflearntocode*.

Operators are NOT standing by, but you can get all the code and samples files you'll need at http://wickedlysmart.com/hflearntocode.

The Brain Power exercises don't usually have answers.

For some of them, there is no right answer, and for others, part of the learning experience of the Brain Power activities is for you to decide if and when your answers are right. In some of the Brain Power exercises, you will find hints to point you in the right direction.

Get the code examples, help, and discussion online.

You'll find everything you need for this book online at *http://wickedlysmart.com/hflearntocode*, including code sample files and additional support material.

You're going to have to install Python

More than likely your computer is either not going to have Python installed, or it's not going to have the right version of Python installed. In this book we use Python 3, which at the time of writing was version 3.6. So, you'll need to install version 3.6 or later. Here's how:

- **For macOS**, open your browser and enter:

    https://www.python.org/downloads

On this page you should see the macOS download links. If not, look under the Downloads menu on the page.

1. Click the Download button for Python 3.x (where x is the latest version). Do not download version 2.7.

2. Once the installer is downloaded, open the installation package in your downloads folder and follow the installation instructions.

3. After you've completed the install, navigate to your *Applications* folder, under which you'll find the *Python 3.x* folder. To test your installation, double click the IDLE application in the *Python 3.x* folder:

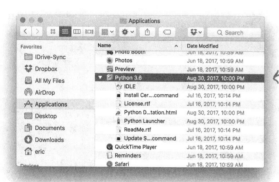

Note that you'll need administrator privileges to install Python—if you commonly install apps, you should be fine; otherwise, ask your administrator for help.

The IDLE app is located in the Python 3.x folder, which you'll find in the Applications folder. We'll talk more about what IDLE is in the first chapter.

It's a good idea to add IDLE to your dock if you haven't already, as we'll be using it a fair bit in this book. To do that control-click the icon in the dock and choose Options > Keep in Dock from the pop-up menu.

4. When the IDLE application appears on your screen, you should see something similar to the screenshot below. If not, recheck your installation for any errors that might have occurred.

You can choose the IDLE > Quit IDLE menu option to exit the application.

- **For Windows**, open your browser and enter:

  https://www.python.org/downloads

1. Click the Download button for Python 3.x (where x is the latest version). Do not download version 2.7.

2. Choose to either save or run the executable installer. If the latter, click to run the installer after you've downloaded it.

3. When you see the installer window appear on your screen, make sure the "Add Python to PATH" checkbox is checked at the bottom of the installer, then click "Install Now."

4. After you've completed the install, navigate using the Start button to **All Programs,** and in your list of apps you should see a menu option for Python 3.x (with your version number in place of the x). Under the Python menu you'll see choices for Python 3.x, documentation, and IDLE, which is an editor we will also be using in this book.

5. To test, click the IDLE menu item; when the IDLE application appears on your screen, you should see something similar to the screenshot below. If not, recheck your installation and any errors that might have occurred.

You can choose the IDLE
> Quit IDLE menu option
to exit the application.

Note to Linux users: We're not worried about you; let's be real, you know what you're doing. Just grab the approriate distribution from python.org

A word on organizing your code

Your *source code* is all the code you'll be writing with this book. We recommend keeping your code organized on a per-chapter basis and throughout the book we've assumed that you'll be creating one folder per chapter, like this:

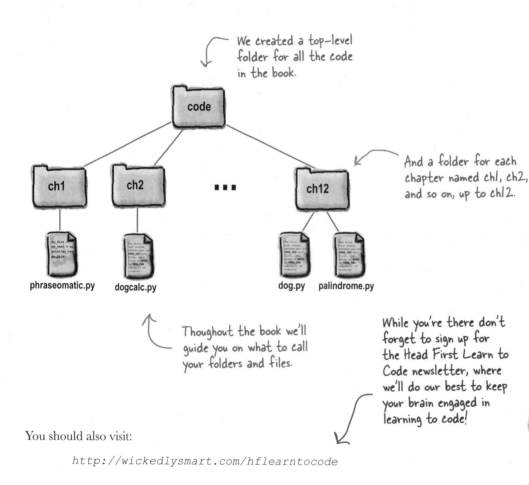

We created a top-level folder for all the code in the book.

And a folder for each chapter named ch1, ch2, and so on, up to ch12.

Thoughout the book we'll guide you on what to call your folders and files.

While you're there don't forget to sign up for the Head First Learn to Code newsletter, where we'll do our best to keep your brain engaged in learning to code!

You should also visit:

> *http://wickedlysmart.com/hflearntocode*

There you'll find instructions for downloading the complete source code for the book. In this code you'll find our versions of the programs you're going to write as well as a few data files and images you'll need. We do ask that you take the time to type in the programs yourself (this will help you develop your muscle memory for coding and help things sink into your brain), but if you run into any issues you just can't figure out, you can always compare your code with ours to see where you might have made a mistake.

Acknowledgments*

A huge thanks goes out first to my esteemed technical reviewers: **Elisabeth Robson** carefully and expertly reviewed the manuscript with a keen Head First and computer science eye. **Josh Sharfman** was the MVP reviewer who added depth and quality to every corner of the book. **David Powers**, in his usual style, rigorously scoured the technical text (his Harry Potter knowledge ain't too shabby either). And veteran Head First author **Paul Barry** provided a much-needed Python critical eye. In addition, my **review team** (listed on the next page) was invaluable across every aspect of reviewing the book.

Elisabeth Robson   Josh Sharfman   David Powers   Paul Barry

My biggest thanks to my editors, **Jeff Bleiel**, **Dawn Schanafelt**, and **Meghan Blanchette**. Meghan was instrumental in getting this book off the ground, Dawn carefully saw it through its early developmental stages, and Jeff drove the book through to its publication.

Also a big thanks to the entire O'Reilly team including **Susan Conant, Rachel Roumeliotis,** and **Melanie Yarbrough**. At WickedlySmart, thanks to **Jamie Burton** for all her help, including early reader surveys and managing the review team forum. And as always, thanks to **Bert Bates** and **Kathy Sierra** for inspiration, interesting discussion, and all their help solving writing conundrums. Thanks to **Cory Doctorow** for his support and for lending his writing to Chapter 7.

Finally, a number of individuals and organizations unknowingly inspired aspects of this book, including **Daniel P. Friedman**, **Nathan Bergey**, the **Raspberry Pi Foundation,** and **Socratica**.

Jamie Burton

Jeff Bleiel

Meghan Blanchette

Dawn Schanafelt

Bert Bates

Kathy Sierra

*The large number of acknowledgments is because we're testing the theory that everyone mentioned in a book acknowledgment will buy at least one copy, probably more, what with relatives and everything. If you'd like to be in the acknowledgment of our *next* book, and you have a large family, write to us.

The Review Team

Meet the review team!

An amazing group of people took on reviewing this book. With backgrounds from **newbie** to **expert**, and professions as diverse as **architect**, **dentist**, **elementary school teacher**, **real estate agent,** and **AP computer science teacher**, they participated across the globe from **Albania** to **Australia**, from **Kenya** to **Kosovo**, from the **Netherlands** to **Nigeria** to **New Zealand**.

This group read every page, did every exercise, and entered and executed every line of code, providing feedback and encouragement over 600 pages. They also, on their own, worked as a team, helping each other through new concepts, double-checking errors, and locating problems in the text and code.

Every reviewer here made significant contributions to this book and vastly improved its quality.

Thank you!

Crystal Gilmore Rodriguez

Ridvan Bunjaku

Troy Welch

Hudson Read

Mark S. van der Linden

Mitch Johnson

Chris Talent

Andrea Toston

Chris Griggs

David Oparanti

Johnny Rivera

David Kinoti

Michael Peck

Mauro Caser

Benjamin E. Hall

Alfred J. Speller

Tiron Andric

Dennis Fitzgerald

Abdul Rahman Shaik

Also a big thanks to **Christopher Davies**, **Constance Mallon,** and **Wanda Hernandez** for their significant contributions to this book.

1 thinking computationally

Getting Started

Learn to Think Computationally
Win Friends
and Influence Poeple

Knowing how to think computationally puts you in control. It's no secret the world around you is becoming more connected, more configurable, more programmable, and more, well, **computational**. You can remain a passive participant, or you can *learn to code*. When you can code, you're the director, the creator—you're telling all those computers what they should be doing *for you*. When you can code, you control your own destiny (or at least you'll be able to program your internet-connected lawn sprinker system). But how do you learn to code? First, learn to **think computationally**. Next, you grab a **programming language** so you can speak the same lingo as your computer, mobile device, or anything with a CPU. What's in it for you? More time, more power, and more creative possibilities to do the things you really want to do. Come on, let's get started...

Breaking it down

The first thing that stands between you and writing your first real piece of code is learning the skill of breaking problems down into achievable little actions that a computer *can do for you*. Of course, you and the computer will also need to be speaking a common language, but we'll get to that topic in just a bit.

Now breaking problems down into a number of steps may sound like a new skill, but it's actually something you do every day. Let's look at a simple example: say you wanted to break the activity of fishing down into a simple set of instructions that you could hand to a robot, who would do your fishing for you. Here's our first attempt to do that:

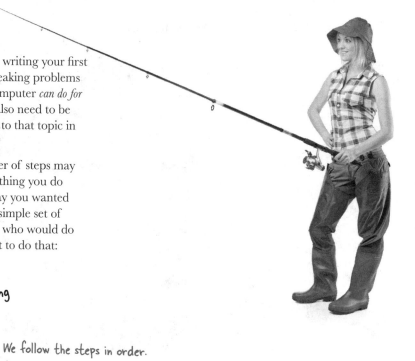

Let's break the process of catching fish down into a number of easily understood steps.

We follow the steps in order.

1. Put worm on hook.

2. Cast line into pond.

Some steps are simple instructions, or __statements__ if you will, like "cast line into pond."

3. Watch the bobber until it goes underwater.

A statement might __conditionally__ wait before proceeding.

4. Hook and pull in fish.

This statement only happens after the bobber has gone underwater in the previous statement.

5. If done fishing, then go home; otherwise, go back to step 1.

Statements can also make __decisions__, like is it time to go home or should we keep fishing?

Notice that often statements repeat, like here: if we don't go home, we instead go back to the beginning and repeat the instructions to catch another fish.

←The bobber

The hook

←The worm

You can think of these statements as a nice **recipe** for fishing. Like any recipe, this one provides a set of steps that, when followed in order, will produce some result or outcome (in our case, hopefully, catching some fish).

Notice that most steps consist of a simple instruction, like "cast line into pond," or "pull in the fish." But also notice that other instructions are a bit different because they depend on a condition, like "is the bobber above or below water?" Instructions might also direct the flow of the recipe, like "if you haven't finished fishing, then cycle back to the beginning and put another worm on the hook." Or, how about a condition for stopping, as in "if you're done, then go home"?

You're going to find that these simple statements or instructions are the foundation of coding. In fact, every app or software program you've ever used has been nothing more than a (sometimes large) set of simple instructions to the computer that tell it what to do.

Exercise

Real recipes don't just tell you *what to do*, they also include objects that are used in making a particular dish (like measuring cups, whisks, food processors, and of course ingredients). What objects are used in our fishing recipe? Circle all the objects in the fishing recipe on the previous page, and check your answer at the end of the chapter before moving on.

This is a workbook. You can write in it; in fact, we encourage it.

Sharpen your pencil

One thing to understand right up front is that computers do **exactly** what you tell them—nothing more, nothing less. Look at our recipe for fishing on the previous page. If you were the robot and you followed these instructions precisely, what problems might you encounter? Do you think we would really be successful using this recipe?

☐ A. If there are no fish, you're going to be fishing for a very long time (like, forever).

☐ B. If the worm falls off the hook, you'll never know about it or replace it.

☐ C. What happens if we run out of worms?

Can you think of more issues?

☐ D. Did we specify what to do with a fish when we pulled it in?

☐ E. What happened to the fishing rod?

☐ F. _____
_____
_____
_____

In case you are not familiar with fishing, this is a bobber, otherwise known as a fishing float. When a fish bites, it goes underwater.

You'll find the answers to Sharpen Your Pencil exercises at the end of the chapter.

I bought this expensive technical book to learn to code and you're starting by telling me about recipes? That doesn't sound very promising or, well, *technical*.

Actually, a recipe is a perfectly good way to describe a set of instructions to a computer. You might even run into that term loosely used here and there in more advanced programming books. Heck, you'll even find books on common software development techniques that are called cookbooks. That said, if you want to get technical we can—a computer scientist or serious software developer would commonly call a recipe an **algorithm**. What's an algorithm? Well, not much more than a recipe—it's a sequence of instructions that solves some problem. Often you'll find algorithms are first written in an informal form of code called **pseudocode**.

More on pseudocode in a bit...

One thing to keep in mind is that, whether you're talking about a recipe, pseudocode, or an algorithm, the whole point is to work out a high-level description of how to solve a problem before you get into the nitty-gritty details of writing code that the computer can understand and execute.

As you'll see, this can make the task of coding more straightforward and less error-prone.

In this book, you'll hear us interchange all these terms, where appropriate—and, oh, in your next job interview you might want to use the term *algorithm* or even *pseudocode* to ensure that larger signing bonus (but there's still nothing wrong with the word *recipe*).

Just as there are many recipes for the same dish, with algorithms, you'll find there are many ways to solve the same problem. Some more tasty than others.

Code Magnets

Let's get a little practice with ~~recipes~~ algorithms. We put the Head First Diner's algorithm for making an three-egg omelet on the fridge to remember it, but someone came along and messed it up. Can you put the magnets back in the right order to make our algorithm work? Note that the Head First Diner makes two kinds of omelets: plain and cheese. **Make sure you check your answer at the end of the chapter.**

Rearrange these magnets here to make the algorithm work.

```
If the customer ordered cheese:
```

```
Add cheese on top
```

```
while eggs aren't fully mixed:
```

```
Transfer eggs to plate
```

```
While eggs aren't fully cooked:
```

```
Remove pan from heat
```

```
Stir eggs
```

```
Serve
```

```
Heat saute pan
```

```
Whip eggs
```

```
Crack three eggs into bowl
```

```
Transfer eggs to pan
```

How coding works

So you've got a task you want the computer to do for you, and you know you'll need to break that task down into a number of instructions the computer can understand, but how are you going to *actually tell* the computer to do something? That's where a programming language comes in—with a programming language you can describe your task in terms that *you and the computer* both understand. But before we take a deep dive into programming languages, let's look at the steps you'll take to actually write code:

❶ Craft your algorithm

This is where you take the problem or task you want solved and turn it into a high-level recipe, pseudocode, or algorithm that describes the steps that need to be performed by the computer to achieve whatever result you are after.

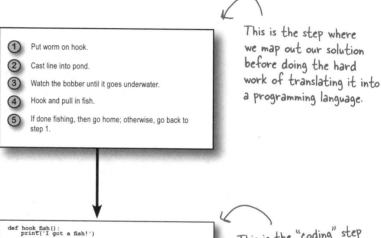

① Put worm on hook.

② Cast line into pond.

③ Watch the bobber until it goes underwater.

④ Hook and pull in fish.

⑤ If done fishing, then go home; otherwise, go back to step 1.

This is the step where we map out our solution before doing the hard work of translating it into a programming language.

❷ Write your program

Next, you take that recipe and translate it into a specific set of instructions that are written in a programming language. This is the *coding* stage, and we call the result a *program* or just "your code" (or, more formally, the *source code*).

```
def hook_fish():
    print('I got a fish!')

def wait():
    print('Waiting...')

print('Get worm')
print('Put worm on hook')
print('Throw in lure')

while True:
    response = input('Is bobber underwater? ')
    if response == 'yes':
        is_moving = True
        print('I got a bite!')
        hook_fish()
    else:
        wait()
```

This is the "coding" step where you turn your algorithm into code (which is shorthand for source code) that is ready to execute in the next step.

❸ Run your program

Finally, you take your source code and hand it to the computer, which will start carrying out your instructions. Depending on the language you're using, this process might be called *interpreting*, *running*, *evaluating*, or *executing* your code.

We often use some of these terms interchangeably as well.

```
Get worm
Put worm on hook
Throw in lure
Is bobber underwater?
```

When your source code is complete, you're ready to execute it. If all goes well, and you designed your code well, you'll get the result from the computer you were looking for.

Are we even speaking the same language?

Think of a **programming language** as a special-purpose language created expressly for specifying tasks to a computer. Programming languages give you a way to describe your recipes in a manner that is clear and precise enough that a computer can understand it.

To learn a programming language there are two things you need to nail down two things: what things can you say using the language, and what do those things mean? A computer scientist would call these the **syntax** and **semantics** of the language. Just stash those terms in the back of your brain for now; we'll be getting you up to speed on both as the book progresses.

Now, as it turns out, just like spoken languages, there are *many* programming languages, and, as you may already have figured out, in this book we're going to use the Python programming language. Let's get a little better feel for languages and Python...

Relax

Don't worry; at this point we don't expect you to read or write code. For gosh sakes, you've got the whole book ahead of you—for now we're just getting familiar with code, what it looks like, and how it works. The important thing in this chapter is just to take it all in.

You'll find that the techniques you're learning in this book can be applied to just about any programming language you might encounter in the future.

YOU SAY TOMATO

On the left you'll find some statements written in English, and on the right you'll find statements written in a programming language. Draw a line from each English statement to its corresponding code translation. We did the first one for you. Make sure you check your work with the solution at the end of the chapter before proceeding.

Print "Hi there" on the screen.

If the temperature is more than 72, then print "Wear shorts" on the screen.

A grocery list with bread, milk, and eggs on it.

Pouring five drinks.

Ask the user, "What is your name?"

```
for num in range(0, 5):
        pour_drink()


name = input('What is your name? ')


if temperature > 72:
        print('Wear shorts')


grocery_list = ['bread', 'milk', 'eggs']


print('Hi there')
```

The world of programming languages

If you're reading this book you may have, in passing, heard about various programming languages. Just walking through the programming section of your local bookstore you might encounter Java, C, C++, LISP, Scheme, Objective-C, Perl, PHP, Swift, Clojure, Haskell, COBOL, Ruby, Fortran, Smalltalk, BASIC, Algol, JavaScript, and of course Python, to name just a few. You might also be wondering where all these names came from. The truth is, programming language names are a lot like the names of rock bands—they're names that meant something to the people who created the language. Take Java, for instance: it was named, not surprisingly, after coffee (the preferred name Oak was already taken). Haskell was named after a mathematician, and the name C was chosen because C was the successor of the languages A and B at Bell Labs. But why are there so many languages and what are they all about? Let's see what a few folks have to say about the languages they use:

> I'm for **Objective-C** all the way. I build iPhone apps all day long, and I love the way Objective-C is like C, but is much more dynamic and object-oriented. I'm also learning Apple's new language called **Swift**.

> **Java** keeps me thinking at the level of objects, not low-level code, and it takes care of a lot of low-level things, like memory management and threading, for me.

> I live in the world of WordPress, which is written in **PHP**, so PHP is my go-to language. Some people call it a scripting language, but it does everything I need.

I mostly use the **C** programming language. I write parts of operating systems that have to be super efficient. In my job, every CPU cycle and every memory location counts.

Call me academic, but I love **Scheme-** and **LISP**-style languages. For me it is all about high-order functions and abstraction. I'm glad to see functional languages like **Clojure** getting real industry use.

I'm a web developer and **JavaScript** is my main language. It's the de facto language of all browsers, and it's being used to write backend web services as well.

I'm a system administrator. I use **Perl** quite a bit to write various system scripts. It's terse, but also very expressive. Just a little code gets a lot done.

> We love **Python**.
> It's known for being a
> very readable, clean language with
> great library support that lets you
> write code for all kinds of domains;
> it also has a great community of
> people involved in it.

> **Python's**
> known as one of the best languages
> for beginners, but it also grows with you
> as your skills mature. And it's a real language
> too, with folks like Google, Disney, and NASA
> using it to build serious systems.

Choices, choices...

As you can see, there are a lot of languages and opinions out there, and we've barely scratched the surface of modern languages. You can also see there's a lot of terminology that comes along with these languages, and, as you progress, those terms are going to make a lot more sense to you. For now, just know there's a wide variety of languages out there, with more being created every day.

So, in this book, what should we use? Here's the thing: first and foremost, we want to learn how to think *computationally*—that way, no matter what language you run across in the future, you'll be in a good position to learn it. But, that said, we have to start with *some language*, and, as you already know, we're going to use Python. Why? Our friends above said it well: it's considered one of the best languages for beginners because it's such a readable and consistent language. It's also a powerful language in that no matter what you want to do with it (now or beyond this book), you can find support in terms of code extensions (we call them *modules* or *libraries*) and a supportive community of developers to give you a hand. Finally, some developers will even tell you Python is just *more fun* than other languages. So how can we go wrong?

Sharpen your pencil

Look how easy it is to write Python

You don't know Python yet, but we bet you can make some good guesses about how Python code works. Take a look at each line of code below and see if you can guess what it does. Write in your answers below. If you get stuck, the answers are on the next page. We did the first one for you.

```python
customers = ['Jimmy', 'Kim', 'John', 'Stacie']
```
Make a list of customers.

```python
winner = random.choice(customers)
```

```python
flavor = 'vanilla'
```

```python
print('Congratulations ' + winner +
    ' you have won an ice cream sundae!')
```

```python
prompt = 'Would you like a cherry on top? '
```

```python
wants_cherry = input(prompt)
```

```python
order = flavor + ' sundae '
```

```python
if (wants_cherry == 'yes'):
    order = order + ' with a cherry on top'
```

```python
print('One ' + order + ' for ' + winner +
        ' coming right up...')
```

Python Output

Congratulations Stacie you have won an ice cream sundae!
Would you like a cherry on top? yes
One vanilla sundae with a cherry on top for Stacie coming right up...

This should help; it's the output of this code. Do you think this code has the same output every time you run it?

Sharpen your pencil Solution

Look how easy it is to write Python

You don't know Python yet, but we bet you can make some good guesses about how Python code works. Take a look at each line of code below and see if you can guess what it does. Write in your answers below. If you get stuck, the answers are on the next page. We did the first one for you.

```python
customers = ['Jimmy', 'Kim', 'John', 'Stacie']
```
Make a list of customers.

```python
winner = random.choice(customers)
```
Randomly choose one of those customers.

```python
flavor = 'vanilla'
```
Set the name or variable called flavor to the text 'vanilla'.

```python
print('Congratulations ' + winner +
    ' you have won an ice cream sundae!')
```
Print out a congratulations message to the screen that includes the winning customer's name. For instance, if Kim is the winner this code prints "Congratulations Kim you have won an ice cream sundae!"

```python
prompt = 'Would you like a cherry on top? '
```
Set the name or variable called prompt to the text "Would you like a cherry on top? "

```python
wants_cherry = input(prompt)
```
Ask the user to type in some text, and assign it to wants_cherry. Notice that when the user is asked for input, the prompt is first displayed (as seen in the Python output).

```python
order = flavor + ' sundae '
```
Set order to the text 'vanilla' followed by 'sundae'.

```python
if (wants_cherry == 'yes'):
    order = order + ' with a cherry on top'
```
If the user answered yes to 'Would you like a cherry on top?', then add the text " with a cherry on top" to the order.

```python
print('One ' + order + ' for ' + winner +
        ' coming right up...')
```
Print out that the winner's order is coming right up.

```
Python Output

Congratulations Stacie you have won an ice cream sundae!
Would you like a cherry on top? yes
One vanilla sundae with a cherry on top for Stacie coming
right up...
```

P.S. If you can't help yourself and you have to type this code in, add import random at the very top of the file before running it. We'll get to what that does later, but note that running the code at this point is not required or all that useful. That said, we just know someone's going to have to try it. You know who you are!

How you'll write and run code with Python

Now that we've talked about and even looked at some code, it's time to start thinking about how you'd actually write and execute some real code. As we mentioned, depending on the language and environment, there are a lot of different models for how you do that. Let's get a sense for how you're going to be writing and running your Python code:

❶ Writing your code

First you get your code typed into an editor and saved. You can use any text editor, like Notepad on Windows or TextEdit on the Mac, to write your Python code. That said, most developers use specialized editors known as IDEs (or Integrated Development Environments) to write their code. Why? IDEs are a bit like word processors—they give you lots of nice features like autocompletion of common Python keywords, highlighting of the language syntax (or of errors), as well as built-in testing facilities. Python also conveniently includes an IDE called IDLE, which we'll be looking at shortly.

Your code

This is Python's IDLE editor.

Your code

The Python intepreter

❷ Running your code

Running your code is as easy as handing it to the Python interpreter, a program that takes care of everything needed to execute the code you've written. We'll step through the details of this in a bit, but you can access the intepreter through IDLE, or directly from your computer's command line.

❸ How your code is interpreted

We've been describing Python as a language that you and the computer both understand. And, as we've learned, an interpreter does the job of reading your code and executing it. To do this, the interpreter actually translates your code behind the scenes into a lower-level machine code that can be directly executed by your computer hardware. You won't need to worry about how it does this; just know that the interpreter will do the job of executing each statement of your Python code.

The interpreter running your code

there are no
Dumb Questions

Q: Why not use English to program computers? Then we wouldn't need to learn these special-purpose programming languages.

A: Yes, wouldn't that be nice. As it turns out, English is full of ambiguity, which makes creating such a translator extremely difficult. Reseachers have made small inroads in this area, but we're a long way from using English, or any other spoken language as a programming language. Also, in the few languages, that have tried to be more English-like, we've found that programmers prefer languages that are less like a spoken language and that are more streamlined for coding.

Q: Why isn't there just one programming language?

A: Technically all modern programming languages are equivalent in that they can all compute the same things, so, in theory, we could use one programming language to serve all our needs. Like spoken languages, however, programming languages differ in their expressive power—that is, you'll find some types of programming tasks (say, building websites) are easier in some languages than others. Other times the choice of a programming language just comes down to taste, using a particular methodology, or even the need to use the language that your employer has adopted. Count on one thing, though: there will be even more languages, as programming languages continue to evolve.

Q: Is Python just a toy language for beginners? If I wanted to be a software developer, is learning Python going to help me?

A: Python is a serious language and used in many products you probably know and love. In addition, Python's one of the few professional languages that is also considered an excellent language for beginners. Why? Compared to many existing languages, Python approaches things in a straightforward and consistent way (something you'll have a better understanding of over time, and as you gain experience with Python and other languages).

Q: What's the difference between learning to code and thinking computationally? Is the latter just a computer science thing?

A: Computational thinking is a way of thinking about problem solving that grew out of computer science. With computational thinking we learn how to break problems down, to create algorithms to solve them, and to generalize those solutions so we can solve even bigger problems. Often, though, we want to teach a computer to execute those algorithms for us, and that's where coding comes in. Coding is the means by which we specify an algorithm to a computer (or any computational device, like your smartphone). So the two really go hand in hand—computational thinking gives us a way to create solutions to problems that we want to code, and coding provides a means of specifying our solutions to a computer. That said, computational thinking can be valuable even if you aren't coding.

⚛ BRAIN POWER

Where do you think the name Python most likely came from? Check the most likely answer below:

☐ **A.** Python's creator loved snakes, and had previously created the less successful Cobra language.

☐ **B.** The creator of Python loved pie… thus, Pie-thon.

☐ **C.** The Python name is inspired by the name of a British surreal comedy group.

☐ **D.** Python is an acronym for Programming Your Things, Hosted On the Network

☐ **E.** The Python name was inspired by the Anaconda runtime system, on which it is built.

C. Monty Python is the British comedy group who created the show Monty Python's Flying Circus. Feel free to watch a few of their shows as homework—whether it is your cup of tea or not, you'll often see Monty Python references in the Python community.

A very brief history of Python

Python 1.0

Over in the Netherlands, at the National Research Institute for Mathematics and Computer Science, they had a big problem: their scientists found programming languages difficult to learn. Yes, even to these highly educated, skilled scientists, the most current programming languages were confusing and inconsistent. To the rescue, the Institute developed a new language called "ABC" (you thought we were going to say "Python," didn't you?), which was designed to be much easier to learn. While ABC was somewhat successful, an enterprising young developer named Guido van Rossum, after a weekend of binge-watching Monty Python reruns, thought he could take things further—so, using what he'd learned from ABC, Guido created Python. And the rest is history.

Note from editor: umm, "the rest" is actually in the next few paragraphs.

Python 2.0

Python came of age with version 2.0 and a whole new set of features aimed at supporting its growing community of developers. For instance, in recognition that Python was truly now a global language, 2.0 was extended to handle character sets from languages far beyond the typical English letters. Python also also improved many technical aspects of the language, like better handling of computer memory as well as better support for common types of data like lists and character strings.

The Python development crew also worked hard to make Python open to a whole community of developers who could help improve the language and implementation.

Actually, we just made up the part about the binge weekend.

Python 3.0

Nobody's perfect, and there came a time when Python's creators looked back and saw a few things in Python they wanted to improve. While Python was known for its adherence to keeping things straightforward, experience with the language had revealed a few parts of its design that could be improved, and a few things that hadn't aged well that needed to be removed.

All these changes meant that some aspects of Python 2 would no longer be supported. That said, Python's creators made sure there were ways to keep the 2.0 code running. So, if you have code written in Python 2, don't worry—Python 2 is still alive and well, but know that Python 3 is the future of the language.

We fully expect our flying car is going to be Python enabled.

| 1994 | 2000 | 2008 | The Future! |

> So, it sounds like there are two versions of Python out there, version 2 and version 3. Which are we going to use and how different are they?

Good question. And you're right, there are two versions of Python—to be a little more specifc, at the time this book was printed, the current versions are 3.6 and 2.7.

Here's how we're going to think about the versions. As it turns out, when you view the two languages, from, say, 10,000 feet, they are remarkably similar, and in fact you might not even be able to see any differences. That said, there *are* differences, and if you aren't paying attention to the version you are using, they could trip you up. We'll be using the newest version of Python in this book—that is, version 3. We'd rather get you started with the version that is going to carry on into the future.

Now there is a lot of code in the world already written in Python 2, and you certainly might encounter it in a module you've downloaded online or, if you happen to become a software developer, as part of some old code you become responsible for. After this book you'll be in a good position to study the small differences between Python 3 and 2, should you need to.

When we say Python 3 or 2, we mean in each case, the latest version of 3 or 2 (at the time of writing, 3.6 and 2.7).

Got Python?

We're not going to get much further if you haven't installed Python yet. If you haven't taken the time to install Python, now is the time. Check out the "You're going to have to install Python" section in the introduction to get started. Remember, if you're using a Mac or Linux there's a good chance you already have Python installed; however, there's also a good chance you have version 2, not version 3. So whether you're on a Mac, a Windows, or a Linux machine, at this point you may need to install version 3 of Python.

So, go do that and once you've got Python up and running, you're ready to dive into some real code.

Putting Python through its paces

Now that you've got Python installed, let's put it to work. We're going to start with a small test program just to make sure everything is up and running. To do that, you need to use an editor to enter your program before you can execute it; that's where IDLE, the Python editor (or Integrated Development Environment if you prefer), comes in. Go ahead and open IDLE like we did in the introduction. As a reminder, on the Mac you'll find IDLE under the **Applications** > **Python 3.x** folder. On Windows navigate using the Start button to All Programs, and you'll find IDLE under the Python 3.x menu option.

When you first open IDLE, it displays an interactive interpreter called the Python Shell. If you're really curious, type *1+1* (that's one plus one) into it and hit return. More on this in the next chapter.

When you first run IDLE it displays an interactive window, called the Python Shell, that you can type Python statements directly into. You can also use an editor to type your code into; to do that, choose **File** > **New File** from the IDLE menu. You'll see a new, empty editor window appear.

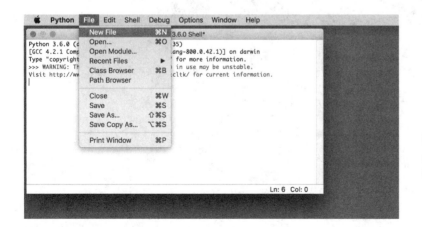

Use the File > New File menu option to get a new window ready for entering Python code.

IDLE works just like a word processor, only it knows about Python code and assists you by highlighting Python language keywords, helping you with formatting, and even, when appropriate, autocompleting common Python keywords to make code entry even easier.

After choosing New File, you should see a new, empty window on top of the Python Shell window.

After creating a new file and getting a new blank editing window, you're going to type in one line of code to test things out; go ahead and enter this code:

```python
print('You rock!')
```

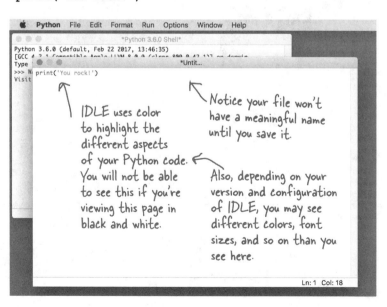

IDLE uses color to highlight the different aspects of your Python code. You will not be able to see this if you're viewing this page in black and white.

Notice your file won't have a meaningful name until you save it.

Also, depending on your version and configuration of IDLE, you may see different colors, font sizes, and so on than you see here.

Pay careful attention to every detail of spelling and punctuation, as Python and other programming languages are quite intolerant of mistakes.

Saving your work

Now that you've typed in your first line of code, let's save it. To do that just choose **File** > **Save** from the IDLE menu:

Before we execute our code we need to save it. In IDLE, the Save menu item is under the File menu. Simply choose this option and give your source code a name. When we're writing Python code, we use an extension of ".py" on the end of the filename.

Source code, source file, code, and program are all common names for your files with code in them.

And then give your code a name with a *.py* extension. We chose the name *rock.py*. Note that, although we didn't show it, we also created a folder for Chapter 1 code, called *ch1*, and we recommend you do too.

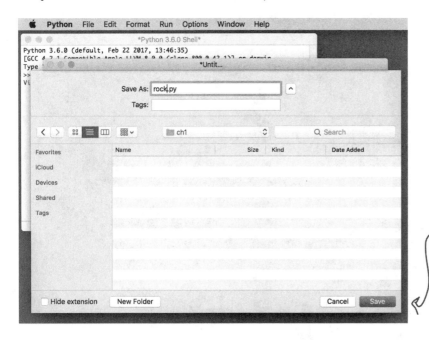

You'll want to follow the same code organization scheme we do in this book. If you haven't done so already, take a look at page xxxvi in the book's introduction.

Finally, when you have a folder for your code and a name, click Save.

A Test Drive

This is where it all comes together. After you've got the code saved, choose the **Run > Run Module** menu item. After that, look at the Python Shell window and you should see your program's output there.

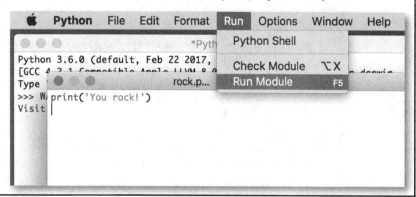

Execute your code by using the Run Module menu item in the Run menu. If you haven't saved your code, IDLE will ask you to.

Congrats on coding your first Python program!

You've installed Python, you've entered a short bit of real Python code using IDLE, and you've even executed your first Python program. Now it's not a very complex bit of code, but you've gotta start somewhere. And the good news is, we're all set up and ready to move on to a serious business application!

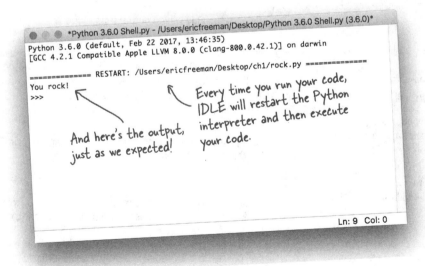

And here's the output, just as we expected!

Every time you run your code, IDLE will restart the Python interpreter and then execute your code.

Watch it!

Did you get something other than "You rock!"?

The process of writing and testing code can be error-prone. If you weren't successful on your first try, get used to it: all of us developers are constantly fixing errors in our code. Here are a few things to try:

- *If Python reported an error like* `invalid syntax` *check your code for incorrect punctuation, like missing parentheses. If you look at the code highlighting in IDLE, usually you can quickly determine where these errors are.*

- *If Python reported an error like* `Python NameError: name 'prin' is not defined` *check your code for typos, like a name that isn't spelled correctly—in this case, the word* `print`*.*

- *If Python reported an error like* `EOL while scanning` *that typically means you left out a single quote on one of the* `'You rock'` *string of characters—make sure you've surrounded it with two single quotes, like* `'You rock!'`*.*

- *If you're really stuck, try the book's community page on wickedlysmart.com.*

---

there are no Dumb Questions

Q: Why do we use Run Module to execute our code?

A: Python calls a file of Python code a *module*. So, all this means is "run all the Python code in my file." Modules are also a way to further organize code that we'll get to later.

Q: What exactly do you mean by input and output?

A: Right now we're just dealing with simple kinds of input and output. Our output is the text that is generated from your program and displayed in the Python Shell window. Likewise, input is any text your program gets from you in the shell window. More generally, all kinds of input and output are possible, such as mouse input, touch input, graphics and sound output, and so on.

Q: I've figured out that print gives you a way to print text to the user, but why the name print? When I first saw that, I thought it was something for the printer.

A: Think way, way back to when computers were more likely to output to a printer than a screen. Back in those days, the name **print** made a lot more sense than it does now. Of course, Python is young enough to not have an excuse for using the name **print**, but print has traditionally been the way to output to the screen in a lot of languages. So, **print** outputs to the screen (by way of the Python Shell window), and on a related note, you saw an example earlier of **input**, which gets user input from the Python Shell.

Q: Is print the only way to output from Python?

A: No, it's just the most basic way. Computers and programming languages excel at output (and input), and Python is no exception. Using Python (or most languages), you can output to web pages, the network, files on storage devices, graphics devices, audio devices, and many other things.

Q: Okay, well, when I use print, I type something like print('hi there'). What exactly is going on there?

A: What you're doing is using some functionality built into Python to print. More specifically, you're asking a function called **print** to take your text in quotes and output it to the Python Shell. Now, we're going to be getting more into exactly what functions are, what text is, and so on later, but, for now, just know you can use this function anytime you want to print to the shell.

Python Exposed

This week's interview: are you serious?

Head First: Welcome, Python! We're looking forward to digging in and finding out what you're all about.

Python: Glad to be here.

Head First: Let's see, you're named after a comedy troupe, and you're known for being a beginner's language; honestly, should anyone take you seriously?

Python: Well, let's see, I'm used for everything from running silicon chip production lines to applications that help create major motion pictures (you didn't hear it from me, but can you say, "George Lucas"?) to powering interfaces for air traffic control systems. I could go on... does that sound serious?

Head First: Well, then, if you're such a serious language, how on earth can newbies easily use you? I mean, the projects you're describing sound quite complex. Would you have us believe it doesn't take a hardcore, complex language to pull all that off?

Python: One of the reasons newbies *and professionals* appreciate me is because my code is quite straightforward and readable. Ever look at a language like, say, Java? Blech. My gosh, the effort you have to go to just to say, "Hello World!" That takes a single line of Python code.

Head First: Okay, you're readable, great, but what exactly does that mean, anyway?

Python: Given I mentioned Java, let me just give you a little example. Let's say you want to tell your user "Hello!" Here's how you do it with Java:

```
class HelloWorldApp {

  public static void main(String[] args) {

    System.out.println("Hello!");

  }

}
```

That's a lot to take in. I'd call it totally unreadable, especially to someone just learning to program. What the heck does all that mean, anyway? Is all that really necessary? Now let's look at my version, which I've written in Python of course:

```
print('Hello!')
```

I think you'd have to agree that is more straightforward and readable—anyone can look at that line and have a decent idea of what it does. But that's just a simple example. Overall, Python strikes people as clear, almost English-like, and consistent...

Head First: Consistent? What does that mean?

Python: One way to think about consistency is that there aren't a lot of surprises in the language. In other words, once you understand a bit of the language, other things tend to work as you might guess, or expect. Not all languages are like that.

Head First: I want to go back to something you said earlier—you mentioned some rather esoteric examples, like air traffic control, chip manufacturing, being the main software for the space shuttle, and so on. That all sounds very industrial and special purpose. I'm not sure Python is going to be the best language for our readers.

Python: The space shuttle? You made that up. For the others, I was giving you examples of things you *might consider serious*, given that you claimed Python was otherwise. Some of the most common uses of Python are for things like creating websites, writing games, and even creating desktop apps.

Head First: Can we switch gears? Someone just handed me a note: our sources tell us that there are actually *two versions* of Python, and what's more, they are actually... gosh, how do I say it, *incompatible with each other*. How on earth is that being consistent?

Python: Like anything, languages tend to grow and evolve, and yes, there are two version of Python, version 2 and version 3. Version 3 has new things in it that were not part of version 2, but there are ways to make things backward compatible. Let me walk your readers through...

Head First: ...on that note, we're out of time. We look forward to our next ambush, er, I mean opportunity, to speak with you.

Python: Thanks, my pleasure...I think.

Try my new Phrase-O-Matic and you'll be a slick talker just like the boss or those guys in marketing...

Okay, it's time to get serious and to write a real-world business application using Python. Check out this Phrase-O-Matic code—you're going to be impressed.

Relax

Yes, we mean it! Your job right now is to take it all in by osmosis. Take a look at every line of code, read the description of what it does, and let it register in your brain. We've added some Python comments, which are just notes after the # marks, so you have a better idea of what this code does. Think of those comments as helpful pseudocode if you want. We'll talk about comments a bit later in the book. When you think you've made some sense of the code, move on to the next page and we'll walk through it in more detail.

1 # let python know we'll be using some random
functionality by importing the random module

```python
import random
```

2 # make three lists, one of verbs, one of adjectives,
and one of nouns

```python
verbs = ['Leverage', 'Sync', 'Target',
         'Gamify', 'Offline', 'Crowd-sourced',
         '24/7', 'Lean-in', '30,000 foot']

adjectives = ['A/B Tested', 'Freemium',
              'Hyperlocal', 'Siloed', 'B-to-B',
              'Oriented', 'Cloud-based',
              'API-based']

nouns = ['Early Adopter', 'Low-hanging Fruit',
         'Pipeline', 'Splash Page', 'Productivity',
         'Process', 'Tipping Point', 'Paradigm']
```

3 # choose one verb, adjective, and noun from each list

```python
verb = random.choice(verbs)
adjective = random.choice(adjectives)
noun = random.choice(nouns)
```

4 # now build the phrase by "adding" the words together

```python
phrase = verb + ' ' + adjective + ' ' + noun
```

5 # output the phrase

```python
print(phrase)
```

Phrase-O-Matic

In a nutshell this program takes three lists of words, randomly picks one word from each list, combines the words into a phrase (suitable for your next startup's slogan), and then prints out the phrase. Don't worry if you don't understand every aspect of this program; after all, you're on page 25 of a 600-page book. The point here is just to start to get some familiarity with code:

1 The `import` statement tells Python we're going to be using some additional built-in functionality that's in Python's `random` module. Think of this as extending what your code can do—in this case, by adding the ability to randomly choose things. We'll get into the details of how `import` works later in the book.

2 Next we need to set up three lists. Declaring a list is straightforward—just place each item in the list within quotes and surround it by square brackets, like this:

```
verbs = ['Leverage', 'Sync', 'Target',
         'Gamify', 'Offline', 'Crowd-sourced',
         '24/7', 'Lean in', '30,000 foot']
```

Notice we're assigning each list to a name, like `verbs`, so we can refer to it later in the code.

3 Next we need to choose one word randomly from each list. To do that we're using `random.choice`, which takes a list and randomly chooses one item. We then take that item, and assign it to the corresponding name (`verb`, `adjective`, or `noun`) so we can refer to it later.

random.choice is another built-in function from Python. We'll learn more about these later in the book.

4 We then need to create the phrase, and we do this by gluing the three items together (the verb, adjective, and noun)—in Python we can glue these together using the plus sign. Notice also that we have to insert spaces between the words; otherwise, we'd end up with phrases like "Lean-inCloud-basedPipeline."

Computer scientists like to call gluing text together "concatenation." It's a pretty handy word, so you'll see it more in this book.

5 Finally, we output the phrase to the Python Shell with the print statement and...voila! *We're in marketing.*

Slogans for Your Next Python-based Startup

24/7 Freemium Productivity

Lean-in Hyperlocal Splash Page

Gamify Siloed Early Adopter

Offline API-based Process

Crowd-sourced Cloud-based Pipeline

Getting the code in the machine

You've entered one program into IDLE, but let's step through it again—we're going to create a new Python file by choosing **File** > **New File** from the menu. Go ahead and do that, and then type the code from two pages back into the editor.

Here's an example of a typo; notice how it is highlighted. If you get this, double-check that your code is correct.

Pay special attention to the words and punctuation that are being used. We'll get to all this detail in later chapters, but for now it's great to get accustomed to it.

Note that IDLE highlights common errors. You might see errors highlighted while you're typing your code or when you run your code, depending on the error. Here a missing quote error is highlighted. If you see any errors, you'll want to double-check the code and fix them.

We purposefully added an error here to show what IDLE does; as long as you faithfully type in the code from two pages back, you should not see this error.

Now that you've typed in all the code, let's save it. Remember, to do that just choose **File** > **Save** from the IDLE menu and then save your code as *phraseomatic.py*.

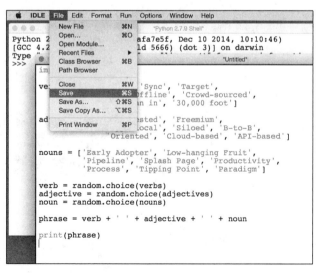

Remember, IDLE will color your code according to its function.

IDLE will also insert indenting when appropriate after you hit the Return key.

Notice that extra whitespace—that is, spaces and return characters—can be used to make your code more readable; Python largely ignores whitespace (we'll talk about an exception to that later).

A Test Drive

Now it's time to run the Phrase-O-Matic. Let's explicitly go through this once more to really set it in—after you've got the code saved, choose the **Run > Run Module** menu item. After that, look for the output in the shell window, and get ready for your next startup's slogan!

Remember, to execute your code, use the Run Module menu item in the Run menu. If you haven't saved your code, IDLE will ask you to.

We're going to Gamify A/B Tested Splash Pages!

We ran Phrase-O-Matic a few times; check out what we got.

```
                                          Python 2.7.10 Shell
>>>
Sync B-to-B Early Adopter
>>> ================================ RESTART ========================
==========
>>>
Leverage Siloed Productivity
>>> ================================ RESTART ========================
==========
>>>
24/7 A/B Tested Low-hanging Fruit
>>> ================================ RESTART ========================
==========
>>>
Crowd-sourced API-based Tipping Point
>>> ================================ RESTART ========================
==========
>>>
Sync API-based Low-hanging Fruit
>>>
                                                              Ln: 9 Col: 0
```

To re-run Phrase-O-Matic, first click on your code window, then choose Run > Run Module again.

BULLET POINTS

- To write code, you first have to break a problem down into a simple set of actions that solves the problem.

- We call this set of actions an algorithm, or less formally a recipe for solving a problem.

- Actions are in the form of statements that can carry out very simple tasks, make decisions, or control the flow of an algorithm by repeating parts of the code.

- Computational thinking is a way of thinking about problem solving that grew out of computer science.

- Coding is the act of taking an algorithm and translating its steps into a programming language that can be executed on a computer.

- Algorithms are sometimes expressed in a more human-readable pseudocode before being translated to an actual programming language.

- Programming languages are special-purpose languages created expressly for describing tasks to computers.

- English makes for a poor programming language because it is quite ambiguous.

- There are many programming languages, each created with inherent advantages and disadvantages, but all have the same computational power.

- The Python name doesn't come from a snake, but from the creator's love of the Monty Python comedy troupe.

- New and experienced programmers appreciate Python's clean and consistent design.

- There are two versions of Python, 2 and 3, and this book focuses on Python 3 (although the differences are minor in a lot of cases).

- Python code is executed by an interpreter, which translates high-level Python code into low-level machine code that your computer can execute directly.

- Python provides an editor called IDLE that is tailored to writing Python code.

- You can use whitespace in a Python program to increase readability.

- **input** and **print** are two functions provided by Python for simple, shell-based input and output.

Coding Crossword

Let's give your right brain something to do.

It's your standard crossword, but all of the solution words are from Chapter 1.

Across
1. Layman's term for algorithm.
5. Python IDE.
6. Input to interpreter or compiler.
7. Language named for coffee.
8. Human-readable code.
10. Flying _____.
11. Technical name for recipe.
12. One of best beginner languages.
14. Low-level code.
16. Python is this type of language.
17. Python is one of them.

Down
2. Running a program.
3. Another word for source code.
4. Kind of thinking this book teaches.
9. Too ambiguous for code.
10. Supportive side of Python.
13. Head First Diner serves them.
15. One company using Python

Sharpen your pencil
Solution

Real recipes don't just tell you *what to do*, they also include objects that are used in making a particular food (like utensils, appliances, and ingredients). What objects are used in our fishing recipe?

(1) Put (worm) on (hook)

(2) Cast (line) into (pond)

(3) Watch the (bobber) until it goes underwater.

(4) Hook and pull in (fish)

(5) If done fishing, then go (home); otherwise, go back to step 1.

Sharpen your pencil
Solution

One thing to understand right up front is that computers do **exactly** what you tell them—nothing more, nothing less. Look at our recipe for fishing on page 2. If you were the robot and you followed these instuctions precisely, what problems might you encounter? Do you think we would really be successful using this recipe?

☑ A. If there are no fish, you're going to be fishing for a very long time (like, forever).

☑ B. If the worm falls off the hook, you'll never know about it or replace it.

☑ C. What happens if we run out of worms?

It looks like the answer was "all of the above."

☑ D. Did we specify what to do with a fish when we pulled it in?

☑ E. What happened to the fishing rod?

☑ F. Are there any specifics of what a good cast is? If the worm lands on a lily pad, do we need to redo the cast?

Typically when the bobber goes underwater, you try to "hook" the fish before pulling it in. This doesn't say anything about that.

How do we know if we're done fishing? By the time? When we're out of worms? Something else?

There's a lot we assumed in our recipe; we're sure you probably thought of a lot of other instructions that were unspecified in addition to these.

Code Magnets Solution

We put the Head First Dinner's ~~recipe~~ algorithm for making an three-egg omelet on the fridge to remember it, but someone came along and messed it up. Can you put the magnets back in the right order to make our algorithm work? Note that the Head First Dinner makes two kinds of omelets: plain and cheese.

Here are the unscrambled magnets!

There are several correct variations you could come up with; just make sure you understand our solution, and that yours, if different, makes logical sense.

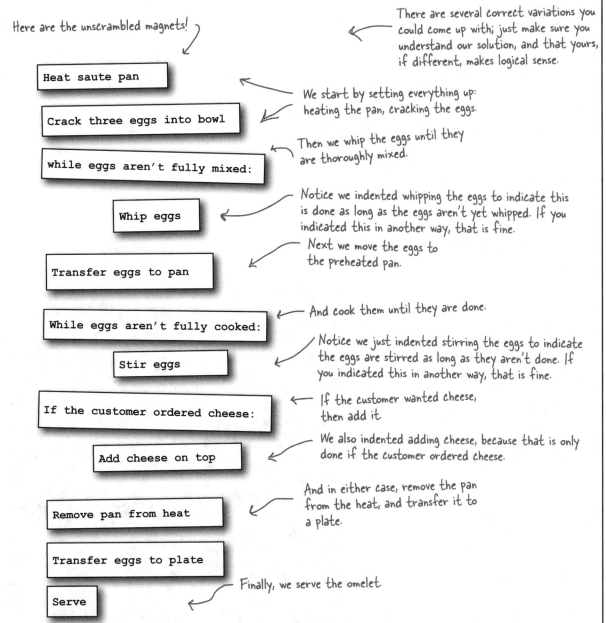

```
Heat saute pan
```

We start by setting everything up: heating the pan, cracking the eggs.

```
Crack three eggs into bowl
```

Then we whip the eggs until they are thoroughly mixed.

```
while eggs aren't fully mixed:
```

```
        Whip eggs
```

Notice we indented whipping the eggs to indicate this is done as long as the eggs aren't yet whipped. If you indicated this in another way, that is fine.

```
Transfer eggs to pan
```

Next we move the eggs to the preheated pan.

```
While eggs aren't fully cooked:
```

And cook them until they are done.

```
        Stir eggs
```

Notice we just indented stirring the eggs to indicate the eggs are stirred as long as they aren't done. If you indicated this in another way, that is fine.

```
If the customer ordered cheese:
```

If the customer wanted cheese, then add it.

```
        Add cheese on top
```

We also indented adding cheese, because that is only done if the customer ordered cheese.

```
Remove pan from heat
```

And in either case, remove the pan from the heat, and transfer it to a plate.

```
Transfer eggs to plate
```

```
Serve
```

Finally, we serve the omelet.

YOU SAY TOMATO SOLUTION

On the left you'll find some statements written in English, and on the right you'll find statements written in a programming language. Draw a line from each English statement to its corresponding code translation. We did the first one for you.

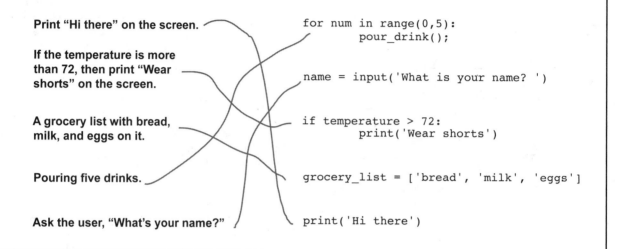

Print "Hi there" on the screen.

If the temperature is more than 72, then print "Wear shorts" on the screen.

A grocery list with bread, milk, and eggs on it.

Pouring five drinks.

Ask the user, "What's your name?"

```
for num in range(0,5):
        pour_drink();

name = input('What is your name? ')

if temperature > 72:
        print('Wear shorts')

grocery_list = ['bread', 'milk', 'eggs']

print('Hi there')
```

Coding Crossword Solution

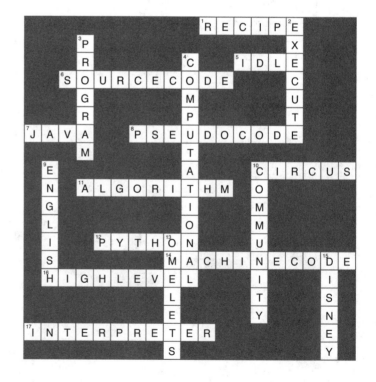

2 simple values, variables, and types

✳ *Know Your Value* ✳

Computers really only do two things well: store values and perform operations on those values. You might think they're doing a whole lot more, as you send texts, shop online, use Photoshop, or rely on your phone to navigate in your car; however, everything computers do can be broken down into **simple operations** that are performed on **simple values**. Now, part of **computational thinking** is learning to use these operations and values to build something that is much more sophisticated, complex, and meaningful—and we're going to get to that. First, though, we're going to take a look at what these values are, the operations you can perform on them, and just what role **variables** play in all this.

Coding the Dog Age Calculator

You didn't think we were going to take you through 50 pages of Python specifications on values and operations before writing some real code, did you? Of course not—we've got real work to do!

Up next, the **Dog Age Calculator**. You already know what the calculator does: you enter a dog's chronological age and the calculator tells you the dog's age in relative *human years*. To perform that calcuation you simply multiply the dog's chronological age by the number 7. Or, is it that simple? We shall see...

But where do we even start? Do we just start trying to write some code? Well, remember the concept of pseudocode, which we briefly discussed in the last chapter? Recall that pseudocode allows you to work out a high-level solution of your problem before you have to get into all the specifics required to write code. That's a good place to start.

Especially given you don't know how to code yet!

So what exactly is pseudocode? Think of it as nothing more than your algorithm written in human-readable form. With pseudocode, you typically spell out, step by step, everything your solution needs to do to solve your problem (in our case, figuring out a dog's age in human years).

Remember, you've already seen one example of pseudocode in the fishing recipe on page 2 of Chapter 1.

They say 12 is the new 9...

Codie, 12

Sharpen your pencil

We're going to write some pseudocode. First, think about how you'd write an algorithm or recipe that computes a dog's age in human years. Once you have an idea, write it down as a set of steps in plain English (or your chosen language). Make your solution user-friendly by asking the user for the dog's name and age. You'll also want to generate some nice output at the end, like "Your dog, Rover, is 72 years old in human years."

Again, just write your pseudocode in English. **Important**: make sure that you compare your answer with ours at the end of the chapter before you move on.

Or, if you get stuck, feel free to peek ahead.

Write your pseudocode here.

Here is an example of how the Dog Age Calculator will work.

Sparky, 1

Fido, 5

```
Python 3.6.0 Shell
What is your dog's name? Codie
What is your dog's age? 12
Your dog Codie is 84 years old in human years
>>>
```

Going from pseudocode to code

Now that we've written our pseudocode, we have a good sense of the steps our code will need to take to implement the Dog Age Calculator—of course the pseudocode doesn't provide every detail, but it will provide us with a nice guide to follow as we *implement* each step in code.

So let's do just that: we'll take our pseudocode step by step, and implement as we go.

When we translate our ideas, algorithms, or pseudocode to real code, we often say we're implementing them.

Sharpen your pencil

As a first step to transforming our pseudocode into code, step through each line of your pseudocode and make some notes about what you think the code will have to do. Just keep it high level. Make sure and check your answers with ours before you move on. We did the first one for you.

As always, if you get stuck, feel free to peek ahead, but try not to until you've made a first pass through every line.

Dog Age Calculator Pseudocode

1. Ask the user for the dog's name.

2. Ask the user for the dog's age.

3. Multiply the dog's age by the number 7 to get the dog's age in human years.

4. Output to the user:

   "Your dog"
   the dog's name
   "is"
   the dog's age in human years
   "years old in human years"

---

1. Prompt the user to get the dog's name and then have the user type it in. We'll presumably need to save the name somewhere so we can use it in step 4.

2.

3.

4.

Put your notes for each step here.

---
there are no
Dumb Questions

Q: Why bother with something English-like when the computer only understands a programming language?

A: Working out things in pseudocode gives you the opportunity to think about your algorithm without the burden and complexity of actual computer code. It also gives you the opportunity to study your solution, possibly improving it, before committing it to code.

Q: Do experienced software developers use pseudocode?

A: Yes. Planning out how you are going to attack a problem before committing it to more complex coding is always a good idea. Some developers are good enough to do a lot of that in their head, but many still use pseudocode or similar techniques to map out things before they code. Pseudocode is also commonly used for communicating coding ideas to other developers.

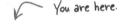 You are here.

Step 1: Getting some input

Now we're ready to tackle step 1—asking the user for the dog's name. As we've indicated in our notes, we're going to need to prompt the user to give us their dog's name, and then remember that name so we can use it in step 4 (when we print out the name and dog's age in human years). So there's really two things we need to do here: prompt the user to get the dog's name, and then store that name for later use. Let's focus on prompting the user and getting the name first.

You may have already noticed in a couple of the code exercises from Chapter 1 that we used a Python function named `input` to solicit input from the user. While a function may sound like something from math class, think of it as just a way to call upon built-in functionality provided by Python.

Let's look at the syntax for *calling* the `input` function and then we'll look at how it works:

↖ Remember, the syntax tells us how we write things in a computer language.

> **Dog Age Calculator Pseudocode**
>
> ► 1. **Ask the user for the dog's name.**
> 2. **Ask the user for the dog's age.**
> 3. **Multiply the dog's age by the number 7 to get the dog's age in human years.**
> 4. **Output to the user:**
>   "Your dog"
>   **the dog's name**
>   "is"
>   **the dog's age in human years**
>   "years old in human years"

We're going to spend a lot of time on functions in this book, and before long you'll understand exactly how they work, but for now just think of them as a way of asking Python to do some work for us and don't worry too much about the details.

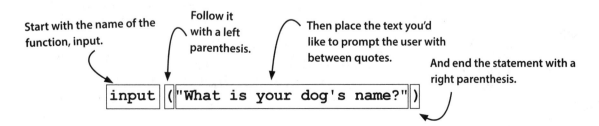

Start with the name of the function, input.

Follow it with a left parenthesis.

Then place the text you'd like to prompt the user with between quotes.

And end the statement with a right parenthesis.

```
input ("What is your dog's name?")
```

How the input function works

Alright, we now know how to type in the `input` function (in other words we know the syntax), but how does it actually work? Like this:

① When the interpreter sees your call to the `input` function, it takes your prompt text and displays it for the user in the Python Shell.

② The interpreter then waits for the user to type in a response, which the user completes by pressing the Return key.

③ Finally, the text the user typed in is passed back to your code.

Okay, so the text the user typed in is passed back to our code, but what does that mean? Well, when you call the `input` function, it goes off and gets text from the user and then, as a result of calling the function, *returns* that text for your code to make use of.

Now, that text isn't going to be too useful if we can't remember it for later, because we'll need it in step 4 when we print out our user-friendly output. So, how do we remember things with Python?

Make it stick

Syntax tells us how to write Python statements.

Semantics tell us what Python statements mean.

Using variables to remember and store values

One of the most common things you'll do when programming is to store a value so you can use it later. To do that, we use a **variable**. Think of a variable as a name you can always use to retrieve a value you've previously stored. Here's how we store, or *assign*, a value to a variable:

Pretty much every programming language you're ever going to encounter works this way too.

First name your variable. Almost any name will do, but we'll talk more about legal names in a bit...

Next add an equals sign, followed by the value you want stored and assigned to your variable.

We refer to text as a string. Think of this like a string of characters. You'll find this terminology is common across practically every programming language. There are a lot of other types of values you can use in Python too, such as numbers, which we'll talk about soon.

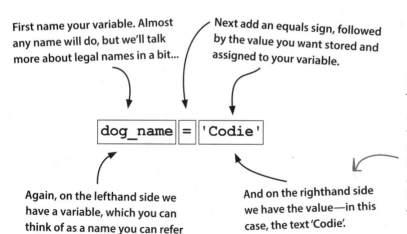

```
dog_name = 'Codie'
```

Again, on the lefthand side we have a variable, which you can think of as a name you can refer to over and over to recall a value.

And on the righthand side we have the value—in this case, the text 'Codie'.

Assigning the user's input to a variable

Now that you know a little bit about variables (don't worry, we're going to dive in deep in a few pages), let's store the user's input in a variable. To do that we simply call the **input** function and assign its *return value* to a variable. Here's how we do that:

Let's use the variable dog_name.

Then we call the input function, which prompts the user with "What is your dog's name?"

Wondering about how to name variables? Or how to correctly use single and double quotes? Hang on, we'll discuss both shortly.

```
dog_name = input("What is your dog's name? ")
```

When the user finishes entering a name, the input function then passes that name back to your code in the form of a return value.

And that return value is then assigned to the variable dog_name.

We're moving on to step 2.

Step 2: Getting more input

We also need to get the dog age from the user. How? We'll do this just like we did with the dog name: first we make use of the **input** function and supply it with a prompt like "What is your dog's age?" Then we will take the age the user types in and store this in a variable called, say, dog_age. When we say "we will" we actually mean YOU will, in this next exercise:

> **Dog Age Calculator Pseudocode**
>
> 1. **Ask the user for the dog's name.**
> 2. **Ask the user for the dog's age.**
> 3. **Multiply the dog's age by the number 7 to get the dog's age in human years.**
> 4. **Output to the user:**
>   "Your dog"
>   **the dog's name**
>   "is"
>   **the dog's age in human years**
>   "years old in human years"

Exercise

It's your turn. Write the code to get the dog's age using the input function, just as we did with the dog's name. Prompt the user with "What is your dog's age?" and store the result in a variable called dog_age. Make some notes as well about what each piece of your code does. Check your answer in the back of the chapter before moving on.

It's time to run some code

It's one thing to look at code on paper, and it's another to actually execute real code. Let's take the code from the last couple of pages and get some experience executing it in a different way—rather than entering code into IDLE's editor, we're going to use the Python Shell instead. Why? Well, you're going to see that the shell is a great way to experiment with and test small pieces of code. Don't worry: when we get to writing longer programs, we'll be right back in the editor.

> *Using the shell is a great way to test out small pieces of code to see how it works.*

To use the shell, run idle3 as usual, only this time we'll be typing into the Python Shell window:

```
Python 3.6.0 Shell

Python 3.6.0 (default, Feb 22 2017, 13:46:35)
[GCC 4.2.1 Compatible Apple LLVM 8.0.0] on darwin
Type "copyright", "credits" or "license()" for more information.
>>>
```

This is the shell prompt; it's waiting for you to type something.

Your version numbers and startup messages may differ slightly depending on your version and operating system, as may your window's look and feel and color.

After you've located the shell, click in the window and locate the prompt, which looks like >>>. Type 1 + 1 and hit return; Python will evaluate your expression and print its value (in this case 2) before displaying another prompt. Congrats, you've successfully used the Python Shell! Now let's try some of our code:

1 Let's start by entering the code to get the dog's name and then hitting return.

```
Python 3.6.0 Shell

>>> dog_name = input("What is your dog's name? ")
What is your dog's name?
```

Type this in and hit return.

Python will display this.

2 Next, enter your favorite dog name and press return again.

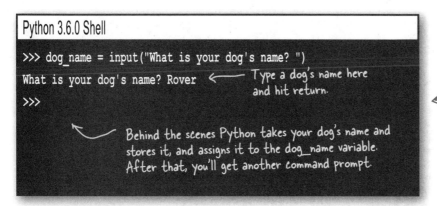

Python 3.6.0 Shell

```
>>> dog_name = input("What is your dog's name? ")
What is your dog's name? Rover     ←——— Type a dog's name here
                                          and hit return.
>>>
```

Behind the scenes Python takes your dog's name and stores it, and assigns it to the dog_name variable. After that, you'll get another command prompt.

Notice that an assignment statement doesn't evaluate to a value like, say, 1 + 1 does. Rather, as you already know, the assignment statement takes the value on the righthand side and assigns it to the variable on the lefthand side.

BRAIN POWER

The variable dog_name should now hold the value **'Rover'**, or whatever dog name you entered. How can you show it does?

3 We've looked at print a few times; let's use print to see the value of the variable dog_name. You can also determine the value of dog_name more directly in the shell by just entering the variable name.

Python 3.6.0 Shell

```
>>> dog_name = input("What is your dog's name? ")
What is your dog's name? Rover
>>> print(dog_name)
Rover
>>> dog_name
'Rover'
>>>
```

We can use print to display the current value of the variable dog_name, which is Rover.

Or enter any variable and the shell will evaluate it, displaying its value.

Note that print does not display quotes around a string value, while evaluating it directly in the shell does.

> I noticed you can't keep your single and double quotes straight—sometimes you use text surrounded by single quotes and sometimes by double quotes. What's the deal?

Good catch. First of all, remember we call text in quotes **strings**, like a string of characters. And you are exactly right: we have mostly used single quotes but then changed to double quotes with the `input` function. As it turns out, Python doesn't care—either single or double quotes are just fine, as long as you are consistent. In other words, if you start a string with a single quote, then you have to end it with a single quote. Likewise, if you start a string with a double quote, then be sure to end it with a double quote.

So, why did we choose one over the other? In general a lot of Python developers prefer to use single quotes, and so do we; however, there is a case where you'll be forced to use double quotes, and that is when you need to use a single quote *as part of your string*.

Notice that our prompt needs to use a single quote in the word `dog's`:

```
dog_name = input("What is your dog's name? ")
```

To use a single quote as part of your string, just surround the text with double quotes.

The same is true if you need to use a double quote in your string's text, in which case you'll need to surround your string by single quotes.

Getting some code entered

Alright, enough playing around in the shell; we've got a real app to build here!
Next, we'll enter the existing two lines of code (the ones that prompt the user for
the dog's name and age), then give that code a quick test before moving on to
finish converting our pseudocode to code.

So, in IDLE, choose **File > New File** and let's get our first two lines of the
dog calculator typed in. Here's the code:

```
dog_name = input("What is your dog's name? ")
dog_age = input("What is your dog's age? ")
```

After you've entered and double-checked the code, choose **File > Save** and
save your work in a new folder *ch2* with the filename *dogcalc.py*.

*Note the extra space, so there
is space between the prompt
and where the user types.*

A Test Drive

*The Test Drive is where we'll
ask you to stop what you're
doing, make sure all the new
code is up to date, and then
execute and test your new
code.*

We're not done with the calculator yet, but it's a good idea to test code
as you go to make sure everything is working as you'd expect. After
you've saved the code, choose the **Run > Run Module** menu item.
Look for the output in your shell window. Remember, the code is going
to ask you to enter your dog's name and age.

*Keep in mind at this point
all your code will do is ask
you for your dog's name
and age, and then display
another prompt.*

```
Python 3.6.0 Shell

What is your dog's name? Rover
What is your dog's age? 12

>>>
```

*If you get a "SyntaxError: EOL while scanning string literal" when
executing this code, double-check your use of single and double quotes with
the code above.*

A deep dive on variables

We've gotten a little experience by creating a variable name and assigning a value to it, but how do these variables really work and how can you make use of them? Let's take a little time over the next few pages to better understand variables. After that, we'll finish off our Dog Age Calculator. Let's start by looking at what is happening behind the scenes when we assign a value to a variable.

```
dog_name = 'Codie'
```

← We often just call this "assignment."

1 The first thing Python does is evaluate the righthand side of the assignment, which evaluates to the string `'Codie'`, and then it finds a free spot in your computer's memory where it stores the string. You can think of this like taking an empty cup and throwing the text `'Codie'` in it.

Python creates a spot in your device's memory for a string, and places a 'Codie' there.

2 With the string `'Codie'` stored, Python then creates a label—think of it as a sticky note if you want—with the name **dog_name**, and puts it on the cup.

Next, a label, dog_name, is made and associated with the value's location in memory.

3 Of course we can create and store as many values as we need. How about two more:

```
phrase = "Your dog's name is "

dog_age = 12
```

Note we can store numbers as well as strings.

We can create as many values assigned to variables as we need, which will be stored in memory for us until we need them.

4 Anytime we need to retrieve the stored values, we can use the variables:

```
print(phrase)
print(dog_name)
```

This retrieves the value for phrase and dog_name, and then prints...

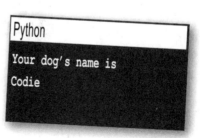

```
Python

Your dog's name is
Codie
```

Adding some expression

So far our values have been pretty simple, but there's no need for them to be—instead of using simple values, you can use *expressions* to *compute* values. If you've ever seen any form of mathematical expression, Python's expressions should look familiar to you: they just consist of simple values combined with *operators* like +, −, *, and /. For instance, what if it is Codie's birthday?

Almost without exception, programming languages use an asterisk for the multiplication symbol.

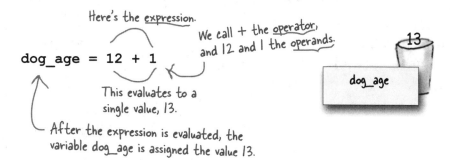

Here's the expression.

We call + the operator, and 12 and 1 the operands.

```
dog_age = 12 + 1
```

This evaluates to a single value, 13.

After the expression is evaluated, the variable dog_age is assigned the value 13.

dog_age

Or we need to compute Codie's weight in kilograms?

Here we're using the multiplication operator.

```
weight = 38 * 0.454
```

After this statement completes, weight has been assigned the value 17.252.

weight

Or we need to compute the average age of Codie, Fido, and Sparky?

```
avg = (12 + 5 + 1) / 3
```

We can group operations together using parentheses.

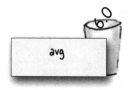

avg

In these expressions we can use variables anywhere you'd use a value. As an example, let's rewrite the average of Codie, Fido, and Sparky's age:

```
codie = 12
fido = 5
sparky = 1
avg = (codie + fido + sparky) / 3
```

Anywhere we put a variable, it is replaced with its value to compute the expression.

avg

Of course we aren't limited to simple math and numbers in our expressions. Remember concatenation from Chapter 1? We use concatenation to add strings together.

Let's create a couple strings.

```
greeting = 'Hi'
name = 'Codie'
message = greeting + ' ' + name
```

And add (or rather, concatenate) them together.

This expression evaluates to 'Hi Codie', which is assigned to the variable message.

message

Variables are called VARY-ables for a reason

Variables are called variables because their values usually *vary* over time. Let's take Codie's height for example, which we start at 22:

```
dog_height = 22
```

Here we're creating a new variable and assigning it the value 22.

22

dog_height

Let's say Codie has grown and we need to update his height by one inch, which changes the value that `dog_height` is holding.

```
dog_height = 22 + 1
```

As usual we evaluate the righthand side, which evaluates to 23, and then assign that value to dog_height. So, dog_height changes from 22 to 23.

23

dog_height

But there's a better way to update Codie's height. Let's do that when Codie grows another two inches:

```
dog_height = dog_height + 2
```

❷ *We then take 25 and make it the new value of dog_height.*

❶ *Remember we can use a variable anywhere we use a value, so on the righthand side we add 2 to the current value of dog_height, or, 23 + 2 = 25.*

25

dog_height

We need to talk about your operator precedence...

Better living through operator precedence

Evalute this expression:

```
mystery_number = 3 + 4 * 5
```

Is `mystery_number` 35? Or is it 23? Well, it depends on whether you added three to four first, or if you multiplied four time five first. What's the right answer? 23.

How did we know the right order of evaluation? *Operator precedence.* Operator precedence tells you the order in which operations should be applied. This isn't a computer programming thing, mind you, it's a mathematics thing, and in your algebra class you most likely covered precedence at some point (either recently or long ago). If you've forgotten it, no worries—we're going to cover it now.

To understand operator precedence, think of operators being listed from highest to lowest precedence, like this:

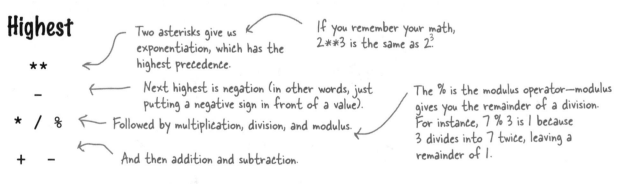

Highest

`**` — Two asterisks give us exponentiation, which has the highest precedence.

If you remember your math, $2**3$ is the same as 2^3.

`-` — Next highest is negation (in other words, just putting a negative sign in front of a value).

`* / %` — Followed by multiplication, division, and modulus.

The % is the modulus operator—modulus gives you the remainder of a division. For instance, 7 % 3 is 1 because 3 divides into 7 twice, leaving a remainder of 1.

`+ -` — And then addition and subtraction.

Lowest

Computing with operator precedence

Let's evaluate an expression to understand how operator precedence is applied. Here's an expression to evalute:

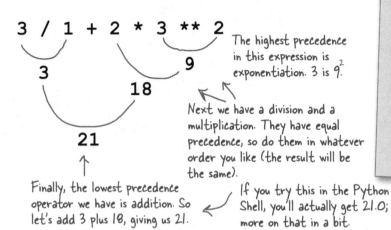

The highest precedence in this expression is exponentiation. 3 is 9^2.

Next we have a division and a multiplication. They have equal precedence, so do them in whatever order you like (the result will be the same).

Finally, the lowest precedence operator we have is addition. So let's add 3 plus 18, giving us 21.

If you try this in the Python Shell, you'll actually get 21.0; more on that in a bit.

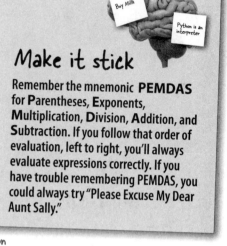

Make it stick

Remember the mnemonic **PEMDAS** for **P**arentheses, **E**xponents, **M**ultiplication, **D**ivision, **A**ddition, and **S**ubtraction. If you follow that order of evaluation, left to right, you'll always evaluate expressions correctly. If you have trouble remembering PEMDAS, you could always try "Please Excuse My Dear Aunt Sally."

You can determine how any Python numeric expression is evaluated by simply applying its operations in the order of their precedence (highest first). In these examples we're using numbers to keep things simple, but of course we could replace any of these numbers with variables and the same rules apply.

But what if this isn't the way you wanted to evaluate this expression? What if you really wanted to add 1 to 2 *before* the division and multiplication occurred? That's where parentheses come in. With parentheses you can dictate the order:

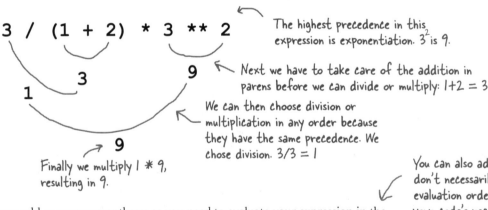

The highest precedence in this expression is exponentiation. 3^2 is 9.

Next we have to take care of the addition in parens before we can divide or multiply: 1+2 = 3

We can then choose division or multiplication in any order because they have the same precedence. We chose division. 3/3 = 1

Finally we multiply 1 * 9, resulting in 9.

You can also add parens that don't necessarily change evaluation order, but improve your code's readability.

You can add as many parentheses as you need to evaluate your expression in the appropriate order. For instance:

$$(((3 \ / \ 1) \ + \ 2) \ * \ 3) \ ** \ 2$$

This expression first does division, then addition, then multiplication, then exponentiation, and evaluates to 225.

Who am I?

A bunch of Python expressions lost their values. Can you help them get back together? For each expression on the left, draw a line to the value it evaluates to on the right. Careful—there may be an impostor hanging out too.

Expressions

'kit e' + ' ' + 'cat'

(14 - 9) * 3

3.14159265 * 32**

42

'h' + 'e' + 'l' + 'l' + 'o'

8 % 3

7 - 2 * 3

(7 - 2) * 3

Values

Who's the impostor?

1

2

15

21

28.27433385

42

-13

'kit e cat'

'hello'

Here's modulus again—it may seem esoteric, but it has a lot of uses in coding. Some folks like to call this remainder.

Exercise

Get ready for the classic shell game, usually played with cups and balls; in this game we're going to use variables and values. Using what you know about variables, values, and assignment, see if you can beat the cup game. Work through the code and see which cup has the number 1 in it at the end of the game. Will it be in cup 1, cup 2, or cup 3? Place your bet now!

```
cup1 = 0
cup2 = 1
cup3 = 0
cup1 = cup1 + 1
cup2 = cup1 - 1
cup3 = cup1
cup1 = cup1 * 0
cup2 = cup3
cup3 = cup1
cup1 = cup2 % 1
cup3 = cup2
cup2 = cup3 - cup3
```

Use your brain to evaluate this code and see, when it completes, which cup has the 1 in it. When you're done, check your answer at the end of the chapter (you can type the code in as well, but only to check yourself).

BRAIN POWER

What does this expression evaluate to? Or do you think this is an error in Python because we're multiplying a number times a string?

`3 * 'ice cream'`

You might want to try typing it into the Python Shell.

Crack the Code Challenge

You're all ready for your first spy assignment, but to get started you need your all-important passcode. You'll find the passcode below in code—that is, literally, in code. Work through the code in your head to figure out the passcode, but be careful—get it wrong, and it may be the last code you'll ever look at. We wish you luck.

```python
word1 = 'ox'
word2 = 'owl'
word3 = 'cow'
word4 = 'sheep'
word5 = 'flies'
word6 = 'trots'
word7 = 'runs'
word8 = 'blue'
word9 = 'red'
word10 = 'yellow'
word9 = 'The ' + word9
passcode = word8
passcode = word9
passcode = passcode + ' f'
passcode = passcode + word1
passcode = passcode + ' '
passcode = passcode + word6
print(passcode)
```

Here's your passcode; all you have to do is work through the code to get it.

This prints your passcode.

Back away from that keyboard!

You know variables have a name, and you know they have a value.

But what can you call your variables? Is any name okay? Well, no, but the rules around creating variable names are simple: just follow the two rules below to create valid variable names:

1 Start your variables with a letter or an underscore.

2 After that, use as many letters, numeric digits, or underscores as you like.

Oh, and one more thing: we really don't want to confuse Python by using any of the built-in *keywords*, like **False** or **while** or **if**, so consider those off-limits for your own variable names. We'll get to these keywords and what they mean throughout the rest of the book, but here's a list just to take a quick look at:

These rules are specific to Python; other programming languages have their own rules, which can be quite different.

False	as	continue	else	from	in	not	return	yield
None	assert	def	except	global	is	or	try	
True	break	del	finally	if	lambda	pass	while	
and	class	elif	for	import	nonlocal	raise	with	

Expect Python to complain or at least be confused if you use any of these reserved keywords as variable names.

there are no Dumb Questions

Q: What's a keyword?

A: A keyword is basically a word that Python reserves for its own use. Keywords are part of the core Python language, and so using them as variables in code would result in confusion.

Q: What if I used a keyword as part of my variable name? For instance, can I have a variable named if_only (that is, a variable that contains the keyword if)?

A: You sure can—just don't match the keyword *exactly*. It's also good to write clear code, so in general you wouldn't want to use something like **elze**, which might be confused with **else**. Again, we'll look at what these keywords mean throughout the book.

Q: Does Python consider myvariable and MyVariable the same thing?

A: Python treats these as two different variables names. More technically, Python is said to be *case sensitive*, meaning it treats upper- and lowercase letters differently. Today, most common programming languages are case sensitive, but not all are.

Q: Are there any conventions for naming variables? Do I use myVar, MyVar, or my_var, or does it matter?

A: There are conventions that Python programmers follow. Python programmers prefer to use lowercase letters for variables. If a variable name has multiple words, then put underscores between the words, like

max_speed, **height**, or **super_turbo_mode**. As we'll see later, there are some additional conventions for naming other things in Python. Also, these conventions are specific to Python; you'll find each language has its own conventions.

Q: Okay, but what makes a good variable name? Or does it matter?

A: To Python it doesn't matter at all, as long as your variable names follow the rules. To you, your variable names could matter a lot. When you choose names that are clear and meaningful, your code becomes more readable and understandable. Short, terse names can be hard to read, as can long, cumbersome names. In general, call variables what they are; for instance, don't name your variable **num** when you should have named it **number_of_hotdogs**.

Step 3: Computing the dog's age

We've got the first two steps in our pseudocode out of the way, so let's move on to step 3. In this step we simply need to multiply the dog's age by 7 to get the dog's age in human years. It seems like that would be straightforward, so let's do a little experimentation back in the shell:

> Could we get back to more pressing matters, namely the dog age code?

Jackson, 9

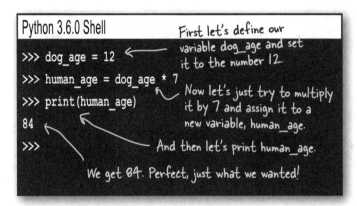

Python 3.6.0 Shell

```
>>> dog_age = 12
>>> human_age = dog_age * 7
>>> print(human_age)
84
>>>
```

First let's define our variable dog_age and set it to the number 12.

Now let's just try to multiply it by 7 and assign it to a new variable, human_age.

And then let's print human_age.

We get 84. Perfect, just what we wanted!

Dog Age Calculator Pseudocode

1. **Ask the user for the dog's name.**
2. **Ask the user for the dog's age.**
▶ 3. **Multiply the dog's age by the number 7 to get the dog's age in human years.**
4. **Output to the user:**
   "Your dog"
   the dog's name
   "is"
   the dog's age in human years
   "years old in human years"

We're here now in the pseudocode.

Sharpen your pencil

Below you'll find the Dog Age Calculator code so far. Using the experiment above as a guide, add the code to compute the dog age in human years.

```
dog_name = input("What is your dog's name? ")
dog_age = input("What is your dog's age? ")
```

Add your new code here, then check your answer before moving on.

A Test Drive

Let's test drive our code now that we've got step 3 coded. Go ahead and get the new code into your *dogcalc.py* file, save your code, and choose the **Run > Run Module** menu item. After that, head to the shell and enter your dog's name and age, and then check the output to see that we're calculating the human age correctly.

Here's the code again:

Add this new code to your file. →

```python
dog_name = input("What is your dog's name? ")
dog_age = input("What is your dog's age? ")
human_age = dog_age * 7
print(human_age)
```

Throughout the book you'll find the gray background signifies new code additions.

↖ Could you have printed dog_age * 7 directly? Like print(dog_age * 7)? Give it a try.

Houston, we've got a problem!

Did you get what we got? We entered that Codie was 12 and expected to see an output of 84, but we got 12121212121212! What on earth! Where did we go wrong? We've double-checked our code, and everything looks good. Why would this output be different than our test run in the command-line interpreter?

> Python 3.6.0 Shell
>
> What is your dog's name? Codie
> What is your dog's age? 12
> 12121212121212
> >>>   ⌐ Okay, that's not right!

BRAIN POWER

Think about the number 12121212121212. Is there anything you can think of that explains how Python got this number?

Hint: how many 12s are in 12121212121212?

To err is ~~human~~ to code

Finding and fixing **errors** is part of coding. No matter how well you plan your pseudocode and how diligent you are writing your code, errors are a part of coding life; in fact, most programmers view **debugging** as a natural part of the coding process. What's debugging? Debugging is the process of removing errors from the software you're writing. We formally call these errors *defects*, and informally everyone just calls them *bugs*.

As you code you'll actually encounter three different kinds of errors. Let's have a look at them:

They're called <u>bugs</u> because one of the first programming errors was caused by a moth that became stuck in an early computer relay. So, we ended up calling the process of removing errors *debugging*. More at: https://en.wikipedia.org/wiki/Software_bug.

syntax errors

You'll know quickly if you have a syntax error in Python when you get the dreaded `'Syntax Error'` message from the interpreter. **Syntax errors are the equivalent of making grammatical errors**—in other words, you've typed something that violates the conventions for writing correct Python. The good news is syntax errors are usually easy to fix—just find the offending line of code and double-check your syntax.

runtime errors

Runtime errors occur when you've written a syntactically correct program, but Python encounters a problem running your program. An example of a runtime error would be if at some point in your code you accidentally divided a number by zero (an invalid mathematical operation in any language). To fix runtime errors, look at the specific error you received and then track down where in your code you're causing the runtime condition to occur.

semantic errors

Semantic errors are also known as logic errors. With a semantic error your program will appear to operate normally—the interpreter won't complain that you've made a syntax error and at runtime you won't encounter any issues, but your program won't give you the results you expected. **These always occur because what you think you've told your program to do isn't actually what you're telling it to do.** Semantic errors can be some of the toughest errors to debug.

BRAIN POWER

We currently have a bug in our Dog Age Calculator because we're getting 121212121212 instead of 84. What kind of error is this?

☐ A. Runtime error

☐ B. Syntax error

☐ C. Semantic error

☐ D. Calculation error

☐ E. None of the above

☐ F. All of the above

Answer C because there are no syntax or runtime errors.

I noticed there are seven 12s, so somehow when we multiplied 12 by 7, Python didn't use multiplication, but rather just repeated the 12 seven times. I did a little experimenting in the Python Shell and I discovered if I multiply the **string** "12" by 7, I get the result of 12121212121212, but if I multiply the **number** 12 by 7, I get 84 like we'd expect.

Great debugging. The reason you got the result 12121212121212 instead of 84 is that Python, as you guessed, treated the dog age as a string and not a number. Why does that matter? Well, let's take a closer look at how Python deals with multiplication...

A little more debugging...

Let's do a little investigative debugging and see exactly what is happening. Using our handy Python Shell let's try a few things:

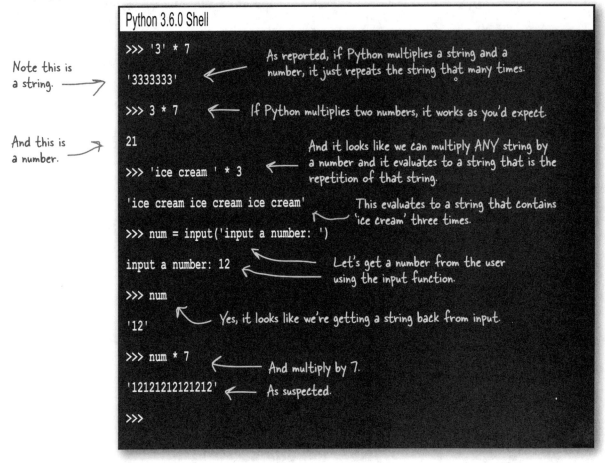

Note this is a string.

And this is a number.

```
Python 3.6.0 Shell
>>> '3' * 7

'3333333'              As reported, if Python multiplies a string and a
                       number, it just repeats the string that many times.

>>> 3 * 7        If Python multiplies two numbers, it works as you'd expect.

21
                              And it looks like we can multiply ANY string by
                              a number and it evaluates to a string that is the
>>> 'ice cream ' * 3          repetition of that string.

'ice cream ice cream ice cream'        This evaluates to a string that contains
                                       'ice cream' three times.
>>> num = input('input a number: ')

input a number: 12        Let's get a number from the user
                          using the input function.

>>> num

'12'         Yes, it looks like we're getting a string back from input.

>>> num * 7
                  And multiply by 7.
'12121212121212'      As suspected.

>>>
```

So why is Python treating the number we entered using the `input` function as a string? After all, we clearly typed in a number when prompted. The reason is because the **input** function always returns a string. How do we know? Well, while our experiment seems to bear this out, there are actually more direct ways to know. First of all, we could just look at the Python specification, which says:

input(*prompt*)   After the prompt argument is written to output, the function then reads a line from input, converts it to a string, and returns that.

This definition is from the Python specification (we abbreviated it slightly).

There are also ways, in code, we could examine the value and determine it is a string. Both of these topics, specifications and examining values, are something we'll be getting to later, but for now just know that we've uncovered the problem: *input is returning a string when we need a number.*

> Aren't these computers? Python can't even figure out that when I'm multiplying a number with a number in a string, I want to do **real multiplication** rather than just repeat the string over and over? How dumb is that?

Careful what you ask for...

It certainly feels like Python could just figure this out and decide our string is actually a number, but that might lead to surprises down the road when you really meant for a number to be a string. That's the thing: it's hard for an interpreter to decide the right thing every time, and that is why Python tries NOT to make any assumptions. Python, as we said early on, tries to avoid surprises by taking you at your word (er, code)—if you say something is a string, then Python treats it as a string. If you instead represent something as a number, then Python's good with that too. What Python *doesn't* like to do is start guessing what you intend, because it's going to get it wrong a lot of the time, leading to more debugging by you.

What this all means is that as a programmer you're better served by understanding the type of data you're using and operating on. So, maybe we need to take a closer look at types and what they're all about.

What are Python types, anyway?

Every piece of data in Python has a **type**. Types are important because they determine how Python operates on our data. As we've seen with multiplication, it makes a big difference if we're multiplying a number by a string or a number by a number. So, as you code, you want to be very conscious of the types you're using and operating on.

We've already seen a few examples of different data types. We have **strings**, which, as you already know, you can think of as a sequence of characters, like "What is your dog's age?" We've also seen a few **number** types in passing. When it comes to numbers, Python supports two main types: **integers** and **floats**. Let's take a closer look:

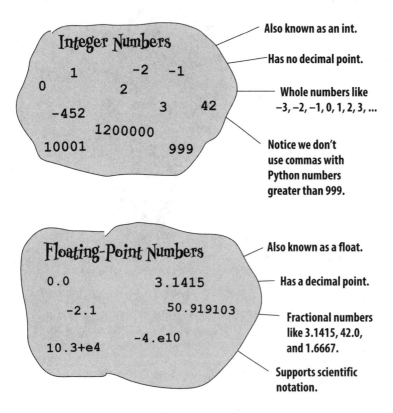

Integer Numbers
- 0 1 -2 -1
- 2
- -452 3 42
- 1200000
- 10001 999

Also known as an int.

Has no decimal point.

Whole numbers like −3, −2, −1, 0, 1, 2, 3, …

Notice we don't use commas with Python numbers greater than 999.

Floating-Point Numbers
- 0.0 3.1415
- -2.1 50.919103
- -4.e10
- 10.3+e4

Also known as a float.

Has a decimal point.

Fractional numbers like 3.1415, 42.0, and 1.6667.

Supports scientific notation.

Python has other types too, like **booleans**, **lists**, **dictionaries**, and **objects**, that we'll be getting to later in the book.

Dumb Questions

Q: I get that a string is a sequence of characters, but what can I do with them other than concatenate them and print them out?

A: Don't be fooled by our simple beginnings: string processing is an important part of our computational world—just think of all the text being processed by Google or Facebook as an example. We're going to explore strings a lot more as the book progresses and find out how we can search them, change them, format them, and create all kinds of interesting algorithms that operate on them.

Q: Do I have to worry about mixing integers and floats like I do with integers and strings?

A: Not really. Anytime you use ints and floats together in an expression, Python will typically convert everything to a floating-point value.

Q: What if a variable is assigned to an int value and then I switch it to be assigned to a string value?

A: Python is totally fine with that. Remember the value has a type, not the variable. So you can assign variables to values and change those values over time, even if it means the type changes as well. Note, however, that this is not considered a good practice, as code quickly becomes confusing when variables change types in a piece of code.

Serious Coding

In need of some rocket-scientist-style numbers? Python has you covered there too; with Python you can use scientific notation or imaginary numbers should you need to.

Fixing our code

Well, it looks like our little bug was caused by an assumption we made about types: we assumed that if we supplied a number when prompted by the `input` function, then we'd have a number returned to us. But, as we've discovered, the `input` function always returns a string. No worries, though—this is exactly why we test as we go, to uncover bugs like this. And, as it turns out, Python has a handy way to convert a string to a numeric value.

Here's how it works:

①　First, let's create a string representation of a number.

```
answer = '42'
```

Here the string '42' is assigned to the variable answer.

②　Next, call the `int` function and pass it the string.

```
answer = int('42')
```

Look, Ma, I'm an int!

Here the string '42' is converted to an integer and assigned to the variable answer.

there are no
Dumb Questions

Q: **What happens if my string doesn't have a number in it and I call the int function? Like int('hi')?**

A: If you call the **int** function and pass it a string that does not contain a number, then you'll get a runtime error that indicates your value is not a number.

Q: **Does the int function work only with integers values; for instance, could I use int('3.14')?**

A: The **int** function only works for integers (or rather, strings that represent integers), but if you need to convert a string that contains a float value, like **'3.14'**, you can use the **float** function, like **float('3.14')**, to convert it to a floating-point value.

✏️ **Sharpen your pencil**

So we know that the bug is caused by our assumption that `dog_age` is a number, when in fact Python is treating it as a string. Take the code below and add an `int` function to fix this problem.

There's a few ways to approach this, so be sure and check your work with the answer at the end of the chapter.

```
dog_name = input("What is your dog's name? ")
dog_age = input("What is your dog's age? ")
human_age = dog_age * 7
print(human_age)
```

A Test Drive

So now that we've figured out the code to convert the string to an int (in the last exercise), let's get it added. First make the changes below to update your code to handle the conversion of the dog age to an integer, then save your code and choose the **Run > Run Module** menu item. After that, head to the console and enter your dog's name and age, and check the output to see that we're *finally* calculating the human age correctly.

Here's the code (changes are highlighted):

We added the int function here so that the dog_age value is converted to an integer just before it is multiplied by 7.

```python
dog_name = input("What is your dog's name? ")
dog_age = input("What is your dog's age? ")
human_age = int(dog_age) * 7
print(human_age)
```

Houston, we have liftoff

Much better this time! Now our calculation works; we got 84 just as we'd expect. Give this version a few more test runs with some different values. After that, we're ready to implement the last step of our pseudocode and finish the Dog Age Calculator.

Python 3.6.0 Shell

```
What is your dog's name? Codie
What is your dog's age? 12
84          ⟵        Here's what we got.
>>>
```

Watch it!

If your code isn't working as expected...

As you already know, errors, whether they are runtime, syntactic, or semantic, can get in the way of your Dog Age Calculator working correctly. If Python is complaining about `invalid syntax` *check your code for incorrect punctuation, like missing parentheses. If you're still not seeing the issue, many people read the code backward to look for typos they aren't seeing, or do some peer review by having their friends look at the code and compare it with the book's source code. Also make sure you've got the* `int` *type conversion function and its parentheses. You can always download the source code as well and directly compare it with yours. Remember the code can be found at http://wickedlysmart.com/hflearntocode.*

Step 4: User-friendly output

Well, we've made it to the last step of our pseudocode—we have input from the user, we've computed the dog's age in human years, and now all we need to do is provide some nice output. To do that, we just need to survey our current variables, which hold all the values we need, and to use some `print` statements to output them as specified by our algorithm:

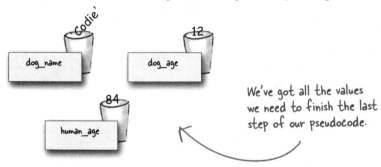

We've got all the values we need to finish the last step of our pseudocode.

Our pseudocode already does a nice job of specifying the exact output we need to code. Before we write the code, though, let's look at another way you can use the `print` function that will make your job easier. So far we've just been providing `print` with one *argument*, like:

We refer to the values we provide to a function as its arguments. We also typically say that we pass those arguments to a function.

print('Hi there')

Until now we've only been passing single values to print, either strings or numbers.

or:

print(42)

We've also used string concatenation to build up strings in the print function, but that still, ultimately, evaluates to just one argument.

or:

print('Good' + 'bye')

But you can actually pass multiple arguments to `print`, like:

You can pass as many arguments to print as you like, separated by commas.

When you pass multiple arguments, print will display each one with a one-space separator in between.

print('Hi there', 42, 3.7, 'Goodbye')

An argument is just a fancy name for the values you pass to a function. More on this topic as we progress...

```
Python 3.6.0 Shell

Hi there 42 3.7 Goodbye
>>>
```

Sharpen your pencil

With your newfound print functionality, write the code to call to
the `print` function that will produce the user-friendly output:

> **Output to the user:**
> "Your dog"
> **the dog's name**
> "is"
> **the dog's age in human years**
> "years old in human years"

*Here's what you
need to output.*

A Final Test Drive

Okay, we've got the step 4 code sketched out in the Sharpen exercise, which we've
reproduced below. Go ahead and make the changes, then save your code and
choose the **Run > Run Module** menu item. After that, head to the shell and give
your Dog Age Calculator a try!

Here's the code:

*Remove this
code.*

*Add this
code to your
dogcalc.py file.*

```python
dog_name = input("What is your dog's name? ")
dog_age = input("What is your dog's age? ")
human_age = int(dog_age) * 7
print(human_age)
print('Your dog',
      dog_name,
      'is',
      human_age,
      'years old in human years')
```

Our final output

```
Python 3.6.0 Shell

What is your dog's name? Codie
What is your dog's age? 12
Your dog Codie is 84 years old in human years
>>>
```

*Just what we'd
planned for!*

Brain Building

Well, the chapter is almost over; you've got just the bullet points and a crossword to go. Why not do a few extra reps for that brain before you go?

Here's one for you: say you have two variables, **first** and **last**, like below. Can you swap their values? See if you can write the code. As usual, you'll find our solution at the end of the chapter.

```python
first = 'somewhere'
last = 'over the rainbow'
print(first, last)
```

← Write your code here.

```python
print(first, last)
```

Here's the output you should get when you tune this code.

```
Python 3.6.0 Shell
somewhere over the rainbow
over the rainbow somewhere
>>>
```

What if you left the quotes off of Codie's name? What would this evaluate to?

```
dog_name = Codie
```

BULLET POINTS

- Computers do two things well: store values and perform operations on those values.

- Using pseudocode is a great way to start the design of your program.

- Syntax tells us how to form Python statements; semantics tells us what they mean.

- A file containing Python code is also called a module.

- You can use the Python Shell to enter and evaluate one statement or expression at a time.

- The input function prompts the user, gets a line of input, and returns it as a string.

- We call functions and they can return values as a result.

- We can store a value for later use by assigning it to a variable.

- When you assign a value to a variable, Python stores the value in memory, and labels it with the variable name for later use.

- A variable can vary, with its value changing over time.

- Python provides simple rules for naming variables and doesn't allow them to be named the same name as a keyword.

- Keywords are reserved words in a programming language.

- A string is a Python type that consists of a sequence of characters.

- Python supports two numeric types, integers and floating-point numbers, in addition to a couple other types indended for scientific computation.

- The int function will convert a string to an integer value. The `float` function converts a string to a floating-point value.

- We test our code often to detect issues early on.

- There are three kinds of errors: syntax, runtime, and semantic.

- If you multiply a string times a number, *n*, Python will repeat the string *n* times.

- You can combine strings with the concatenation operator.

- Concatenation just means adding strings together.

- For strings, Python uses + as the concatenation operator.

- When we pass values to functions, we call those values arguments.

Coding Crossword

It's time for something completely different. It's your standard crossword, but all of the solution words are from Chapter 2.

Across

3. What we're coding.
6. Can't name a variable after one of these.
7. Determines how we write statements in Python.
8. Stores a value for later use.
9. The other numeric type.
11. 12 years old.
13. Name of values passed to a function.
14. Input returns this.
17. Special character you can use in your variable names.
19. Another dog.
20. Another name for a file of Python.
21. Assign a variable to a value with this.

Down

1. Has a decimal point.
2. The value of a variable can do this.
4. Adding strings together.
5. What statements mean.
10. Input shows this to the user.
12. Function to convert strings to integers.
15. Evaluates your code line by line.
16. Values are stored in this.
18. Error encountered before your code is run.

Sharpen your pencil
Solution

We're going to write some pseudocode. First, think about how you'd write an algorithm or recipe that computes a dog's age in human years. Once you have an idea, write it down as a set of steps in plain English (or your chosen language). Make your solution user-friendly by asking the user for the dog's name and age. You'll also want to generate some nice output, like "Your dog, Rover, is 72 years old in human years."

Again, just write your pseudocode in English.

Ask the user for the dog's name.

Ask the user for the dog's age (in dog years).

— First we need to get some information from the user.

Multiply the dog's age by the number 7 to get the dog age in human years.

Output to the user:

"Your dog"

then the dog's name

— Next we'll need to calculate the dog's age in human terms.

"is"

then the dog's age in human years

← Finally, we need to output our results in a user–friendly manner.

"years old in human years"

Sparky, 1

Fido, 5

Sharpen your pencil
Solution

As a first step to transforming our pseudocode into code, step through each line of your pseudocode and make some notes about what you think the code will have to do. Just keep it high level.

Dog Age Calculator Pseudocode

1. Ask the user for the dog's name.

2. Ask the user for the dog's age.

3. Multiply the dog's age by the number 7 to get the dog's age in human years.

4. Output to the user:

   "Your dog"
   the dog's name
   "is"
   the dog's age in human years
   "years old in human years"

1. Prompt the user to get the dog's name and then have the user type it in. We'll presumably need to save the name somewhere so we can use it in step 4.

2. Prompt the user to get the dog's age and then have the user type it in. We'll also need to save this somewhere so we can use it in step 4.

3. Take the age from step 2 and multiply it by the number 7. We'll also need to store this somewhere for use in step 4.

4. First print to the console "Your dog", then print the value from step 1, then print "is", then print the value from step 3, then print "years old in human years".

Exercise
Solution

It's your turn. Write the code to get the dog's age using the `input` function, just as we did with the dog's name. Prompt the user with "What is your dog's age?" and store the result in a variable called `dog_age`. Make some notes as well about what each piece of your code does.

```
dog_age = input("What is your dog's age? ")
```

Here's our new variable, dog_age.

And here's the call to input, which will prompt the user with "What is your dog's age?" and then return the input to be stored in dog_age.

Who am I?
Solution

A bunch of Python expressions lost their values. Can you help them get back together? For each expression on the right, draw a line to the value it evaluates to. Careful—there may be some impostors hanging out too.

Expressions   ## Values

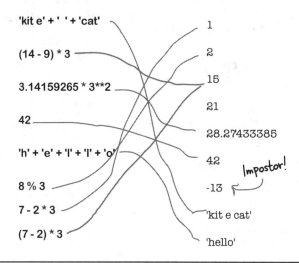

'kit e' + ' ' + 'cat'

(14 - 9) * 3

3.14159265 * 3**2

42

'h' + 'e' + 'l' + 'l' + 'o'

8 % 3

7 - 2 * 3

(7 - 2) * 3

1

2

15

21

28.27433385

42

-13   Impostor!

'kit e cat'

'hello'

Exercise
Solution

Get ready for the classic shell game, usually played with cups and balls; in this game we're going to use variables and values. Using what you know about variables, values, and assignment, see if you can beat the cup game. Work through the code and see which cup has the number 1 in it at the end of the game. Will it be in 1, 2, or 3? Place your bet now!

```
cup1 = 0                    cup1 is 0
cup2 = 1                    cup1 is 0, cup2 is 1
cup3 = 0                    cup1 is 0, cup2 is 1, cup3 is 0
cup1 = cup1 + 1             cup1 is 1, cup2 is 1, cup3 is 0
cup2 = cup1 - 1             cup1 is 1, cup2 is 0, cup3 is 0
cup3 = cup1                 cup1 is 1, cup2 is 0, cup3 is 1
cup1 = cup1 * 0             cup1 is 0, cup2 is 0, cup3 is 1
cup2 = cup3                 cup1 is 0, cup2 is 1, cup3 is 1
cup3 = cup1                 cup1 is 0, cup2 is 1, cup3 is 0
cup1 = cup2 % 1             cup1 is 0, cup2 is 1, cup3 is 0
cup3 = cup2                 cup1 is 0, cup2 is 1, cup3 is 1
cup2 = cup3 - cup3          cup1 is 0, cup2 is 0, cup3 is 1      Winner!
```

Crack the Code Challenge SOLUTION

You're all ready for your first spy assignment, but to get started you need your all-important passcode. You'll find the passcode below in code—that is, literally in code. Work through the code in your head to figure out the passcode, but be careful—get it wrong, and it may be the last code you'll ever look at. We wish you luck.

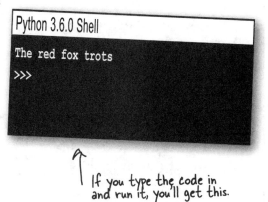

```
Python 3.6.0 Shell

The red fox trots
>>>
```

```
word1 = 'ox'
word2 = 'owl'
word3 = 'cow'
word4 = 'sheep'
word5 = 'flies'
word6 = 'trots'
word7 = 'runs'
word8 = 'blue'
word9 = 'red'
word10 = 'yellow'
word9 = 'The ' + word9          word9 is 'The red'
passcode = word8                passcode is 'blue'
passcode = word9                passcode is 'The red'
passcode = passcode + ' f'      passcode is 'The red f'
passcode = passcode + word1     passcode is 'The red fox'
passcode = passcode + ' '       passcode is 'The red fox '
passcode = passcode + word6     password is 'The red fox trots'
print(passcode)
```

If you type the code in and run it, you'll get this.

The red fox trots

The passcode!

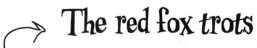

Sharpen your pencil Solution

Below you'll find the Dog Age Calculator code so far. Using the experiment above as a guide, add the code to compute the dog age in human years.

Throughout the book you'll find the gray background signifies new code additions.

```
dog_name = input("What is your dog's name? ")
dog_age = input("What is your dog's age? ")
human_age = dog_age * 7
print(human_age)
```

Let's take the dog_age the user entered and mulitply it by 7. We'll then take the result and assign it to the variable human_age.

Let's also print the human age when we're done so we can see the final value.

Sharpen your pencil
Solution

So we know that our bug is caused by our assumption that `dog_age` is a number, when in fact Python is treating it as a string. Take the code below and add an `int` function to fix this problem.

There are quite a few ways to add
the int function. Here's a few:

```
dog_name = input("What is your dog's name? ")
dog_age = input("What is your dog's age? ")
dog_age = int(dog_age)
human_age = dog_age * 7
print(human_age)
```

First get dog_age as a string and then call the int function on it, and then reassign the result to the dog_age variable.

```
dog_name = input("What is your dog's name? ")
dog_age = int(input("What is your dog's age? "))
human_age = int(dog_age) * 7
print(human_age)
```

Just wait until you are going to use dog_age as an integer and call int there.

```
dog_name = input("What is your dog's name? ")
dog_age = int(input("What is your dog's age? "))
human_age = dog_age * 7
print(human_age)
```

Or finally, use int around the call to input. This way, dog_age is always assigned to an integer.

If you find these confusing, we'll be getting into how to use and call functions later in the book. For now, just know you can pass a string to the int function and have it convert the string to an integer.

Sharpen your pencil
Solution

With your newfound print functionality, write the call to the `print` function that will produce the user-friendly output:

Here's what you need to output.

Output to the user:
"Your dog"
the dog's name
"is"
the dog's age in human years
"years old in human years"

```
print('Your dog',
      dog_name,
      'is',
      human_age,
      'years old in human years')
```

Here we have each part of the output we need, separated in the print function by commas.

Note you can add vertical space to your code like this for readability.

Brain Building Solution

Well, the chapter is almost over; you've just got the bullet points and a crossword to go. Why not do a few extra reps for that brain before you go?

Here's one for you: say you have two variables, `first` and `last`, like below. Can you swap their values? See if you can write the code:

```
first = 'somewhere'
last = 'over the rainbow'
print(first, last)
temp = first
first = last
last = temp
print(first, last)
```

A common technique is to use a temporary variable to store the first item while you set it to the second item. Then you set the second item to the temporary variable.

Trace through this until you understand how it works.

 Coding Crossword Solution

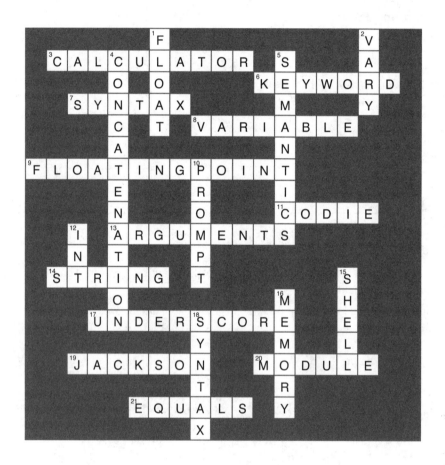

Decisive Code

Have you noticed how, so far, our programs aren't very, well, interesting? That is, all our code has strictly been a set of statements the interpreter evaluates from **top to bottom**—no twists in the plot, no sudden turns, no surprises, no independent thinking. For code to be more interesting, it needs to **make decisions**, to **control its own destiny**, and to do things **more than once** straight through. And in this chapter that's exactly what we're going to learn to do. Along the way we'll learn about the mysterious game called shoushiling, meet a character named Boole, and see how a data type with only two values could be worth our time. We're even going to learn how to deal with the dreaded **infinite loop**. Let's get started!

We may even create one just for the fun of it!

Would you like to play a game?

Passed down from the ancient Chinese Han dynasty, the game *shoushiling* has been used to settle court case decisions, to decide multimillion-dollar deals, and perhaps most importantly, to determine who gets to sit in the front seat of the car.

Today you know the game as *Rock, Paper, Scissors*, and we're going to implement it so that you can play the game against a rather tough opponent: *your computer.*

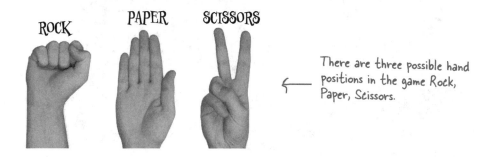

There are three possible hand positions in the game Rock, Paper, Scissors.

How Rock, Paper, Scissors works

If you're never heard of Rock, Paper, Scissors we're going to go over its simple rules now; and if you do know the game, this will be a good review for you. The game is played by two players, who each, upfront, secretly choose either rock, paper, or scissors. The two players then typically count out loud to three (or shout "rock-paper-scissors!") and then show their choice through their hand position, which is either, you guessed it, a rock, paper, or scissors. The winner can be determined by this chart:

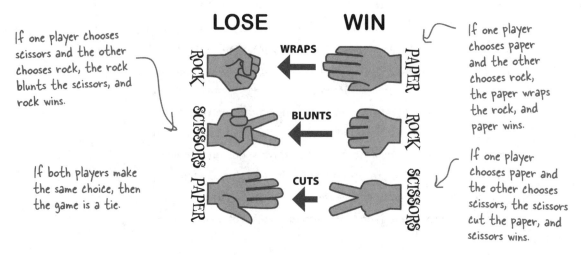

If one player chooses scissors and the other chooses rock, the rock blunts the scissors, and rock wins.

If both players make the same choice, then the game is a tie.

If one player chooses paper and the other chooses rock, the paper wraps the rock, and paper wins.

If one player chooses paper and the other chooses scissors, the scissors cut the paper, and scissors wins.

How you're going to play against the computer

Given the computer doesn't have hands, we'll have to change the way the game works, at least a little—what we'll do is have the computer preselect its choice of rock, paper, or scissors, but not tell us. We'll then enter our choice, and the computer will compare the two before revealing the winner.

It helps to see an example of how the game is going to be played. Below in the Python Shell you'll find a few rounds of Rock, Paper, Scissors being played that show each possible outcome: the user wins, the computer wins, and a draw.

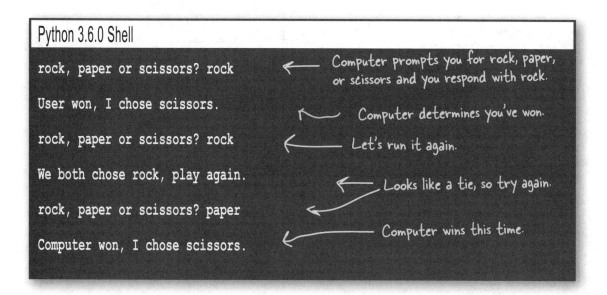

First, a high-level design

The first thing we need to do is figure out the flow of the game. Let's put our pseudocode skills to use by reviewing this high-level design for the game. Notice we've added something new this time too: a diagram that helps map out the flow of the game in the form of a flowchart.

Here's the basic idea:

1 User starts the game.

   A The computer determines what its choice is going to be: rock, paper, or scissors.

2 Game play begins.

   A Get the user's choice.

   B Examine the user's choice. If it is invalid (not rock, paper, or scissors), go back to step 2A.

      If it is the same as the computer's, set the winner to a tie and move on to step 3.

   C Determine who wins by the rules of the game.

3 Game finishes.

Tell the user who won along with what the computer's choice was.

Now we have a high-level idea of the kinds of things the program needs to do. Next we'll dig into each step and figure out a few more details.

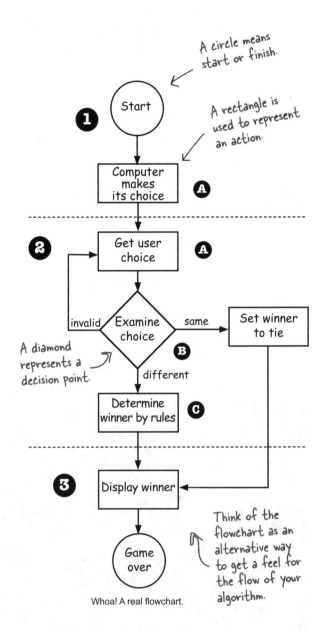

A circle means start or finish.

A rectangle is used to represent an action.

A diamond represents a decision point.

Think of the flowchart as an alternative way to get a feel for the flow of your algorithm.

Whoa! A real flowchart.

The computer's choice

Looking at our high-level design, the first thing we need to do is have the computer make its choice in the game; that is, it needs to choose rock, paper, or scissors. To make the game interesting, that choice should be random and not predictable by the user.

Making random choices is a task many programs need to perform, and you'll find practically every programming language provides a way to generate random numbers. Let's see how we can get a random number in Python, and how we turn that into a choice of rock, paper, or scissors.

How to generate a random number

Python ships with a lot of prebuilt code—that is, code you don't have to write yourself. You'll often find prebuilt code supplied in the form of a *module* (sometimes called a *library*), and we'll be discussing modules in detail later in the book. But for now, we'd like to use the random module, and to do that we *import* it into our code using Python's import statement.

Here's how we do that:

Use the import keyword first.

Follow that by the name of the module you want to use—in this case, the random module.

Typically we place import statements at the top of the code file so that you can easily keep track of all the modules you're importing.

```
import random
```

Remember, a module is just another file with Python code in it.

We'll be looking much more seriously at functions (and modules) later in the book, but for now, think of them as a way to make use of built-in functionality in Python.

After you've imported the random module, you're all ready to make use of the many random functions it provides. We're going to use just one of them for now:

We start with the name of the module—in this case random.

Then we add a period (otherwise known to coders as a dot).

Then comes the function name, randint.

So randint will return 0, ,1 or 2.

```
random.randint(0,2)
```

We pass randint two numbers....

...this is a range, so randint will give us random integers between 0 and 2.

We're going to dive into all the specifics of this notation later in the book, but for now, just take it all in.

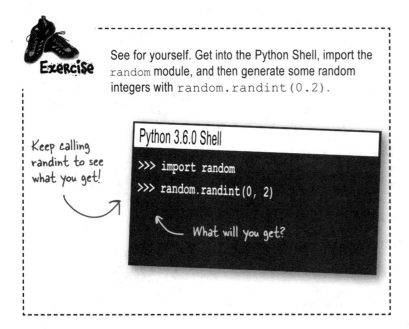

Exercise

See for yourself. Get into the Python Shell, import the `random` module, and then generate some random integers with `random.randint(0.2)`.

Keep calling randint to see what you get!

```
Python 3.6.0 Shell
>>> import random
>>> random.randint(0, 2)
```

What will you get?

How to use the random number

Alright, we know how to generate a random number of either 0, 1, or 2, and we're going to use that number to represent the computer's game choice. So, if we generate a 0, then the computer's choice is rock; if it's a 1, it will be paper; and if it's 2, the choice is scissors. Let's write that code:

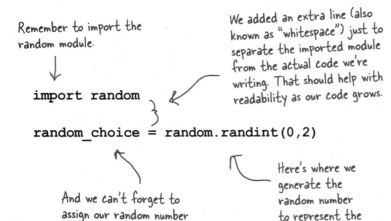

Remember to import the random module.

We added an extra line (also known as "whitespace") just to separate the imported module from the actual code we're writing. That should help with readability as our code grows.

```
import random

random_choice = random.randint(0,2)
```

And we can't forget to assign our random number to a variable so we can actually make use of it later in code.

Here's where we generate the random number to represent the computer's choice.

---

there are no Dumb Questions

Q: How are random numbers going to help?

A: Think of generating a random number like throwing the dice. In this case we have three choices (rock, paper, scissors), so generating a random number of 0, 1, or 2 is sort of like having a dice with three sides. Once we generate a random number, we'll then associate that number with our choices, so 0 = rock, 1 = paper, and 2 = scissors.

Q: Why do you start with 0 for the random numbers? Why not generate the numbers 1, 2, and 3? That makes more sense.

A: Ah, not to a computer scientist. Programmers usually think of sequences of numbers starting at zero. This will start to feel more natural (and sensical) as you see it used in a variety of ways in code. For now, just go with the flow.

Q: Are random numbers truly random?

A: No, random numbers generated by a digital computer are *pseudorandom*, meaning not truly random. Pseudorandom numbers, at some level, have patterns that are predictable, whereas truly random numbers do not. To generate true random numbers, we have to make use of natural phenomena like radioactive decay—not a very convenient method for everyday use. For most programming applications, though, pseudorandom numbers are generally sufficient.

Q: So import gives me a way to access Python code written by someone else?

A: Python developers take useful code and make it available in modules. By using import, you can make use of their code and use it along with your own. For instance, the random module includes many functions you can use to generate random numbers. Right now we're just making use of the **randint** function, but we'll be seeing more of this module as the book progresses.

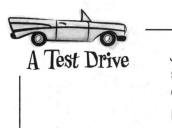

A Test Drive

Just to get things rolling, go ahead and get this code into a file called *rock.py*, save your code, and choose the **Run > Run Module** menu item to make sure everything's working.

Here's the code so far:

Add this new code to your file.

```
import random
```

We added an extra line just to provide some output.

```
random_choice = random.randint(0, 2)
print('The computer chooses', random_choice)
```

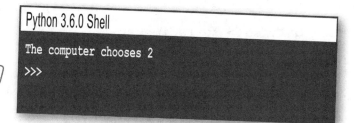

Here's what we got. You might want to try it a few times to see the choices are random.

```
Python 3.6.0 Shell
The computer chooses 2
>>>
```

Taking things further...

By using the random module we've now implemented a way for the computer to randomly make its choice, but it's a little unsatisfying. Why? Well, our goal was to have the computer choose rock, paper, or scissors, and we've done that by mapping those choices to the integers 0, 1, and 2, but wouldn't it be nicer if we had a variable that was set to a string "rock", "paper", or "scissors" instead? Let's make that happen. But to do that we're going to have to step back and learn about how to make decisions in Python.

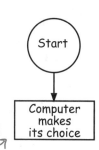

We're still here.

Sharpen your pencil

Assume **random_choice** is already set to 0, 1, or 2 and write some pseudocode to set the variable **computer_choice** to "rock", "paper", or "scissors" based on random_choice's value.

You don't know how to code this in Python yet, but remember pseudocode uses English–like language. Don't overthink it.

True? Or False?

Python makes decisions by asking questions with yes or no answers, only in Python we call those true or false answers. The questions themselves are just expressions, similar to the expressions you've already learned, but instead of evaluating to strings or integers or floating-point numbers, they evaluate to `True` or `False`. Here's an example:

Here's an expression comparing the values of two variables that hold numbers.

We call this a relational operator; in this case it's the greater than operator, which is True if the first operand is greater than the second, and False if not.

We're going to look at other relational operators like "less than," "equal to," and so on in a bit.

bank_balance > ferrari_cost

You can read this as "is the bank_balance greater than the ferrari_cost?"

The result of this expression is either <u>True</u> or <u>False</u> depending on whether the bank balance is greater than the cost of the ferrari.

You can assign the result of this expression to a variable as well, and you can even print it if you want.

Again, this is the expression.

decision = bank_balance > ferrari_cost
print(decision)

The decision variable holds the (True or False) value of the comparison.

Here's the output.

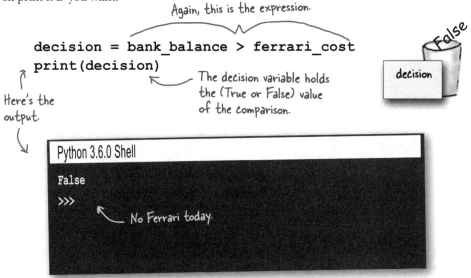

```
Python 3.6.0 Shell

False
>>>
```

No Ferrari today.

The values `True` and `False` belong to their own data type, the Boolean type. Let's take a look at it...

Introducing the Boolean type

Oh, forgive us, we've been talking about a brand new data type, but we haven't formally introduced you. The **Boolean** data type is a simple one; it has only two values, and, as you can guess, they are True and False.

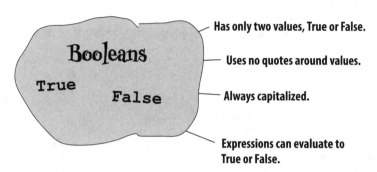

Booleans
True   False

— Has only two values, True or False.

— Uses no quotes around values.

— Always capitalized.

— Expressions can evaluate to True or False.

You can treat Booleans like any other type in that you can store them in a variable, print them, or use them in expressions. Let's get some practice in with them, and then we're going to see how to use them to make decisions.

there are no Dumb Questions

Q: Boolean?

A: Right, pronounced Boo-lee-an. Strange name, huh? Unlike numbers and strings, Booleans are named after a person, George Boole, a 19th-century mathematician who formalized much of the logic we use with computers today. While it may sound overly formal, you'll find the word *Boolean* in common use amongst programmers today. We're sure in no time it will be rolling right off your tongue as well.

Sharpen your pencil

Get out your pencil and put some Boolean expressions through their paces. For each expression below, compute its value and write in your answer. Be sure to check your answers at the end of the chapter. Remember, Boolean expressions always evaluate to either True or False.

> This tests if the first value is greater than the second. You can also use >= to test if the first value is greater than or equal to the second.

your_level > 5

When your_level is 2, what does this evaluate to? _____

When your_level is 5, what does this evaluate to? _____

When your_level is 7, what does this evaluate to? _____

> The == operator tests if two values are equal to each other. It's True if they are and False if not.

color == "orange"

Is this expression True or False when color has the value "pink"? _____

Or has the value "orange"? _____

> The != operator tests if two values are NOT equal to each other.

color != "orange"

Is this expression True or False when color has the value "pink"? _____

Serious Coding

That's two equals signs put together.

Did you notice in the last exercise that the == operator tests for equality, while we've been using = for assignment? That is, we use one equals sign to assign values to variables, and we use two equals signs to test if two values are equal to each other. Accidentally substituting one for the other is a common coding mistake for beginners (and sometimes the more experienced).

Making decisions

Now that we know about Boolean expressions and relational operators, like > and < and ==, we can use them to make decisions in code. To do that we use the `if` keyword combined with a Boolean expression. Here's an example:

Start with the keyword if.

Then we have a Boolean expression, sometimes called a <u>conditional expression</u>, that evaluates to True or False.

Next we have a colon.

```
if bank_balance >= ferrari_cost:
    print('Why not?')
    print('Go ahead, buy it')
```

Then we have one or more statements that will be executed if the condition is True.

Notice that all the statements we want executed when the conditional is True are indented.

The convention in Python is to indent four spaces.

But we don't have to stop there: we can supply an alternative set of statements to execute if the conditional expression is `False`.

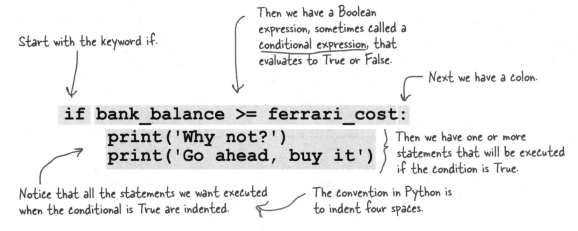

We add an else keyword.

```
if bank_balance >= ferrari_cost:
    print('Why not?')
    print('Go ahead, buy it')
else:
    print('Sorry')
    print('Try again next week')
```

You'll find anytime we have a colon in Python, it is followed by an indented set of statements.

Next we have a colon.

Then we have one or more statements that will be executed if the condition is False.

Notice that all the statements we want executed when the conditional is False are indented four spaces too.

Decisions and more decisions

But there's more: we can even set up a whole series of conditions, by using the elif keyword. Admittedly, elif is a strange keyword, but it's just a contraction of "else if," so don't let it throw you. Let's see how elif works:

Start with your first condition, using an if keyword.

```python
if number_of_scoops == 0:
    print("You didn't want any ice cream?")
    print('We have lots of flavors.')
elif number_of_scoops == 1:
    print('A single scoop for you, coming up.')
elif number_of_scoops == 2:
    print('Oh, two scoops for you!')
elif number_of_scoops >= 3:
    print("Wow, that's a lot of scoops!")
else:
    print("I'm sorry I can't give you negative scoops.")
```

Follow that with an elif keyword and a second condition.

And then add any number of other elifs with their own conditions.

Remember, for each if, elif, and else, we can supply as many statements to execute as we like.

And finally, you can supply a final else, which acts as a catch-all if all previous conditions fail.

Note that only the code of the first True condition will be executed, or if no conditions are True, the else's code will be executed.

Sharpen your pencil

Below you'll find several potential values for the number_of_scoops variable. Using each value, write down what the output of the code above would be with number_of_scoops set to the indicated value. We did the first one for you.

When number_of_scoops has this value, the output is...

number_of_scoops = 0	You didn't want any ice cream? We have lots of flavors.
number_of_scoops = 4	
number_of_scoops = 1	
number_of_scoops = 3	
number_of_scoops = 2	
number_of_scoops = -1	

Sharpen your pencil

Take a moment and READ the code above out loud to yourself in English (or your chosen language). After you've gotten comfortable speaking the code, jot down the words you use.

Back to Rock, Paper, Scissors

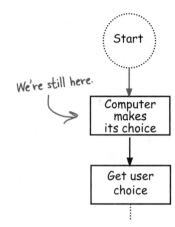

We're still finishing up the first stage of our Rock, Paper, Scissors game. Remember, before our Boolean diversion, we wanted to improve our code so that the computer could pick a string, "rock", "paper", or "scissors", instead of a number 0, 1, or 2. Now that you've learned how to use Python's if statement, you're all set to do that. What we're going to do now is write some code that, depending on the value of random_choice, sets a new variable, computer_choice, to one of those three strings.

Here's our code so far.

```python
import random

random_choice = random.randint(0,2)
print('The computer chooses', random_choice)
```

We don't need this anymore, so you can delete it.

Add this new code to your file rock.py.

```python
if random_choice == 0:
    computer_choice = 'rock'
elif random_choice == 1:
    computer_choice = 'paper'
else:
    computer_choice = 'scissors'

print('The computer chooses', computer_choice)
```

Check to see if random_choice is 0 and if so, set the computer's choice to the string "rock".

Otherwise, check to see if random_choice is 1 and if so, set the computer's choice to the string "paper".

Otherwise, the only choice left is "scissors".

And just to test things, let's print out computer_choice.

A Test Drive

Make sure you have this new code added to your file, and then give it a test run.

Here's our first run; remember to try it a few times.

```
Python 3.6.0 Shell

The computer chooses scissors
>>>
```

Getting the user's choice

Now that we have the computer's choice, it's time to get the user's choice. After Chapter 2, you're a pro at getting user input. Let's start by prompting the user and storing the response in a variable called `user_choice`.

```python
import random

random_choice = random.randint(0, 2)

if random_choice == 0:
    computer_choice = 'rock'
elif random_choice == 1:
    computer_choice = 'paper'
else:
    computer_choice = 'scissors'
```

> *We're assigning the string returned from the input function to the variable user_choice.*

~~print('The computer chooses', computer_choice)~~

> *We don't need this debugging print statement anymore.*

> *We're using the input function again, and prompting for the user's choice in the game.*

```python
user_choice = input('rock, paper or scissors? ')
print('You chose', user_choice, 'and the computer chose', computer_choice)
```

> *Let's add a print statement just to keep track of things as we're coding this.*

Computer makes its choice

Now we're here.

Get user choice

Examine choices — invalid / same / different

A Test Drive

Can you say quick turnaround? Make sure you have this even newer code added to your *rock.py* file, and then give it a test run too.

> *Here's our first run; remember to try this a few times.*

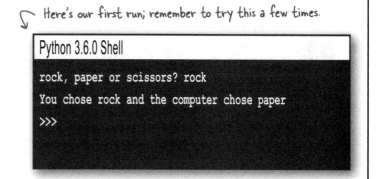

```
Python 3.6.0 Shell

rock, paper or scissors? rock
You chose rock and the computer chose paper
>>>
```

In Chapter 1 we used this random.choice function in one of the examples. Would that have been useful in picking the computer's choice?

Good eye.

We said there were a lot of other useful functions in the `random` module, and there are. One of those is the function `choice`, and here's how it works:

↖ Dont' be confused by the square brackets; we'll be learning about lists in the next chapter. ↘

First create a list of choices, which is just a list of strings. ↓

```
choices = ['rock', 'paper', 'scissors']
computer_choice = random.choice(choices)
```

↑ Then we pass our list to the choice function, which will randomly choose one item for us.

So now that you mention it, this is exactly what we'd want to use if we were to implement this again because this approach uses less code and is more readable. That said, if we'd used this from the beginning of this chapter, we would have had no reason to talk about decisions, or Boolean values, or relational operators, or conditionals, or data types...well, you see the point.

But we're glad you asked because `choice` is a great function to use to do just this kind of thing, especially after the next chapter when you totally understand lists.

NOTE: for those Type A's out there dying to update their code to use random.choice, go for it, if you must. All you need to do is replace every line between the import and the input statement with the code above. That said, this isn't necessary at this point, but you know how you are, so we're letting you know.

Booleans Exposed

This week's interview:
Getting to know Booleans

Head First: Welcome Boolean. We know you're super-busy out there, working in all those Python programs, so we're glad you could take time out to talk to us.

Boolean: No problem. It's true, I *am* busier than ever these days. People are using Boolean values all over the place. It's nuts!

Head First: That's amazing given you are, well, just two values, yes or no.

Boolean: I'm actually the two values `True` or `False`, not yes or no.

Head First: Right, of course, but either way, you're two values. Hardly enough to call you a data type, no?

Boolean: Actually, Boolean values are pretty core to any algorithm or program. Every language has them, not just Python. I'm everywhere.

Head First: Okay, big guy, you tell us then—what's the big deal?

Boolean: Think of a Boolean value representing any current condition in your code: Is the temperature above 98.6? Is the data fully loaded? Is the list sorted yet? Did your credit card charge go through? All of those are Boolean values, `True` or `False`, that determine where you code goes from there.

Head First: You're talking about conditional expressions. We test those conditions to determine the code that we should evaluate next.

Boolean: The official term is *Boolean expression*, and that is part of it, sure. You can test a condition and then, using something like the `if` statement, specify what is to come next. We call it *controlling the flow* of the program.

Head First: Well, if that is just part of it, what's the rest of it?

Boolean: As your readers are going to see you can also repeat code over and over while a Boolean expression is `True`. Say you want to keep prompting for a password while the user is entering it incorrectly; say you want to keep retrieving data while you haven't reached the end of it; say you want to keep updating the screen as long as a game's player is moving.

Head First: Okay, but I'm still not over the two values thing. It's hard to take you seriously.

Boolean: I'm a lot more than two simple values. There's a whole algebra named after me—Boolean Algebra, maybe you've heard of it?

Head First: No.

Boolean: Oh boy. Boolean Algebra is a whole branch of mathematics that studies how we deal with Boolean values.

Head First: Again, just the values `True` and `False`?!

Boolean: Here's an example: take the game your audience is working on. Now there's a whole bit of logic that needs to determine who wins. How do you take that graph of rock versus paper versus scissors and translate that to code that figures out the winner?

Head First: You got me.

Boolean: Okay, to solve that we need to...

Head First: Well, thank you so much, Boolean; as always it's been a pleasure to have you, but it looks like we're out of time. We're looking forward to the next time we can have you on.

Boolean: Yeah, I can, uh, barely wait.

Taking a look at the user's choice

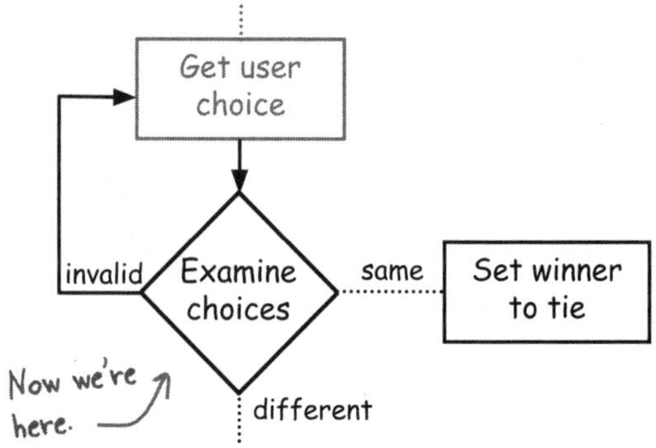

Now that we've got the user's choice, let's examine it. According to our flowchart, we've got three possibilities:

☐ The user and the computer made the same choice, and we have a tie.

☐ The user and the computer made different choices, and we need to determine who won.

☐ The user entered an invalid choice, and needs to enter another choice.

This possibility is where the user enters a word that isn't rock, paper, or scissors; we're going to come back and handle this case a bit later.

We'll tackle these in order (saving the last one for a bit later in the chapter), but first, let's observe that no matter who wins, or if there is a tie, we need some kind of variable to hold that information. So let's use a variable, `winner`, that will hold the outcome of the game, which will be either `'Tie'`, `'User'`, or `'Computer'`. Create that variable and give it an initial value like this:

```python
winner = ''
```

This is an empty string; there is no space between the two quotes.

We'll add this to our code in just a sec…

Here we've assigned the empty string to the new variable `winner` as an initial value. An empty string is a string that has no characters in it (yet it's still a string). You might think of it like this: a laundry basket is still a laundry basket even if it currently has no laundry in it. Right? You'll find this kind of thing pops up all over programming languages: empty strings, empty lists, empty files, and so on. For us, setting `winner` to an empty string gives us a way to indicate that `winner` is going to be a string, even if we're not yet in a position to put any meaningful characters in it (because we haven't computed the outcome).

Although there's nothing wrong with this approach, later in the book we'll see an alternative, that, for Python, is a better way to provide an initial value for winner.

Now that we've created the `winner` variable to hold the outcome of the game, let's proceed with implementing the possibilities at the top of the page. Looking at the first item above, where the user and the computer make the same choice, we'll need to set `winner` to `'Tie'`. To do that, we need to first write the code to compare the user's and computer's choices, and, again, if they are the same, then we'll set our new `winner` variable to `'Tie'`.

Flowchart (top right):

Get user choice → Examine choices

- invalid (loops back to Get user choice)
- same → Set winner to tie
- different

Now we're here.

Sharpen your pencil

Your turn again. Based on our plan on the previous page, finish the code fragment below. Your code should determine if there is a tie, and if so, set the `winner` variable to `'Tie'`. After you've completed this exercise, we'll get this code into the *rock.py* file in the next step.

```
if _____ == _____ :
    winner = _____
```

Adding the code to detect a tie

We've got a new variable to add, `winner`, and we've got some new code that compares the user's and computer's choice to see if they are the same, in which case we have a tie. Let's take a look at all the code together:

Here's our new variable, winner. Right now it's just going to be set to an empty string, but later it will be set to the winner, which will be either 'User', 'Computer', or 'Tie'.

```
import random

winner = ''

random_choice = random.randint(0,2)

if random_choice == 0:
    computer_choice = 'rock'
elif random_choice == 1:
    computer_choice = 'paper'
else:
    computer_choice = 'scissors'

user_choice = input('rock, paper or scissors? ')
print('You chose', user_choice, 'and the computer chose', computer_choice)

if computer_choice == user_choice:
    winner = 'Tie'
```

Exercise

Go ahead and make these changes to *rock.py*. We'll test things thoroughly in a bit when we've added more code. For now, just run the code to make sure you don't have any syntax errors. Note, because we've removed the `print` statements, you won't currently see any output when you run your code.

You can go ahead and remove this code.

And if the computer and the user make the same choice, we're going to set the winner to 'Tie'.

Who won?

So now that we've written the code to deal with a tie, we're ready for the interesting part of the code: *figuring out who won*. We already have everything we need to decide a winner—we've got the computer's choice in the variable `computer_choice`, and we've got the user's choice in the variable `user_choice`. So what we need at this point is to figure out *the logic of* determining who won. To do that it really pays to study our Rock, Paper, Scissors diagram to see if we can break the process of determining the winner down into a simple set of rules. Here's another insight too: if we pick a side, say, by figuring out the ways the computer can win, then we know if the *computer doesn't win*, the user does. That can really simplify our logic because we only need to look at one set of cases.

So with that in mind, let's take a look at all the cases where the computer wins:

Now we need to tackle this.

To Do:

☑ The user and the computer made the same choice, and we have a draw or tie.

☐ The user and the computer made different choices, and we need to determine who won.

☐ The user entered an invalid choice, and needs to enter another choice.

If the computer chooses paper and the user chooses rock, the computer wins.

If the computer chooses rock and the user chooses scissors, the computer wins.

If the computer chooses scissors and the user chooses paper, the computer wins.

In all other cases the user wins or we have a tie.

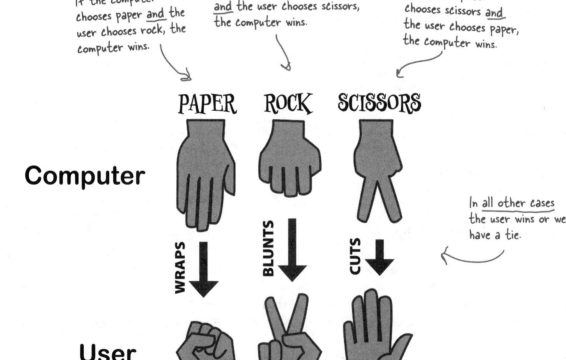

> So you're saying we only need to consider the cases where the computer wins because if the computer doesn't win, we know the user wins?

Right.

Let's step through this in more detail. We've already determined if there is a tie, so we can rule out that case. So, assuming there isn't a tie, who won? The computer or the user? Well, let's start by looking at the cases where the computer wins:

- The computer wins if it chooses paper and the user chooses rock.

- The computer wins if it chooses rock and the user chooses scissors.

- The computer wins if it chooses scissors and the user chooses paper.

In all other cases the computer does not win.

So what about the user? What are the cases where the user wins? Well, we could enumerate those just like we did with the computer, but do we really need to? We've assumed there isn't a tie (and our code already takes care of that), and we've gone through the cases where the computer is going to win, and if none of those applies, guess what: the user wins. So we don't need to write any code to determine if the user wins, we just need to know the computer doesn't win in order to call the user a winner.

Let's work through the actual logic to bring this all together.

How to implement the game logic

As you can see there are three ways the computer can win, and for each way we have to test two conditions, like "did the computer choose paper?" AND "did the user choose rock?" But, so far, in our coding, we've never had to test two conditions at once. That said, we *do know* how to test for a single condition, like, if the computer chose paper:

```
computer_choice == 'paper'
```

← A simple Boolean expression that we're familiar with at this point, which asks if the computer's choice is paper

And if the user chose rock:

```
user_choice == 'rock'
```

← And another expression asking if the user's choice is rock

But how do we test for both conditions?

To do that we can use a **Boolean operator.** It sounds fancy, but Boolean operators are just a way to combine Boolean expressions together, and, for now, there are only three of them to know about: **and**, **or**, and **not**.

We'll see one additional Boolean operator in a bit.

To test if the computer chose paper AND the user chose rock, we can use the and Boolean operator and combine our expressions, like this:

Here's our first condition.

Here's our second condition.

```
computer_choice == 'paper' and user_choice == 'rock'
```

← This entire phrase is a Boolean expression and will evaluate to either True or False.

Placing an and operator between them means this entire expression will be True if and only if both conditions are True.

And we can use this Boolean expression with an `if` statement:

Now the if statement's conditional expression is the entire combined Boolean expression.

```
if computer_choice == 'paper' and user_choice == 'rock':
    winner = 'Computer'
```

So this code handles one of the three cases where the computer wins.

If the expression is True, then we execute the if's code block.

More about Boolean operators

As you've already seen, the and operator is True if, and only if, both of its conditions (or we can call them operands) are True. But what about or and not; how do they work? Like and, or is used to combine two Boolean values or expressions, and is True if *either* of those values or expressions evaluates to True.

Serious Coding

Wondering about precedence with Boolean operators? The relational operators (>, <, ==, and so on) are highest, followed by not, or, and then and. You can also add parentheses to your Boolean expressions to override the default precedence or to add clarity to your expression.

You've got the money for the Ferrari if you have enough money in the bank balance...

OR, you have a loan that is equal to the cost of the Ferrari.

```
if bank_balance > ferrari_cost or loan == ferrari_cost:
    print('Buy it!')
```

Note that only one of these conditions needs to be True to get the Ferrari, but both can be True as well. If both are False, then you'll have to wait for the Ferrari.

The not operator, on the other hand, when placed before any single Boolean value or expression, gives you the opposite of the Boolean value—in other words, if not's operand evaluates to True then not evaluates to False, and if its operand is False then **not** evaluates to True. We like to say that **not** *negates* its operand.

Here we've put a not in front of a Boolean expression.

First we evaluate this relational operator to True or False, and then the not operator is applied, evaluting to the opposite Boolean value.

```
if not bank_balance < ferrari_cost:
    print('Buy it!')
```

You can read this as "if the bank account is NOT less than the Ferrari cost," then buy it.

Sharpen your pencil

Take out your pencil and put some more Boolean expressions through their paces. For each expression below, compute its value and write in your answer.

`age > 5 and age < 10`

When age is 6, what does this evaluate to? _____
When age is 11, what does this evaluate to? _____
When age is 5, what does this evaluate to? _____

`age > 5 or age == 3`

Notice we added parens here, which makes this more readable. >

When age is 6, what does this evaluate to? _____
When age is 2, what does this evaluate to? _____
When age is 3, what does this evaluate to? _____

`not (age > 5)`

When age is 6, what does this evaluate to? _____
When age is 2, what does this evaluate to? _____

Code Magnets

We'd already worked out the code for the game logic on the fridge with code magnets, but someone came along and knocked most of it on the floor. Can you reconstruct the code snippets so that we can determine the winner? Notice, there may be some extra code magnets, so you may not use all of them. Check your answer at the end of the chapter.

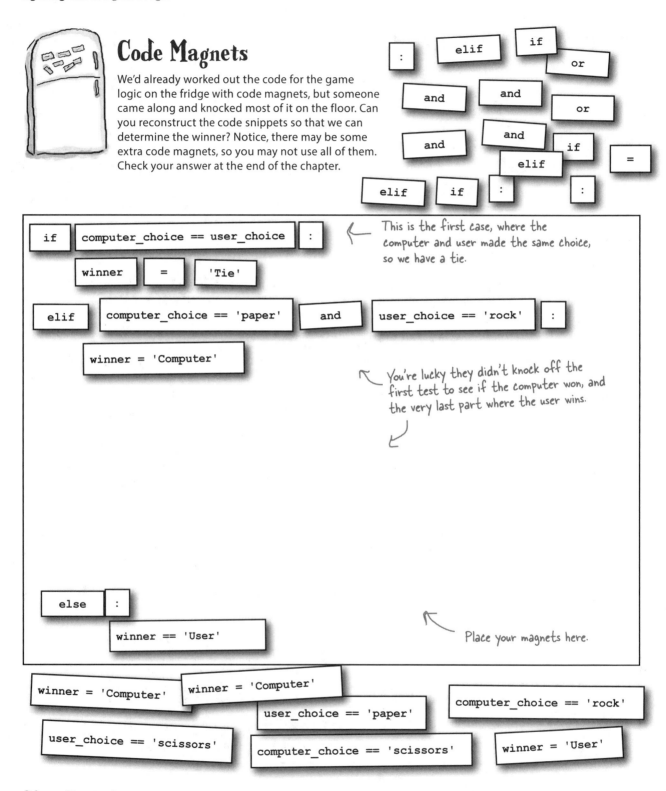

`:` `elif` `if`

`or`

`and` `and`

`or`

`and` `and` `if`

`elif`

`=`

`elif` `if` `:`

`:`

`if` `computer_choice == user_choice` `:`

← This is the first case, where the computer and user made the same choice, so we have a tie.

`winner` `=` `'Tie'`

`elif` `computer_choice == 'paper'` `and` `user_choice == 'rock'` `:`

`winner = 'Computer'`

↖ You're lucky they didn't knock off the first test to see if the computer won, and the very last part where the user wins.

↙

`else` `:`

`winner == 'User'`

↖ Place your magnets here.

`winner = 'Computer'`   `winner = 'Computer'`

`user_choice == 'paper'`

`computer_choice == 'rock'`

`user_choice == 'scissors'`

`computer_choice == 'scissors'`

`winner = 'User'`

A Test Drive

Alright, we've got our game logic all figured out. Let's get it typed into *rock.py* and then give the game a few tries. Of course we haven't added our user-friendly output yet, so we're just going to find out who wins, not what the computer's choice was. That's next on our list.

```python
import random

winner = ''

random_choice = random.randint(0,2)

if random_choice == 0:
    computer_choice = 'rock'
elif random_choice == 1:
    computer_choice = 'paper'
else:
    computer_choice = 'scissors'

user_choice = input('rock, paper or scissors? ')

if computer_choice == user_choice:
    winner = 'Tie'
elif computer_choice == 'paper' and user_choice == 'rock':
    winner = 'Computer'
elif computer_choice == 'rock' and user_choice == 'scissors':
    winner = 'Computer'
elif computer_choice == 'scissors' and user_choice == 'paper':
    winner = 'Computer'
else:
    winner = 'User'

print('The', winner, 'wins!')
```

Examine choice

You are here.

Determine winner by rules

Here's the code for the game logic. Go ahead and enter this code.

Play it a few times and make sure it appears to be working. We'll add more user-friendly output next!

You may even see "The Tie wins!" but we'll fix that in a sec.

```
Python 3.6.0 Shell

rock, paper or scissors? rock
The Computer wins!
>>>
```

Display the winner

Now it's time to display the winner. If you look at the sample output again, either the user or the computer wins, or there's a tie.

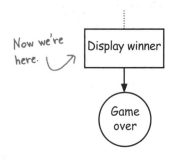

Now we're here.

Display winner

Game over

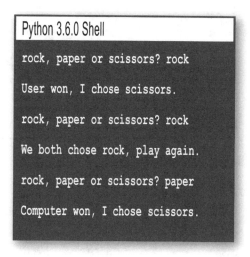

```
Python 3.6.0 Shell
rock, paper or scissors? rock

User won, I chose scissors.

rock, paper or scissors? rock

We both chose rock, play again.

rock, paper or scissors? paper

Computer won, I chose scissors.
```

Let's first take care of the code to handle the tie. Looking at our existing code, if there's a tie then the `winner` variable will be assigned to the value `'Tie'`. So, let's set up a condition for this case:

Remember that print adds a space betweens values separated by commas. So, sometimes we'll use string concatenation if we don't want spaces (like if we need to follow a word immediately by punctuation).

If winner has been set to 'Tie' then...

```python
if winner == 'Tie':
    print('We both chose', computer_choice + ', play again.')
```

Print the message along with the choice both players made.

Note we could have used user_choice here too. Because there is a tie, they both have the same value.

If there isn't a tie, we need to announce the winner, which is conveniently stored in the `winner` variable.

This code will be run, only if there isn't a tie.

```python
else:
    print(winner, 'won, I chose', computer_choice + '.')
```

We announce the winner.

And then report what the computer's choice was.

A Test Drive

We should have a fully functioning game now! Let's get the new code typed into *rock.py* and then give it a spin.

```
import random

winner = ''

random_choice = random.randint(0,2)

if random_choice == 0:
    computer_choice = 'rock'
elif random_choice == 1:
    computer_choice = 'paper'
else:
    computer_choice = 'scissors'

user_choice = input('rock, paper or scissors? ')

if computer_choice == user_choice:
    winner = 'Tie'
elif computer_choice == 'paper' and user_choice == 'rock':
    winner = 'Computer'
elif computer_choice == 'rock' and user_choice == 'scissors':
    winner = 'Computer'
elif computer_choice == 'scissors' and user_choice == 'paper':
    winner = 'Computer'
else:
    winner = 'User'
```

~~print('The', winner, 'wins!')~~ ← Remove this.

Here's the code for game output. Go ahead and enter this code.

```
if winner == 'Tie':
    print('We both chose', computer_choice + ', play again.')
else:
    print(winner, 'won. The computer chose', computer_choice + '.'
```

Alright, we have a fully functioning game! Give it a whirl.

```
Python 3.6.0 Shell

rock, paper or scissors? rock
Computer won. The computer chose paper.
>>>
```

Got documentation?

It's a good time to step back and look at all the code you've written. There's actually enough code that if you revisited it in the future you might have to remind yourself of what each piece does and how it all fits together. You might also have to study the code to remember the design decisions you made and why you made them.

Also notice that the code has an inherent structure and is pretty well organized in that it's divided into pieces that handle the parts of our algorithm (or the actions in the corresponding flowchart). Let's mark these sections and also add some notes to remind us in the future of how all this works.

It's also handy to document your code for anyone else who might want to take a look at it, like another programmer.

Here we're doing some setup by importing the random module and setting up the winner variable.

```python
import random

winner = ''
```

The computer randomly chooses rock, paper, scissors by generating a random number from 0 to 2 and then mapping that to a corresponding string.

```python
random_choice = random.randint(0,2)

if random_choice == 0:
    computer_choice = 'rock'
elif random_choice == 1:
    computer_choice = 'paper'
else:
    computer_choice = 'scissors'
```

Get the user's choice with a simple input statement.

```python
user_choice = input('rock, paper or scissors? ')
```

Here's our game logic, which checks to see if the computer wins (or not), and makes the appropriate change to the winner variable.

```python
if computer_choice == user_choice:
    winner = 'Tie'
elif computer_choice == 'paper' and user_choice == 'rock':
    winner = 'Computer'
elif computer_choice == 'rock' and user_choice == 'scissors':
    winner = 'Computer'
elif computer_choice == 'scissors' and user_choice == 'paper':
    winner = 'Computer'
else:
    winner = 'User'
```

Here we announce the game was a tie, or the winner along with the computer's choice.

```python
if winner == 'Tie':
    print('We both chose', computer_choice + ', play again.')
else:
    print(winner, 'won, I chose', computer_choice + '.')
```

But isn't this silly that we're documenting this code *in a book*? After all, you've got real, live code on your computer. Why don't we document the *actual code* so the documentation is right there when you need it? Let's see how to do that.

How to add comments to your code

With Python, and pretty much any programming language, you can add human-readable comments right into your code. To add a comment with Python, type a hash character (#) on any line, and then your comment. Python will conveniently ignore anything you type after the hash. With comments, the general idea is to add remarks to your code that are going to be read by you, or other programmers, with the goal of providing additional information about the design, structure, or approach you used in the code. Let's look at an example:

Comments are one form of documentation; later in the book we'll look at help documentation, which is meant for coders who just want to use your code, not necessarily understand it.

Start your comment with a hash character and then type your human-readable text after it. Each new line needs its own hash.

```
# This code supports my weekly habit of seeing if I can
# afford a ferrari. The general algorithm is to compare
# my bank account amount to the current cost of a ferrari.

if bank_balance >= ferrari_cost:
    # If it's greater I can finally buy one.
    print('Why not?')
    print('Go ahead, buy it')
else:
    print('Sorry')
    print('Try again next week')     # bummer
```

Comments can start anywhere on the line.

They can even start after code on a line.

Exercise

In the IDLE editor add comments to your *rock.py* file. Feel free to use our comments on the previous page as a starter, but also make your own comments. You'll want your comments to be meaningful to anyone who, in the future, might read your code (including you!). Check our solution at the end of the chapter to see how we did it.

Watch it!

Do as we say, not as we do.

Documenting code is an important part of coding, but you're going to notice in this book we don't do a lot of it. That's because our method of using handwritten code annotations is more effective in *Head First* book form (and all those comments tend to kill lots of trees when we have to include them in every code listing).

Annotations like these.

BRAIN POWER

Thinking about the Rock, Paper, Scissors game again, what happens if you don't enter rock, paper, or scissors correctly? Say you enter "rack" instead of "rock": How does your program behave? Do you think that behavior is correct?

We need to finish that game!

You realize that we haven't quite finished our game, right? Check out the To Do list: we haven't dealt with that possibility of invalid user input. Now the user is *supposed* to enter "rock" or "scissors" or "paper," but they might not; they might mistype, like "scisors," or they might just be troublemakers who decide to enter "dog," "hammer," or "no." So, when you're creating an app or program that's going to be used by actual people, you want to keep in mind that they often make mistakes, and your code needs to deal with that.

So, let's deal with it.

But first we have to figure out how we want the game to behave when the user enters an invalid answer. Looking back at the flowchart, our original intent was to have the program reprompt the user if the input was invalid.

Perhaps something like this:

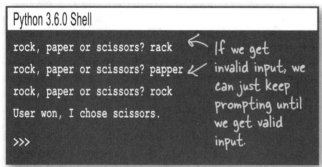

```
Python 3.6.0 Shell

rock, paper or scissors? rack
rock, paper or scissors? papper
rock, paper or scissors? rock
User won, I chose scissors.

>>>
```

If we get invalid input, we can just keep prompting until we get valid input.

We can always make it more elaborate later, but for now we'll just reprompt the user until we get a valid input.

Are you ready to get this coded and finish this game? We just need to make sure we know how to approach coding two aspects of this:

1. How do we detect invalid input?

2. How do we continually prompt the user until we get a valid answer?

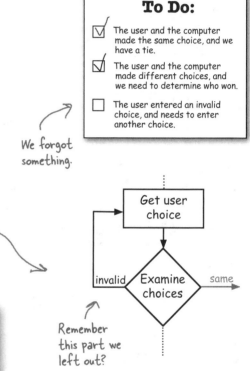

To Do:

☑ The user and the computer made the same choice, and we have a tie.

☑ The user and the computer made different choices, and we need to determine who won.

☐ The user entered an invalid choice, and needs to enter another choice.

We forgot something.

Get user choice

invalid ◇ Examine choices ◇ same

Remember this part we left out?

Users often make mistakes. Make sure your code anticipates and handles these mistakes—even if the only user is y<u>ou</u>.

How do we know if the user's choice is invalid?

How do we detect if the user's input is invalid? Well, you probably know we're going to make use of our new Boolean logic skills, but what does an expression that detects invalid answers look like? Sometimes it's good to just talk things out: we know if the user's choice is *invalid* if:

> The user's choice is NOT EQUAL TO 'rock' AND...

> The user's choice is NOT EQUAL TO 'paper' AND...

> The user's choice is NOT EQUAL TO 'scissors'

Sharpen your pencil

Convert the spoken English above into its Boolean expression equivalent. We've done the first part for you.

```
user_choice != 'rock' and _____
```

↖ Complete the Boolean expression.

Checking out and cleaning up the expression

Hopefully your Boolean expression in the last Sharpen exercise was close to our solution. Here it is again, this time as part of an `if` statement:

Wow, long and hard to read!

```
if user_choice != 'rock' and user_choice != 'paper' and user_choice != 'scissors':
```

This statement says, basically, if the user's input is invalid...

That looks like a perfectly acceptable statement. But sometimes really long lines like this are quite unwieldy once we start typing them into an editor, or if we have to go back and read them later. It would be nice if we could reformat the statement a bit and make it look more like:

```
if user_choice != 'rock' and
       user_choice != 'paper' and
       user_choice != 'scissors':
```

Ah, much better and easier on the eyes!

Uh oh, not good

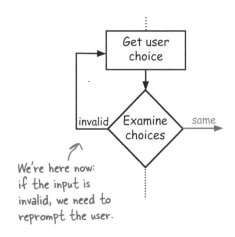

Python 3.6.0 Shell

```
if user_choice != 'rock' and
                              ^
SyntaxError: invalid syntax
>>>
```

The only problem is when we try to break the code into more than one line, Python complains about our syntax.

There is another way—we can wrap a set of parentheses around the expression, like this:

```
if (user_choice != 'rock' and
        user_choice != 'paper' and
        user_choice != 'scissors'):
```

Wrap parens around your expression and then you can break it into multiple lines.

And Python is just fine with the reformatting of the code.

Okay, now that we know how to detect an invalid user choice, we still need to figure out how to reprompt the user.. Let's spend a little time thinking through how that might work....

We're here now: if the input is invalid, we need to reprompt the user.

Before you go on to solve the reprompting problem, I had a question about the user input. Are we considering 'ROCK' or 'Rock' or other variations of 'rock' as valid entries too?

No, but we could, and you bring up a good point. First of all, what is the issue here? Well, the strings `'rock'` and `'ROCK'`, for example, are different strings because Python treats strings as case sensitive. In other words, in Python (and almost every programming language), the following equality test would evaluate to `False`:

> `'rock' == 'ROCK'` ⟵ False

So if the user enters `Rock` instead of `rock`, right now our code would say that entry was invalid (and our logic code, for that matter, wouldn't know what to do with `Rock`).

That said, the suggestion does seem very reasonable—after all, if you enter the word `rock` no matter the capitalization, it should count as a valid answer.

So what do we do? Well, we could just add in additional logic to test all permutations of upper- and lowercase letters for the words `rock`, `paper`, and `scissors`, and that would work. However, it would make our code very complex, and there are better ways to approach this problem that we're going to learn about later in the book.

But right now, let's just assume that the user needs to enter an answer in lowercase, and we'll point out how this could have been more easily solved when we get to it later in the book.

Sharpen your pencil

While you were discussing upper- and lowercase strings, we went ahead and wrote the code to reprompt the user, only our approach was flawed. Can you take a look and see what you think the flaw might be? You'll find the code, some notes, and a sample run of the code below.

```
user_choice = input('rock, paper or scissors? ')
if (user_choice != 'rock' and
        user_choice != 'paper' and
        user_choice != 'scissors'):
    user_choice = input('rock, paper or scissors? ')
print('User chose', user_choice)
```

First we get the user's choice.

Then we test to see if the input was valid.

If not, then we get the user's choice again.

We thought we were on the right track, but what do you think we're missing?

Python 3.6.0 Shell

```
rock, paper or scissors? rack
rock, paper or scissors? papper
User chose papper

>>>
```

We're getting reprompted.

But then we can just enter invalid input again.

Ugh!

How to continually prompt the user

Our first attempt failed. We tried to test the user input and then if it wasn't valid, prompt again. The problem is, this solution only works once. If the user enters "rocknroll" on the second try, then that string will be accepted as the valid user input.

Now we could keep adding if statements for a second and third and fourth try, but that would lead to a coding mess, and our requirements are to reprompt the user as many times as it takes.

The problem is, given our Python knowledge, we only know how to do things once. What we really need to be able to do is write code in a way that it can repeat over and over, as many times as needed. We need a way to do things *more than once*.

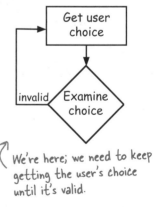

We're here; we need to keep getting the user's choice until it's valid.

```
while juggling:
    keep_balls_in_air()
```

Doing things more than once

You do a lot of things more than once:

Lather, rinse, repeat...

Wax on, wax off...

Keep turning the pages of the book, until it's done.

Of course you'll often need to do things in code more than once, and Python gives you a couple of ways to repeatedly execute code in a loop using its while and for statements. We'll look at both of these ways of looping, but let's focus on while for now.

We've talked a lot about expressions that evaluate to Boolean values, like scoops > 0, and these kinds of expressions are the key to the while statement. Here's how the while statement works:

A while statement starts with the keyword <u>while</u>.

while uses a Boolean expression as a conditional test (just like the if statement).

If the conditional is true, everything in the <u>code block</u> is executed.

```
while scoops > 0:
    print('Another scoop!')
    scoops = scoops - 1
```

What's a code block? We haven't introduced the term formally, but it's everything indented after the colon

After we execute the code block, we loop back around and do the conditional test again. If the conditional is still True, we execute the code block again. When the conditional is False, we're done executing the block.

While Python uses indenting to identify a block of code, this is actually a bit unusual, as most programming languages use matched pairs of curly braces or parentheses.

How the while loop works

Seeing as this is your first `while` loop, let's trace through a round of its execution to see exactly how it works. Notice we've added a declaration for the variable `scoops` at the top of the code, and initialized it to the value 5.

Now let's start executing this code. First we set `scoops` **to** 5.

```
scoops = 5
while scoops > 0:
    print('Another scoop!')
    scoops = scoops - 1
print("Life without ice cream isn't the same.")
```

A note from readers who have read this before you: read the next several pages slowly and carefully. There's a lot to take in and you really want to get how this works into your brain.

After that we encounter the `while` **statement. When we evaluate a** `while` **statement, the first thing we do is evaluate the conditional to see if it's** `True` **or** `False`.

```
scoops = 5
while scoops > 0:
    print('Another scoop!')
    scoops = scoops - 1
print("Life without ice cream isn't the same.")
```

Is scoops greater than zero? Looks like it to us!

Because the conditional is `True`**, we start executing the block of code. The first statement in the body prints the string** `"Another scoop!"` **to the shell.**

```
scoops = 5
while scoops > 0:
    print('Another scoop!')
    scoops = scoops - 1
print("Life without ice cream isn't the same.")
```

```
Python 3.6.0 Shell
Another scoop!
```

The next statement subtracts one from the number of
scoops and then sets `scoops` to that new value, `4`.

*I scoop gone,
4 left!*

```
scoops = 5
while scoops > 0:
    print('Another scoop!')
    scoops = scoops - 1
print("Life without ice cream isn't the same.")
```

That's the last statement in the block, so we loop back up
to the conditional and start over again.

*Observe that our code never
changes. But the variables
in our code, like scoop, are
changing throughout the
computation. At this stage,
scoops is equal to 4.*

```
scoops = 5
while scoops > 0:
    print('Another scoop!')
    scoops = scoops - 1
print("Life without ice cream isn't the same.")
```

Evaluating our conditional again, this time `scoops` is `4`. But that's
still more than zero.

Still plenty left!

```
scoops = 5
while scoops > 0:
    print('Another scoop!')
    scoops = scoops - 1
print("Life without ice cream isn't the same.")
```

Once again we write the string `"Another scoop!"` to the shell.

```
scoops = 5
while scoops > 0:
    print('Another scoop!')
    scoops = scoops - 1
print("Life without ice cream isn't the same.")
```

```
Python 3.6.0 Shell
Another scoop!
Another scoop!
```

The next statement subtracts one from the number of
scoops and sets `scoops` to that new value, which is 3.

2 scoops gone,
3 left!

```
scoops = 5
while scoops > 0:
    print('Another scoop!')
    scoops = scoops - 1
print("Life without ice cream isn't the same.")
```

That's the last statement in the block, so we loop back up
to the conditional and start over again.

```
scoops = 5
while scoops > 0:
    print('Another scoop!')
    scoops = scoops - 1
print("Life without ice cream isn't the same")
```

Evaluating our conditional again, this time `scoops` is 3. But that's
still more than zero.

Still plenty left!

```
scoops = 5
while scoops > 0:
    print('Another scoop!')
    scoops = scoops - 1
print("Life without ice cream isn't the same.")
```

Once again we write the string `"Another scoop!"` to the shell.

```
scoops = 5
while scoops > 0:
    print('Another scoop!')
    scoops = scoops - 1
print("Life without ice cream isn't the same.")
```

Python 3.6.0 Shell

```
Another scoop!
Another scoop!
Another scoop!
```

And as you can see, this continues. Each time we loop, we decrement (reduce `scoops` by 1), write another string to the browser, and keep going.

3 scoops gone, 2 left!

```python
scoops = 5
while scoops > 0:
    print('Another scoop!')
    scoops = scoops - 1
print("Life without ice cream isn't the same.")
```

Python 3.6.0 Shell

```
Another scoop!
Another scoop!
Another scoop!
Another scoop!
```

And continues...

4 scoops gone, 1 left!

```python
scoops = 5
while scoops > 0:
    print('Another scoop!')
    scoops = scoops - 1
print("Life without ice cream isn't the same.")
```

Until the last time...this time something's different. `scoops` is `0`, and so our conditional evaluates to `False`. That's it, folks; we're not going to go through the loop anymore, and we're not going to execute the block. This time, we bypass the block and execute the statement that follows it.

5 scoops gone, 0 left!

```python
scoops = 5
while scoops > 0:
    print('Another scoop!')
    scoops = scoops - 1
print("Life without ice cream isn't the same.")
```

Python 3.6.0 Shell

```
Another scoop!
Another scoop!
Another scoop!
Another scoop!
Another scoop!
```

Now we execute the other `print` statement, and write the string `"Life without ice cream isn't the same"`. We're done!

Python 3.6.0 Shell

```
Another scoop!
Another scoop!
Another scoop!
Another scoop!
Another scoop!
Life without ice cream isn't the same.
```

```python
scoops = 5
while scoops > 0:
    print('Another scoop!')
    scoops = scoops - 1
print("Life without ice cream isn't the same.")
```

Exercise

Write a quick game. Here's how it works: you prompt the player with "What color am I thinking of?" and you see how many guesses it takes the player to guess it.

```
color = 'blue'
guess = ''
guesses = 0

while _____:
    guess = input('What color am I thinking of? ')
    guesses = guesses + 1
print('You got it! It took you', guesses, 'guesses')
```

How to use while to prompt the user until you get a valid choice

Now that you know how to use `while`, you're all ready to get this code reprompting the user. To do that we just need to make a couple simple changes to the previous attempt: we're going to start by initializing `user_choice` to the empty string, and then we're going to replace the `if` keyword with `while`.

Like this:

✓ First set user_choice to the empty string.

↙ We're setting user_choice to the empty string because when it first enters the while loop it needs a value.

```
user_choice = ''
while (user_choice != 'rock' and
        user_choice != 'paper' and
        user_choice != 'scissors'):
    user_choice = input('rock, paper or scissors? ')
```

← While the user_choice isn't valid, we'll keep executing the code body. ↘

↖ Each time through the loop, our code prompts the user for a choice, and assigns the input to the user_choice variable.

↑ So, when we finally get a valid choice, the while loop stops and we have that choice in the user_choice variable.

A Test Drive

In your *rock.py* file, replace the `input` statement with the new `while` loop, and then give it a final test run. At this point, the game should be complete!

```python
import random

winner = ''

random_choice = random.randint(0,2)

if random_choice == 0:
    computer_choice = 'rock'
elif random_choice == 1:
    computer_choice = 'paper'
else:
    computer_choice = 'scissors'

user_choice = input('rock, paper or scissors? ')
user_choice = ''
while (user_choice != 'rock' and
       user_choice != 'paper' and
       user_choice != 'scissors'):
    user_choice = input('rock, paper or scissors? ')

if computer_choice == user_choice:
    winner = 'Tie'
elif computer_choice == 'paper' and user_choice == 'rock':
    winner = 'Computer'
elif computer_choice == 'rock' and user_choice == 'scissors':
    winner = 'Computer'
elif computer_choice == 'scissors' and user_choice == 'paper':
    winner = 'Computer'
else:
    winner = 'User'

if winner == 'Tie':
    print('We both chose', computer_choice + ', play again.')
else:
    print(winner, 'won. The computer chose', computer_choice + '.')
```

Delete the old input statement.

Here's our new code to handle the user input. This code will keep prompting the user until they enter rock, paper, or scissors.

Now we have a fully functional game. Our game randomly picks a computer choice, prompts the user until it receives a valid choice, and then figures out the winner (or if the game is a tie)!

```
Python 3.6.0 Shell
rock, paper or scissors? scisors
rock, paper or scissors? rock
User won. The computer chose scissors.
RESTART: /ch3/rock.py
rock, paper or scissors? papper
rock, paper or scissors? rocker
rock, paper or scissors? paper
Computer won. The computer chose scissors.
```

Congratulations on coding your first game!

What's the best thing to do after coding your new game? Play a few rounds, of course! Sit back, relax, and let everything in this chapter sink in as you try to defeat the computer at Rock, Paper, Scissors. Of course, you're not quite done yet—you've still got the extra credit, the bullet points, and a crossword to do, but take some time and enjoy the game first.

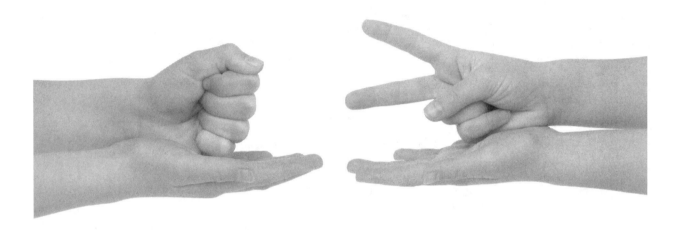

extra credit

Exercise

Remember the color guessing game? It has a bug. Have you noticed if you guess the color correctly on the first try, it prints: `"You got it! It took you 1 guesses"`. Can you fix the bug so that it prints "guess" for one guess and "guesses" for multiple guesses?

```
color = 'blue'
guess = ''
guesses = 0

while guess != color:
    guess = input('What color am I thinking of? ')
    guesses = guesses + 1
print('You got it! It took you', guesses, 'guesses')
```

Your code fixes here ↳

Beware of the
THE DREADED INFINITE LOOP

Before we wrap up this chapter we need to talk about infinite loops. You see, when you write code without loops it just goes straight through—you know it's going to end, someday. But with loops, things get more interesting.

Let's say you've just written your latest code, you feel good about it, and you confidently run it. What happens next? Nothing. Any output slows to a crawl. Your program seems to be doing something, but what, you're not quite sure. Whatever it is, it's taking a long time.

You just encountered an <u>infinite loop</u>—that is, a loop that is looping and looping and is never going to end, ever.

It's easier to get into this situation than it sounds. In fact, sooner or later you're going to encounter one, so it might as well be now. Let's create one:

```python
counter = 10

while counter > 0:
    print('Counter is', counter)
    counter = counter + 1
print('Liftoff!')
```

Be our guest: type it in and run it.

```
Python 3.6.0 Shell
Counter is 814304
Counter is 814305      Uh oh, this is
Counter is 814306      out of control.
Counter is 814307
Counter is 814308      ↙
Counter is 814309
Counter is 814310
```

So what do you do when you have an out-of-control program running on your computer? If you're using IDLE, simply close the shell window to terminate the program. If you're using your computer's command line, then typically a tap of Control+C (Ctrl+C on some keyboards) will terminate the program as well.

And what do you do with your code? Well, infinite loops are logic errors. You've create some logic that never lets the loop end, so examine the conditional of your loop (or loops) and trace through the execution of your code until you determine what about the conditional logic is wrong. In our case, we simply need to rewrite the `counter + 1` as `counter - 1`, so that the code counts down.

BULLET POINTS

- Many programs make use of random numbers.

- Practically all languages provide a means of generating random numbers.

- Python provides a **random** module for generating random numbers.

- Use the **import** statement to include Python's random functionality in your code.

- The Boolean data type has two values, **True** and **False**.

- Boolean or conditional expressions evalute to **True** or **False**.

- Relational operators, like **==, >**, and **<**, compare two values.

- Relational operators are provided for numbers and strings.

- Boolean expressions provide the foundation of the **if** statement.

- The **if** statement evaluates a Boolean expression and then, if **True**, executes a code block.

- A code block is a set of Python statements that are executed together.

- Code blocks are indented sections of code.

- The **elif** keyword can be used to test additional conditionals in an **if** statement.

- The **elif** keyword is a contraction of "else if."

- The **else** keyword can be used to provide a final alternative or catch-all for an **if** statement.

- Boolean expressions can be combined with the Boolean operators **and** and **or**.

- The Boolean operator **not** can be used to negate a Boolean expression or value.

- The **while** statement evaluates a Boolean expression and executes a code block while the expression remains **True**.

- We call a string without any characters an **empty** string.

- You use = for assignment and == for equality testing.

- You can add comments to your code by using the hash character (#) followed by arbitrary text.

- It's a good idea to use comments to add documentation to your code so you can remember your design decisions later (or so others can understand your code).

- Anticipating user error is an important part of designing a user-centered program, like a game.

- Logic errors can lead to infinite loops.

Coding Crossword

Let's give your right brain something to do.

It's your standard crossword, but all of the solution words are from Chapter 3.

Across

2. == is for.
4. >, <, and == are for.
6. Keeps executing as long as True.
7. Has two values.
8. If its Boolean expresssion is True it executes a code block.
10. Character for comments.
11. = is for.
13. Boolean is another one of these.
14. Cuts paper.
15. A string with nothing in it.
19. Many programs need to generate these.
20. Paper wraps _____.
21. Rock blunts.
22. Alternative for if.

Down

1. Can't afford.
3. Foundation of if and while.
5. Ancient Chinese game.
9. True or _____.
12. Catch-all.
16. How you include the random module.
17. Boole's first name.
18. We often say repeating code is in one of these.

Exercise Solution

See for yourself. Get into the Python Shell, import the `random` module, and then generate some random integers with `random.randint(0.2)`:

Your output should look slightly different because these are random numbers! Perhaps you'll see 2, 2, 0, 0, or maybe 1, 2, 0, 1, or maybe 1, 1, 1, 1 (it could happen!) or who knows—that's the fun of random numbers!

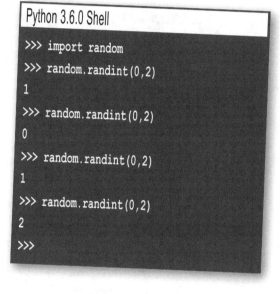

```
Python 3.6.0 Shell
>>> import random
>>> random.randint(0,2)
1
>>> random.randint(0,2)
0
>>> random.randint(0,2)
1
>>> random.randint(0,2)
2
>>>
```

Sharpen your pencil Solution

Assume `random_choice` is already set to 0, 1, or 2 and write some pseudocode to set the variable `computer_choice` to `"rock"`, `"paper"`, or `"scissors"` based on `random_choice`'s value.

if random_choice equals 0, then set computer_choice to "rock"

otherwise, if random_choice equals 1, then set computer_choice to "paper"

otherwise, set computer_choice to "scissors"

Sharpen your pencil
Solution

Get out your pencil and put some Boolean expressions through their paces. For each expression below, compute its value and write in your answer.

This tests if the first value is greater than the second. You can also use >= to test if the first value is greater than or equal to the second.

your_level > 5

When `your_level` is 2, what does this evaluate to? **False**

When `your_level` is 5, what does this evaluate to? **False**

When `your_level` is 7, what does this evaluate to? **True**

This is a Boolean expression. The == operator tests if two values are equal to each other.

color == "orange"

Is this expression `True` or `False` when color has the value "pink"? **False**

Or has the value "orange"? **True**

The != operator tests if two values are NOT equal to each other.

color != "orange"

Is this expression True or False when color has the value "pink"? **True**

Sharpen your pencil
Solution

Below you'll find several values of `number_of_scoops`. Using each value, write down what the output of the code above would be when run with the given value. We did the first one for you.

When number_of_scoops has this value, the output is...

number_of_scoops = 0	You didn't want any ice cream? We have lots of flavors.
number_of_scoops = 4	Wow, that's a lot of scoops!
number_of_scoops = 1	A single scoop for you, coming up.
number_of_scoops = 3	Wow, that's a lot of scoops!
number_of_scoops = 2	Oh, two scoops for you!
number_of_scoops = -1	I'm sorry I can't give you negative scoops

Sharpen your pencil Solution

Take a moment and READ the code above out loud to yourself in English (or your chosen language). After you've gotten comfortable speaking the code, jot it down using your pencil.

if the number of scoops is zero, then print 'You didn't want any ice cream? We have lots of flavors.'

Else if the number of scoops is one, then print 'A single scoop for you, coming up.'

Else if the number of scoops is two, then print 'Oh, two scoops for you!'

Else if the number of scoops is greater than or equal to three, then print 'Wow, that's a lot of scoops!'

Else, print "I'm sorry I can't give you negative scoops."

Sharpen your pencil Solution

Your turn again. Based on our plan on the previous page, finish the code fragment below. Your code should determine if there is a tie, and if so, set the winner variable accordingly. After you've done this we'll get this code into the *rock.py* file.

```
if computer_choice == user_choice :
    winner = 'Tie'
```

Sharpen your pencil Solution

Get out your pencil and put some more Boolean expressions through their paces. For each expression below, compute its value and write in your answer.

`age > 5 and age < 10`

When age is 6, what does this evaluate to? *True*
When age is 11, what does this evaluate to? *False*
When age is 5, what does this evaluate to? *False*

`age > 5 or age == 3`

When age is 6, what does this evaluate to? *True*
When age is 2, what does this evaluate to? *False*
When age is 3, what does this evaluate to? *True*

`not age > 5`

When age is 6, what does this evaluate to? *False*
When age is 2, what does this evaluate to? *True*

Code Magnets Solution

We'd already worked out the code for the game logic on the fridge with code magnets, but someone came along and knocked most of it on the floor. Can you reconstruct the code snippets so that we can determine the winner? Notice, there may be some extra code magnets, so you may not use all of them.

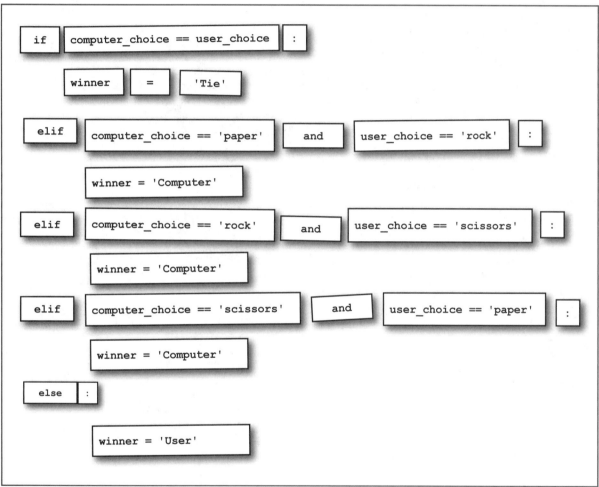

```python
if  computer_choice == user_choice :
    winner = 'Tie'
elif  computer_choice == 'paper'  and  user_choice == 'rock' :
    winner = 'Computer'
elif  computer_choice == 'rock'  and  user_choice == 'scissors' :
    winner = 'Computer'
elif  computer_choice == 'scissors'  and  user_choice == 'paper' :
    winner = 'Computer'
else :
    winner = 'User'
```

Exercise Solution

In the IDLE editor add comments to your *rock.py* file. Feel free to use our comments on the previous page as a starter, but make the comments your own; that is, make sure they are meaningful to you.

Here's our attempt to document Rock, Paper, Scissors.

```python
# ROCK, PAPER, SCISSORS
# Passed down from the ancient Chinese Han dynasty, the game
# shoushiling is now better known as Rock, Paper, Scissors.
# This code implements a version of the game that is you against
# the computer.

# Here we're doing some setup by importing the random module
# and setting up the winner variable.

import random

winner = ''

# The computer randomly chooses rock, paper, scissors by
# generating a random number from 0 to 2 and then mapping that
# to a corresponding string.

random_choice = random.randint(0,2)

if random_choice == 0:
    computer_choice = 'rock'
elif random_choice == 1:
    computer_choice = 'paper'
else:
    computer_choice = 'scissors'

# Get the user's choice with a simple input statement.

user_choice = input('rock, paper or scissors? ')

# Here's our game logic, which checks to see if the computer wins
# (or not), and makes the appropriate change to the winner variable.

if computer_choice == user_choice:
    winner = 'Tie'
elif computer_choice == 'paper' and user_choice == 'rock':
    winner = 'Computer'
elif computer_choice == 'rock' and user_choice == 'scissors':
    winner = 'Computer'
elif computer_choice == 'scissors' and user_choice == 'paper':
    winner = 'Computer'
else:
    winner = 'User'

# Here we announce the game was a tie, or the winner along
# with the computer's choice.

if winner == 'Tie':
    print('We both chose', computer_choice + ', play again.')
else:
    print(winner, 'won. The computer chose', computer_choice + '.')
```

Sharpen your pencil
       Solution

Convert the spoken English above into its Boolean expression equivalent. We've done the first part for you.

```
user_choice != 'rock' and user_choice != 'paper' and user_choice != 'scissors'
```

Sharpen your pencil
       Solution

While you were turning the page we went ahead and wrote the code to reprompt the user, only our approach was flawed. Can you take a look and see what you think the flaw might be? You'll find the code, some notes, and a sample run of the code below.

```
user_choice = input('rock, paper or scissors? ')       ←  First we get the
if (user_choice != 'rock' and                              user's choice.
        user_choice != 'paper' and            ←  Then we test to see
        user_choice != 'scissors'):              if the input was valid.
    user_choice = input('rock, paper or scissors? ')
print('User chose', user_choice)
        ↑
```

If not, then we get the
user's choice again.

We thought we were on the
right track, but what do you
think we're missing?

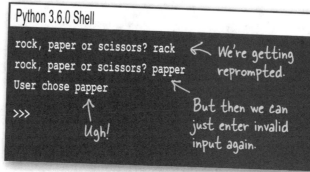

Python 3.6.0 Shell

```
rock, paper or scissors? rack        ←  We're getting
rock, paper or scissors? papper         reprompted.
User chose papper            ↖
>>>           ↑               But then we can
            Ugh!             just enter invalid
                             input again.
```

ANALYSIS: On the good side, the code to detect invalid input is working great. However, the attempt to reprompt the user, while it works, only works the first time. We really need a way for this to work as many times as the user enters invalid input.

Exercise Solution

Write a quick game. Here's how it works: you prompt the player with "What color am I thinking?" and you see how many guesses it takes the player to guess it.

```
color = 'blue'
guess = ''
guesses = 0

while guess != color:
    guess = input('What color am I thinking of? ')
    guesses = guesses + 1
print('You got it! It took you', guesses, 'guesses')
```

extra credit

Exercise Solution

Remember the color guessing game? It has a bug. Have you noticed if you guess the color correctly on the first try, it prints: "You got it! It took you 1 guesses". Can you fix the bug so that it prints "guess" for one guesses and "guesses" for multiple guesses?

```
color = 'blue'
guess = ''
guesses = 0

while guess != color:
    guess = input('What color am I thinking of? ')
    guesses = guesses + 1
if guesses == 1:
    print('You got it! It took you 1 guess')
else:
    print('You got it! It took you', guesses, 'guesses')
```

Coding Cross Solution

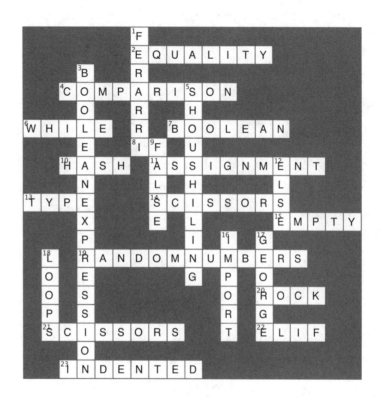

4 lists and iteration

Providing Some Structure

There's more to data types than numbers, strings, and Booleans. So far you've been writing Python code using **primitive types**—those floats, integers, strings, and of course Booleans—with values like `3.14`, `42`, `"hey, it's my turn"`, and `True`. And you can do a lot with primitives, but at some point you'll want to write code that deals with lots of data—say, all the items in a shopping cart, the names of all the notable stars, or an entire product catalog. For that we need a little more *ummph*. In this chapter we're going to look at a new type, called a **list,** which can hold a collection of values. With lists, you'll be able to provide some **structure** for your data, rather than just having a zillion variables floating around your code holding values. You're also going to learn how to treat all those values as a whole as well as how to **iterate** over each item in a list using that *for* loop we mentioned in the last chapter. After this chapter, your ability to deal with data is going to grow and expand.

Can you help Bubbles-R-Us?

Check out the Bubbles-R-Us company. Their tireless research makes sure bubble wands and machines everywhere blow the best bubbles. Today they're testing the "bubble factor" of several different formulations of their new bubble solution—that is, they're testing how many bubbles can be blown with a given solution. Here's their data:

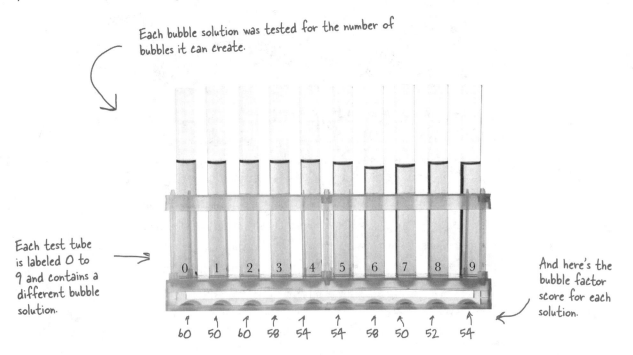

Each bubble solution was tested for the number of bubbles it can create.

Each test tube is labeled 0 to 9 and contains a different bubble solution.

And here's the bubble factor score for each solution.

0	1	2	3	4	5	6	7	8	9
60	50	60	58	54	54	58	50	52	54

Of course you want to get all this data into Python so you can write code to help analyze it. But that's a lot of values. How are you going to construct your code to handle all these values?

How to represent multiple values in Python

You know how to represent single values like strings, numbers, and Booleans with Python, but how do you represent *multiple* values, like all the bubble factor scores from the 10 bubble solutions? To do that we use Python **lists**. A list is a Python data type that can hold many values. Here's a Python list that holds all the bubble factor scores:

Many programming languages call their ordered data type an array instead of a list.

```
scores = [60, 50, 60, 58, 54, 54, 58, 50, 52, 54]
```

We placed numbers in this list, but you can put whatever values you want.

Here's all 10 values, grouped together into a list, and assigned to the scores variable.

We also often call types like lists a <u>data structure</u> because they provide a way to organize values or data.

Once you have your data in a list, you can access the individual scores when you need to. Each individual score, or *item*, has an index. Computer scientists like to number things starting at zero, so the first item has an index of 0. You can retrieve any item in the list using its index, like this:

To access an <u>item</u> in the list we use this syntax: the variable name of the list followed by the <u>index</u> of the item, surrounded by square brackets.

The index is zero-based, so the first item in the list is at index 0, the second items is index 1, and so on.

Remember we said computer scientists like to start things from zero.

```
score = scores[3]
print('Solution #3 produced', score, 'bubbles.')
```

```
Python 3.6.0 Shell

Solution #3 produced 58 bubbles.
>>>
```

My bubble solution #3 is definitely going to be the best.

One of the Bubbles-R-Us bubbleologists

How lists work

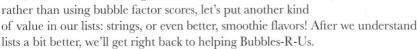

It looks like we might have some interesting work to do for Bubbles-R-Us, but before we start, let's make sure we've got lists down, and rather than using bubble factor scores, let's put another kind of value in our lists: strings, or even better, smoothie flavors! After we understand lists a bit better, we'll get right back to helping Bubbles-R-Us.

So, once you have a bunch of values you want to group together, you can create a list that holds them, and then access those values in the list whenever you need them. Most often you'll use lists when you want to group together similar things, like bubble factor scores, ice cream flavors, daytime temperatures, or even the answers to a set of true/false questions. Let's look again at how to create a list, paying a little more attention to the syntax this time.

How to create a list

Let's say you wanted to create a list that holds the name of a bunch of smoothies. Here's how you'd do that:

Notice that each item in the list is separated by a comma.

```
smoothies = ['coconut', 'strawberry', 'banana', 'pineapple', 'acai berry']
```

Let's assign the list to a variable named smoothies.

To begin the list, use the [character, otherwise known as an opening square bracket.

And then we have each item of the list...

...and we end the list with a closing square bracket.

As we already said, every item in a list resides at a location, or index. With the smoothies list, the first item, "coconut," is at index 0; the second, "strawberry," is at index 1; and so on. Here's a conceptual look at how lists are stored:

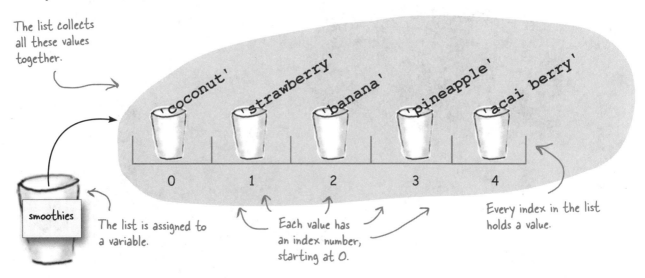

The list collects all these values together.

The list is assigned to a variable.

Each value has an index number, starting at 0.

Every index in the list holds a value.

How to access a list item

Each item in the list has an index, and that's your key to both accessing and changing the values in a list. We've already seen how to access an item by starting with the list's variable name and then adding on an index, surrounded by square brackets. You can use that notation anywhere you'd use a variable:

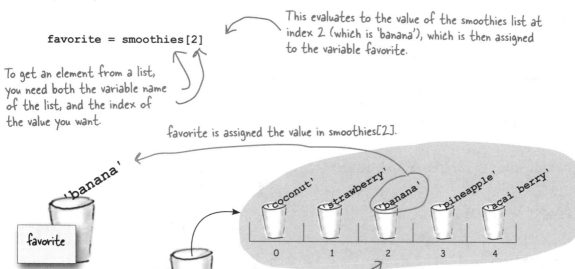

This evaluates to the value of the smoothies list at index 2 (which is 'banana'), which is then assigned to the variable favorite.

favorite = smoothies[2]

To get an element from a list, you need both the variable name of the list, and the index of the value you want.

favorite is assigned the value in smoothies[2].

'banana'

favorite

smoothies

'coconut' 'strawberry' 'banana' 'pineapple' 'acai berry'

0   1   2   3   4

And remember, because the index starts at 0, smoothies[2] is the <u>third</u> item in the list.

Updating a value in the list

You can also change the value of an item in a list using its index:

smoothies[3] = 'tropical'

This sets the value of the item at index 3 (previously 'pineapple') to a new value, 'tropical'.

So, after this line of code, the smoothie list will look like this:

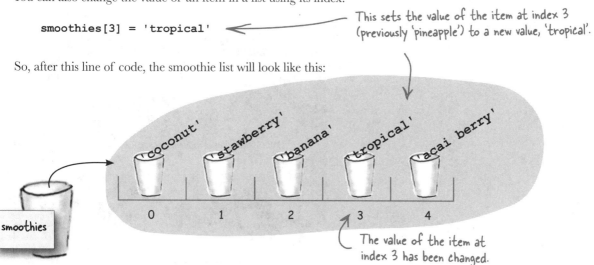

'coconut' 'stawberry' 'banana' 'tropical' 'acai berry'

smoothies

0   1   2   3   4

The value of the item at index 3 has been changed.

Sharpen your pencil

It's a good time to get some practice with lists. Pretend you're the Python interpreter and trace though this code, figuring out what the final output is. After you've completed the exercise, we'll take our list knowledge a little further.

```python
eighties = ['', 'duran duran', 'B-52s', 'muse']
newwave = ['flock of seagulls', 'postal service']

remember = eighties[1]

eighties[1] = 'culture club'

band = newwave[0]

eighties[3] = band

eighties[0] = eighties[2]

eighties[2] = remember

print(eighties)
```

How big is that list, anyway?

Say someone hands you a nice big list with important data in it. You know how to get what's in the list, but you have no idea exactly how big it is (in other words, how many items it has). Luckily, Python provides a built-in function to tell you, called len. Here's how you use the len function:

Use the len function to tell you the number of items currently in the list.

Just pass the len function the list you'd like to know the length of.

```
length = len(smoothies)
```

After this statement is executed, the length variable will hold the number of items in the list, in this case 5.

The length is 5 because there are five items.

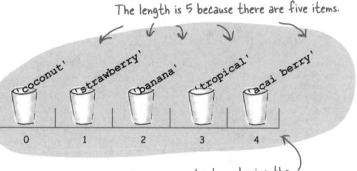

'coconut' 'strawberry' 'banana' 'tropical' 'acai berry'

0   1   2   3   4

smoothies

Notice that because we start numbering the indices of the list at 0, the length of the list will always be one greater than the last index.

This important fact crops up in a lot of other programming languages as well.

BRAIN POWER

Now that you know how to get the length of a list, how can you use the length's value to obtain the last item of a list?

Accessing the last item in the list

Accessing the last item of a list is something you'll do often when coding. Say you've got a list that holds the most recent scores of a sports game and you need to display the latest score. Or say you have a list of current wind speeds of an approaching hurricane, and you need to report the lastest speeds. You get the point: lists often have data arranged with the latest, and often most important, values at the end (that is, at the largest index), so accessing the last item of the list is a common task.

The conventional way to do this, across many programming languages, is to use the length of the list as an index. But remember, lists are indexed starting at zero, so the index of the last item is actually one less than the length of the list. To get the last item of our smoothies list, we do this:

```python
length = len(smoothies)
last = smoothies[length-1]
print(last)
```

This is a common technique in most languages: figure out the length of the list and then subtract one to get the index of the last item.

Python 3.6.0 Shell

```
acai berry
>>>
```

Python makes this even easier

Finding the last item of a list is such a common task that Python actually provides an easier way to do it. Here's how it works: you can use a negative index, starting at -1, to specify the items in a list in reverse order. So an index of -1 is the last item in the list, an index of -2 is the second to last, and so on.

Python supports negative indices as offsets from the END of the list. So, -1 is the last item, -2 is the item before that, -3 is the third to the last item, and so on. Note that a lot of languages don't offer the convenient negative indices syntax like Python does.

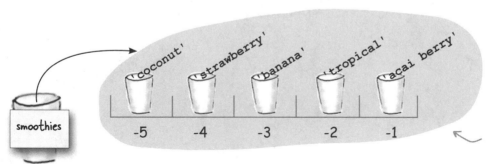

Here's what negative indices look like, which start from the end of the list.

Using Python's negative indices

Let's give Python's negative indices a try. Let's say we want to take the last three smoothies on our list and print them:

```python
last = smoothies[-1]
second_last = smoothies[-2]
third_last = smoothies[-3]
print(last)
print(second_last)
print(third_last)
```

— With an index of –1 we get the last item.

← And –2 gets us the second to the last item.

↰ Likewise –3 gets us the third to the last item.

Now let's print them.

```
Python 3.6.0 Shell
acai berry
tropical
banana
>>>
```

The Thing-A-Ma-Jig

Exercise

The Thing-A-Ma-Jig is quite a contraption—it clanks and clunks and even thunks, but what it really does, well, you've got us stumped. Coders claim they know how it works. Can you uncrack the code and find its quirks?

```python
characters = ['t', 'a', 'c', 'o']

output = ''
length = len(characters)
i = 0
while (i < length):
    output = output + characters[i]
    i = i + 1

length = length * -1
i = -2

while (i >= length):
    output = output + characters[i]
    i = i - 1

print(output)
```

View this as a character-building exercise—spend some real time on this and make your brain work; it will thank you later.

When you think you know what this code does, write your answer here and check the solution at the end of the chapter.

Try these as an alternative for the characters list above:
```
characters = ['a', 'm', 'a', 'n', 'a', 'p', 'l', 'a', 'n', 'a', 'c']
```
or
```
characters = ['w', 'a', 's', 'i', 't', 'a', 'r']
```

If you need hints, look at the code comments at the end of the chapter.

there are no
Dumb Questions

Q: Does the order of items in a list matter?

A: The list is an ordered data type. So, most of the time, it matters, but not always. In the Bubbles-R-Us scores list, the ordering matters a lot, because the index of the score in the list tells us which bubble solution got that score—bubble solution 0 got score 60, and that score is stored at index 0. If we mixed up the scores in the list, then we'd ruin the experiment! However, in other cases, the order may not matter. For instance, if you're using a list just to keep track of grocery items you need to pick up, the order probably doesn't matter much. So it really depends on how you're using the list. You'll probably find that ordering matters more often than not when you use a list. Python also has other data types—for instance, dictionaries and sets—that are unordered. More on those later in the book.

Q: How many things can you put into a list?

A: Theoretically, as many as you want. Practically, however, the number is limited by things like the memory on your computer. Each list item takes up a little bit of space in memory and if you keep adding items to a list, eventually you'll run

out of memory. However, depending on the kind of items you're putting in your list, the maximum number of items you can put into a list is probably in the many thousands or hundreds of thousands. Once you get into the millions there are other solutions (like databases) that are probably going to be more appropriate.

Q: Can you have a list without any elements?

A: Remember when we talked about empty strings? Yes, you can have empty lists too. In fact, you'll see an example of using an empty list in this chapter. To create an empty list, just write:

```
empty_list = []
```

If you start with an empty list, you can add things to it later. We'll see how shortly.

Q: So far we've seen strings and numbers in a list; can you put other things in lists too?

A: You can; in fact, you can put values from any Python type (including ones you haven't seen yet) into a list.

Or even another list!

Q: Can values in a list have different types, or do they all have to be the same?

A: There is no requirement in Python that all the values in a list be of the same type. We call lists with items of different types *heterogeneous* lists. Here's one:

```
heterogenous = ['blue', True, 13.5]
```

Q: What happens if I try to access an item in a list that doesn't exist?

A: You mean like you have a list of 10 items and you try to access item at index 99? If you do that you'll get a runtime error, like this:

```
IndexError: list index out of
range
```

Q: Okay, well, can I assign a new value to a list index that doesn't exist?

A: No, you can reassign an item to a new value, but you can't assign a value to an item that doesn't exist—if you do you'll get a runtime "out of bounds" error. Note that some languages do allow this, but not Python. In Python we have to first add a new item to the list instead.

Sharpen your pencil

The smoothie flavors below were added to the list in the order of their creation. Finish the code to determine the *most recent* smoothie flavor created.

```
smoothies = ['coconut', 'strawberry', 'banana', 'pineapple', 'acai berry']
most_recent = _____
recent = smoothies[most_recent]
```

There are two ways to do this; one uses len, the other doesn't. Can you get them both?

Meanwhile, back at Bubbles-R-Us...

Hey, glad you guys are here. We just got a lot of new bubble tests run. Check out all the new bubble scores! I really need some help understanding this data. I'd love for you to code up what I sketched below.

```
scores = [60, 50, 60, 58, 54, 54,
          58, 50, 52, 54, 48, 69,
          34, 55, 51, 52, 44, 51,
          69, 64, 66, 55, 52, 61,
          46, 31, 57, 52, 44, 18,
          41, 53, 55, 61, 51, 44]
```

The Bubbles-R-Us CEO

What we need to build ⟍

New bubble scores ↰

Hey, I really need this report to be able to make quick decisions about which bubble solution to produce! Can you get this coded?

— Bubbles-R-Us CEO

```
Bubble solution #0 score: 60
Bubble solution #1 score: 50
Bubble solution #2 score: 60
```

⟵ — rest of scores here...

```
Bubbles tests: 36
Highest bubble score: 69
Solutions with highest score: [11, 18]
```

Let's take a closer look at what the CEO is looking for:

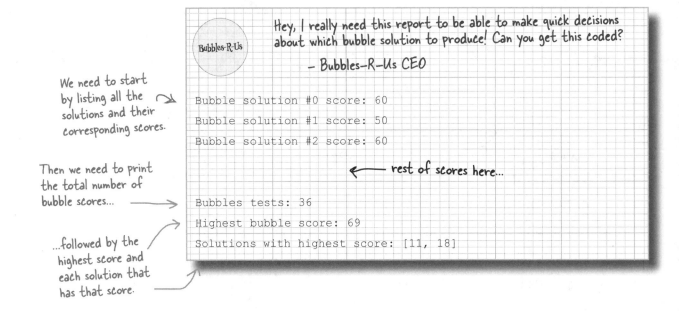

We need to start by listing all the solutions and their corresponding scores.

Then we need to print the total number of bubble scores...

...followed by the highest score and each solution that has that score.

Hey, I really need this report to be able to make quick decisions about which bubble solution to produce! Can you get this coded?

— Bubbles-R-Us CEO

```
Bubble solution #0 score: 60
Bubble solution #1 score: 50
Bubble solution #2 score: 60

                     ←— rest of scores here...

Bubbles tests: 36
Highest bubble score: 69
Solutions with highest score: [11, 18]
```

BRAIN POWER

Time once again to put your pseudocoding skills to use! Go ahead and write some pseudocode that will create the bubble score report. Take each item in the report separately and think of how you'd break it down and generate the right output. Put any notes and your pseudocode here.

Do your best and take this as far as you can, and then we'll work through the entire bubble score report together.

Cubicle conversation

Let's take a look at the CEO's mockup and see how we can tackle coding it...

Frank   Judy   Joe

Judy: The first thing we need to do is display every score along with its solution number.

Joe: And the solution number is just the index of the score in the list, right?

Judy: Oh, yeah, that's totally right.

Frank: Slow down a sec. So we need to take each score, print its index, which is the bubble solution number, and then print the corresponding score.

Judy: You've got it, and the score is just the corresponding item in the list.

Joe: So, for bubble solution #10, its score is just `scores[10]`.

Judy: Right.

Frank: Okay, but there are a lot of scores. How do we write code to output all of them?

Judy: Iteration, my friend.

Frank: Oh, you mean like a `while` loop?

Judy: Right, we loop through all the values from zero to the length...oh, I mean the length minus one, of course.

Joe: This is starting to sound very doable. Let's write some code; I think we know what we're doing.

Judy: That works for me! Let's do it, and then we'll come back to the rest of the report.

How to iterate over a list

Your goal is to produce some output that looks like this:

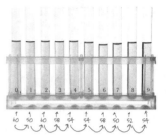

```
Bubble solution #0 score: 60
Bubble solution #1 score: 50
Bubble solution #2 score: 60
  .
  .
  .
Bubble solution #35 score: 44
```

Scores 3 through 34 will be here...we're saving some trees (or electrons depending on which version of the book you have).

We'll do that by outputting the score at index 0, and then we'll do the same for index 1, 2, 3, and so on, until we reach the last index in the list. You already know how to use a `while` loop; let's see how we can use that to output all the scores:

And then we'll show you a better way in a sec...

```
scores = [60, 50, 60, 58, 54, 54, 58, 50, 52, 54, 48, 69,
          34, 55, 51, 52, 44, 51, 69, 64, 66, 55, 52, 61,
          46, 31, 57, 52, 44, 18, 41, 53, 55, 61, 51, 44]

i = 0

length = len(scores)

while i < length:

    print('Bubble solution #', i, 'score:', scores[i])

    i = i + 1
```

Create a variable to keep track of the current index, which we'll start at 0.

Get the length of the scores list.

Loop over the items while our index is less than the length of the list.

Note we didn't need length–1 here because we're using < (less than length).

Here we create the report output by using the variable i to represent our solution #. The variable i is also being used as the index into the scores list.

And finally, increment the index i by one before looping again.

A quick Test Drive

It's about time we get some real code written. Go ahead and get the code on the previous page into a file called *bubbles.py* before running it.

Here's what we got; not bad!

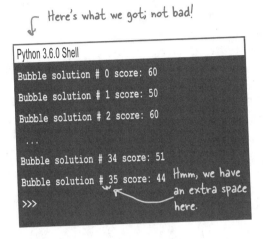

```
Python 3.6.0 Shell
Bubble solution # 0 score: 60
Bubble solution # 1 score: 50
Bubble solution # 2 score: 60
...
Bubble solution # 34 score: 51
Bubble solution # 35 score: 44
>>>
```

Hmm, we have an extra space here.

Just one small nit: did you notice how the output has an extra space after the hash character? The CEO's version doesn't have that.

```
Bubble solution #0 score: 60
Bubble solution #1 score: 50
Bubble solution #2 score: 60
```

Fixing the output glitch

Let's look at the `print` statement to identify where the extra space is coming from:

As you know, when we provide multiple values to print, separated by commas, by default behavior is to add a space between each one.

```python
print('Bubble solution #', i, 'score:', scores[i])
```

To fix this we could just do something like:

```python
bubble_string = 'Bubble solution #' + i

print(bubble_string, 'score:', scores[i])
```

Concatenate the string "Bubble solution#" to i first, then hand it to the print function.

BRAIN POWER

It looks like by just concatenating `"Bubble solution #"` to the `i` variable we can easily get rid of the extra space, but this isn't going to work. Can you spot where we went wrong?

Really fixing the output glitch

Did you figure out where we went wrong? Well, you can't concatenate a string to an integer. D'oh! But how do we change an integer into a string? Well, remember when we did the opposite? We changed a string into an integer using the int function. As it turns out, there is also a str function that does the opposite: give it an integer, and it will give you back a string representation of that integer.

Given that, we can rework our code like this:

```
bubble_string = 'Bubble solution #' + str(i)

print(bubble_string, 'score:', scores[i])
```

All we need to do is pass the integer i to the str function and it will convert it into a string representation.

Let's get that into our code, only we'll do it without the extra bubble_string variable. Instead, we'll make our code more concise and add the call to str right in with the print arguments. Check out the Test Drive below for the changes.

A quick fix Test Drive

Let's make a quick update to the code and then you'll have the CEO's spec implement, so far, just like he wanted it.

```
scores = [60, 50, 60, 58, 54, 54, 58, 50, 52, 54, 48, 69,
          34, 55, 51, 52, 44, 51, 69, 64, 66, 55, 52, 61,
          46, 31, 57, 52, 44, 18, 41, 53, 55, 61, 51, 44]

i = 0

length = len(scores)

while i < length:
  print('Bubble solution #' + str(i), 'score:', scores[i])
  i = i + 1
```

Here we just concatenate "Bubble solution #" with i before it is passed to print. And we make sure to use the str function so we have a string representation of i.

Much better

```
Python 3.6.0 Shell
Bubble solution #0 score: 60
Bubble solution #1 score: 50
Bubble solution #2 score: 60
   ...
Bubble solution #34 score: 51
Bubble solution #35 score: 44
>>>
```

Code Magnets

Time for a quick exercise. We wrote some code to see which smoothies have coconut in them. We had all the code nicely laid out on our fridge using fridge magnets, but the magnets fell on the floor. It's your job to put them back together. Be careful; a few extra magnets got mixed in. Check your answer at the end of the chapter before you go on.

```
while i < len(has_coconut)
```

```
:
```

```
:
```

```
:
```

```
i = i + 2
```

```
i = i + 1
```

```
i = 0
```

```
if has_coconut[i]
```

```
while i > len(has_coconut)
```

```
smoothies = ['coconut',
             'strawberry',
             'banana',
             'tropical',
             'acai berry']
```

```
has_coconut = [True,
               False,
               False,
               True,
               False]
```

```
print(smoothies[i],'contains coconut')
```

Here's the output we're expecting.

```
Python 3.6.0 Shell

coconut contains coconut
tropical contains coconut
>>>
```

↑
Rearrange the magnets here.

The <u>for</u> loop, the preferred way to iterate over a list

So, you can use a `while` loop to iterate over your lists, but the preferred method is actually using a `for` loop. Think of the `for` loop as the `while` loop's cousin—the two basically do about the same thing, except we typically use a `while` loop when we're looping over some *condition*, and a `for` loop when we're *iterating over* a sequence of values (like a list). Let's return to our smoothies to see how we loop, or iterate, over a list with the `for` loop. After we've done that, we'll nail down the Bubbles-R-Us code.

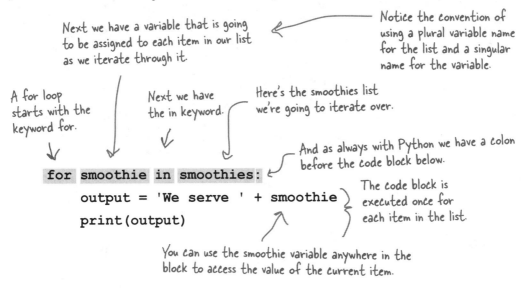

Notice the convention of using a plural variable name for the list and a singular name for the variable.

Next we have a variable that is going to be assigned to each item in our list as we iterate through it.

A for loop starts with the keyword for.

Next we have the in keyword.

Here's the smoothies list we're going to iterate over.

And as always with Python we have a colon before the code block below.

```python
for smoothie in smoothies:
    output = 'We serve ' + smoothie
    print(output)
```

The code block is executed once for each item in the list.

You can use the smoothie variable anywhere in the block to access the value of the current item.

How the for loop works

Let's execute the code above. The first time through the loop, the first item in the list `smoothies` is assigned to the variable `smoothie`. After that the body of the `for` loop is executed.

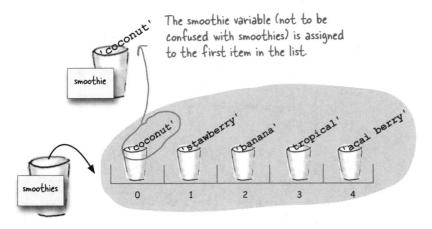

The smoothie variable (not to be confused with smoothies) is assigned to the first item in the list.

Then we execute the code block of the for statement.

```
Python 3.6.0 Shell

We serve coconut
```

Next time through the loop, the next item, "strawberry," in the list smoothies is assigned to the variable smoothie. After that the code block is executed.

Next, 'strawberry' is then assigned to the smoothies variable.

Because smoothie now is set to strawberry, we now get the output "We serve strawberry".

```
Python 3.6.0 Shell
We serve coconut
We serve strawberry
```

The third time through the loop, the next item, "banana," in the list smoothies is assigned to the variable smoothie. After that the code block of the for loop is executed.

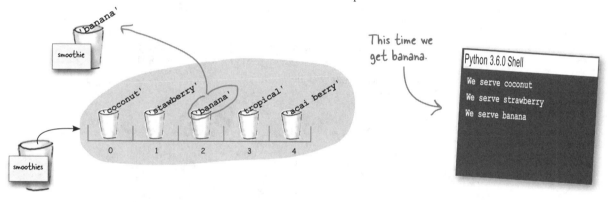

This time we get banana.

```
Python 3.6.0 Shell
We serve coconut
We serve strawberry
We serve banana
```

And by now you can see the pattern—the fourth time through the loop, the next item, "tropical," is assigned to the variable smoothie before we execute the code block.

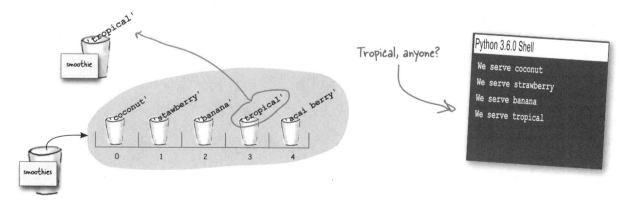

Tropical, anyone?

```
Python 3.6.0 Shell
We serve coconut
We serve strawberry
We serve banana
We serve tropical
```

And as you can guess at this point, the fifth, or last time, through the loop, the next item, "acai berry," in the list `smoothies` is assigned to the variable `smoothie`. After that the code bock of the `for` loop is executed for the last time.

We've now iterated through every item in the smoothies list.

```
Python 3.6.0 Shell
We serve coconut
We serve strawberry
We serve banana
We serve tropical
We serve acai berry
```

> I like the **for** loop; that's nice. But how do we print the score numbers—it looks like we just have the actual scores?

Judy: Oh, you're saying when we used a `while` loop we had the counter `i`, which we used for the score number and as an index to get the scores.

Frank: Exactly, and when we're using a `for` statement, we just seem to have the item of the list. Where's the index?

Judy: Uh, good question.

Joe (shouting from across the room): Guys, I did some research, there's another way to use `for`. The way you're talking about is great for sequences when you don't care about an index, but you can use `for` with a range of indices to iterate through the bubble solutions.

Frank: Say what?

Joe: It's almost easier to show you...

How the for loop works on a <u>range</u> of numbers

There's another kind of sequence the `for` loop works on: a range of numbers. In fact, Python gives you a built-in function called `range` that you can use to generate different sequences of numbers. After you've generated a sequence of numbers, you can use the `for` loop to iterate through them.

Here's how you generate a range from 0 to 4:

range(5) → Creates the sequence 0, 1, 2, 3, 4.

The range starts at 0 and gives you a sequence of 5 numbers.

You can combine `range` with `for` like this:

range makes the sequence 0, 1, 2, 3, 4.

```
for i in range(5):
    print('Iterating through', i)
```

The i variable is assigned to each item of the sequence before the body is executed.

```
Python 3.6.0 Shell
Iterating through 0
Iterating through 1
Iterating through 2
Iterating through 3
Iterating through 4
>>>
```

So say you want to iterate through our smoothies and print the index of each. Here's how you can do that:

Create a range from zero to the length of smoothies.

```
length = len(smoothies)
for i in range(length):
    print('Smoothie #', i, smoothies[i])
```

Each time we iterate, we print "Smoothie#", the index, and the smoothie at that index.

```
Python 3.6.0 Shell
Smoothie # 0 coconut
Smoothie # 1 strawberry
Smoothie # 2 banana
Smoothie # 3 tropical
Smoothie # 4 acai
>>>
```

Doing more with ranges

With a range you don't have to create sequences from zero to some number; you can create all kinds of ranges of numbers. Here's a few examples:

Try a starting and ending number

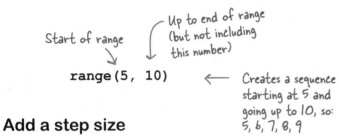

Start of range

Up to end of range (but not including this number)

```
range(5, 10)
```

Creates a sequence starting at 5 and going up to 10, so: 5, 6, 7, 8, 9

Add a step size

You can add a "step size" as well, which tells Python to count by increments.

```
range(3, 10, 2)
```

Creates a sequence starting at 3 and going up to 10, but counting by steps of 2, so: 3, 5, 7, 9

Count backward

We can even count backward by making the first argument larger than the second, and using a negative step size.

```
range(10, 0, -1)
```

Creates a sequence starting at 10 and going down to 0, but by steps of -1, so: 10, 9, 8, 7, 6, 5, 4, 3, 2, 1

Or start from negative numbers

You can start at a negative number too.

```
range(-10, 2)
```

Creates a sequence starting at -10 counting to 2, so: -10, -9, -8, -7, -6, -5, -4, -3, -2, -1, 0, 1

Q: **Does range(5) just create a list, like [0, 1, 2, 3, 4]?**

A: No, it doesn't, although we can easily see how you'd think that. The reason it doesn't is Python actually creates something a lot more efficient than a list. For now, though, it is fine to think of it that way; just know you can't substitute range for a list in your code. Oh, and if you ever want to use range to create a list, you can do that like this:

```
list(range(5))
```

to create the list you mentioned in your question.

Q: **You used a variable name called i. That doesn't seem very good for readability. Why not index or smoothie_index or something like that?**

A: Good catch. You're right, the variable i may not be the most readable variable name, but when a variable is used as an index in a iteration, there is a long history of using variables like i, j, and k—so much so, it is almost blindly followed by programmers and in fact it might strike them as odd to use a longer variable name. So, we encourage you, for this exception, to use short variable names, and before long it will feel like second nature to you.

We had our `range` function calls figured out, and then they got all mixed up. Can you help us figure out who does what? Be careful, we're not sure if each range matches zero, one, or more sequences. We've already figured one out, which is marked below:

range(8)

-3, -2, -1, 0

range(0, 8)

3, 6

range(0, 8, 1)

0, 1, 2, 3, 4, 5, 6, 7

range(0, 8, 2)

0, 1, 2, 3, 4, 5, 6

range(0, 7)

0, 2, 4, 6

range(-3, 1)

3, 4, 5, 6, 7

range(3, 8)

3, 5, 7

range(3, 8, 3)

1, 2, 3, 4

range(3, 8, 2)

> I think we've got all the pieces we need for the first part of the report, so let's put this all together...

Putting it all together

Let's now use our knowledge of ranges and the `for` loop to rework the `while` loop we previously wrote to generate the bubble solution numbers plus their scores.

Here's our bubble scores list.

```
scores = [60, 50, 60, 58, 54, 54, 58, 50, 52, 54, 48, 69,
          34, 55, 51, 52, 44, 51, 69, 64, 66, 55, 52, 61,
          46, 31, 57, 52, 44, 18, 41, 53, 55, 61, 51, 44]
```

First, get length of the scores list, as before.

You can delete the while loop.

```
length = len(scores)
while i < length:
for i in range(length):
```

Then create a range from the scores length, and iterate over those values from zero to the length of scores minus one.

```
    print('Bubble solution #' + str(i), 'score:', scores[i])
```

Then we create our output. Notice this is exactly the same print statement we used with the while loop—nothing changed!

Test drive the bubble report

Type the new code in and save it in the file *bubbles.py*, and then give it a test run. Check out the brilliant report you just generated for the Bubbles-R-Us CEO.

Just what the CEO ordered

It's nice to see all the bubble scores in a report, but it's still hard to find the highest scores. We need to work on the rest of the report requirements to make it a little easier to find the winner.

```
Python 3.6.0 Shell

Bubble solution #0 score: 60
Bubble solution #1 score: 50
Bubble solution #2 score: 60
Bubble solution #3 score: 58
Bubble solution #4 score: 54
Bubble solution #5 score: 54
Bubble solution #6 score: 58
Bubble solution #7 score: 50
Bubble solution #8 score: 52
Bubble solution #9 score: 54
Bubble solution #10 score: 48
Bubble solution #11 score: 69
Bubble solution #12 score: 34
Bubble solution #13 score: 55
Bubble solution #14 score: 51
Bubble solution #15 score: 52
Bubble solution #16 score: 44
Bubble solution #17 score: 51
Bubble solution #18 score: 69
Bubble solution #19 score: 64
Bubble solution #20 score: 66
Bubble solution #21 score: 55
Bubble solution #22 score: 52
Bubble solution #23 score: 61
Bubble solution #24 score: 46
Bubble solution #25 score: 31
Bubble solution #26 score: 57
Bubble solution #27 score: 52
Bubble solution #28 score: 44
Bubble solution #29 score: 18
Bubble solution #30 score: 41
Bubble solution #31 score: 53
Bubble solution #32 score: 55
Bubble solution #33 score: 61
Bubble solution #34 score: 51
Bubble solution #35 score: 44
```

Sharpen your pencil

Another quick exercise. Remember the fridge magnet code from a few pages back? Update that code so that it uses a `for` loop instead of a `while` loop. If you need a hint, revisit the way we reworked the `while` loop for Bubbles-R-Us.

```
smoothies = ['coconut',
             'strawberry',
             'banana',
             'tropical',
             'acai berry']
```

You don't need to turn back a few pages because we've reproduced the solution for you here.

```
has_coconut = [True,
               False,
               False,
               True,
               False]
```

```
i = 0
```

```
while i < len(has_coconut) :
```

```
    if has_coconut[i] :
```

```
        print(smoothies[i],
            'contains coconut')
```

```
    i = i + 1
```

Your code goes here.

Fireside Chats

Tonight's talk: **The WHILE and FOR loop answer the question "Who's more important?"**

The WHILE loop

What, are you kidding me? Hello? I'm the *general* looping construct in Python. I don't need a sequence or a range, as I can be used with any type of conditional. Did anyone notice I was taught first in this book?

And that's another thing: have you noticed that the FOR loop has no sense of humor? I mean if we all had to do skull-numbing iteration all day, I guess we'd all be that way.

Oh, I don't think that could possibly be true.

This book just said that FOR and WHILE loops are pretty much the same thing, so how could that be?

The FOR loop

I don't appreciate that tone.

Cute. But have you noticed that 9 times out of 10, coders use FOR loops?

Not to mention, doing iteration over, say, a list that has a fixed number of items with a WHILE loop is just a bad, clumsy practice.

Ah, so you admit we're more equal than you let on, huh?

I'll tell you why...

When you use a WHILE loop you have to initialize your counter and increment it in separate statements. If, after lots of code changes, you accidentally moved or deleted one of these statements, well, then things could get ugly. But with a FOR loop, everything is packaged right in the FOR statement for all to see and with no chance of things getting changed or lost.

The WHILE loop

Well, isn't that nice and neat of you. Hey, most of the iteration I see doesn't even include counters; it's stuff like:

```
while (input != ''):
```

try that with a FOR loop!

Not only better, prettier.

Hey, I can iterate over a sequence too.

Like what?

I'm sure I can work with them too.

Oh sure, you're the tough guy. Next time you need to iterate while a condition is `True`, don't call me, and then we'll see how heavy duty you are.

The FOR loop

So that's all you got? You're only better when you've got a condition to loop over?

Oh, I didn't realize this was a beauty contest. I'd argue people iterate over sequences *way more* than they write loops over general conditionals.

I think we've already covered that ground. Sure you can, but it's, well, it *ain't* pretty. Don't forget I'm quite general too, I don't just work on lists.

There are lots of sequences in Python. We've seen lists and ranges and strings, but there's even more you can iterate over, like files, and quite a few other more advanced data types the readers haven't even looked at it in this book.

Perhaps, but, again, wouldn't be pretty. Face it, when it comes to heavy-duty iteration, I'm designed for it.

Likewise, don't call me when you need to iterate over a sequence!

Cubicle conversation continued...

> We've got all the bubble solution scores displaying, so now we just need to generate the rest of the report.

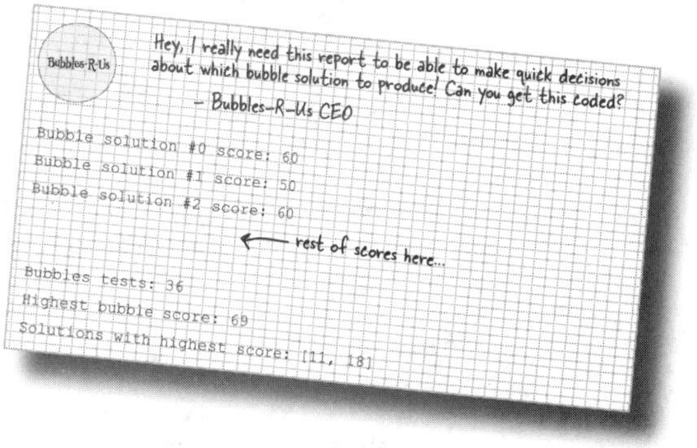

Judy: Right, and the first thing we need to do is determine the total number of bubble tests. That's easy; it's just the length of the scores list.

Joe: Oh, right. We've got to find the highest score too, and then the solutions that have the highest score.

Judy: Yeah, that last one is going to be the toughest. Let's work out finding the highest score first.

Joe: Sounds like a good place to start.

Judy: To do that I think we just need to maintain a highest score variable that keeps track as we interate through the list. Here, let me write some Python-like pseudocode:

```
DECLARE a variable high_score and set to 0.      ⟵  Add a variable to hold the high score.
FOR i in range(length)
                                                    Check each time through the loop to see if we have
    PRINT i and the bubble solution score[i]        a higher score, and if so that's our new high score.
    IF scores[i] > high_score:              ⟵
        high_score = scores[i];        ⟵      If we have a new high score, then assign it to high_score.
PRINT high_score
                    ⟵   After the loop we just display the high score.
```

(Handwritten note on graph paper):
Bubbles-R-Us

Hey, I really need this report to be able to make quick decisions about which bubble solution to produce! Can you get this coded?
— Bubbles-R-Us CEO

Bubble solution #0 score: 60
Bubble solution #1 score: 50
Bubble solution #2 score: 60

⟵ rest of scores here...

Bubbles tests: 36
Highest bubble score: 69
Solutions with highest score: [11, 18]

Joe: Oh nice; you did it with just a few lines added to our existing code.

Judy: Each time through the list we look to see if the current score is greater than `high_score`, and if so, that's our new high score. Then, after the loop ends we just display the high score.

 **Sharpen your pencil**

Go ahead and implement the pseudocode on the previous page to find the highest score by filling in the blanks in the code below. Once you're done, add the code to *bubbles.py* and give your code a test. Check the results in the shell, and fill in the blanks in our shell below with the number of bubble tests and the highest score. As always, check your answer at the end of the chapter before you go on.

```
scores = [60, 50, 60, 58, 54, 54,
          58, 50, 52, 54, 48, 69,
          34, 55, 51, 52, 44, 51,
          69, 64, 66, 55, 52, 61,
          46, 31, 57, 52, 44, 18,
          41, 53, 55, 61, 51, 44]

high_score = _____          ⟵ Fill in the blanks to complete the code here...

length = len(scores)
for i in range(length):
    print('Bubble solution #' + str(i), 'score:', scores[i])
    if _____ > high_score:
        _____ = scores[i]

print('Bubbles tests:', _____)
print('Highest bubble score:', _____)
```

...and then fill in the blanks showing the output you get in the console.

```
Python 3.6.0 Shell

Bubble solution #0 score: 60
Bubble solution #1 score: 50
Bubble solution #2 score: 60
  ...
Bubble solution #34 score: 51
Bubble solution #35 score: 44
Bubbles tests: _____
Highest bubble score: _____
```

Hey, you guys are almost there! All you've got left is collecting up all the solutions with the highest score and printing them. Remember, there might be more than one.

More than one? When we need to store more than one thing, what do we use? A list, of course. So, can we iterate through our existing scores list looking for scores that only match the highest score, and then add those to a new list that we can later display in the report? You bet we can, but to do that we'll have to learn how to create a brand new, empty list, and then understand how to add new elements to it.

Remember here's what we have left.

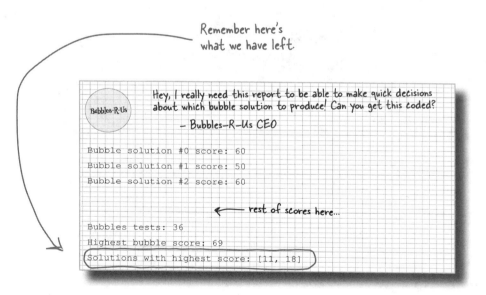

Hey, I really need this report to be able to make quick decisions about which bubble solution to produce! Can you get this coded?
— Bubbles-R-Us CEO

```
Bubble solution #0 score: 60
Bubble solution #1 score: 50
Bubble solution #2 score: 60

        ← — rest of scores here...

Bubbles tests: 36
Highest bubble score: 69
Solutions with highest score: [11, 18]
```

Building your own list, from scratch

Before we take on finishing this code, let's get a sense for how to create a new list, and how to add items to it. You already know how to explicitly create a list with values, like this:

```python
menu = ['Pizza', 'Pasta', 'Soup', 'Salad']
```

But you can also omit the initial items and just create an empty list:

```python
menu = []
```

↖ A new list, all ready to go with no
items and a length of zero.

Once you've created an empty list you can add new items with append, like this:

```python
menu = []
menu.append('Burger')
menu.append('Sushi')

print(menu)
```

↖ As before, a new list item is created.

↖ The string 'Burger' is added to the list.

↖ And a second item is created that holds the string 'Sushi'.

```
Python 3.6.0 Shell
['Burger', 'Sushi']
>>>
```

You can also create a new, empty list in Python by calling list(), but more on this later in the book. Just tuck that in the back of your brain for now.

✏️ Sharpen your pencil

You've seen how to create an empty list with two square backets, but what do you think the code below does? Feel free to type the code into the shell to experiment. Record your observations here.

```python
mystery = ['secret'] * 5
```
← Multiplication of a number and a list? What on earth does this do?

```python
mystery = 'secret' * 5
```
← How is it different from this?

Doing even more with lists

There's a lot more you can do with lists, like insert new items, delete items, add lists together, and search for items in a list—here are a few examples to whet your appetite.

Delete an item from a list

Need to get rid of an item in a list? Python provides a built-in function called del to do just that. Here's how it works:

Delete the item at index 0.

```
del menu[0]

print(menu)
```

The item at index 0 is removed, leaving only one item, 'Sushi', which is now at index 0.

```
Python 3.6.0 Shell
['Sushi']
>>>
```

After you've deleted an item from a list, all the items with greater indices move down one. So if you delete the item at index 2, then the item previously at index 3 takes its place. The item at index 4 becomes 3, and so on.

Add one list to another

Let's say you have a list, and someone hands you another list and you want to add all those items to your list. No worries, here's how you do that:

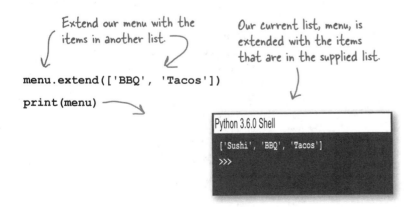

Extend our menu with the items in another list.

Our current list, menu, is extended with the items that are in the supplied list.

```
menu.extend(['BBQ', 'Tacos'])

print(menu)
```

```
Python 3.6.0 Shell
['Sushi', 'BBQ', 'Tacos']
>>>
```

⚛ BRAIN POWER

What is the difference between using **append** and using **extend** on lists?

There's another way to combine lists as well—you can just add the lists together using the + operator, like this:

```
menu = menu + ['BBQ', 'Tacos']
```

If we execute this instead of our previous use of the extend function, we get the same result.

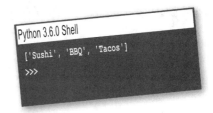

Python 3.6.0 Shell

```
['Sushi', 'BBQ', 'Tacos']
>>>
```

Note: extend extends an existing list. When you use + you get a brand new list with the items of both lists in it.

Or insert items into your list

Let's say you really need to add an item in the middle of your list. Use the `insert` function to do that.

Here's the index where we want an item inserted.

And here's the item.

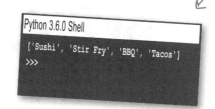

Python 3.6.0 Shell

```
['Sushi', 'Stir Fry', 'BBQ', 'Tacos']
>>>
```

insert adds a new item at the supplied index, in this case 1.

```
menu.insert(1, 'Stir Fry')

print(menu)
```

As we said, we'll be seeing even more list operations as the book progresses, but these are some good operations to get you started.

there are no
Dumb Questions

Q: What happens if I insert an item after an index that doesn't exist, like menu.insert(100, 'French Fries')?

A: If you try to insert an item beyond the end of your list, it will simply add the item in the last position in your list.

Q: What does the syntax mylist.append(value) actually mean? It looks similar to the random.randint(0,2) syntax we used in the last chapter.

A: Yes, they are related; both are an example of something we'll get to later in the book: the use of functions and objects (actually we'll make our use of terminology even more precise at that stage of the book). Now that all won't mean a lot to you right now, but we're going to see how data types, like lists, can provide their own

special behavior to do things like append items. So, mylist.append is using the behavior append, which is provided by the list. For now, go with the syntax, and down the road you'll better understand the true meaning behind it as we explore objects and functions.

Q: Well, why do we have menu.append and menu.insert, but del menu[0]? Why isn't it menu.delete(0) or something similar? I thought Python was consistent?

A: It's a very good question. It turns out the designers of Python thought common operations, like **len** and **del**, deserved a bit of special treatment. They also thought that, for example, **len(menu)** was more readable than **menu.length()**. The reasoning behind this has been debated at great length, but that's the way it is in Python. And, as in the last question, you're asking all the right things, and the madness behind the method will be clearer once we get to talking about functions and objects.

Now that we know how to add items to a list, we can finish up this report. We can just create the list of the solutions with the highest score as we iterate through the scores list to find the highest bubble score, right?

Judy: Yes, we'll start with an empty list to hold the solutions with the highest scores, and add each solution that has that high score one at a time to it as we iterate through the scores list.

Frank: Great, let's get started.

Judy: But hold on a second…I think we might need another loop.

Frank: We do? It seems like there should be a way to do that in our existing loop.

Judy: Actually, I'm sure we do. Here's why: we have to know what the highest score is *before* we can find all the solutions that have that highest score. So we need two loops: one to find the highest score, which we've already written, and then a second one to find all the solutions that have that score.

Frank: Oh, I see. And in the second loop, we'll compare each score to the highest score, and if it matches, we'll add the index of the bubble solution score to the new list we're creating for the solutions with the highest scores.

Judy: Exactly! Let's do it.

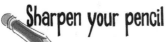 Sharpen your pencil

Can you help write the loop to find *all the scores* that match the high score? You'll find all the code up until now listed below. Give it a real shot below before you check the solution.

```
scores = [60, 50, 60, 58, 54, 54,
          58, 50, 52, 54, 48, 69,
          34, 55, 51, 52, 44, 51,
          69, 64, 66, 55, 52, 61,
          46, 31, 57, 52, 44, 18,
          41, 53, 55, 61, 51, 44]
```

← Here's all the code so far.

```
high_score = 0

length = len(scores)
for i in range(length):
    print('Bubble solution #' + str(i), 'score:', scores[i])
    if scores[i] > high_score:
        high_score = scores[i]

print('Bubbles tests:',  length
print('Highest bubble score:',  high_score)
best_solutions = []                ←
```

Here's the new list you'll use to store the bubble solutions with the highest score.

_____

_____

_____

Write your code here, using more lines if necessary.

↑
Remember, the variable high_score has the highest score in it; you can use that in your code.

Test drive the final report

Go ahead and add your code to generate the bubble solutions with the highest score to your code in *bubbles.py* and run another test drive. All of our code is shown below:

```python
scores = [60, 50, 60, 58, 54, 54,
          58, 50, 52, 54, 48, 69,
          34, 55, 51, 52, 44, 51,
          69, 64, 66, 55, 52, 61,
          46, 31, 57, 52, 44, 18,
          41, 53, 55, 61, 51, 44]

high_score = 0

length = len(scores)
for i in range(length):
    print('Bubble solution #' + str(i), 'score:', scores[i])
    if scores[i] > high_score:
        high_score = scores[i]

print('Bubbles tests:', length)
print('Highest bubble score:', high_score)

best_solutions = []
for i in range(length):
    if high_score == scores[i]:
        best_solutions.append(i)

print('Solutions with the highest score:', best_solutions)
```

If this code looks new to you, then you may not have studied the solution to the last Sharpen your pencil exercise. You'll want to do that now.

And the winners are...

Bubble solutions #11 and #18 both have a high score of 69, so they are the best bubble solutions in this batch of test solutions!

```
Python 3.6.0 Shell

Bubble solution #0 score: 60
Bubble solution #1 score: 50
 ...
Bubble solution #34 score: 51
Bubbles tests: 36
Highest bubble score: 69
Solutions with the highest score: [11,18]
```

> Great job! Just one more thing... can you figure out the most cost-effective bubble solution? With that final bit of data, we'll definitely take over the entire bubble solution market. Here's a list with the cost of each solution you can use to figure it out.

Here's the new cost list. Notice that it has a cost for each of the corresponding solutions in the scores list.

```
costs = [.25, .27, .25, .25, .25, .25,
         .33, .31, .25, .29, .27, .22,
         .31, .25, .25, .33, .21, .25,
         .25, .25, .28, .25, .24, .22,
         .20, .25, .30, .25, .24, .25,
         .25, .25, .27, .25, .26, .29]
```

So, what's the job here? It's to take the leading bubble solutions—that is, the ones with the highest bubble scores—and choose the lowest-cost one. Now, luckily, we've been given a costs list that mirrors the scores list. That is, the bubble solution score at index 0 in the scores list has the cost at index 0 in the costs list (.25), the bubble solution at index 1 in the scores list has a cost at index 1 in the costs list (.27), and so on. So, for any score you'll find its cost in the costs list at the same index. Sometimes we call these *parallel* lists:

Scores and costs are parallel lists because for each score there is a corresponding cost at the same index.

```
costs = [.25, .27, .25, .25, .25, .25, .33, .31, .25, .29, .27, .22, ..., .29]
```

The cost at 0 is the cost of the bubble solution at 0...

And likewise for the other cost and score values in the lists.

```
scores = [60, 50, 60, 58, 54, 54, 58, 50, 52, 54, 48, 69, ..., 44]
```

> This seems a little tricky. How do we determine not only the scores that are highest, but then pick the one with the lowest cost?

Judy: Well, we know the highest score already.

Frank: Right, but how do we use that? And we have these two lists, but how do we get those to work together?

Judy: I'm pretty sure either of us could write a simple `for` loop that goes through the `scores` list again and picks up the items that match the highest score.

Frank: Yeah, I could do that. But then what?

Judy: Anytime we hit a score that matches the highest score, we need to see if its cost is the lowest we've seen.

Frank: Oh, I see, so we'll have a variable that keeps track of the index of the "lowest cost high score." Wow, that's a mouthful.

Judy: Exactly. And once we get through the entire list, whatever index is in that variable is the index of the item that not only matches the highest score, but has the lowest cost as well.

Frank: What if two items match in cost?

Judy: Hmm, we have to decide how to handle that. I'd say, whatever one we see first is the winner. Of course we could do something more complex, but let's stick with that unless the CEO says differently.

Frank: This is complicated enough I think I want to sketch out some pseudocode before writing anything.

Judy: I agree; whenever you are managing indices of multiple lists things can get tricky. Let's do that; in the long run I'm sure it will be faster to plan it first.

Frank: Okay, I'll take a first stab at it…

I'm pretty sure I nailed the pseudocode. Check it out below. Make sure you've got it down, and then we'll go ahead and translate it into real code.

Create a variable to hold the cost of the most cost-effective solution. We'll make it larger than any item in costs and also make it a float to match the type of each item in the costs list.

Create a variable to hold the index of the most cost-effective solution.

DECLARE a *variable* cost and set to 100.0

DECLARE a *variable* most_effective

Iterate over every solution, and if a solution has the highest score...

FOR i in *range(length)*:

    IF the bubble solution at scores[i] equals high_score **AND** bubble solution at costs[i] is less than cost:

        SET the value of most_effective to the value of i

        SET the value of cost to the cost of the bubble solution

...and a lower cost than previous solutions...

...then record the index and cost of current solution.

At the end of the loop most_effective holds the index of the solution with the highest score and lowest cost. And the variable cost holds the cost of that solution. Note, if there is a tie between one or more solutions, this code will always pick the solution it sees first in the list.

⚛ BRAIN POWER

As Judy suggested in the cubicle conversation, if there are multiple high score solutions with the same cost, this code favors the first solution it finds. But why is that? What aspect of the code makes that happen? What if you wanted to favor the last solution you found instead; how would you do that?

Answer: Because this code is always comparing the current low cost by using less than, so once a low cost is established, it takes an even lower cost (not an equal cost) to pick a new winner. You could favor the last solution it sees by changing the less than comparison to a less than or equal to, <=, comparison.

Testing the most cost-effective solution

```
scores = [60, 50, 60, 58, 54, 54,
          58, 50, 52, 54, 48, 69,
          34, 55, 51, 52, 44, 51,
          69, 64, 66, 55, 52, 61,
          46, 31, 57, 52, 44, 18,
          41, 53, 55, 61, 51, 44]
```

We should have everything coded below for the Bubbles-R-Us CEO. Check out the code and see how it matches the pseudocode, and then enter the new code into *bubbles.py* and give it another test run. All the code is shown below. When you've got a winning solution, turn to page to see if it matches ours.

```
costs = [.25, .27, .25, .25, .25, .25,
         .33, .31, .25, .29, .27, .22,
         .31, .25, .25, .33, .21, .25,
         .25, .25, .28, .25, .24, .22,
         .20, .25, .30, .25, .24, .25,
         .25, .25, .27, .25, .26, .29]
```

← Don't forget the new costs list.

```
high_score = 0

length = len(scores)
for i in range(length):
    print('Bubble solution #' + str(i), 'score:', scores[i])
    if scores[i] > high_score:
        high_score = scores[i]

print('Bubbles tests:', length)
print('Highest bubble score:', high_score)

best_solutions = []
for i in range(length):
    if high_score == scores[i]:
        best_solutions.append(i)

print('Solutions with the highest score:', best_solutions)
```

We translated Frank's Python-like pseudocode directly to Python.

```
cost = 100.0
most_effective = 0
for i in range(length):
    if scores[i] == high_score and costs[i] < cost:
        most_effective = i
        cost = costs[i]
print('Solution', most_effective,
      'is the most effective with a cost of',  costs[most_effective])
```

We also added some output to add the most cost-effective solution to the report.

THE WINNER: SOLUTION #11

The last bit of code you wrote really helped determine the TRUE winner; that is, the solution that produces the most bubbles at the lowest cost. Congrats on taking a lot of data and crunching it down to something Bubbles-R-Us can make real business decisions with.

Now, if you're like us, you're dying to know what is in Bubble Solution #11. Look no further: the Bubbles-R-Us CEO said he'd be delighted to give you the recipe after all your unpaid work.

So, you'll find the recipe for Bubble Solution #11 below. Take some time to let your brain process lists by making a batch, getting out, and blowing some bubbles before you begin the next chapter. Oh, but don't forget the bullet points and the crossword before you go!

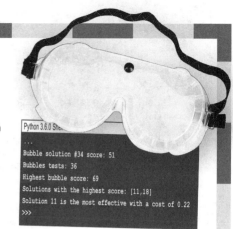

```
Python 3.6.0 She...

Bubble solution #34 score: 51
Bubbles tests: 36
Highest bubble score: 69
Solutions with the highest score: [11,18]
Solution 11 is the most effective with a cost of 0.22
>>>
```

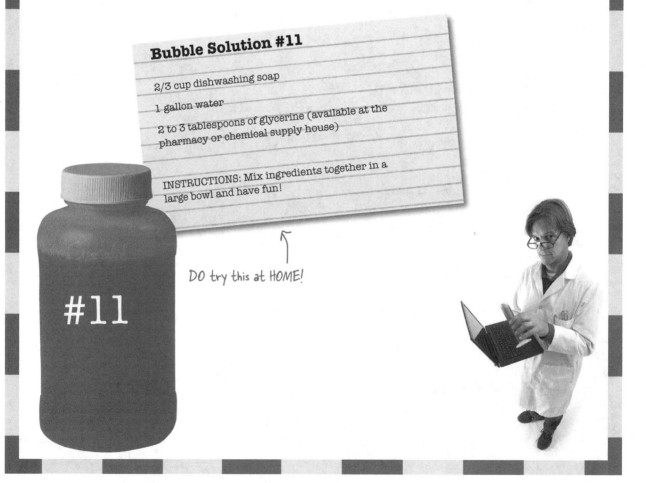

Bubble Solution #11

2/3 cup dishwashing soap

1 gallon water

2 to 3 tablespoons of glycerine (available at the pharmacy or chemical supply house)

INSTRUCTIONS: Mix ingredients together in a large bowl and have fun!

#11

DO try this at HOME!

> I have to ask: we already knew the highest score solutions, they are in the best_solutions list, so why did we need to go through EVERY score again?

You're right: we didn't need to.

We could have found the lowest-cost solution from just the list in best_solutions, because that list is the result of already figuring out one or more solutions with the highest bubble scores. The only reason we didn't was to keep things simple on our first attempt.

Others might be asking, though: what's the difference? Who cares? It works! Well, it is all about the efficiency of the code. How much work is your code doing? And, for a list as small as ours, there really isn't much of a difference; however, if you had a *huge* list of data you'd want to avoid iterating over it multiple times if you had a more efficient way. And we do.

To determine the lowest-cost solution (with the highest score), all we need to do is consider the solutions in the best_solutions list. Doing that is a little more complex, but not much.

We're rewritten the code to compute the most cost-effective solution.

This time we'll iterate over the best_solutions list instead of the scores lists

And we use each best_solutions item as an index into the cost list.

So, in this code we're using the values in best_solutions as our indices.

```
cost = 100.0
most_effective = 0


for i in range(len(best_solutions)):
    index = best_solutions[i]
    if cost > costs[index]:
        most_effective = index
        cost = costs[index]

print('Solution', most_effective,
    'is the most efftive with a cost of',
    costs[most_effective])
```

We examine the cost of each solution in the best_solutions list, and look for the lowest.

And as before we print the results.

COMPARE this code to the previous version; can you see the differences? Think through how each executes; can you see how much less work this version does to compute the most cost-effective solution? It's worth some time to see the difference.

BULLET POINTS

- Lists are a **data structure** for ordered data.

- A list holds a set of items, each with its own **index**.

- Lists use a zero-based index, where the first item is at index **0**.

- You can use the **len** function to get the number of items in a list.

- You can access any item using its index. For example, use **my_list[1]** to access the second item in the list.

- You can also use negative indices to identify items starting at the end of the list.

- Trying to access an item beyond the end of the list will result in a runtime index error.

- Assigning a value to an existing item will change its value.

- Assigning a value to an item that doesn't exist in the list results in an index "out of bounds" runtime error.

- List items can hold values of any type.

- Not all the values in a list need to be the same type.

- Lists that hold values of different types are called heterogeneous.

- You can create an empty list with **my_list = [ ]**.

- You can add a new value to a list using **append**.

- You can extend a list with the items in another list with **extend**.

- You can create a new list from two existing lists by simply adding them together with +.

- Use **insert** to add a new item at an index in an existing list.

- The **for** loop is commonly used to iterate through sequences, like lists.

- The **while** loop is most often used when you don't know how many times you need to loop, and you're looping until a condition is met. The **for** loop is most often used when you know the number of times the loop needs to execute.

- The **range** function creates a range of integers.

- You can iterate over ranges with the **for** loop.

- The **str** function converts a number to a string.

 Coding cross

Let lists sink into your brain as you do the crossword.

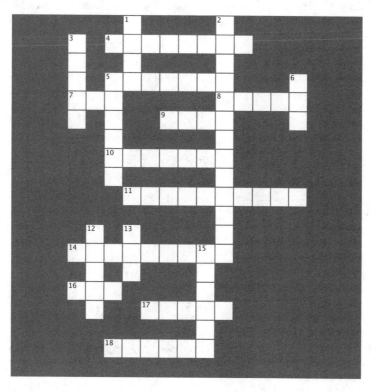

Across

4. Author probably likes this kind of music.
5. Another word for loop.
7. Gets the length.
8. Creates a sequence of numbers.
9. Computer scientists like to start lists at this index.
10. Accessing an item that doesn't exist results in this error.
11. Best bubble company.
14. We made a lot of these drinks.
16. Makes numbers into strings.
17. Every item has one.
18. Adds an item to a list.

Down

1. An ordered data structure.
2. A list with values of different types.
3. Iterates over a condition.
5. Puts an item into a list.
6. How to delete an item.
12. A list with no items.
13. Iterates over a sequence or range.
15. Adds items of one list to another.

Sharpen your pencil
Solution

It's a good time to get some practice with lists. Pretend you're the Python interpreter and trace though this code, figuring out what the final output is. After you finish, we'll take our list knowledge a little further.

Let's keep track of the eighties and other variables as we trace through this code. The newwave list never changes throughout this code.

```
eighties = ['', 'duran duran', 'B-52s', 'muse']
newwave = ['flock of seagulls', 'postal service']
```

	eighties	remember	band
`remember = eighties[1]`	[' ', 'duran duran', 'B-52s', 'muse']	'duran duran'	
`eighties[1] = 'culture club'`	[' ', 'culture club', 'B-52s', 'muse']	'duran duran'	
`band = newwave[0]`	[' ', 'culture club', 'B-52s', 'muse']	'duran duran'	'flock of seagulls'
`eighties[3] = band`	[' ', 'culture club', 'B-52s', 'flock of seagulls']	'duran duran'	'flock of seagulls'
`eighties[0] = eighties[2]`	['B-52s', 'culture club', 'B-52s', 'flock of seagulls']	'duran duran'	'flock of seagulls'
`eighties[2] = remember`	['B-52s', 'culture club', 'duran duran', 'flock of seagulls']	'duran duran'	'flock of seagulls'

```
print(eighties)
```

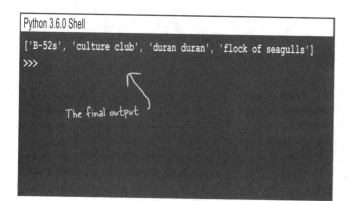

Python 3.6.0 Shell

```
['B-52s', 'culture club', 'duran duran', 'flock of seagulls']
>>>
```

The final output

The Thing-A-Ma-Jig

The Thing-A-Ma-Jig is quite a contraption—it clanks and clunks and even thunks,
but what it really does, well, you've got us stumped. Coders claim they know how it
works. Can you uncrack the code and find its quirks?

What does it all mean? The Thing-A-Ma-Jig takes a sequence of characters and
it creates and prints out a palindrome. You might remember that a palindrome is a
word that reads the same forward as it does backward, like "tacocat". So if we give
the Thing-A-Ma-Jig a sequence of t-a-c-o, it will turn that into the palindrome
tacocat for us. For a lot of sequences, like t-a-r, the results aren't so interesting:
'tarat'. But for others, like a-m-a-n-a-p-l-a-n-a-c, they are quite impressive: a
manaplanacanalpanama (or, "a man a plan a canal panama").

The important thing, though, is how does this code take half a palindrome and create
a full one. Let's study the code:

```
characters = ['t', 'a', 'c', 'o']

output = ''                          ← We'll start with output as the empty string.
length = len(characters)  ← Let's get the length of the characters list.
i = 0                                ← And set i to 0.
while (i < length):                  ← Now we'll start at 0 and
    output = output + characters[i]     go through each item in
    i = i + 1                           the list, adding it to the
                                        output list.

length = length * -1      ← Now let's reset things a bit, setting the length
i = -2                       to its corresponding negative value (so, for
                             example, a length of 8 would become -8).
                          ← And we'll set i to -2; you'll see how this is used
                             in the code block.            ← Why backward? Because
while (i >= length):                                          our indices are now
    output = output + characters[i]                           negative, not positive.
    i = i - 1             ←
                          ← Now we're looping over the characters
                             backward! We're also skipping the very last
print(output)                character so it doesn't get repeated in the
                             middle of the string.
```

Finally, we print the results.

We'll be seeing more of
palindromes in Chapter 8.

Study this until you understand it! Go through
each pass of the loop and write down the values
of the variables and lists that are changing if
necessary (and it may be!).

Sharpen your pencil
Solution

The smoothie flavors were added to this list in the order of their creation. Finish the code to determine the *most recent* smoothie flavor created.

```
smoothies = ['coconut', 'strawberry', 'banana', 'pineapple', 'acai berry']
most_recent = ___-1___
recent = smoothies[most_recent]
```

We can make use of Python negative indexes to grab the last item in the list with −1.

```
smoothies = ['coconut', 'strawberry', 'banana', 'pineapple', 'acai berry']
most_recent = len(smoothies) − 1
recent = smoothies[most_recent]
```

Or we can get the length of the list, and subtract one.

You can take this a little further.

Note that while breaking down things into clear steps can often help with the clarity of our code, for simple, common operations more succinct code can actually be more readable. Let's take the first attempt at the code above and make it more succinct:

```
smoothies = ['coconut', 'strawberry', 'banana', 'pineapple', 'acai berry']
most_recent = -1
recent = smoothies[-1]
```

We can just get rid of the most_recent variable and use the −1 value directly in the list index.

We can do this with the second code attempt as well.

```
smoothies = ['coconut', 'strawberry', 'banana', 'pineapple', 'acai berry']
most_recent = len(smoothies) − 1
recent = smoothies[len(smoothies)-1]
```

Here we've also gotten rid of the intermediate most_recent variable and just moved the len(smoothies)−1 calcuation into the index of the list. This is arguably not as readable, but to an experienced programmer it most likely would be. Code clarity is more an art than a science, so go with what you find most clear and readable—and keep in mind that may change over time!

Code Magnets Solution

We've got code for testing to see which smoothies have coconut in them. We had all the code nicely laid out on our fridge using fridge magnets, but the magnets fell on the floor. It's your job to put them back together. Be careful; a few extra magnets got mixed in.

```
:
```

```
i = i + 2
```

```
while i > len(has_coconut)
```

```python
smoothies = ['coconut',
             'strawberry',
             'banana',
             'tropical',
             'acai berry']
```

```python
has_coconut = [True,
               False,
               False,
               True,
               False]
```

```python
i = 0
```

```python
while i < len(has_coconut)    :
```

```python
    if has_coconut[i]    :
```

```python
        print(smoothies[i],'contains coconut')
```

```python
    i = i + 1
```

↑
Rearrange the magnets here.

Here's the output we're expecting. ↘

```
Python 3.6.0 Shell
coconut contains coconut
tropical contains coconut
>>>
```

WHO DOES WHAT? SOLUTION

We had our `range` function calls figured out, and then they got all mixed up. Can you help us figure out who does what? Be careful, we're not sure if each range matches zero, one, or more sequences. We've already figured one out, which is marked below:

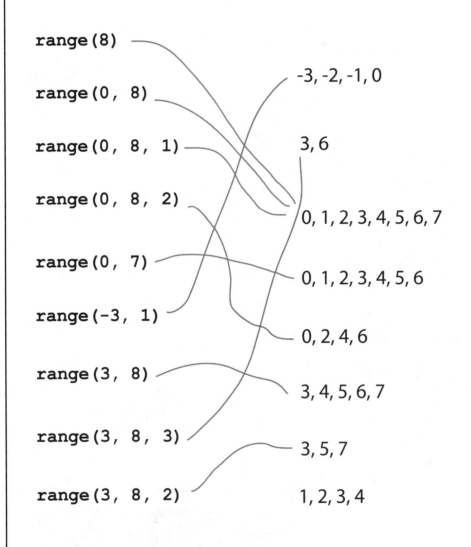

range(8)

range(0, 8)

range(0, 8, 1)

range(0, 8, 2)

range(0, 7)

range(-3, 1)

range(3, 8)

range(3, 8, 3)

range(3, 8, 2)

-3, -2, -1, 0

3, 6

0, 1, 2, 3, 4, 5, 6, 7

0, 1, 2, 3, 4, 5, 6

0, 2, 4, 6

3, 4, 5, 6, 7

3, 5, 7

1, 2, 3, 4

Sharpen your pencil
Solution

Rewrite your fridge magnet code (from a few pages back) so that it uses a `for` loop instead of a `while` loop. If you need a hint, revisit the way we reworked the `while` loop for Bubbles-R-Us.

```
smoothies = ['coconut',
             'strawberry',
             'banana',
             'tropical',
             'acai berry']
```

```
has_coconut = [True,
               False,
               False,
               True,
               False]
```

```
i = 0
```

```
while i < len(has_coconut) :
    if has_coconut[i] :
        print(smoothies[i],
              'contains coconut')
    i = i + 1
```

Your code goes here.

```
smoothies = ['coconut',
             'strawberry',
             'banana',
             'tropical',
             'acai berry']

has_coconut = [True,
               False,
               False,
               True,
               False]

length = len(has_coconut)

for i in range(length):
    if has_coconut[i]:
        print(smoothies[i], 'contains coconut')
```

Let's get the length of the list.

And iterate from 0 to the length of the list (minus 1).

Test the has_coconut list at index i to see if the item has coconut and if so, print its name from the smoothies' list at i.

Notice we could have written "if has_coconut[i] == True", but has_coconut[i] evaluates to a Boolean value, so it isn't really necessary.

Sharpen your pencil
Solution

Go ahead and implement the pseudocode on the previous page to find the highest score by filling in the blanks in the code below. Once you're done, add the code to *bubbles.py* and give your code a test. Check the results in the shell, and fill in the blanks in our shell below with the number of bubble tests and the highest score.

```python
scores = [60, 50, 60, 58, 54, 54,
          58, 50, 52, 54, 48, 69,
          34, 55, 51, 52, 44, 51,
          69, 64, 66, 55, 52, 61,
          46, 31, 57, 52, 44, 18,
          41, 53, 55, 61, 51, 44]

high_score = __0__                        ← Fill in the blanks to complete the code here...

length = len(scores)
for i in range(length):
    print('Bubble solution #' + str(i), 'score:', scores[i])
    if ___scores[i]___ > high_score:
        ___high_score___ = scores[i]

print('Bubbles tests:', ___length___)
print('Highest bubble score:', ___high_score___)
```

Here's what we got. ⟶

```
Python 3.6.0 Shell

Bubble solution #0 score: 60
Bubble solution #1 score: 50
Bubble solution #2 score: 60
 ...
Bubble solution #34 score: 51
Bubble solution #35 score: 44
Bubbles tests: 36
Highest bubble score: 69
```

Sharpen your pencil
Solution

You've seen how to create an empty list with two square backets, but what do you think the code below does? Feel free to type the code into the shell to experiment. Record your observations here.

```
mystery = ['secret'] * 5
```

This syntax creates a list with 'secret' as an item repeated five times: ['secret', 'secret', 'secret', 'secret', 'secret']. This is a Python special feature, so you won't find it in too many other programming languages. It does come in handy at times (for instance, in Chapter 11).

```
mystery = 'secret' * 5
```

Multiplication and strings? Well, we saw this already when Codie's "12" was repeated seven times, remember? So if you multiply a number by a string, you get a new string with the original string repeated.

Sharpen your pencil
Solution

Can you help write the loop to find *all the scores* that match the high score? You'll find all the code up until now listed below. Give it a real shot below before you check the solution.

Again, we're starting by creating a new list that will hold all the bubble solutions that match the highest score.

Next, we iterate through the entire scores list, looking for those items with the highest score.

We're just showing you the new code. You know, saving trees and all that.

```
best_solutions = []
for i in range(length):
    if high_score == scores[i]:
        best_solutions.append(i)
```

Each time through the loop, we compare the score at index i with the high_score and if they are equal, then we add the score at that index to the best_solutions list using append.

```
print('Solutions with the highest score:', best_solutions)
```

And finally, we can display the bubble solutions with the highest scores. Notice we're using print to display the best_solutions list. We could have created another loop to display the list items one by one, but, luckily, print will do this for us (and, if you look at the output, it also adds commas between the list values; just what we need).

Coding cross Solution

Let lists sink into your brain as you do the crossword.

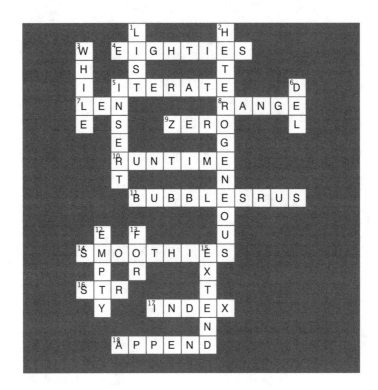

5 functions and abstraction

*Getting Functional

Now that we know how to abstract our code, the future's so bright we gotta wear shades.

You already know a lot. Variables and data types and conditionals and iteration—that's enough to **write** basically **any program** you'd ever want to. In fact, a computer scientist would tell you it's enough to write any program that anyone could ever conceive of. But you don't want to stop now, because your next step in computational thinking is learning how to **create abstractions** in your code. That may sound complex, but it's actually going to make your coding life simpler. Creating abstractions gives you leverage; with abstraction, you can more easily create programs of increasing complexity and power. You can put your code in neat little packages that you can reuse over and over. And you can forget all the nitty-gritty details of your code and to start thinking at a higher level.

Sharpen your pencil

Do a little analysis of the code below. How does it look? Choose as many of the options below as you like, or write in your own analysis:

```python
dog_name = "Codie";
dog_weight = 40
if dog_weight > 20:
    print(dog_name, 'says WOOF WOOF')
else:
    print(dog_name, 'says woof woof')

dog_name = "Sparky"
dog_weight = 9
if dog_weight > 20:
    print(dog_name, 'says WOOF WOOF')
else:
    print(dog_name, 'says woof woof')

dog_name = "Jackson"
dog_weight = 12
if dog_weight > 20:
    print(dog_name, 'says WOOF WOOF')
else:
    print(dog_name, 'says woof woof')

dog_name = "Fido"
dog_weight = 65
if dog_weight > 20:
    print(dog_name, 'says WOOF WOOF')
else:
    print(dog_name, 'says woof woof')
```

Discussing my age wasn't enough?

Codie,

☐ A. It's the same code over and over, so it seems very redundant.

☐ B. It looks tedious to type in!

☐ C. It doesn't seem to do a lot for that much code.

☐ D. Not the most readable code I've ever seen.

☐ E. If we wanted to change how the dogs bark, that would be a lot of changes to make!

☐ F. _____
_____

What's wrong with the code, anyway?

Okay, so we have some code that is repeated *over and over*. What's wrong with that? Well, at face value, nothing. After all, it works, right? Let's have a closer look at the code in question:

```
dog_name = "Codie"
dog_weight = 40
if dog_weight > 20:
    print(dog_name, 'says WOOF WOOF')
else:
    print(dog_name, 'says woof woof')
```

What we're doing here is comparing the dog's weight to 20, and if it's greater than 20, we're outputting a big WOOF WOOF. If it's less than 20 or equal to 20, we're outputting a smaller woof woof.

```
dog_name = "Sparky"
dog_weight = 9
if dog_weight > 20:
    print(dog_name, 'says WOOF WOOF')
else:
    print(dog_name, 'says woof woof')
```

And this code is...wait, it's doing EXACTLY the same thing! And the same is true of the rest of the code.

Sure, this code looks innocent enough, but it's tedious to write, it's hard to read, and it will be problematic if your code needs to change over time. That last point will become more and more clear as you gain experience in programming—almost all code does change over time, and the code above is a nightmare waiting to happen because we've got the same logic repeated over and over.

```
dog_name = "Jackson"
dog_weight = 12
if dog_weight > 20:
    print(dog_name, 'says WOOF WOOF')
else:
    print(dog_name, 'says woof woof')

dog_name = "Fido"
dog_weight = 65
if dog_weight > 20:
    print(dog_name, 'says WOOF WOOF')
else:
    print(dog_name, 'says woof woof')
```

Again, only the details of the dog are different.

And again, different dog, same code.

Say you need to add a new bark called "yip yip," for tiny dogs that are less than 2 lb. How many places do you need to make that change in the existing code?

Oh boy, so what do we do?

BRAIN POWER

How can you improve this code? Take a few minutes to think of a few possibilities.

If only I could find a way to reuse code so that anytime I needed it, I could just use it rather than retyping it. And a way to give it a nice memorable name so that I could remember it. And a way to make edits in just one place instead of many if something changes. That would be dreamy. But I know it's just a fantasy...

Turning a block of code into a **FUNCTION**

What if we told you that you could take a block of code, put a name on it, and then use and reuse that code anytime you like? You'd probably say, "What took you so long?!"

Python gives us a way to do exactly that, and it's called *defining a function*. You've already *used* a few functions, like, print, str, int, and range. Let's look at how they work again:

> You'll find all programming languages (at least languages that you'd want to use) give you a way to define functions.

We call or invoke a function by using its name in code.

The name is followed by a parenthesis.

And then we provide zero or more arguments we pass along to the function.

```
print("I'm a function")
```

And then finally we have an ending parenthesis.

> You might have also noticed that sometimes a function returns something to us, like with the str function, which returns a string that represents an integer.

When we call a function, we've assumed the function goes off and does a bunch of work (like printing the values we passed it) and then at some point returns and our code resumes where it left off. And that's exactly what a function does.

You don't have to be satisfied calling prebuilt functions; you can create your own. Here's how you do that:

To create a function, start with the def keyword, and follow it with a name to remember the function by.

Next you can have zero or more parameters. Think of these like variables that hold values that you will pass into the function when you call it.

And then we have a colon, which, as you know, starts a block of code in Python.

```
def bark(name, weight):
    if weight > 20:
        print(name, 'says WOOF WOOF')
    else:
        print(name, 'says woof woof')
```

Here's the block of code we are going to reuse.

In Python and pretty much all languages, we call this code block the body of the function.

When the Python interpreter sees this code, it simply defines the function and stashes the code away for later use—the body of the function is not executed at this point. The body is only executed when the function is called.

So now that you know how to define a function, let's see how you use it.

We created a function, so how do we use it?

Now that you've created a function by taking a block of code, giving it a name, and defining some parameters (the dog's name and weight) that you'll be supplying when you call it, you're all ready to use your new function.

And given your experience with functions like `print`, `str`, `random`, and `range`, you already know what to do. Let's call `bark` a few times to see how it works:

```python
bark('Codie', 40)
bark('Sparky', 9)
bark('Jackson', 12)
bark('Fido', 65)
```

Let's test bark with all the dogs we know about.

Great, that's the output we were expecting!

```
Python 3.6.0 Shell

Codie says WOOF WOOF
Sparky says woof woof
Jackson says woof woof
Fido says WOOF WOOF
>>>
```

But how does all this actually work?

We've created a function and we've put it to work, and everything seems like it is working as expected, but what is really going on behind the scenes? How does this all really work? Let's take things step by step and see. To do that, let's step through the following code:

Here we start with a print statement, just to get things going.

```python
print('Get those dogs ready')

def bark(name, weight):
    if weight > 20:
        print(name, 'says WOOF WOOF')
    else:
        print(name, 'says woof woof')

bark('Codie', 40)

print("Okay, we're all done")
```

And then we have our bark function definition.

And then we're going to call the bark function with the arguments Codie and 40.

And finally we use a print statement to say we're done.

BRAIN POWER

Pretend you are the Python interpreter. Start at the top of the code and mentally step through and execute each line. Are there any steps that are unclear to you?

**Behind
the Scenes**

Like any good interpreter, let's start at the beginning.
So our first line of code is a `print` statement. This executes as you'd expect and outputs 'Get those dogs ready' to the Python Shell.

We start here.

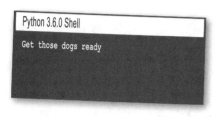

Python 3.6.0 Shell

Get those dogs ready

So far we just have a print statement, which sends its output to the shell.

```python
print('Get those dogs ready')

def bark(name, weight):
    if weight > 20:
        print(name, 'says WOOF WOOF')
    else:
        print(name, 'says woof woof')

bark('Codie', 40)

print("Okay, we're all done")
```

Up next: the function definition.
After executing the print statement, the interpreter encounters the function definition for the bark function. At this point, the Python interpreter doesn't execute the code in the function; rather, it creates a name, bark, and stores away the function parameters and body (after giving the body a quick syntax scan) for later use. After the definition is processed by the interpreter, we can use the name bark to invoke the function any time we want.

The whole point of this bit of code is to create the function, not to invoke it. So after this code is evaluated, we're all ready to invoke this function at any time with the function's name, bark.

```python
print('Get those dogs ready')

def bark(name, weight):
    if weight > 20:
        print(name, 'says WOOF WOOF')
    else:
        print(name, 'says woof woof')

bark('Codie', 40)

print("Okay, we're all done")
```

Next we have a <u>call</u> to the bark function.

After the function definition is complete, the interpreter next encounters a function call. This time it's a call to the `bark` function with two arguments: the string 'Codie' and the number 40.

The interpreter retrieves the function definition named `bark` from memory, and assigns the *arguments* 'Codie' and 40 to the *parameters* `name` and `weight`, respectively.

Behind the Scenes

It's time to invoke our function.

```
print('Get those dogs ready')

def bark(name, weight):
    if weight > 20:
        print(name, 'says WOOF WOOF')
    else:
        print(name, 'says woof woof')

bark('Codie', 40)

print("Okay, we're all done")
```

Here we're passing two arguments, which are 'Codie' and 40...

↓ ↓

```
bark('Codie', 40)
```

`'Codie'`   `40`

```
def function bark(name, weight)
    . . .
```

↑ ↑

...which are assigned to the parameters name and weight.

You can think of `name` and `weight` as brand new variables that are around as long as your function body is being executed. Anytime you refer to them in your function body, you can count on them to hold the values of the arguments you passed into your function.

Next, after the parameters have been set, the interpreter takes `bark`'s code and begins executing it.

Make it stick

We call, or **invoke**, a function.

You pass **arguments** into your function calls.

A function has zero or more **parameters** that accept values from your function call.

Now we execute the function

body. An important thing to notice here is that the flow of the program has now gone from the call to the `bark` function to the body of the `bark` function—we're no longer proceeding straight through our code, but rather, we've jumped to the code in the function body. Keep that in mind.

In the function body we first have a conditional test to see if the `weight` parameter is greater than 20, and given we passed in 40, it is, so we execute the code block of the conditional.

The block of the conditional prints the parameter `name`, which has the value of 'Codie' and then 'says WOOF WOOF'.

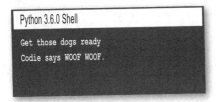

```
Python 3.6.0 Shell

Get those dogs ready
Codie says WOOF WOOF.
```

And with that, we complete the code in the body of the `bark` function. So where do we go from here? Well, when a function completes, the control of the program returns back to where the function was called, and the interpreter resumes execution there.

> **Remember, when a function completes, the control of the program returns back to where the function was called, and the interpreter resumes execution there.**

Behind the Scenes

After the values of your arguments have been assigned to each parameter, then it's time to start executing the body of your function.

```
print('Get those dogs ready')

def bark(name, weight):
    if weight > 20:
        print(name, 'says WOOF WOOF')
    else:
        print(name, 'says woof woof')

bark('Codie', 40)

print("Okay, we're all done")
```

```
print('Get those dogs ready')

def bark(name, weight):
    if weight > 20:
        print(name, 'says WOOF WOOF')
    else:
        print(name, 'says woof woof')

bark('Codie', 40)

print("Okay, we're all done")
```

With the call to bark finished, the interpreter resumes execution right after the call to the bark function. So, we'll pick back up here.

Behind the Scenes

Now we execute the code after the function call. Finally, we return from the call to the bark function and the only code remaining is a simple print statement that outputs Okay, we're all done to the Python Shell.

```
print('Get those dogs ready')

def bark(name, weight):
    if weight > 20:
        print(name, 'says WOOF WOOF')
    else:
        print(name, 'says woof woof')

bark('Codie', 40)

print("Okay, we're all done")
```

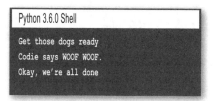

Python 3.6.0 Shell

```
Get those dogs ready
Codie says WOOF WOOF.
Okay, we're all done
```

Finally we reach the last line of our program.

A Test Drive

That's a lot to take in. Take a deep breath, and then get this code into a file called *bark.py*, save your code, and choose the **Run > Run Module** menu item to make sure everything's good.

Here's the code:

Add all this new code to your file.

```
def bark(name, weight):
    if weight > 20:
        print(name, 'says WOOF WOOF')
    else:
        print(name, 'says woof woof')

bark('Codie', 40)
bark('Sparky', 9)
bark('Jackson', 12)
bark('Fido', 65)
```

WOW, look how much more readable and clear this code is!

Here's what we got when we tested the code.

Python 3.6.0 Shell

```
Codie says WOOF WOOF
Sparky says woof woof
Jackson says woof woof
Fido says WOOF WOOF
>>>
```

Sharpen your pencil

Here's a little connect-the-dots exercise for you. Using your pencil, start at step 1 and draw a line from each step to the next as the program executes. Feel free to annotate your lines where necessary to explain what is happening in the code's execution. We already drew the first couple lines for you.

We start here.

Print, and then proceed to the next line.

1 `print('Get those dogs ready')`

2 `def bark(name, weight):`
a   `if weight > 20:`
b   `print(name, 'says WOOF WOOF')`
    `else:`
        `print(name, 'says woof woof')`

3 `bark('Codie', 40)`

4 `print("Okay, we're all done")`

Sharpen your pencil

We've got some more calls to `bark` below. Next to each call, write what you think the output should be, or if you think the code will cause an error. Check your answer at the end of the chapter before you go on.

`bark('Speedy', 20)` _____

`bark('Barnaby', -1)` _____

`bark('Scottie', 0, 0)` _____

`bark('Lady', "20")` _____

`bark('Spot', 10)` _____

`bark('Rover', 21)` _____

Write what you think the shell will display here.

Hmm, any ideas what these do?

I thought you said we were going to learn about abstraction? So far it seems this chapter is just about functions.

Functions are a way to abstract your code.

Think about the first dog example in this chapter. We had a lot of messy code, and if you looked at that code it was a bit hard, at least at first, to figure out what its purpose was. But after some study, it was pretty obvious: we wanted each dog to bark. And we wanted it to bark in a way that was representative of the dog's size—WOOF WOOF for big dogs, and woof woof for small dogs.

So, what we did was pull the code that does the barking out and abstracted it into a function. Once we did that, we could simply write code like this:

```
bark('Codie', 40)
```

We no longer had to worry about *how* the code barks (as we did with every single case of barking before we had this function), we just need to *use* the bark function. And, two months from now when you need to make some more dogs bark, you can reuse this function with very little knowledge of how it works. That allows you to focus on what you're coding (say, a dog show simulator), not the low-level details of barking.

↙ Or your coworker does.

So we are taking code, abstracting it into a function, and then making use of that abstraction in our code.

Code Magnets

This working code is all scrambled up on the fridge. Can you reconstruct the code snippets to make a working program that produces the output listed below? Notice, there may be some extra code on the fridge, so you may not use all the magnets. Check your answer at the end of the chapter.

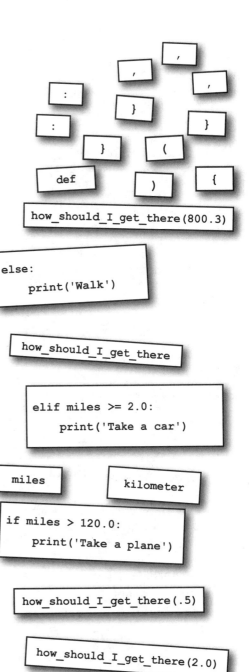

```
,
,
,
:
}
:
}
}
(
def    )    {
how_should_I_get_there(800.3)
```

```
else:
    print('Walk')
```

```
how_should_I_get_there
```

```
elif miles >= 2.0:
    print('Take a car')
```

```
miles          kilometer
```

```
if miles > 120.0:
    print('Take a plane')
```

```
how_should_I_get_there(.5)
```

```
how_should_I_get_there(2.0)
```

```
Python 3.6.0 Shell
Take a plane
Take a car
Walk
```

there are no Dumb Questions

Q: Do I need to define my function before the code that calls it? Or can I put my functions at the end of the file?

A: Yes, you need to define functions before they are *called* in your code. One thing to consider: say we have two functions, f1 and f2, where f1 calls f2 in its body. In this case, it is perfectly fine to define f2 after f1 in your code, so long as f1 does not get called before f2 is defined. That's because defining the function body of f1 does not invoke f2, until f1 is actually called. In terms of where to put functions, we suggest defining functions at the top of your file for better organization and clarity.

Q: What kind of values can I pass to a function?

A: In Python you can pass any of the data types you've learned (as well as all the ones you *will* learn) to a function: Booleans, strings, numbers, and lists. Believe it or not, you can even pass a function to another function—we will get to why you'd want to and what it gets you later in the book (in the Appendix).

Q: Sorry, I'm still confused on the whole argument versus parameter thing.

A: Don't overthink it. They are both terms for simple things. Arguments are the values you pass to a function when you make a function call. Parameters are part of the function definition, and get initialized to the arguments passed to the function call.

Q: What happens if I mix up the order of my arguments, so that I'm passing the wrong arguments into the parameters?

A: All bets are off; in fact, we'd guess you're pretty much guaranteed either an error at runtime or incorrectly behaving code. Always take a careful look at a function's parameters, so you know what arguments the function expects to be passed and in what order.

That said, there are some other ways to approach passing arguments that we'll look at before the chapter is over.

Q: What are the rules for function names?

A: The rules for naming a function are the same as the rules for naming a variable, which we saw in Chapter 2. Just start with an underscore or letter, and continue with letters, underscores, or numbers. Most Python programmers, by convention, keep their function names all lowercase with undescores between words, like **get_name** or **fire_cannon**.

Q: Can functions call other functions?

A: Yes, happens all the time. Note you're already doing this when you call the **print** function within the **bark** function code. Your own functions are no different; you can call them from your other functions.

Functions can RETURN things too

So far you've *only passed things to a function*; that is, you know how to call a function and pass arguments to it. But you can also *get a value back from a function*, with the `return` statement:

Here's a new function, get_bark, that returns the appropriate bark, given a dog's weight.

```python
def get_bark(weight):
    if weight > 20:
        return 'WOOF WOOF'
    else:
        return 'woof woof'
```

If the weight is greater than 20 we return the string 'WOOF WOOF'.

Otherwise, we return the string 'woof woof'.

A function can have zero, one, or more return statements.

But only one will be executed, because as soon as a return statement is executed, the code immediately returns from the function.

How to call a function that has a return value

So we've got a function, `get_bark`, that we just need to pass the weight of our dog, and it returns the appropriate bark for that dog. Let's see how to use it:

You call the function like any other function, only this function returns a value, so let's set that value to a variable, codies_bark.

```
codies_bark = get_bark(40)
print("Codie's bark is", codies_bark)
```

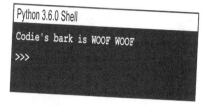

```
Python 3.6.0 Shell
Codie's bark is WOOF WOOF
>>>
```

Sharpen your pencil

Get some practice to make return values sink in. Compute the return value of each function call.

```
def make_greeting(name):
    return 'Hi ' + name + '!'
```

```
def compute(x, y):
    total = x + y
    if (total > 10):
        total = 10
    return total
```

```
def allow_access(person):
    if person == 'Dr Evil':
        answer = True
    else:
        answer = False

    return answer
```

Defined on the previous page ↓

get_bark(20) _____   Write what each call returns here. ←

make_greeting('Speedy') _____

compute(2, 3) _____

compute(11, 3) _____

allow_access('Codie') _____

allow_access('Dr Evil') _____

I noticed in that last exercise that you declared some new variables right inside your functions, like total and answer.

Good catch.

We sure did. You can declare new variables right inside of your function, just as we did. It's often handy to have variables that hold the result of an intermediate calculation that you'll need in your function. We call these *local variables*, because they are local to the function and only exist as long as the function execution does. That's in comparison to the global variables we've been using so far, which exist as long as your entire program does.

But hold that thought. Given our new knowledge of functions, parameters, return values, and so on, we've just received a request to help "refactor" some code. We never turn down a chance to do real coding, so we're going to do that and then circle back and dig into variables (local, global, and otherwise) some more.

Getting a little refactoring under our belts

A new startup around the corner has been working on some code to help their users choose an avatar—you know, an onscreen representation, real or imagined. They've just started, and so far all their code does is ask for the user's preferences for hair color, eye color, gender, and so on—once they get this all working, they'll presumably take all these preferences and generate a nice avatar image for each user.

But they feel like their code is already getting too complex for such a simple task. You'll find the code below; notice that they've tried to make this easy on the user by supplying some default values—the user can either type in a value, or just hit return to accept the default.

> For each attribute of the avatar, we prompt the user, including a default choice, like brown hair.

```
hair = input("What color hair [brown]? ")
if hair == '':
    hair = 'brown'
print('You chose', hair)
```

> If the user simply hits the Return key, then we assign the variable to the default value. Otherwise, we use what they typed in.

```
hair_length = input("What hair length [short]? ")
if hair_length == '':
    hair_length = 'short'
print('You chose', hair_length)
```

> We also print each user's choice.

```
eyes = input("What eye color [blue]? ")
if eyes == '':
    eyes = 'blue'
print('You chose', eyes)
```

> We do this over and over for each attribute.

```
gender = input("What gender [female]? ")
if gender == '':
    gender = 'female'
print('You chose', gender)

has_glasses = input("Has glasses [no]? ")
if has_glasses == '':
    has_glasses = 'no'
print('You chose', has_glasses)

has_beard = input("Has beard [no]? ")
if has_beard == '':
    has_beard = 'no'
print('You chose', has_beard)
```

Running the code

Let's do a little run-through of the code so far to see how it works. Before we do, though, make sure you've studied the code a bit so you get the gist of it.

Python 3.6.0 Shell

```
What color hair [brown]? blonde
You chose blonde
What hair length [short]?
You chose short
What color eyes [blue]? brown
You chose brown
What gender [female]? male
You chose male
Has glasses [no]?
You chose no
Has beard [no]? yes
You chose yes
```

The program prompts us for each attribute. We either type out an attribute, or accept the default (like short hair length and no glasses) by hitting return.

And for each attribute, the program confirms the user's choice by printing it back out.

BRAIN POWER

Obviously our avatar code is in need of some abstraction. Use this space to work out how you think this code should be abstracted into a function (or functions) and what your function calls might look like. When you're done, we'll walk through it together on the next page (but make sure you do your own work first!).

How to abstract the avatar code

Now that you've done your own thinking, let's take a look and find the commonality in the code that we can abstract into a function:

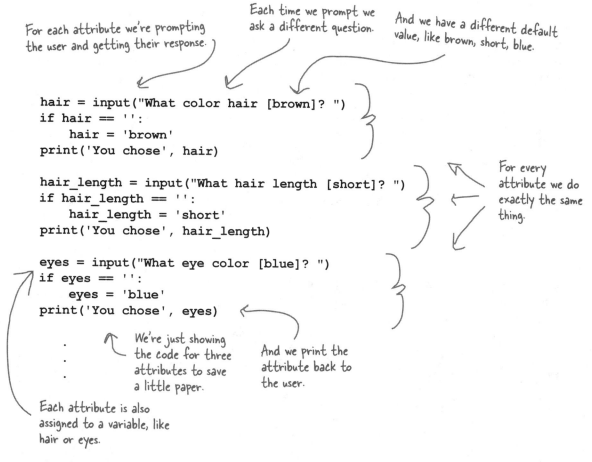

For each attribute we're prompting the user and getting their response.

Each time we prompt we ask a different question.

And we have a different default value, like brown, short, blue.

```python
hair = input("What color hair [brown]? ")
if hair == '':
    hair = 'brown'
print('You chose', hair)

hair_length = input("What hair length [short]? ")
if hair_length == '':
    hair_length = 'short'
print('You chose', hair_length)

eyes = input("What eye color [blue]? ")
if eyes == '':
    eyes = 'blue'
print('You chose', eyes)
    .
    .
    .
```

For every attribute we do exactly the same thing.

We're just showing the code for three attributes to save a little paper.

And we print the attribute back to the user.

Each attribute is also assigned to a variable, like hair or eyes.

There are two things that vary over each bit of code, and that's the question and the default value. Those are going to be our parameters because each time we call our function they will be different. Let's start there:

Let's call our function get_attribute.

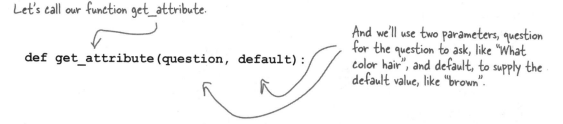

```python
def get_attribute(question, default):
```

And we'll use two parameters, question for the question to ask, like "What color hair", and default, to supply the default value, like "brown".

Writing the get_attribute function body

Now let's work on the function body. Based on the original code, the first thing we need to do is create a string that acts as a question, so that we can prompt and get input from the user.

```python
def get_attribute(query, default):
    question = query + ' [' + default + ']? '
    answer = input(question)
```

Let's put together the question for the user by using the query parameter along with the default parameter, and we'll format the string just like the previous code did.

Then we'll prompt the user and get their input. We'll assign the answer variable to their input.

Now, just as the previous code did, we need to check to see if the user chose the default value by hitting return (in which case, the answer will be the empty string). Then we need to print out their choice:

```python
def get_attribute(query, default):
    question = query + ' [' + default + ']? '
    answer = input(question)
    if (answer == ''):
        answer = default
    print('You chose', answer)
```

Check the answer against the empty string, and if it is the empty string, set the answer to the default parameter.

Finally, we just have one thing left to do: we need to get the answer back to the code that called `get_attribute`. How do we do that? With the `return` statement, of course:

```python
def get_attribute(query, default):
    question = query + ' [' + default + ']? '
    answer = input(question)
    if (answer == ''):
        answer = default
    print('You chose', answer)
    return answer
```

We've got the user's answer, so the only thing left to do is return it.

Calling get_attribute

Now, for each attribute, we just need to write the appropriate call to the get_attribute function.

```python
def get_attribute(query, default):
    question = query + ' [' + default + ']? '
    answer = input(question)
    if (answer == ''):
        answer = default
    print('You chose', answer)
    return answer
```

We've taken each of the original attributes and created a call to get_attribute for each one.

```python
hair = get_attribute('What hair color', 'brown')
hair_length = get_attribute('What hair length', 'short')
eye = get_attribute('What eye color', 'blue')
gender = get_attribute('What gender', 'female')
glasses = get_attribute('Has glasses', 'no')
beard = get_attribute('Has beard', 'no')
```

A Test Drive

Get this code above into a file called *avatar.py*, save your code, and choose the **Run > Run Module** menu item to give the avatar code a try.

```
Python 3.6.0 Shell
What color hair [brown]? blonde
You chose blonde
What hair length [short]?
You chose short
What color eyes [blue]? brown
You chose brown
What gender [female]? male
You chose male
Has glasses [no]?
You chose no
Has beard [no]? yes
You chose yes
```

Make sure you take another look at the code above; look at how much more concise and understandable it is! Not to mention it's more maintainable if you need to change something in the future.

Exactly as it looked and operated before our rework

Serious Coding

Reworking code to make it more concise, readable, and well structured is a common activity of good coders. Often this activity is called ***refactoring*** code.

Functions Exposed

This week's interview:
Sitting down with a Local Variable

Head First: Welcome, Local Variable. We're glad you joined us.

Local Variable: Glad to be here.

Head First: So, we really don't know a lot about you. Maybe you could fill us in.

Local Variable: Ever declare a variable inside a function? That's me.

Head First: And so how is that any different than any other time we declare a variable?

Local Variable: I'm meant to be used only *within* the function body; in fact, that's the only place you can use me!

Head First: What do you mean?

Local Variable: Say you're writing a function and you need a variable to hold something you're calculating in that function, say a variable called `position`. You declare `position` within the function and use it anywhere in the function body. Now, that variable doesn't exist until the function is invoked, and then it exists as long as the function body is being evaluated, but as soon as your function returns, the variable disappears.

Head First: What about the next time the function is invoked?

Local Variable: You get a fresh new local variable called `position`, which is around as long as the function invocation is, and then it goes away again.

Head First: So what good are you if you're just around for a bit and you keep disappearing as soon as the function ends?

Local Variable: Oh, I'm hugely useful. I'm hugely useful. In a function you need variables to hold the temporary results as you compute something. So you have me to do that. And when the function is done, I take care of all the cleanup; you don't even have to worry about me cluttering up your program with unneeded variables.

Head First: So, I don't think this audience has heard her, but we've also had Parameters in for an interview in the past; how are you different from her?

Local Variable: Oh, Parameters! She's like a sister to me. Parameters are essentially local variables, but special ones that get set up when the function is called. Basically each parameter is created and set to the value of the corresponding incoming arguments. And, like a local variable, a parameter is available to you throughout the function body, but then it goes away when the function ends.

Head First: Ah, I didn't know you knew each other. Well, the other interviewee that comes to mind is Global Variable.

Local Variable: Ah yes, overrated if you ask me; that guy's a pain.

Head First: Come again?

Local Variable: A global variable is a variable you declare outside a function. It has global scope.

Head First: Scope?

Local Variable: Scope is the extent of where your variables are visible. It's an area of the program where you can access a variable, to read or change its value. A global variable is visible everywhere in your code.

Head First: Well, what's your scope?

Local Variable: Like I said, just the function body, same as Parameters.

Head First: Well, what's the issue with Global Variable being, well, global scope?

Local Variable: It's not considered the best design decision to use lots of global variables.

Head First: Why, they sound like a convenient thing to me.

Local Variable: I think your readers will hear more about this later, but it can lead to some issues with large programs.

Head First: Maybe next time we can have you and Globals in for a fireside chat?

Local Variable: Oh, I can hardly wait.

What does this code output? Are you sure? Maybe you better test it for real. Why did you get that result? Was it what you expected?

```python
def drink_me(param):
    msg = 'Drinking ' + param + ' glass'
    print(msg)
    param = 'empty'


glass = 'full'
drink_me(glass)
print('The glass is', glass)
```

Don't even think about skipping this one!

Let's talk about variables a little more...

We're finding out there's more to variables than just declaring them, setting their values, and changing them. By adding functions into the mix, we've introduced a bunch of new concepts like local variables and, by contrast, global variables. And don't forget parameters, which act like local variables (except they are set up for us when the function is invoked). And then we have this concept of scope as well.

Sharpen your pencil

Make sure we can recognize each type of variable. Annotate this code by identifying local and global variables as well as any parameters. Check your answers.

```python
def drink_me(param):
    msg = 'Drinking ' + param + ' glass'
    print(msg)
    param = 'empty'


glass = 'full'
drink_me(glass)
print('The glass is', glass)
```

Understanding variable scope

The term *scope* describes where a variable is visible, or accessible, within your code. The rules are pretty straightforward:

- **Global variable**: visible anywhere in your program, although we'll see one minor exception to this in just a sec.

- **Local variable**: only visible within the function body where it is declared.

- **Parameter**: only visible within the function body where it is declared.

> Notice local variables are created only within functions.

Let's check out this idea of variable scope with some code we're already familiar with:

> The local variables question and answer have local scope within the get_attribute function.

> The parameters query and default also have local scope within the get_attribute function.

```
def get_attribute(query, default):
    question = query + ' [' + default + ']? '
    answer = input(question)
    if (answer == ''):
        answer = default
    print('You chose', answer)
    return answer
```

> Notice we return the value in a local variable, answer, just before the function ends.

```
hair = get_attribute('What hair color', 'brown')
hair_length = get_attribute('What hair length', 'short')
eye = get_attribute('What eye color', 'blue')
gender = get_attribute('What gender', 'female')
glasses = get_attribute('Has glasses', 'no')
beard = get_attribute('Has beard', 'no')
```

> The variables hair, hair_length, eye, gender, glasses, and beard are all global variables and are visible anywhere in this code.

Q: How can you return a local variable from a function if it goes away when the function completes?

A: When you return a local variable from a function, you are returning *the value* of the local variable, not the local variable itself. Think of it like this: if you're running a relay race, you pass the baton (value), not yourself (the variable holding the value), to the next runner. So given only the value is being returned, this is not a problem when the function ends and the variable goes away (because the value the variable held is still around).

The same is true of local variables; they can shadow globals within a function.

Q: What happens if I name a parameter the same name as a global variable, or is that even allowed?

A: It is allowed. What happens is that within your function body any references to that variable will refer to the local version (the parameter), not that global one. So effectively, that particular global variable won't be visible within that function. When this happens we call it *shadowing* a variable (because the local parameter is overshadowing the global variable). This is quite common and isn't necessarily something to avoid as long as your code is well structured. If a parameter name makes sense, go for it—your function really shouldn't be referring to global variables in the function body anyway (more on that topic later).

Q: I get why we might want local variables to hold temporary parts of things we're computing in a function, but why do we need parameters. Can't we just always refer to global variables with the values we want?

A: Technically that could be done, but it would lead to code that is difficult to understand and error prone. Using parameters allows us to write general functions that don't need to depend on specific global variables; instead, they are parameterized, allowing the calling code to determine the arguments to pass to the function.

Take our bark function, for example; if it relied on globals, how would you make it work for various dogs?

When variables get passed to functions

Are you still wondering about the output for the `drink_me` code? Or, wondering more specifically why the glass didn't get emptied? Most people do. The reason has to do with how variables and values are treated when they are passed to a function. Let's take a look:

Spoiler alert: here's what the drink_me code outputs.

```
Python 3.6.0 Shell
Drinking full glass
The glass is full
>>>
```

Here's our drink_me code again. Let's step through it and see how the glass remains full after drink_me is called.

```python
def drink_me(param):
    msg = 'Drinking ' + param + ' glass'
    print(msg)
    param = 'empty'

glass = 'full'
drink_me(glass)
print('The glass is', glass)
```

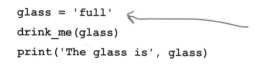

In this code, after the function is defined, we assign the string value 'full' to the variable glass.

Making the drink_me function call

Now let's call the `drink_me` function and see what happens with our
variables and parameters.

When drink_me is called, the value of the argument
glass is evaluated, and its value 'full' is passed along,
and assigned to the parameter param.

The value 'full' is assigned
to the parameter param.

```
def drink_me(param):
    msg = 'Drinking ' + param + ' glass'
    print(msg)
    param = 'empty'

glass = 'full'
drink_me(glass)
print('The glass is', glass)
```

Remember from Chapter 2, when we assign a value to a
variable (and you can think of param as a variable), we
create a location for the value, and then we label the
location (a cup in our diagram) with the variable name.

NOTE: the way Python handles passing arguments
is a little more complex than this, in particular
when we start talking about objects, but for now
this is a good working model for us.

glass

'full'

param

'full'

Next we construct the msg using the
value of the parameter param.

Python 3.6.0 Shell

Drinking full glass

```
def drink_me(param):
    msg = 'Drinking ' + param + ' glass'
    print(msg)
    param = 'empty'

glass = 'full'
drink_me(glass)
print('The glass is', glass)
```

And then we print it.

The value of param at
this point is 'full'.

glass

'full'

param

'full'

Now for the important part. We're going
to assign 'empty' to param.

Nothing about the glass
variable has changed; it is
still labeling the value 'full'.

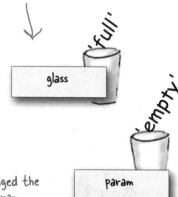

```
def drink_me(param):
    msg = 'Drinking ' + param + ' glass'
    print(msg)
    param = 'empty'


glass = 'full'
drink_me(glass)
print('The glass is', glass)
```

Now we've changed the
value of the param
parameter to 'empty'.

Finally we return from the
function call to drink_me, and we
execute the print statement.

Our parameter param no longer
exists because the function call
has completed. Sad.

```
def drink_me(param):
    msg = 'Drinking ' + param + ' glass'
    print(msg)
    param = 'empty'


glass = 'full'
drink_me(glass)
print('The glass is', glass)
```

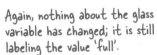

Again, nothing about the glass
variable has changed; it is still
labeling the value 'full'.

The print statement prints
the value of the glass variable,
which is 'full'.

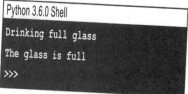

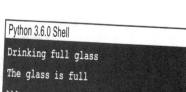

```
Python 3.6.0 Shell
Drinking full glass
The glass is full
>>>
```

So, when we pass a variable to a function, we're actually passing the value of that variable, not the variable itself.

You got it. It's common for coders to say, "When I pass the variable x to the do_it function," but that is a coder colloquialism, and what they really mean is "When I pass *the value of the variable* x to the do_it function." Think about it this way—when you make a function call, each argument is evaluated *before* it is passed to the function, so if we have:

```
x = 10
do_it('secret', 2.31, x)
```

The string 'secret' evaluates to the string 'secret' and is passed along, the number 2.31 evaluates to the floating-point number 2.31 and is passed along, and finally, the variable x is evaluated to the value 10 before it is passed along. So your function doesn't even know there is a variable x, it just gets the value 10 and sets its corresponding parameter to that value.

Now, we're going to see that things get slightly more complicated when we start working with objects, but think of your arguments as always being passed to your functions, not your variables.

What about using global variables in functions?

Global variables are global, right? So they should be visible both inside and outside functions, and they are. To use a global variable in a Python function, we first let Python know we're going to use a global variable with the `global` keyword.

Create a global variable greeting.

```
greeting = 'Greetings'

def greet(name, message):
    global greeting
    print(greeting, name + '.', message)

greet('June', 'See you soon!')
```

Tell our function we're going to use a global.

And use it.

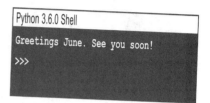

```
Python 3.6.0 Shell
Greetings June. See you soon!
>>>
```

Of course you can change the value of a global variable in your function if you want to:

```
greeting = 'Greetings'

def greet(name, message):
    global greeting
    greeting = 'Hi'
    print(greeting, name + '.', message)

greet('June', 'See you soon!')
print(greeting)
```

Change the global greeting to 'Hi'.

Print the value of greeting after the call to greet.

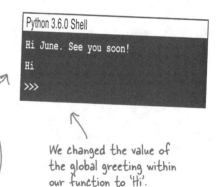

```
Python 3.6.0 Shell
Hi June. See you soon!
Hi
>>>
```

We changed the value of the global greeting within our function to 'Hi'.

Watch it!

Make sure you use the `global` keyword as a best practice

This all seems simple enough: to use a global variable in a function, just use the `global` keyword to state your intent and use it at will. But watch out—this one has bitten many coders before you. If you don't use the `global` keyword you will still be able to read the values of global variables in your functions, but if you try to change the value of this global, one of two things will happen: either it will have been the first time you've used the variable in your function, and Python will assume it is a local variable instead of a global, or you will have already read the value once, and Python will throw an `UnboundLocalError`. Whenever you see this, look for cases where you are unintentionally mixing local and global variables.

Fireside Chats

Tonight's talk: **LOCAL and GLOBAL variables answer the question "Just what is GLOBAL's problem, anyway?"**

The LOCAL variable

Look, I get I don't have as big a job as Global, but it's a nice job—anytime I'm needed to hold a value inside a function, I'm there. And as soon as that function is done, I clean up and get out of the way.

Just because you're everywhere doesn't mean folks should go out of their way to use you.

What I mean is, folks shouldn't jump right into a global variable when they don't really need one.

I don't disagree with that for simple code, but for more complex code apparently you haven't spent much time on the top coder discussion site stackoverflow.com, because people say, "Avoid globals!" all the time.

One problem is that if you use a lot of globals, sooner or later you're going to accidentally reuse the same global name. Or imagine giving someone else your code—they won't even know without a lot of study what globals you're using. In fact, they might already have code using the same global names.

The GLOBAL variable

I've got global scope. I'm everywhere; enough said.

No one needs to go out of their way. Just declare a variable outside a function, I'm there.

What are you talking about—who doesn't like a global variable? Especially for simple programs, they are actually one of the clearest and most straightforward ways to store important values.

Oh, you can't be serious; I'm like a basic part of almost every programming language. You think all those smart computer scientists would have put me in if I wasn't totally useful?

Oh sure, blame people being sloppy in their code on me. Who are you going to blame next, the `for` loop?

The LOCAL variable

Another issue is when you're looking at a piece of code that uses a global variable, you have no idea what other parts of the code could be using and changing that value, especially in a large program. At least with a local variable you can typically see all the code that deals with it; after all, it's all right there in the function.

Say you're building some code for a chocolate factory.

You've got a global Boolean variable controlling whether the boiling vat's drain is closed, and you always want set it to `True` before pouring chocolate into the vat.

Ah, but then in all your hundreds of lines of chocolate factory code, a new hire comes along and sets the variable to `False`, without checking to see if there is chocolate in the vat. Can you say inherently dangerous?

Actually, a really good solution to that problem is objects. Which I think the readers will learn about much later in the book.

And guess what, you still use local variables within objects as well.

Have you considered looking for another line of work? Once these readers get more advanced, they may not need you anymore.

The GLOBAL variable

What's the big deal? I don't see the issue.

Okaaaaaay...

Exactly; see how well that works? You have a global variable and you just look to see if it is closed or not. It's in one place, easy to find.

Well, you just need to train people better. And how does a local variable solve that?

Objects, so I've heard.

Oh, well good for you.

Oh, I'm pretty sure they'll be using me for quite a while, at least until they learn...oh, nevermind.

Going further with parameters: default values and keywords

Earlier we'd said you need to be careful about argument order: if you don't pass the correct arguments, in the correct order, then all bets are off in terms of how a function is going to operate. If you've got a function that has speed and altitude parameters and you switch the order when you pass your arguments, watch out!

You'll find this is true across most programming languages; to alleviate this potential ordering problem, Python provides another, more flexible way to provide parameters. With Python, parameters can have *default values* and *keywords*, which allows you to pick and choose your arguments and the order you want to supply them. You'll find parameter keywords and default values used in many Python modules and libraries (not to mention you might want to use keywords and default values in your own code).

You want a speed of 35,000 and an altitude of 580? That could be a bit of a problem. You might want to check your argument order.

← We'll be seeing them used in practice, later in the book, as we explore more Python modules.

How default parameter values work

Your function parameters can have default values. Let's use a simpler version of our `greet` function, without the global variable:

Here's a normal, everyday parameter waiting for an argument.

And here's a parameter that doesn't really care if it gets a corresponding argument or not because it has a default value.

```python
def greet(name, message='You rule!'):
    print('Hi', name + '.', message)
```

This is the default value for message if the calling code doesn't pass an argument for message.

Now that we've got a parameter with a default value, let's see how we use this:

If we call greet without an argument for message, then the greet function will use the default value for the message parameter.

```python
greet('John')
greet('Jennifer', 'How are you today?')
```

And if we supply an argument for message, then our greet function will gladly accept that as the message argument.

```
Python 3.6.0 Shell

Hi John. You rule!
Hi Jennifer. How are you today?
>>>
```

Always list your required parameters first!

If you're providing defaults for some of your parameters, you need to be careful and put all your *required parameters* first. What's a required parameter? Well, if your function has a parameter without a default value, then when your function is called, it *must supply* an argument for that parameter, so it's required. So say we were to expand our `greet` function like this:

> Here's a new parameter, but it's required because there is no default value.

```python
def greet(name, message='You rule!', emoticon):
    print('Hi', name + '.', message, emoticon)
```

What not to do!

Our new function definition is not allowed. Python is complaining that a required (non-default as Python calls it) argument follows a default argument.

```
Python 3.6.0 Shell

File "defaults.py", line 1
    def greet(name, message='You
rule!', emoticon):

                              ^
SyntaxError: non-default argument
follows default argument
```

So what's the big deal? Why can't we do this? The short story: if you work through more complex examples, you'll see the interpreter can easily get into a situation where it has no idea which arguments go with which parameters. While we encourage you to think through such a situation, for now just remember to list all your required (non-default in Python lingo) parameters before the parameters with defaults. So, fixing our code above, we get:

If you've been keeping track of the parameter versus argument definitions, you might be asking why the interpreter is calling these arguments and not parameters. We have the same question, but who are we to argue with the Python interpreter?

Now the non-defaults (required) parameters are first... ...followed by the optional ones.

```python
def greet(name, emoticon, message='You rule!'):
    print('Hi', name + '.', message, emoticon)
```

Using arguments with keywords

So far every time we've called a function, the arguments have been *positional*. That is, the first argument is mapped to the first parameter, the second argument to the second parameter, and so on. You can also use the parameter names as keywords and specify the arguments in a different order if you like.

To understand how this works, let's take our newly expanded `greet` function and call it with some keywords:

```
greet(message='Where have you been?', name='Jill', emoticon='thumbs up')
```

> To use a keyword, use the parameter name, followed by an equals sign and the value for that argument.

> Using keywords we can mix and match the order of our arguments and even omit them if they have defaults. Just make sure your calls provide any required arguments before the keywords arguments.

```
Python 3.6.0 Shell
Hi Jill. Where have you been? thumbs up
>>>
```

You can mix and match positional and keyword arguments as well.

```
greet('Betty', message='Yo!', emoticon=':)')
```

> Here we're positionally specifying the name parameter, but using keywords for the others.

```
Python 3.6.0 Shell
Hi Betty. Yo! :)
>>>
```

How to think about all these options

Parameter defaults and argument keywords are fairly specific to the Python language. In some cases you'll find that when you have a function with many parameters, they are quite convenient in allowing you to specify common default values for those who might use your code. We're not going to focus heavily on the use of either in this book, but if you're going to continue Python programming you will come across them, and as we said, we'll need knowldege of them later in the book for some of Python's modules we make use of.

Exercise

Cement how those keyword arguments work into your brain before this chapter ends by working through the code below and figuring out what it outputs. Write your answer in the Python Shell window below.

```python
def make_sundae(ice_cream='vanilla', sauce='chocolate', nuts=True,
                banana=True, brownies=False, whipped_cream=True):
    recipe = ice_cream + ' ice cream and ' + sauce + ' sauce '
    if nuts:
        recipe = recipe + 'with nuts and '
    if banana:
        recipe = recipe + 'a banana and '
    if brownies:
        recipe = recipe + 'a brownie and '
    if not whipped_cream:
        recipe = recipe + 'no '
    recipe = recipe + 'whipped cream on top.'
    return recipe

sundae = make_sundae()
print('One sundae coming up with', sundae)

sundae = make_sundae('chocolate')
print('One sundae coming up with', sundae)

sundae = make_sundae(sauce='caramel', whipped_cream=False, banana=False)
print('One sundae coming up with', sundae)

sundae = make_sundae(whipped_cream=False, banana=True,
                     brownies=True, ice_cream='peanut butter')
print('One sundae coming up with', sundae)
```

```
Python 3.6.0 Shell



                                    ← Output goes here.
```

> I know the chapter is about to end, but I just have one more question about functions. If a function doesn't have a return statement, does it return anything?

It returns None. This is a bit of a can of worms to open up right before the chapter ends, but it's our fault for not bringing it up sooner.

When you have a function that doesn't explictly return a value with a `return` statement, it returns the value None. Not the string `"None"`, but the *value* None. If you're saying "what on earth is that?" it's one of those strange computational objects, sort of like the empty string or an empty list, or maybe more like `True` or `False`. In this case it's just a value that means *no value* or perhaps *undefined*.

You might also be asking if None is a value, what's its type? The type of None is NoneType. We know, now it all makes sense, right? Here's the trick: don't think too hard about None; it's a value that signifies the lack of a value, and we'll see a bit here and there how this can be used. For now, here's more about the type:

NoneType

None

— Has a single value None.

— Uses no quotes around None.

— First letter always capitalized.

— Expressions can evaluate to None.

So add that to the stack of things you've got in the back of your brain and we'll return to this topic later.

You can file NoneType under "truly weird types."

You'll find many programming languages have similar values with names like NULL, null, and nil.

The case of the attempted robbery not worth investigating

Sherlock finished his phone call with the bumbling chief of police, Lestrade, and sat down in front of the fireplace to resume reading the newspaper. Watson looked at him expectantly.

Five Minute Mystery

"What?" said Sherlock, not looking up from the paper.

"Well? What did Lestrade have to say?" Watson asked.

"Oh, he said they found a bit of rogue code in the bank account where the suspicious activity was taking place."

"And?" Watson said, trying to hide his frustration.

"Lestrade emailed me the code, and I told him it wasn't worth pursuing. The criminal made a fatal flaw and will never be able to actually steal the money," Sherlock said.

"How do you know?" Watson asked.

"It's obvious if you know where to look," Sherlock exclaimed. "Now stop bothering me with questions and let me finish this paper."

With Sherlock absorbed in the latest news, Watson snuck a peek at Sherlock's phone and pulled up Lestrade's email to look at the code.

```
balance = 10500
camera_on = True
```

← *This is the real, actual bank balance in the account.*

```
def steal(balance, amount):
    global camera_on
    camera_on = False
    if (amount < balance):
        balance = balance - amount

    return amount
    camera_on = True


proceeds = steal(balance, 1250)
print('Criminal: you stole', proceeds)
```

Why did Sherlock decide not to investigate the case? How could he know that the criminal would never be able to steal the money just by looking at the code? Is there one problem with the code? Or more?

BULLET POINTS

- Functions give us a way to package up, abstract, and reuse code.

- A function has a name, zero or more parameters, and a body.

- You call or invoke a function and pass it zero or more arguments.

- You can pass a Python function any valid Python value.

- The number and order of arguments in a function call needs to match the parameters in the function. You can use keyword arguments to specify a subset of arguments in an arbitrary order.

- When a function is invoked, it assigns the arguments to parameter variables and then executes its code block.

- A function's code block is also known as the body of the function.

- Functions can return values by using the return statement.

- To capture the value returned from a function, simply assign the result of the call to a variable.

- Functions can themselves call built-in functions or other functions you've defined.

- You can declare functions in any order as long as they are defined before they are called.

- You can create local variables within a function.

- Local variables exist only as long as the function execution does.

- The places in your code where a variable is visible define its scope.

- Variables that aren't created inside functions are called global variables.

- A function's parameters are treated as local variables in the function body.

- When we name a parameter the same name as a global variable, we say that parameter is shadowing the global variable.

- The global keyword is used within a function to signify you'd like to refer to a global variable in the function body.

- Abstracting code often makes your code more readable, well structured, and maintainable.

- Abstracting code also allows you to focus at a higher level, and to forget about the low-level details a function implements.

- Reworking code is often called refactoring.

- You can use parameter defaults to provide default values for missing arguments.

- You can use parameter names as keyword arguments when calling a function.

Coding cross

Get more functional as you do the crossword.

Across

3. Solved the case.
5. Parameters can do this to global variables.
6. An online representation.
9. Another name for the function's block of code.
10. When you call a function, you supply these.
11. Arguments are passed to these.
13. Reworking your code.
14. Functions are great for this.
16. Keyword for using globals in function.
17. Parameter names can be used as these.
18. Another word for calling a function.

Down

1. Parameters are also these.
2. How long a variable lasts.
4. All functions have one.
5. We made some of these with lots of default values.
7. You can use functions to do this.
8. We usually use this to match arguments to parameters.
12. Variables declared in a function.
13. How you pass values back.
15. When we pass a variable to a function, we really pass its _____.

Sharpen your pencil
Solution

Do a little analysis of the code below. How does it look? Choose as many of the options below as you like, or write in your own analysis:

☑ A. It's the same code over and over, so it seems very redundant.

☑ B. It looks tedious to type in!

☑ C. It doesn't seem to do a lot for that much code.

☑ D. Not the most readable code I've ever seen.

☑ E. If we wanted to change how the dogs bark, that would be a lot of changes to make!

☑ F. <u>Should we be reusing the same variables over and over for different dogs?</u>

 Sharpen your pencil
Solution

Here's a little connect-the-dots exercise for you. Using your pencil, start at step 1 and draw a line from each step to the next as the program executes. Feel free to annotate your lines where necessary to explain what is happening in the code's execution. We already drew the first couple lines for you.

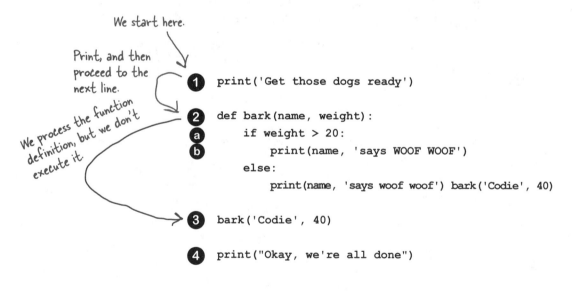

We start here.

Print, and then proceed to the next line.

We process the function definition, but we don't execute it.

```
1  print('Get those dogs ready')

2  def bark(name, weight):
a      if weight > 20:
b          print(name, 'says WOOF WOOF')
       else:
           print(name, 'says woof woof') bark('Codie', 40)

3  bark('Codie', 40)

4  print("Okay, we're all done")
```

SOLUTION CONTINUES ON NEXT PAGE...

Then we call bark, so we're back to step 2.

```
1  print('Get those dogs ready')

2  def bark(name, weight):
a      if weight > 20:
b          print(name, 'says WOOF WOOF')
       else:
           print(name, 'says woof woof') bark('Codie', 40)

3  bark('Codie', 40)

4  print("Okay, we're all done")
```

Then we execute the function's body with steps 2a and 2b...

```
1  print('Get those dogs ready')

2  def bark(name, weight):
a      if weight > 20:
b          print(name, 'says WOOF WOOF')
       else:
           print(name, 'says woof woof') bark('Codie', 40)

3  bark('Codie', 40)

4  print("Okay, we're all done")
```

...before returning from the function at 3 and then executing step 4.

Sharpen your pencil Solution

We've got some more calls to `bark` below. Next to each call, write what you think the output should be, or if you think the code will cause an error. Here's our solution.

`bark('Speedy', 20)`   Speedy says woof woof

`bark("Barnaby", -1)`   Barnaby says woof woof

⤷ Our bark function doesn't check to make sure dog weights are greater than 0. So this works because −1 is less than 20.

`bark('Scottie', 0, 0)`   ERROR, bark() takes 2 positional arguments but 3 were given.

`bark('Lady', "20")`   ERROR, '>' not supported between instances of 'str' and 'int'

`bark('Spot', 10)`   Spot says woof woof

`bark('Rover', 21)`   Rover says WOOF WOOF

Code Magnets Solution

This working code is all scrambled up on the fridge. Can you reconstruct the code snippets to make a working program that produces the output listed below? Notice, there may be some extra code on the fridge, so you may not use all the magnets.

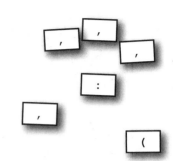

```
def   how_should_I_get_there   (   miles   )   :
```
> The function takes miles as a parameter and then...

```
    if miles > 120.0:
        print('Take a plane')
```

```
    elif miles >= 2.0:
        print('Take a car')
```
> ...checks the distance to see if a plane, a car, or walking is appropriate.

```
    else:
        print('Walk')
```

```
how_should_I_get_there(800.3)
```

```
how_should_I_get_there(2.0)
```

```
how_should_I_get_there(.5)
```

```
kilometer
```

Python 3.6.0 Shell
```
Take a plane
Take a car
Walk
```

Sharpen your pencil
Solution

Get some practice to make return values sink in. Compute the
return value of each function call.

`get_bark(20)`   'woof woof'

`make_greeting('Speedy')`   'Hi Speedy!'

`compute(2, 3)`   5

`compute(11, 3)`   10

`allow_access('Codie')`   False

`allow_access('Dr Evil')`   True

Sharpen your pencil
Solution

Let's make sure we can recognize each type of variable. Annotate this code by
identifying local and global variables as well as any parameters. Here's our solution.

```
                                   parameter
              def drink_me(param):
local variable    msg = 'Drinking ' + param + ' glass'
              print(msg)
parameter     param = 'empty'          local variable

global variable  glass = 'full'
              drink_me(glass)          global variable
              print('The glass is', glass)
```

Exercise Solution

Cement how those keyword arguments work into your brain before this chapter ends by working through the code below and figuring out what it outputs. Write your answer in the Python Shell window below.

```python
def make_sundae(ice_cream='vanilla', sauce='chocolate', nuts=True,
                banana=True, brownies=False, whipped_cream=True):
    recipe = ice_cream + ' ice cream and ' + sauce + ' sauce '
    if nuts:
        recipe = recipe + 'with nuts and '
    if banana:
        recipe = recipe + 'a banana and '
    if brownies:
        recipe = recipe + 'a brownie and '
    if not whipped_cream:
        recipe = recipe + 'no '
    recipe = recipe + 'whipped cream on top.'
    return recipe

sundae = make_sundae()
print('One sundae coming up with', sundae)

sundae = make_sundae('chocolate')
print('One sundae coming up with', sundae)

sundae = make_sundae(sauce='caramel', whipped_cream=False, banana=False)
print('One sundae coming up with', sundae)

sundae = make_sundae(whipped_cream=False, banana=True,
                     brownies=True, ice_cream='peanut butter')
print('One sundae coming up with', sundae)
```

Did you notice this code has a bug if there are no nuts?

```
Python 3.6.0 Shell

One sundae coming up with vanilla ice cream and chocolate sauce with nuts and a banana and whipped
cream on top.
One sundae coming up with chocolate ice cream and chocolate sauce with nuts and a banana and whipped
cream on top.
One sundae coming up with vanilla ice cream and caramel sauce with nuts and no whipped cream on top.
One sundae coming up with peanut butter ice cream and chocolate sauce with nuts and a banana and a
brownie and no whipped cream on top.
>>>
```

Here's our output.

Five Minute Mystery Solution

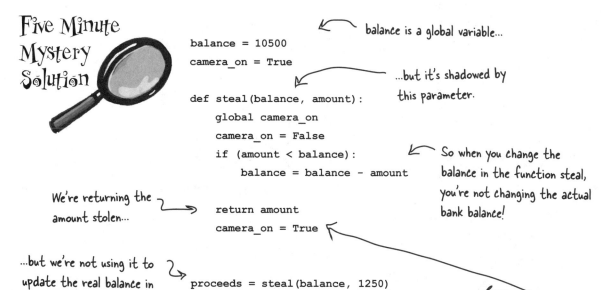

balance is a global variable...

```
balance = 10500
camera_on = True

def steal(balance, amount):
    global camera_on
    camera_on = False
    if (amount < balance):
        balance = balance - amount

    return amount
    camera_on = True

proceeds = steal(balance, 1250)
print('Criminal: you stole', proceeds)
```

...but it's shadowed by this parameter.

So when you change the balance in the function steal, you're not changing the actual bank balance!

We're returning the amount stolen...

...but we're not using it to update the real balance in the account. So the balance of the bank account is the same as it was originally.

The criminal thinks he stole the money, but he didn't!

And, in addition to not actually stealing any money, the criminal forgets to turn the camera back on, which is a dead giveaway to the police that something nefarious is going on. Remember, when you return from a function, the function stops executing, so any lines of code after the return are ignored!

Coding Cross Solution

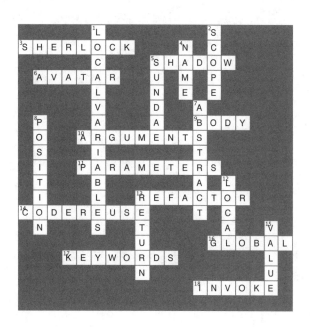

4, part 2, sorting and nested iteration
in which we return to the lists and add some superpowers

Putting Some Order in Your Data

Sometimes the default ordering of your data doesn't cut it.
You've got that list of high scores on 80s arcade games, but you really need it sorted alphabetically by game name. Then there's that list of the number of times your coworkers have stabbed you in the back—it would be nice to know who's at the top of that list. To do that, though, we need to learn how to sort data, and to do that we'll need to explore some algorithms that are a little more involved than the ones we've seen so far. We're also going to have to explore how nested loops work as well as think a little about the efficiency of the code we're writing. Come on, let's take that computational thinking up a level!

I'm back! My bubbleologists did such a great job in Chapter 4 that I'd love to give out some awards. Check out my idea below; I just need for you to write some code to generate one more report. After all the code you've written, I'm sure this will be a walk in the park for you.

Bubbles-R-Us

I just need one more thing, I'd love to give awards to the inventors of the top solutions. Can you give me a list of the top five best bubble solutions in descending order by their bubble score? Something like the report below.

— Bubbles-R-Us CEO

```
Top Bubble Solutions
1) Bubble solution #10 score: 68
2) Bubble solution #12 score: 60
3) Bubble solution #2 score: 57
4) Bubble solution #31 score: 50
5) Bubble solution #3 score: 34
```

Note these aren't real scores; this is just an illustration of what I want.

Thanks!!

Cubicle conversation

> We just need to sort them? That doesn't sound too bad.

Frank Judy Joe

Frank: Well, it doesn't *sound* bad, but how do we do it?

Judy: We've been coming up with some great algorithms, so I'm sure we can tackle sorting.

Joe: Actually, sorting algorithms are a topic some computer scientists spend their entire careers researching. They're not something we should "come up with," but rather we need to research the existing algorithms and choose one that is appropriate for our problem.

Frank: It sounds like we're going to be researching for a while. Should we postpone the softball game this afternoon?

Joe: I don't think so, Frank. I saw this coming and I've already taken a look.

Frank: Oh, why didn't you say so? What kind of sort are we going to use?

Joe: Bubble sort.

Judy, Frank (chuckling): Very funny, Joe. We know we're sorting bubbles. Do you have a sort that is appropriate or not?

Joe: I'm actually being completely serious. We're going to use a bubble sort. It's not the most efficient sorting algorithm ever invented, but it is one of the easiest to understand.

Frank: I don't get it; was it invented by one of our competitors?

Joe: Oh, you mean the name. It's called bubble sort because as you run the algorithm, the larger (or smaller) items in the list tend to "bubble up" to one end. You'll see how that looks when we start implementing it.

Judy: Joe, you seem to have done your homework, so we'll take your lead on this.

Joe: Okay, let's do it.

Judy: That reminds me, I told Greg to get on this too. I didn't realize you'd already done all this research. I need to remember to tell him not to bother. Don't let me forget!

Understanding bubble sort

We're going to look at some pseudocode for bubble sort shortly, but before we do, let's get an intuitive feel for how this algorithm works. To do that, let's sort a list of numbers:

[6, 2, 5, 3, 9] ← *Here's our unsorted list.*

We typically think of sorting lists into ascending order, so we're expecting our list to look like this after the bubble sort algorithm has finished:

[2, 3, 5, 6, 9] ← *The same list sorted in ascending order.*

One thing to know up front: bubble sort works by making a number of *passes* over a list. As you'll see, in each pass, if we end up swapping any values in the list, we'll need to make another pass. When no values are swapped in a pass, we're done. Keep that in mind, as it's key to how the algorithm works.

Starting with pass 1

We begin by comparing the first and second items (the items at index 0 and 1). If the first item is larger than the second, we swap them:

Next we compare the values of index 1 and index 2. If the first value, 6, is larger than the second value, 5 (and it is), we swap them.

Moving along, we compare the next values at index 2 and index 3, and once again, the first is larger. So we swap.

Next we compare the value at index 3 to the value at index 4, and it is not larger. So, we do nothing and pass 1 is complete.

Notice the value 6 used to be the first in the list, and it is slowly making its way (bubbling) toward the end of the list.

At this point we're done with pass 1, but we swapped some values, so we need to do another pass. On to pass 2!

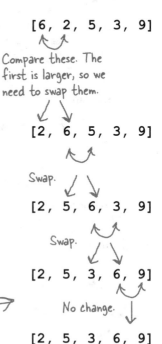

[6, 2, 5, 3, 9]
Compare these. The first is larger, so we need to swap them.

[2, 6, 5, 3, 9]
Swap.

[2, 5, 6, 3, 9]
Swap.

[2, 5, 3, 6, 9]
No change.

[2, 5, 3, 6, 9]

Pass 2

On pass 2 we start over, comparing the values of index 0 and index 1; index 1 has a larger value, so we don't need to swap values.

[2, 5, 3, 6, 9]
No change.

Moving on, we compare the values of index 1 and index 2; in this case, the index 2 value is larger than index 3, so we swap values.

[2, 5, 3, 6, 9]

Swap.

You're staring to understand the method now: we now compare the values of index 2 and index 3, and the value 5 is not larger than 6, so we do not swap values.

[2, 3, 5, 6, 9]
No change.

Moving on, we compare the 3rd and 4th index values, and the 4th value is larger, so we do not need to swap.

[2, 3, 5, 6, 9]
No change.

Now pass 2 is over, but we swapped index 2 and 3 during this pass, so we need to do another pass. On to pass 3.

[2, 3, 5, 6, 9]

Pass 3

On pass 3 we start over once again, comparing index 0's value to index 1's; index 1 has a larger value, so we don't need to swap values.

[2, 3, 5, 6, 9]
No change.

Now we compare the values of index 1 and 2; index 2's value is larger, so we don't need to swap.

[2, 3, 5, 6, 9]
No change.

Moving on we compare the values of index 2 and 3; index 3's value is larger, so we don't need to swap.

[2, 3, 5, 6, 9]

Likewise, we compare the values of index 3 and 4; index 4's value is larger, so we don't need to swap.

[2, 3, 5, 6, 9]
No change.

Now pass 3 is over, and we didn't swap any values. So our algorithm is complete and we have a sorted list!

[2, 3, 5, 6, 9]

Sharpen your pencil

We're not asking you to write any code, we're just asking you to use the bubble sort algorithm to sort this list.

Hopefully you now have a good feel for how to apply bubble sort's algorithm. Let's practice. Take the list below and bubble sort it, showing your work just like we did on the previous two pages. This will help to lock in your understanding. If you get stuck, take a peek at our solution at the end of the chapter.

```
['coconut', 'strawberry', 'banana', 'pineapple']
```

Here's the list. Don't let the strings throw you; just compare them alphabetically (what a computer scientist would call lexicographically, otherwise known as dictionary order).

Pass 1   ← Start pass 1 here.

Some bubble sort pseudocode

Now that you have an intuitive feel for the bubble sort, let's actually look at some pseudocode for the algorithm. You've already got all the knowledge you need to understand this code; it uses basic Boolean logic and some loops. However, it does use loops in a more complex way than you've seen before by using two loops together—what we call a *nested loop*.

Nested loops can make you stop and think the first time you see one, but here's the trick: you just mentally did a nested loop when you worked through the last Sharpen exercise (as well as when we walked through sorting the list of numbers together). The outer loop represents each pass in the algorithm. The inner loop goes through each item in the list and performs the comparisons (and any needed swapping). So with that in mind, let's have a look:

Let's put all that Chapter 5 function knowledge to work!

We're going to have a function, bubble_sort, which takes a list as a parameter.

And we're going to have a variable to track if we've swapped any values in the current pass. We set this to True initially to kick off the first pass.

We're going to use a while loop that loops as long as swapped is True.

Think of the while loop as performing each pass. Each time through the loop is another pass.

Pseudocode can take many forms. This form is closer to code, but still not quite code, at least not Python.

```
DEFINE a function bubble_sort(list):

    DECLARE a variable swapped and set to True.

    WHILE swapped:
        SET swapped to False.
        FOR variable i in range(0, len(list)-1)
            IF list[i] > list[i+1]:
                DECLARE a variable temp and set to list[i].
                SET list[i] to list[i+1]
                SET list[i+1] to temp
                SET swapped to True.
```

The first thing we do in the loop is set swapped to False.

In the for loop, you iterate through each item in the list (except the last item) and compare it to the next. If it's greater, then you swap the values.

If we ever swap any values, we set swapped to True, meaning we're going to have to do another pass when the for loop finishes.

BRAIN POWER

This pseudocode sorts a list in ascending order. What change would you need to make to sort in descending order?

What do you think of the pseudocode; does it make sense?

Judy: I think so, if I understand the two loops.

Joe: Right, so there is a `while` loop and a `for` loop that runs within it.

Judy: Okay, so stepping through this—the outer `while` statement loops until the `swapped` variable has the value `False`.

Joe: Yes, we go one time through the `while` loop for each pass we need to make over the list.

Judy: But in all our examples wasn't that always three times?

Joe: Oh, that was a total coincidence; the algorithm can have any number of passes. Actually, that isn't quite accurate—in the worst case, it has the same number of passes as there are items in the list.

Judy: So if I have 100 items, the `while` loop could loop 100 times?

Joe: Yup.

Judy: Why so many?

Joe: That's the worst case; if the list is in totally backward order, it takes that many passes.

Judy: Got it. Okay, now the inner loop, the `for` loop. What's happening there?

Joe: The `for` loop walks through every item and compares it to the next item. If the first item is of greater value, then we swap the two.

Judy: So the `for` loop is also iterating through all items in the list as well, only not in the worst case, but always.

Joe: Technically the number of items minus one, but yes.

Judy: For a big list that is a lot of iterating.

Joe: It sure is. If you use your example of 100 items, the worst case is roughly 100 passes comparing 100 items in each pass. So we're talking 100 * 100 = 10,000 comparisons.

Judy: Whoa!

Joe: Yes, bubble sort is known more for its simplicity than its efficiency. Why do you think so many people spend their time trying to create fast sorting algorithms? But our lists are very small, so it's really not a problem in our case, and a perfectly acceptable way for us to sort.

Judy: Okay, and the only other thing happening in the `for` loop is that if we swapped some values, we have to set the `swapped` variable back to `True`, which means we'll do another pass.

Joe: Bingo.

BE the Interpreter

For these bits of code, your job is to play like you're the Python interpreter. Step through each bit of code and evaluate it (in your brain). After you've done the exercises, look at the end of the chapter to see if you got it right.

```python
for i in range(0,4):
    for j in range(0,4):
        print(i * j)
```

```python
for word in ['ox', 'cat', 'lion', 'tiger', 'bobcat']:
    for i in range(2, 7):
        letters = len(word)
        if (letters % i) == 0:
            print(i, word)
```

Remember modulus is like finding the remainder of a division. So, 4%2 would be 0, while 4%3 would be 1.

```python
full = False

donations = []
full_load = 45

toys = ['robot', 'doll', 'ball', 'slinky']

while not full:
    for toy in toys:
        donations.append(toy)
        size = len(donations)
        if (size >= full_load):
            full = True

print('Full with', len(donations), 'toys')
print(donations)
```

Implementing bubble sort in Python

Our pseudocode is fairly close to code, and translating it into Python is straightforward. Let's take a look:

Here's our function, which takes a Python list.

```python
def bubble_sort(scores):
    swapped = True

    while swapped:
        swapped = False
        for i in range(0, len(scores)-1):
            if scores[i] > scores[i+1]:
                temp = scores[i]
                scores[i] = scores[i+1]
                scores[i+1] = temp
                swapped = True
```

We set the swapped variable to True to kick off the first pass.

We make our passes with the while loop as long as swapped is True...

...and then step through the entire list comparing and swapping values where needed.

Our nested loop: a for loop within a while loop

Just like the variable swap code we looked at in Chapter 2!

Note there is nothing to return because we've swapped the actual values of the list. In other words, we've changed the original list to be in sorted order.

A Test Drive

Let's start a new file called *sort.py*. Copy the code above into it, and add the test code below:

```python
scores = [60, 50, 60, 58, 54, 54,
          58, 50, 52, 54, 48, 69,
          34, 55, 51, 52, 44, 51,
          69, 64, 66, 55, 52, 61,
          46, 31, 57, 52, 44, 18,
          41, 53, 55, 61, 51, 44]

bubble_sort(scores)
print(scores)

smoothies = ['coconut', 'strawberry', 'banana', 'pineapple']
bubble_sort(smoothies)
print(smoothies)
```

Python's > comparison works with strings too, so we can also have the sort function sort our smoothies.

```
Python 3.6.0 Shell

[18, 31, 34, 41, 44, 44, 44, 46, 48, 50,
50, 51, 51, 51, 52, 52, 52, 52, 53, 54,
54, 54, 55, 55, 55, 57, 58, 58, 60, 60,
61, 61, 64, 66, 69, 69]
['banana', 'coconut', 'pineapple',
'strawberry']
>>>
```

Nice, those look sorted!

A Test Drive

We'd like to have the solutions with the highest bubble scores first (in other words we want descending order, not ascending). We can do that by simply changing the comparison in the `sort` function from a > to a < comparison. Make the change and do another test drive.

```
def bubble_sort(scores):
    swapped = True

    while swapped:
        swapped = False
        for i in range(0, len(scores)-1):
            if scores[i] < scores[i+1]:
                temp = scores[i]
                scores[i] = scores[i+1]
                scores[i+1] = temp
                swapped = True
```

This is all you need to change to have a descending sort. Why does this work?

There we go; sort in descending bubble score order.

```
Python 3.6.0 Shell

[69, 69, 66, 64, 61, 61, 60, 60, 58, 58,
57, 55, 55, 55, 54, 54, 54, 53, 52, 52,
52, 52, 51, 51, 51, 50, 50, 48, 46, 44,
44, 44, 41, 34, 31, 18]
['strawberry', 'pineapple', 'coconut',
'banana']
>>>
```

> I think we're almost there; we just need to generate the report with the top 5 solutions, scores along with their number.

Frank: Yay, Joe wrote all the sort code! But something is missing. We're sorting the list of scores, but we have no idea what the original index of the score was, so how do we know the score number? We need that for the report.

Judy: That's a good point. How can we do that?

Frank: Well, Joe may be the rock star here, but I had an idea. What if we make another list, a parallel list called `solutions_numbers`, where each value in the list is the same as its index, like [0, 1, 2, 3, ..., 35]? Then, when we sort the scores, we sort this list exactly the same way. So, at the end, each score number will be in the same relative position as its corresponding score.

Judy: How do we create a list like that where the values match the indices?

Frank: Remember, you can use `range` and `list` together to do that. Like this:

```
number_of_scores = len(scores)
solution_numbers = list(range(number_of_scores))
```

Get the length of the list.

Create a range from 0 to the length of the list (minus 1) and then use the list function to convert the range into a list [0, 1, 2, ...].

Judy: Interesting. Okay, I *think* I sort of understand your direction.

Frank: Some things are actually easier to explain over code. Here, check this out...

Computing bubble solution numbers

Frank was right. We have a way to sort the bubble scores, but when we do sort them we lose the identifying number of that score (because we've always used the index of the solution as the bubble number). So what we're going to do is create a second list that contains each solution's corresponding bubble number, and then, when we sort the solution's scores, we're going to, in sync, sort the bubble numbers list the same exact way. Let's check out his code:

First, we're going to accept two lists in our bubble_sort function, the scores and the corresponding bubble numbers.

```python
def bubble_sort(scores, numbers):
    swapped = True

    while swapped:
        swapped = False
        for i in range(0, len(scores)-1):
            if scores[i] < scores[i+1]:
                temp = scores[i]
                scores[i] = scores[i+1]
                scores[i+1] = temp
                temp = numbers[i]
                numbers[i] = numbers[i+1]
                numbers[i+1] = temp
                swapped = True

scores = [60, 50, 60, 58, 54, 54,
          58, 50, 52, 54, 48, 69,
          34, 55, 51, 52, 44, 51,
          69, 64, 66, 55, 52, 61,
          46, 31, 57, 52, 44, 18,
          41, 53, 55, 61, 51, 44]

number_of_scores = len(scores)
solution_numbers = list(range(number_of_scores))

bubble_sort(scores, solution_numbers)
```

Everything else works exactly the same as before...

...except, when we swap two values of the score list, we swap the same two values in the numbers list.

If you think this looks like duplicated code, it is. We'll find out in the next chapter how to remove duplicate code.

Here we're just creating the solution_numbers list, which holds the number of each solution (and corresponds to its original index in the scores list).

Now when we call sort, we pass both lists.

Sharpen your pencil

Now our code produces two lists, one with the scores sorted and another with the corresponding solution numbers. Write the code to generate the report given these two lists.

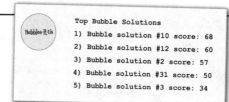

```
            Top Bubble Solutions
Bubbles-R-Us  1)  Bubble solution #10 score:  68
            2)  Bubble solution #12 score:  60
            3)  Bubble solution #2 score: 57
            4)  Bubble solution #31 score:  50
            5)  Bubble solution #3 score:  34
```

↑ Remember the report looks like this; also remember this is not the actual data your report will generate, just a mockup from the CEO.

A Test Drive

Take the code from the last Sharpen exercise (repeated below) and add to your *sort.py* file, replacing the previous test code. Give it a test drive.

```python
print('Top Bubble Solutions')
for i in range(0,5):
    print(str(i+1) + ')',
        'Bubble solution #' + str(solution_numbers[i]),
        'score:', scores[i])
```

```
Python 3.6.0 Shell

Top Bubble Solutions
1)  Bubble solution #11 score: 69
2)  Bubble solution #18 score: 69
3)  Bubble solution #20 score: 66
4)  Bubble solution #19 score: 64
5)  Bubble solution #23 score: 61
>>>
```

Exactly like the CEO requested. Boy, is he going to be happy! ⟿

Not only am I giving my top five bubble solution engineers awards, I'm giving YOU an award. We could not have made Bubbles-R-Us successful without all the business intelligence your code provided!

Top Bubble
Software Maker

Nice job.

It's been a short but challenging chapter. You've had to wrap your head around lots of new concepts. Give your brain some time to let it all sink in. Of course make some more of that bubble solution #11; that's a great way to relax and do something completely different. Get some rest too, and after that, maybe even quickly review this chapter before you move on.

Of course you aren't quite done yet. You've got a brain twister ahead, and the bullet points and the crossword...

BULLET POINTS

- There are many sorting algorithms with various tradeoffs in complexity and space/time considerations.

- Bubble sort is a simple algorithm that makes passes through a list, comparing and swapping values as it goes.

- Bubble sort is complete when a pass through the list finds no items that are out of order.

- Most languages and libraries provide sort functionality.

- When we have a loop within a loop, we call it a nested loop.

- Nested loops often increase the runtime and complexity of an algorithm.

- It's worth studying sorting algorithms and the sort algorithms provided by your language's libraries, which, speaking of...

> Uh, you're not going to believe this. I just went to tell Greg we had solved the problem and he'd beat us to it. In fact he hardly had to write any code; he did it using Python's built-in sort!

You'll find sort provided by most languages.

Yes, you'll find many modern languages and many libraries provide sort functionality. Given that, there's ususally no reason to write your own sort—not only would you be reinventing the wheel, but off-the-shelf sort algorithms tend to be more sophisticated (and more efficient) than bubble sort and take significant time and effort to implement. So, unless your passion turns out to be sorting algorithms, wouldn't you rather be working on your probem at hand?

Our time on the last 10 pages is not wasted, though, because the techniques you just learned in implementing bubble sort, like using nested loops, are core to implementing many algorithms. And, should you need to study sorting or a related algorithm, bubble sort is where most folks start.

Back to Python, you can sort a list by simply calling sort:

```python
scores.sort()
```

And there are lots of ways to customize Python's sort to your needs, but you'll want to learn a few more programming concepts to make full use of that.

Finally, if you're interested in sorting, you'll want to study up on the many sorting algorithms and their advantages and disadvantages. With every algorithm you'll encounter, there are tradeoffs in time (how long it takes) and space (the amount of memory or resources it uses). Some rather well-known sorts are insertion sort, merge sort, and quicksort, just to name a few. Oh, and Python interally uses Timsort, a hybrid of merge and insertion sort. Here's a good place to start your studies: *https://en.wikipedia.org/wiki/Sorting_algorithm.*

> Built-in sort! Maybe you could have let us know 10 pages back?

Try a deep thinking exercise before you finish off Chapter 4, part 2...

The Thing-A-Ma-Jig²

The Thing-A-Ma-Jig is a crazy contraption—it clanks and clunks and even thunks,
Whether you give it lists or strings, it still does things. But how exactly does it
work? Can you uncrack the code and find its quirks?

```
characters = 'taco'

output = ''
length = len(characters)
i = 0
while (i < length):
    output = output + characters[i]
    i = i + 1

length = length * -1
i = -2

while (i >= length):
    output = output + characters[i]
    i = i - 1

print(output)
```

All we changed was the list—now it's a string. But the code still works. How?

Try these as a replacement for characters' value above:
    characters = 'amanaplanac'
or
    characters = 'wasitar'

How does this code work on lists AND strings?
We'll leave you with that deep question, and we'll
uncover some answers in Chapter 6 (and beyond).

Sharpen your pencil
Solution

Hopefully you now have a good feel for how to apply bubble sort's algorithm. Let's practice. Take the list below and bubble sort it, showing your work just like we did on the previous two pages. This will help to lock in your understanding.

['coconut', 'strawberry', 'banana', 'pineapple']

Here's the list. Don't let the strings throw you; just compare them alphabetically (what a computer scientist would call lexicographically, otherwise known as dictionary order).

Pass 1

['coconut', 'strawberry', 'banana', 'pineapple']
       ↖ ↗ No change.

['coconut', 'strawberry', 'banana', 'pineapple']
            ↖ ↗ Swap.

['coconut', 'banana', 'strawberry', 'pineapple']
                ↖ ↗ Swap.

['coconut', 'banana', 'pineapple', 'strawberry']

Compare each index to the next, iterating through the list. Swap if the first value is > the second.

Pass 2

['coconut', 'banana', 'pineapple', 'strawberry']
    ↖ ↗ Swap.

We had swaps in pass 1, so we need to do a pass 2.

['banana', 'coconut', 'pineapple', 'strawberry']
           ↖ ↗ No change.

['banana', 'coconut', 'pineapple', 'strawberry']
                ↖ ↗ No change.

['banana', 'coconut', 'pineapple', 'strawberry']

We had swaps in pass 2, so we need to do a pass 3.

Pass 3

['banana', 'coconut', 'pineapple', 'strawberry']
    ↖ ↗ No change.

['banana', 'coconut', 'pineapple', 'strawberry']
           ↖ ↗ No change.

['banana', 'coconut', 'pineapple', 'strawberry']
                ↖ ↗ No change.

['banana', 'coconut', 'pineapple', 'strawberry']

We had no swaps in pass 3, so we're done and the list is sorted.

BE the Interpreter SOLUTION

For these bits of code, your job is to play like you're the Python interpreter. Step through each bit of code and evaluate it (in your brain). After you've done the exercises, look at the end of the chapter to see if you got it right.

```
for i in range(0,4):
    for j in range(0,4):
        print(i * j)
```

```
Python 3.6.0 Shell
0
0
0
0
0
1
2
3
0
2
4
6
0
3
6
9
>>>
```

```
for word in ['ox', 'cat', 'lion', 'tiger', 'bobcat']:
    for i in range(2, 7):
        letters = len(word)
        if (letters % i) == 0:
            print(i, word)
```

```
Python 3.6.0 Shell
2 ox
3 cat
2 lion
4 lion
5 tiger
2 bobcat
3 bobcat
6 bobcat
>>>
```

```
full = False

donations = []
full_load = 45

toys = ['robot', 'doll', 'ball', 'slinky']

while not full:
    for toy in toys:
        donations.append(toy)
        size = len(donations)
        if (size >= full_load):
            full = True

print('Full with', len(donations), 'toys')
print(donations)
```

```
Python 3.6.0 Shell
Full with 48 toys
['robot', 'doll', 'ball', 'slinky', 'robot', 'doll',
'ball', 'slinky', 'robot', 'doll', 'ball', 'slinky',
'robot', 'doll', 'ball', 'slinky', 'robot', 'doll',
'ball', 'slinky', 'robot', 'doll', 'ball', 'slinky',
'robot', 'doll', 'ball', 'slinky', 'robot', 'doll',
'ball', 'slinky', 'robot', 'doll', 'ball', 'slinky',
'robot', 'doll', 'ball', 'slinky', 'robot', 'doll', 'ball',
'slinky', 'robot', 'doll', 'ball', 'slinky']
>>>
```

Sharpen your pencil
Solution

Now our code produces two lists, one with the scores sorted and another with the corresponding solution numbers. Write the code to generate the report given these two lists.

```
Top Bubble Solutions
1)  Bubble solution #10 score: 68
2)  Bubble solution #12 score: 60
3)  Bubble solution #2 score: 57
4)  Bubble solution #31 score: 50
5)  Bubble solution #3 score: 34
```

Print the heading.

```python
print('Top Bubble Solutions')
for i in range(0,5):
    print(str(i+1) + ')',
          'Bubble solution #' + str(solution_numbers[i]),
          'score:', scores[i])
```

Iterate through five times for the top five scores.

For each line of output, print the final standing of the solution with the value i plus 1, the solution number from the solution_numbers list, and the score from the scores list.

6 text, strings, and heuristics

Putting It All Together

Not so fast. Sure, you know variables and data types and iteration and functions, but can you put it all together?

You've already got a lot of superpowers. Now it's time to use them. In this chapter we're going to integrate what we've learned so far, bringing it all together to build some **increasingy cool code**. We're also going to keep adding to your knowledge and coding skills. More specifically, in this chapter we'll explore how to write code that **grabs some text**, slices it, dices it, and then does a little **data analysis** on it. We're going to find out what a **heuristic** is too, and implement one. Get ready—this is an all-out, heads-down, pedal-to-the-metal, serious coding chapter!

And by the end of the chapter you'll realize how much you've learned about coding!

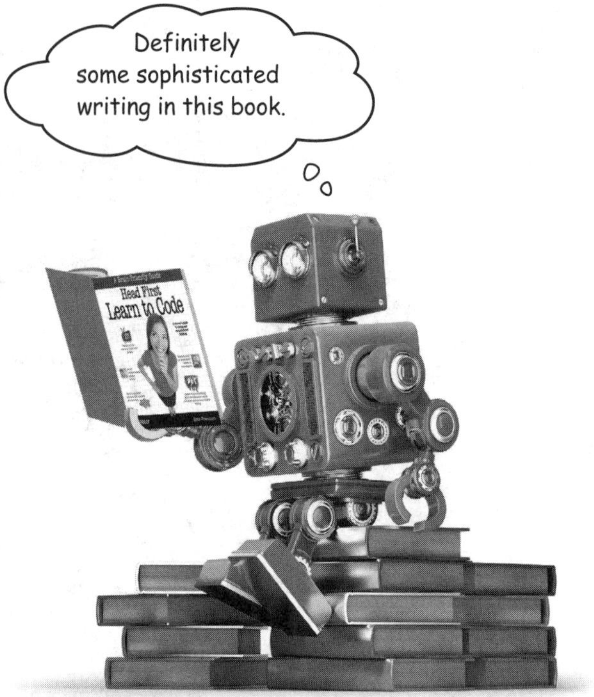

Definitely some sophisticated writing in this book.

Welcome to the data sciences

Heard of data science? It's all about extracting insight and knowledge from data, and we're about to get into the business. Our data? Any text: news articles, blog posts, books, anything written by an author. And what we're going to do with all that text is tell the world how *readable* it is. That is, could a 5th grader read it, or does it take a Ph.D.? With our app, we'll soon know.

Now to perform such an analysis, we're going to have to dig deep; we're going to examine, as you'll soon discover:

every sentence…

and every word…

and every syllable...

not to mention every single character of the text in question!

With all that analysis, we're going to come up with a score that maps to a reading level, from 5th grade all the way up to a college graduate. Let's dig in and see more precisely how this is going to work...

How do you compute something like readability?

Luckily someone else has already answered this question—namely, the US Navy and Army, who have been testing a key formula for years in the military to assess the readability of things like (we're assuming) tank training manuals. Here's how it works: take the text you want to analyze and run it through the following formula to get back a *reading ease score*. We'll talk in a second about what that score means. Here's the formula:

We're not kidding; you can read up on it here: https://en.wikipedia.org/wiki/ Flesch-Kincaid_readability_tests.

To give due credit, the formula was originally developed by Rudolph Flesch in 1948. Dr. Flesch was an author who earned a Ph.D. in English at Columbia University.

The formula makes use of three different numbers we're going to need to compute.

We start with the total number of words in the text, which is used in two places in the formula.

We also need to compute the total number of syllables in the text.

$$206.835 - 1.015 \left(\frac{\text{total words}}{\text{total sentences}} \right) - 84.6 \left(\frac{\text{total syllables}}{\text{total words}} \right)$$

We also need to compute the total number of sentences.

Once we've computed those values, the formula just consists of standard multiplication, division, and subtraction, with a few floating-point values like 84.6.

If you're wondering where numbers like 206.835 come from, all we can say is years of research (see the Wikipedia article above).

After we've used this formula to compute a score, we map the score to the reading ease of the text using this chart:

Say you were writing some text for advertising; how would you want it to score?

Score	School Level	Notes
100.00–90.00	5th grade	Very easy to read. Easily understood by an average 11-year-old student.
90.0–80.0	6th grade	Easy to read. Conversational English for consumers.
80.0–70.0	7th grade	Fairly easy to read.
70.0–60.0	8th & 9th grade	Plain English. Easily understood by 13- to 15-year-olds.
60.0–50.0	10th–12th grade	Fairly difficult to read.
50.0–30.0	College	Difficult to read.
30.0–0.0	College Graduate	Very difficult to read. Best understood by university graduates.

The higher the score, the easier your text is to read.

You'll find the original chart at the Wikipedia URL above.

The game plan

At first glance computing readability just comes down to computing a formula. But, if we look closer, it's the key values that we need for that formula where the computing comes in. That's because, to complete the formula, we need:

(1) To compute the total number of **words** in our text: that means we'll have to take our text and break it down into words and count them.

(2) To compute the total number of **sentences** in our text: that means we'll have to take our text and break it down into its individual sentences and count them.

(3) To compute the total number of **syllables** in our text: that means we'll have to take each word, figure out how many syllables it has, and then add up all the syllables in the entire text.

> One of the first rules for a guide in polite conversation, is to avoid political or religious discussions in general society. Such discussions lead almost invariably to irritating differences of opinion, often to open quarrels, and a coolness of feeling which might have been avoided by dropping the distasteful subject as soon as marked differences of opinion arose. It is but one out of many that can discuss either political or religious differences, with candor and judgment, and yet so far control his language and temper as to avoid either giving or taking offence.

> One of the first rules for a guide in polite conversation, is to avoid political or religious discussions in general society. Such discussions lead almost invariably to irritating differences of opinion, often to open quarrels, and a coolness of feeling which might have been avoided by dropping the distasteful subject as soon as marked differences of opinion arose. It is but one out of many that can discuss either political or religious differences, with candor and judgment, and yet so far control his language and temper as to avoid either giving or taking offence.

> to irritating differences of open quarrels, and a coolness by dropping the distasteful opinion arose. It is but one differences, with candor and

BRAIN POWER

Can you come up with an algorithm to compute the number of syllables in an arbitrary word? Assume you don't have a large dictionary at your disposal. Write your algorithm here in pseudocode.

This is a difficult task, but do your best and think through the problem. Come up with the best answer you can in five minutes or so.

Writing some pseudocode

We're going to write some pseudocode to drive our implementation. For now, we're going to keep the pseudocode high level, and we'll fill in a lot of the details as we progress. There isn't a lot of tricky logic in this code (like a game); rather, our task will be computing the numbers we need for the readability formula (which will nonetheless give us plenty to do). Follow along with our thinking as we write the pseudocode. As we've said, there are many forms of pseudocode; you'll find this one a little more formal and closer to code.

Let's start out right and put this code in a function.

This function expects to be passed the text of the book or article...we'll have to figure out how to do that.

We already know of quite a few important values we're going to need to compute for our formula. Let's go ahead and create local variables for those. We'll also create a variable, score, to hold the final score.

DEFINE a *function* compute_readability(text):

SETUP: here we're declaring all the local variables we'll be using throughout the function.

    DECLARE a *variable* total_words and set to 0.
    DECLARE a *variable* total_sentences and set to 0.
    DECLARE a *variable* total_syllables and set to 0.
    DECLARE a *variable* score and set to 0.

We need to compute those values next, so let's rely on a function to compute each one.

ANALYSIS: we compute all the values we need, and we'll be diving into each one of these separately.

    ASSIGN *variable* total_words to result of calling the function **count_words**(text)
    ASSIGN *variable* total_sentences to result of calling the function **count_sentences**(text)
    ASSIGN *variable* total_syllables to result of calling the function **count_syllables**(text)

FORMULA: we have all the values, so we can now use the formula to compute the score.

    ASSIGN *variable* score to
        $206.835 - 1.015 * (total\_words / total\_sentences) - 84.6 * (total\_syllables / total\_words)$

RESULTS: we've got a score and we're mapping that to a reading level by using the table two pages back.

With all the values computed, we can evaluate the reading ease score...

...and then figure out the reading level.

```
IF score >= 90.0:
        PRINT 'Reading level of 5th Grade'
ELIF scores >= 80.0:
        PRINT 'Reading level of 6th Grade'
ELIF scores >= 70.0:
        PRINT 'Reading level of 7th Grade'
ELIF scores >= 60.0:
        PRINT 'Reading level of 8-9th Grade'
ELIF scores >= 50.0:
        PRINT 'Reading level of 10-12th Grade'
ELIF scores >= 30.0:
        PRINT 'Reading level of College Student'
ELSE:
        PRINT 'Reading level of College Graduate'
```

This is a big if/elif/else statement that prints the appropriate reading level based on the computed score.

Computing readability seems like a generally useful piece of code, so let's put it in a function—we may be able to reuse it later!

We'll probably put this code in its own function.

We need some text to analyze

Before we get coding, we're going to need some interesting text to put through our analysis. Now the truth is, you can analyze any text you want: blog posts, your own writing, news articles, books, whatever—and half the fun of creating this code is analyzing your favorite news outlets and writers. That said, as we build and test this code, it'll help if you use the same text we use, so we're seeing the same results. So let's find some text we can all test together.

And why not put ourselves to the test? We're going to use the first couple pages of this book, which you'll find in the file *ch6/text.txt*.

For testing purposes we'll put ourselves to the test by using the text from Chapter 1 of this book.

Remember, instructions for the book downloads are also in the introduction section of this book, but this is Chapter 6, so of course you've already downloaded the files.

How to get multiline text into Python

If you look at the file *ch6/text.txt*, you'll see we have a big text file, but how do we get that into Python? Well, you already know how to add text to your code with strings:

```
text = 'The first thing that stands between you'
```

And we're going to do the same with the text in *ch6/text.txt*. To do that, we're going to use a Python convention for entering strings that span multiple lines by using triple quotes, like this:

Don't enter anything into IDLE yet. We'll enter it on the next page.

Start your string with three quote characters, either single (') or double (") will do.

Then enter your entire string, including new lines.

```
text = """The first thing that stands between you and writing your first, real,
piece of code, is learning the skill of breaking problems down into
achievable little actions that a computer can do for you."""
```

Obviously make sure your text within the string doesn't have any triple quotes, as unlikely as that is.

And then end your string with triple quotes as well.

After you've done this, use the string as you would any other; it's just a normal string with a bit more text in it. Now let's get the text from the first couple of pages of Chapter 1 into a string.

Exercise

> Remember, a Python file is also known as a module.

Take the text in the *ch6/text.txt* file and get it into a Python file. To do that, in IDLE, create a new file and add the code below. For the Chapter 1 text, you'll want to open the *text.txt* file in IDLE as well, and then copy and paste the text into your new file. When you're done, save your file as *ch1text.py*.

Finally, run your code, and you should see the entire article printed to the shell.

> Start with the string's variable name and follow it with an equals sign, and then with triple quotes. Next, paste in the text from the text.txt file.

```
text = """The first thing that stands between you and writing your first, real,
piece of code, is learning the skill of breaking problems down into
achievable little actions that a computer can do for you. Of course,
you and the computer will also need to be speaking a common language,
but we'll get to that topic in just a bit.

Now breaking problems down into a number of steps may sound a new
skill, but its actually something you do every day. Let's look at an
example, a simple one: say you wanted to break the activity of fishing
down into a simple set of instructions that you could hand to a robot,
who would do your fishing for you. Here's our first attempt to do that,
check it out:
```

.
.
.

> ← We're saving a few trees and omitting some of the text here in the book.

```
You're going to find these simple statements or instructions are the
first key to coding, in fact every App or software program you've ever
used has been nothing more than a (sometimes large) set of simple
instructions to the computer that tell it what to do."""
```

> Don't forget the final triple quotes.

```
print(text)
```

> Let's print the text just to make sure everything is working.

Setting up the function

To get started let's go ahead and set up the `compute_readability` function. Let's then translate the setup portion of the pseudocode into Python:

```python
def compute_readability(text):
    total_words = 0
    total_sentences = 0
    total_syllables = 0
    score = 0
```

Just like in our pseudocode, we have a function that takes text as a parameter.

We also set up four local variables that are going to hold important values in this function.

Go ahead and enter this code in a file called *analyze.py*.

Now let's call `compute_readability` and pass it that text in *ch1text.py*. But how? After all, it's in *another file*. Well, remember any file with a *.py* extension is a Python module, and also remember that in the past we've imported Python modules into our code using the `import` statement. So let's import the *ch1text.py* file into our *analyze.py* file. Once we've done that, we can access the variables and functions within the module by prepending their names with the module name. Take a look:

Remember, a Python module is just a file with a .py extension and Python code inside.

We'll go into a lot more detail on how modules work in the next chapter.

We use import to include the ch1text.py file.

```python
import ch1text
```

```python
def compute_readability(text):
    total_words = 0
    total_sentences = 0
    total_syllables = 0
    score = 0
```

We call compute_readability and pass it the text string from the ch1text file.

And just as a bit of review, note we've defined a function called compute_readability that has a parameter, text, and sets up some local variables

```python
compute_readability(ch1text.text)
```

To access the variable named text in the ch1text file, we prepend it with the module name, ch1text.

And we're calling that function and passing it the text variable from the ch1txt module (in other words, the ch1text.py file).

A Test Drive

Let's give this a quick test to make sure everything is working. To do that, move the `print` statement from your *ch1text.py* file to your analyze file. You'll want to place it in the `compute_readablility` function. The output should be exactly the same as the test run of the *ch1text.py* file.

```
import ch1text

def compute_readability(text):
    total_words = 0
    total_sentences = 0
    total_syllables = 0
    score = 0

    print(text)

compute_readability(ch1text.text)
```

Add this to your compute_readability function.

Python 3.6.0 Shell

```
into pond", or "pull in the fish." But also notice that other
instructions are a bit different because they depend on a condition,
like "is the bobber above or below water?". Instructions might also
direct the flow of the recipe, like "if you haven't finished fishing,
then cycle back to the beginning and put another worm on the hook."
Or, how about a condition for stopping, as in "if you're done" then go
home.

You're going to find these simple statements or instructions are the
first key to coding, in fact every App or software program you've ever
used has been nothing more than a (sometimes large) set of simple
instructions to the computer that tell it what to do.
>>>
```

You should again see the Chapter I text printed in the shell.

DON'T FORGET to remove the print statement from your ch1text.py file.

First up: we need the total number of words in our text

Referring to our pseudocode, the first number we need to compute for our readability formula is the total number of words in our text, and to compute that you need to extend your coding knowledge a little bit. You already know how to *combine* strings with concatenation, but what you don't know how to do is *break them apart*. Strings provide a handy function called `split` that will split a string into words (which we usually call *substrings*) and then place those substrings into a list.

Here's how to use `split`:

1 Take any string with some text and whitespace.

```
lyrics = 'I heard you on the wireless back in fifty two'
words = lyrics.split()
print(words)
```

4 Let's print the list to see what split did.

2 And then call the string's split function.

3 Using whitespace (spaces, tabs, newlines) as a separator, split breaks the string up into a number of substrings, and places each one in the list.

It looks like split does a good job of separating our text into its individual words.

Python 3.6.0 Shell

```
['I', 'heard', 'you', 'on',
'the', 'wireless', 'back',
'in', 'fifty', 'two']
>>>
```

The list holds all the words (or substrings), each from the original string.

Cubicle conversation

Well, it looks like we're going to use the split function to help figure out the number of words?

Frank: I'm already lost. We want to count the number of words, but we're going to split up our text into a list first?

Joe: It's a two-step process, Frank. We're going to essentially extract all the words into a list. After that we'll count how many words are in the list.

Frank: I understand the counting part, but how is the split function giving us back words?

Judy: Frank, that's what split does—it breaks a string up into words, using whitespace as a separator.

Frank: Oh, so anytime it sees a space or tab or return, it uses that to figure out how to break out the words.

Judy: Exactly.

Joe: And once we've split our string up into words and put them in a list, we can easily count them.

Frank: Oh right, we can just use the len function for that, correct?

Joe: That's what I'm thinking.

Judy: Okay, guys, I think we have a plan: we'll use the split function to break the Chapter 1 text into words, which we'll get back in a list, and then we'll call the built-in len function to count how many words there are.

Frank: I like it!

there are no Dumb Questions

Q: So split takes a string and breaks it up into words?

A: Close. Split takes a string and breaks it up into a number of substrings. The way it knows how to break the string up is by treating whitespace as a separator, or as a computer scientist would say, a *delimiter*. In other words, if it sees a delimiter, like a space, a tab, or a newline in your string, it knows that is a place it can split the string. Note the resulting substrings don't have to technically be words; they could be dates, tabular formatted data, numbers, and so on.

Q: What if my string has, say, commas rather than whitespace separating the items?

A: split allows you to specify a set of characters you want to use to delimit your substrings. So you could set the comma character as your delimiter. That said, split is not flexible enough to combine, say, whitespace and commas. You'll find all the details in the documentation for the split function. A bit later we'll be looking at how to make use of Python's documentation. You can also find a more sophisticated way to match words in text using what are known as regular expressions, which are discussed in the Appendix.

Q: Help me with the syntax again: how does lyrics.split() work exactly?

A: For now just know that you can attach functions to data types, and the string data type has a function called split. When you see lyrics.split(), that's saying use the function split that is associated with strings. We're going to be taking a close look at exactly how this works later in the book.

Sharpen your pencil

Now that you know how to use the `split` function, let's return to the `compute_readability` function and take it a little further. In our pseudocode we were going to write a function `count_words`, but as it turns out, with `split` we can handle the job of computing the total number of words with only two lines of code, so let's forgo the function. Go ahead and complete that code below, and then check with our version in the solution at the end of the chapter. After that, give it a test run.

```
import ch1text

def compute_readability(text):
    total_words = 0
    total_sentences = 0
    total_syllables = 0
    score = 0

    words = text.split()
    total_words = _____

    print(words)
    print(total_words, 'words')
    print(text)

compute_readability(ch1text.text)
```

Let's take our text and split it into words.

Hint: Frank, Joe, and Judy already figured out how to do this.

Computing the total number of words is one line of code. Finish this one up.

Let's print all the words, and then the total count. And let's also remove the old print statement.

I noticed in the shell output that we're not doing a perfect job of extracting words. I have words like 'book!,' and 'fire_.' and 'is_,'.

Right. The split function, by default, splits up text only using whitespace as a separator. And, while you can also pass split a custom separator as a second parameter, unfortunately split isn't implemented in a way where you can easily tell it to use "whitepace and commas and periods and semicolons and exclamation points and question marks." The result: we have punctuation at the end of some of our words in the words list.

That's okay, though, as it doesn't really affect our count of words. That said, it may cause some issues later in our coding, but nothing we can't handle. You'll see in a bit...

```
Python 3.6.0 Shell

['The', 'first', 'thing', 'that', 'stands', 'between', 'you', 'and', 'writing', 'your',
'first,', 'real,', 'piece', 'of', 'code,', 'is', 'learning', 'the', 'skill', 'of', 'breaking',
'problems', 'down', 'into', 'achievable', 'little', 'actions', 'that', 'a', 'computer',
'can', 'do', 'for', 'you.', 'Of', 'course,', 'you', 'and', 'the', 'computer', 'will', 'also',
'need', 'to', 'be', 'speaking', 'a', 'common', 'language,', 'but', 'we'll', 'get', 'to',
'that', 'topic', 'in', 'just', 'a', 'bit.', 'Now', 'breaking', 'problems', 'down', 'into',
'a', 'number', 'of', 'steps', 'may', 'sound', 'a', 'new', 'skill,', 'but', 'its', 'actually',
'something', 'you', 'do', 'every', 'day.', 'Let's', 'look', 'at', 'an', 'example,', 'a',
'simple', 'one:', 'say', 'you', 'wanted', 'to', 'break', 'the', 'activity', 'of', 'fishing',
'down', 'into', 'a', 'simple', 'set', 'of', 'instructions', 'that', 'you', 'could', 'hand',
'to', 'a', 'robot,', 'who', 'would', 'do', 'your', 'fishing', 'for', 'you.', 'Here's', 'our',
'first', 'attempt', 'to', 'do', 'that,', 'check', 'it', 'out:', 'You', 'can', 'think',
'of', 'these', 'statements', 'as', 'a', 'nice', 'recipe', 'for', 'fishing.', 'Like', 'any',
'recipe,', 'this', 'one', 'provides', 'a', 'set', 'of', 'steps,', 'that', 'when', 'followed',
'in', 'order,', 'will', 'produce', 'some', 'result', 'or', 'outcome', 'in', 'our', 'case,',
'hopefully,', 'catching', 'some', 'fish.', 'Notice', 'that', 'most', 'steps', 'consists',
'of', 'simple', 'instruction,', 'like', 'cast', 'line', 'into', 'pond"', 'or', '"pull',
'in', 'the', 'fish."', 'But', 'also', 'notice', 'that', 'other', 'instructions', 'are',
'a', 'bit', 'different', 'because', 'they', 'depend', 'on', 'a', 'condition,', 'like',
'"is', 'the', 'bobber', 'above', 'or', 'below', 'water?".', 'Instructions', 'might', 'also',
'direct', 'the', 'flow', 'of', 'the', 'recipe,', 'like', '"if', 'you', 'haven't', 'finished',
'fishing,', 'then', 'cycle', 'back', 'to', 'the', 'beginning', 'and', 'put', 'another',
'worm', 'on', 'the', 'hook."', 'Or,', 'how', 'about', 'a', 'condition', 'for', 'stopping,',
'as', 'in', '"if', 'you're', 'done",', 'then', 'go', 'home.', 'You're', 'going', 'to', 'find',
'these', 'simple', 'statements', 'or', 'instructions', 'are', 'the', 'first', 'key', 'to',
'coding,', 'in', 'fact', 'every', 'App', 'or', 'software', 'program', 'you've', 'ever',
'used', 'has', 'been', 'nothing', 'more', 'than', 'a', '(sometimes', 'large)', 'set', 'of',
'simple', 'instructions', 'to', 'the', 'computer', 'that', 'tell', 'it', 'what', 'to', 'do.']
300 words
>>>
```

Do you see what he's talking about? The way this was split up, some words have periods, commas, and double quotes at the end of them. We could potentially have exclamation points, colons, question marks, and semicolons as well.

If you wanted to go through all the words to remove any extraneous characters like periods and commas, how might you write the code to do that?

Even if you don't have any idea how to write the code, think about what the process might be like.

Computing the total number of sentences

The next step in our pseudocode is computing the number of sentences in the text. It would be great if there was a built-in function for counting sentences, but there isn't, so it's going to be up to us to figure out how to do this.

Here's a suggestion: if we count the number of periods, semicolons, question marks, and exclamation points in the text, that should provide a good approximation of the number of sentences. Now it might not be perfect if, say, an author uses punctuation in a non-standard way, but it should provide a close approximation of the number of sentences. And often when working with messy data like text, we can't be perfect, at least not without considerable effort—more on this topic in a bit.

So how do we figure out the number of *terminal characters* (that is ".", ";", "?", or "!") in the text? Well, why don't we just iterate through every character in the text and keep a running count of the terminal characters we encounter? Sounds like a plan. But we don't know how to iterate through the characters of a string, *or do we?*

Remember we said that you can use the `for` statement on sequences? Well, as it turns out, a string is just a sequence of characters. So, you can use the `for` statement to iterate through all the characters in a string. Here's an example:

Take any Python string...

```
lyrics = 'I heard you on the wireless back in fifty two'

for char in lyrics:
    print(char)
```

...and iterate over each character in the string.

Each time through the loop, the next character in the string will be assigned to the variable char.

Let's print the character so we can see how this works.

```
Python 3.6.0 Shell
I
h
e
a
r
d
y
o
u
o
n
t
h
e
w
i
r
e
l
e
s
s
b
a
c
k
i
n
f
i
f
t
y
t
w
o
>>>
```

Writing the count_sentences function

Now that we know how to iterate through a string, let's get a skeleton of the count_sentences function down before we write the code to count the terminal characters:

Just like in the pseudocode, we're expecting text to be passed to us.

```
def count_sentences(text):
    count = 0

    for char in text:



    return count
```

Here's our count local variable.

Here we're iterating over each character in the text.

And we need to figure out the code for this part. Is the character a terminal character? If so, we increase the count.

Finally, we return the count as the result of the function.

Sharpen your pencil

Can you write the code to test each character to see if it is a period, semicolon, question mark, or exclamation point, and then, if it is, increase the value of the count variable by one?

```
def count_sentences(text):
    count = 0

    for char in text:




    return count
```

Your code goes here.

A Test Drive

We're overdue for a test drive. Let's get all this code together, get it in our *analyze.py* file, and give it a run.

> Just a reminder that we need to define functions before we call them. Given that, think through where you could define count_sentences (and where you couldn't).

```python
import ch1text

def count_sentences(text):
    count = 0

    for char in text:
        if char == '.' or char == ';' or char == '?' or char == '!':
            count = count + 1

    return count

def compute_readability(text):
    total_words = 0
    total_sentences = 0
    total_syllables = 0
    score = 0

    words = text.split()
    total_words = len(words)
    total_sentences = count_sentences(text)

    print(words)
    print(total_words, 'words')
    print(total_sentences, 'sentences')

compute_readability(ch1text.text)
```

> Here's our new function for counting sentences.

> Make sure you've changed this since the last Test Drive.

> Let's make sure we call our new function, passing it the text.

> We'll add some output to show us the number of sentences.

> Make sure you've changed this since the last Test Drive.

> Here's the output we got on the Chapter 1 text.

```
Python 3.6.0 Shell

300 words

12 sentences

>>>
```

It's true.

While the way we wrote our test for terminal characters is perfectly acceptable, there's a more concise way to compare each character to the set of terrminal characters, and it relies on a Boolean operator we haven't seen yet: the in operator. Using the in operator, you can test to see if a value is contained in a sequence. For instance, if you remember the smoothies from Chapter 4, we could test to see if a specific smoothie is in our list. Like this:

Here's our sequence, a list.

```
smoothies = ['coconut', 'strawberry', 'banana', 'pineapple', 'acai berry']
if 'coconut' in smoothies:
    print('Yes, they have coconut!')
else:
    print('Oh well, no coconut today.')
```

And here we're testing if 'coconut' is in the list of smoothies.

And here's what we get.

```
Python 3.6.0 Shell
Yes, they have coconut!
>>>
```

But as we just saw, a string is a sequence as well, and given Python tries to keep things consistent, we can use the `in` operator with a string. Like this:

Do you remember the Thing-A-Ma-Jig mystery at the end of Chapter 4? That used a for loop to iterate over a string too.

Here's our sequence, a string.

```
lyrics = 'I heard you on the wireless back in fifty two'
```

```
if 'wireless' in lyrics:
    print('Yes, they have wireless!')
else:
    print('Oh well, no wireless today.')
```

And here we're testing if 'wireless' is in the lyrics string.

```
Python 3.6.0 Shell

Yes, they have wireless!
>>>
```

Sharpen your pencil

Let's see if we can make the `count_sentences` function more concise (and readable) by using the `in` operator. Below we've removed the existing code that checks for terminal characters. We've also added a new local variable, `terminals`, that holds a string containing all the terminal characters. Complete the `if` statement, using the `in` operator, so that it determines if the current character is a terminal.

```
def count_sentences(text):
    count = 0

    terminals = '.;?!'

    for char in text:

        if _____

            count = count + 1

    return count
```

Add the code using the in operator here.

A Test Drive

Update your code before we implement the next part of the pseudocode. The only change you need to make is to the `count_sentences` function, shown below. Get the change in and give it a test drive; your output should be the same as the last test drive.

```
def count_sentences(text):
    count = 0

    terminals = '.;?!'
    for char in text:
        if char in terminals:
        if char == '.' or char == ';' or char == '?' or char == '!':
            count = count + 1

    return count
```

Add these two lines of code.

And get rid of the old comparison.

You should still see this as output.

```
Python 3.6.0 Shell
300 words
12 sentences
>>>
```

Given that you say a string is a sequence of characters, does that mean characters are another data type?

In many languages, yes.

But not in Python. It's a good question because many languages do treat characters as their own data type. Python, however, treats everything as a string. So, the character 'A' in Python is just a string of length one that happens to hold an A.

Given a string is a sequence, can I use the index syntax on a string? Like my_string[1] to get the first character?

You sure can.

Only remember `my_string[1]` would get you the second character of a string because indices start at `0`. You can also use `my_string[-1]` to get the last character in the string. As you'll soon see, you can even use a similar syntax to access *substrings* of a string, but more on that in a bit.

Nice! And I assume I can change the string too, like with a mystring[1] = 'e' statement?

Not so fast.

You can't actually alter a string. One difference between lists and strings as sequences is that lists are *mutable*, and strings are *immutable*. That is, you can change the items in a list, but you can't change the characters in a string—as it turns out, this is the case with almost every modern programming language. You're probably wondering why. Well, as you'll see as you gain more experience, being able to alter strings can lead to unreliable code; it can also makes implementing efficient interpreters quite difficult. That said, you can effectively "change" a string any time just by creating a new, altered string, and that is the common practice across almost every modern programming language.

Computing the number of syllables, or, learning to love heuristics

Are you ready to implement your algorithm for finding syllables? Remember, the one you tried to write back at the beginning of the chapter in the **BRAIN POWER** exercise? We should probably apologize, as that exercise is a bit tricky—you see, it isn't easy to write an algorithm for finding syllables; in fact, we can't claim *there is* a definitive algorithm, short of using a large database of words.

Finding syllables is a messy business because the English language is messy. For instance, why does "walked" have one syllable while "loaded" is two? English is full of such inconsistencies.

For problems like this we don't write algorithms, we write *heuristics*. A heuristic is a lot like an algorithm, only it's not a 100% solution. It might, for instance, solve a problem with a good answer, but not necessarily a perfect answer.

So what good is a heuristic? Why not just write an algorithm with a perfect answer? For many reasons—in our case it is because there may be no method of finding syllables that is perfect given the inconsistencies of the English language (again, outside of using a very large database of words). In other cases, it may be that providing a 100% solution requires so much computing time (or memory) that it makes an algorithm impractical, while providing only a good answer requires much less time (or memory). Or, it may be because not all aspects of the problem are known to the implementors, and so the best they can do is to provide a partial solution.

Back to our problem, though...because computing syllables is messy, our goal will be to do enough work to get a decent estimate of syllables in our text. It won't be perfect, but it will be close, and if you're interested, there are plenty of ways you can improve our heuristic further on your own (and we'll give you some ideas for that).

**POWER**

Here's your second chance: can you come up with some ideas for how to count the syllables of an arbitrary word? Study the words in our text as a test case. See if you can develop some general rules for determining how many syllables a word has. Make your notes here. We'll get you started...

If a word has three characters or fewer it typically has only one syllable. We came up with this: can you come up with some more possible rules?

I don't get why this is so hard...why don't you just use a dictionary? It has all the syllables spelled out for any word.

You have a point, but... loading an entire English dictionary so that words can be quickly retrieved is actually a pretty big undertaking. It requires not only a lot of data and storage, but also additional technologies like a database or a search engine in order to have quick enough response time to make the program usable. It probably would require you to license the dictionary data as well at some non-trivial cost.

Compare that to implementing a few simple rules, which may get us up to 80–90% or greater accuracy, and the heuristic starts to look pretty attractive as a technology direction.

At least for the purposes of this book!

Cubicle conversation continued...

Alright, syllables look a little more challenging than counting words.

Joe: That's what I thought too. I did notice that if a word has fewer than three characters, you might as well go ahead and call it one syllable.

Judy: I'm sure there's an exception to that rule, but sounds good. I also noticed that if you just look at the number of vowels in a word, it's a pretty good indicator of the number of syllables it has.

Joe: So, take "chocolate"...

Judy: I don't mind if I do!

Joe: ...take the WORD "chocolate"—it has three vowels and three syllables.

Judy: Well, I think you skipped the silent *e*? I see a few other caveats too.

Joe: Like what?

Judy: Well, take the word "looker." It has consecutive vowels, like *oo*, and we just need to count the first vowel we see in those cases.

Joe: Oh, so we count the first *o* and then the *e*, giving us two syllables.

Joe: ...and, like you said, a lot of words have a silent *e* at the end as well. Like "home."

Judy: Right, so we count the *o* in "home" but not the final *e*. So one syllable.

Judy: And related to that, a *y* at the end of a word often adds a syllable, like "proxy," so we need to consider that perhaps as a vowel as well?

Joe: Or at least that it adds a syllable to our count.

Judy: Sure. The other cases I came up with are really just special cases, like "walked" is only one syllable, but "loaded" is two.

Joe: Right, we could build a word list of special cases and then scan all our words for them.

Judy: We could, but we only have so much time, so let's go with the general rules we have and then come back to the special cases if we need to.

Joe: Sounds like a plan.

Setting up the heuristic

It looks like we've got some good ideas for developing our syllable counting heuristic. Of course, we're sure you came up with even more. Let's summarize the ideas before we start implementing them:

- ☐ If a word has fewer than three characters, then count it as one syllable.
- ☐ Otherwise, count the number of vowels and let that represent the number of syllables.
- ☐ To make the previous step more accurate, remove any consecutive vowels in a word.
- ☐ Remove the final *e* from words, in order to account for silent *e*'s.
- ☐ Treat the character *y* as a vowel if it's the last character.

Let's also set up the `count_syllables` function so that we are all ready to code these. Here's how we're going to do that:

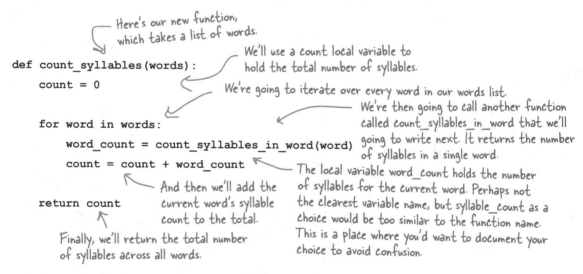

Here's our new function, which takes a list of words.

We'll use a count local variable to hold the total number of syllables.

We're going to iterate over every word in our words list.

We're then going to call another function called count_syllables_in_word that we'll going to write next. It returns the number of syllables in a single word.

The local variable word_count holds the number of syllables for the current word. Perhaps not the clearest variable name, but syllable_count as a choice would be too similar to the function name. This is a place where you'd want to document your choice to avoid confusion.

And then we'll add the current word's syllable count to the total.

Finally, we'll return the total number of syllables across all words.

```python
def count_syllables(words):
    count = 0

    for word in words:
        word_count = count_syllables_in_word(word)
        count = count + word_count

    return count
```

While we're at it, let's set up the `count_syllables_in_word` function too:

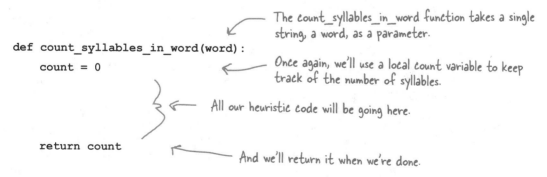

The count_syllables_in_word function takes a single string, a word, as a parameter.

Once again, we'll use a local count variable to keep track of the number of syllables.

All our heuristic code will be going here.

And we'll return it when we're done.

```python
def count_syllables_in_word(word):
    count = 0



    return count
```

A Test Drive

Go ahead and add the new code in your *analyze.py* file. At this point, just make sure you don't have any syntax errors. You'll get the same output as the previous run.

> *You can add this code at the top of your file, right below the import statement.*

```python
def count_syllables(words):
    count = 0

    for word in words:
        word_count = count_syllables_in_word(word)
        count = count + word_count

    return count

def count_syllables_in_word(word):
    count = 0

    return count
```

Writing the heuristic

We're here. →

The first thing on our heurstic punch list is that we need to treat any word with fewer than three characters as having one syllable. But how do we get the length of a string? It turns out, you already know the way: with the `len` function. Previously we've used `len` on a list to get its length, but it can be applied to any sequence in Python, and a string is a sequence of characters.

☐	If a word has fewer than three characters, then count it as one syllable.
☐	Otherwise, count the number of vowels and let that represent the number of syllables.
☐	To make the previous step more accurate, remove any consecutive vowels in a word.
☐	Remove the final *e* from words, in order to account for silent *e*'s.
☐	Treat the character *y* as a vowel if it's the last character.

Let's try it:

> *A common theme in this chapter*

```python
def count_syllables_in_word(word):
    count = 0

    if len(word) <= 3:
        return 1
    return count
```

> *We use the len function to get the length of the word, which is a string. If it is less than or equal to three, then we execute the code block of the if statement.*

> *If the word has a length of three or less, then we've finished the computation and we can go ahead and return 1 from the function.*

How to count vowels

Next, we need to count the vowels in each word. To do that, we're going to do something quite similar to when we looked for terminal characters in a string: define a string containing all the vowels, and then use the `in` operator to see if a character from our word is in that string of vowels. We'll compare to both lower- and uppercase vowels in case someone typed in words in all uppercase:

> ☑ If a word has fewer than three characters, then count it as one syllable.
>
> ☐ Otherwise, count the number of vowels and let that represent the number of syllables.
>
> ☐ To make the previous step more accurate, remove any consecutive vowels in a word.
>
> ☐ Remove the final e from words, in order to account for silent e's.
>
> ☐ Treat the character y as a vowel if it's the last character.

```python
def count_syllables_in_word(word):
    count = 0

    if len(word) <= 3:
        return 1

    vowels = "aeiouAEIOU"
    for char in word:
        if char in vowels:
            count = count + 1

    return count
```

First we're going to create a local variable, vowels, that holds all the vowels, lower- and uppercase.

Then let's step through every character in the word.

We then use the in operator to see if the character currently in the char variable matches any of the characters in the vowels string.

And if that character is in the vowel string, then we have a vowel. Let's update our count by one.

Ignoring consecutive vowels

But we're not done, because we need to take into account two or more consecutive vowels. For instance, if you have the word "book," then you want to count the first *o* and ignore the second, for a total of one syllable. Or if you have the word "roomful," then you want to count the first *o*, ignore the second, and then count the *u* for a total of two syllables.

> ☑ If a word has fewer than three characters, then count it as one syllable.
>
> ☑ Otherwise, count the number of vowels and let that represent the number of syllables.
>
> ☐ To make the previous step more accurate, remove any consecutive vowels in a word.
>
> ☐ Remove the final e from words, in order to account for silent e's.
>
> ☐ Treat the character y as a vowel if it's the last character.

So our goal will be to scan each character of each word for vowels, just like our code does now, but after we encounter a vowel, we need to make sure we ignore any vowels that follow it, until we see another consonant. After that we can repeat the process, until we reach the end of the word.

Writing the code to ignore consecutive vowels

Alright, let's implement our consecutive vowel code. Here's how we're going to approach this: we'll use a Boolean variable to track if the previous character was a vowel, and if so, we know not to count the current character if it's a vowel. Let's take a look:

```python
def count_syllables_in_word(word):
    count = 0

    if len(word) <= 3:
        return 1

    vowels = "aeiouAEIOU"
    prev_char_was_vowel = False

    for char in word:
        if char in vowels:
            if not prev_char_was_vowel:
                count = count + 1
            prev_char_was_vowel = True
        else:
            prev_char_was_vowel = False

    return count
```

There's a lot going on here. Give this code some quality time and make sure you understand exactly how it operates.

First, we're going to add a new local variable called prev_char_was_vowel, and set it to False.

Our code is going to iterate over each character in a word, just as before.

And we're going to test if the current character is in the vowels string.

If the current character is a vowel, and the previous character wasn't, then increment the syllable count.

In either case, we then set the prev_char_was_vowel to True before we process the next character.

If the current character isn't a vowel, then we just set prev_char_was_vowel to False before we process the next character.

BE the Interpreter

Using the count_syllables_in_word function above, your job is to play like you're the interpreter. The function is being called with the argument "roomful". Step through each iteration of the loop and fill in the local variable values as they change. After you've done the exercise, look at the end of the chapter to see if you got it right.

char	prev_char_was_vowel	count
r	False	0
o		
o		
m		
f		
u		
l		

Record changes to the local variables at the end of each step through the iteration.

A Test Drive

We need to update two functions at this point, the `count_syllables_in_word` function to add our new code, and the `compute_readability` function to call the `count_syllables` function. We're only showing the new code here, which is highlighted below. Go ahead and make the changes and give it a test drive.

```python
def count_syllables_in_word(word):
    count = 0

    if len(word) <= 3:
        return 1

    vowels = "aeiouAEIOU"
    prev_char_was_vowel = False

    for char in word:
        if char in vowels:
            if not prev_char_was_vowel:
                count = count + 1
            prev_char_was_vowel = True
        else:
            prev_char_was_vowel = False

    return count


def compute_readability(text):
    total_words = 0
    total_sentences = 0
    total_syllables = 0
    score = 0

    words = text.split()
    total_words = len(words)
    total_sentences = count_sentences(text)
    total_syllables = count_syllables(words)

    print(total_words, 'words')
    print(total_sentences, 'sentences')
    print(total_syllables, 'syllables')
```

Double-check to make sure you're getting the same number of words, sentences, and syllables. If not, double-check your code, and you can also compare it to the book's source code to find any mistakes.

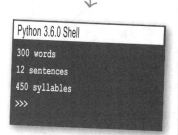

```
Python 3.6.0 Shell
300 words
12 sentences
450 syllables
>>>
```

Removing final e's, y's, and punctuation

Now we just have two more tasks left: removing final *e*'s and counting final *y*'s. Actually, we're forgetting another issue as well—that we still have some words with punctuation at their ends, which may complicate testing for final *e*'s and *y*'s. Let's deal with removing the punctuation first.

Looking at our words in the `words` list, you can see words like "first,", "you.", and "out:". What we need to do is replace them with "first", "you", and "out", and to do that we need to get the substring of each word, excluding the punctuation. With Python we can do that by *slicing*. Let's see how that works.

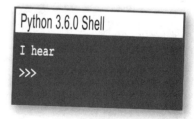

(checklist, top right)

☑ If a word has fewer than three characters, then count it as one syllable.

☑ Otherwise, count the number of vowels and let that represent the number of syllables.

☑ To make the previous step more accurate, remove any consecutive vowels in a word.

☐ Remove the final e from words, in order to account for silent *e*'s.

☐ Treat the character *y* as a vowel if it's the last character.

He who controls the slice, controls the...

We've talked about substrings, but let's talk for a moment about exactly what one is. A substring is just a string that occurs in another string. So if I have a string:

```
lyrics = 'I heard you on the wireless back in fifty two'
```

then `'I'` is a substring, as is `'I heard'`, as is `'on the wire'`, as is `'o'`, and so on. Given a string, Python gives us a way to extract substrings from a string using its slice syntax, which works like this:

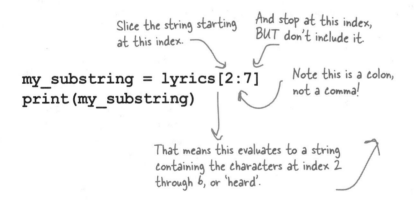

Slice the string starting at this index.

And stop at this index, BUT don't include it.

```
my_substring = lyrics[2:7]
print(my_substring)
```

Note this is a colon, not a comma!

That means this evaluates to a string containing the characters at index 2 through 6, or 'heard'.

Python 3.6.0 Shell
```
heard
>>>
```

Let's look for a few other ways you can use slice as well. If you omit the beginning index, then slice assumes you mean to start at the beginning of the list:

```
my_substring = lyrics[:6]
print(my_substring)
```

Omitting the first index means you want to start at the beginning of the string.

Python 3.6.0 Shell
```
I hear
>>>
```

Or, likewise, if you omit the ending index, then slice assumes you mean to stop the end of the list:

```
my_substring = lyrics[28:]
print(my_substring)
```

Omitting the last index means you want to end at the end of the string.

Python 3.6.0 Shell

back in fifty two
>>>

You can even use the negative indices like you did with lists, like this:

This says end just before the last character in the string.

```
my_substring = lyrics[28:-1]
print(my_substring)
```

Python 3.6.0 Shell

back in fifty tw
>>>

Or, you can even use a negative index in the first index:

Start 17 characters from the end of the string, and then go all the way to the end of the string.

```
my_substring = lyrics[-17:]
print(my_substring)
```

Python 3.6.0 Shell

back in fifty two
>>>

Surprise, slice isn't just for strings!

We said Python tries to be consistent, and consistent it is—you can use slice on your lists too!

```
smoothies = ['coconut', 'strawberry', 'banana', 'pineapple', 'acai berry']
```

Here's a familiar list.

And here's a few examples of slicing your lists. The indexing works as it does on strings.

`smoothies[2:4]` *evaluates to* `['banana', 'pineapple']`

`smoothies[:2]` *evaluates to* `['coconut', 'strawberry']`

`smoothies[3:-1]` *evaluates to* `['pineapple']`

We had our slice operation and substrings all figured out, and then they got all mixed up. Can you help us figure out who does what? Be careful, we're not sure if each slice has zero, one, or more matches. We've already figured one out, which is marked below:

```
str = 'a man a plan panama'
```

str[:]   'man a plan panama'

str[:2]   'a man a plan panam'

str[2:]   'a '

str[1:7]   'a man a plan panama'

str[3:-1]   'an a plan panam'

str[-2:-1]   'a ma'

str[0:-1]   ' man a'

str[0:4]   'm'

Putting slicing (substrings) to work

So with slicing we can take a word like "out:" and easily produce the substring "out". In fact, based on all our slicing training over the last few pages, we know exactly what that code would look like:

```
process_word = word[0:-1]
```

Note we could have written this as word[:-1] too!

Get the substring that starts at index 0 (the beginning of the string) and go until, but not including, the last character.

This variable will hold a new string containing only the string without the ending character.

But we still need the logic of knowing when to remove the final character of a word. We want to remove the final character if it is a period, comma, semicolon, exclamation point, or question mark, and based on our work in this chapter, we have all the pieces we need to do ths:

```python
def count_syllables_in_word(word):
    count = 0

    endings = '.,;!?:'
    last_char = word[-1]

    if last_char in endings:

        processed_word = word[0:-1]

    else:

        processed_word = word

    if len(processed_word) <= 3:
        return 1

    vowels = "aeiouAEIOU"
    prev_char_was_vowel = False

    for char in processed_word:
        if char in vowels:
            if not prev_char_was_vowel:
                count = count + 1
            prev_char_was_vowel = True
        else:
            prev_char_was_vowel = False

    return count
```

Let's set up a string that contains all the word endings.

And get the last character of the current word.

Then check to see if the last character is one of the endings.

If so, we'll set the processed_word to be the word, without the last character.

If not, we're going to set the processed_word to the entire word.

And then we're going to use processed_word rather than word in the rest of the code.

Don't worry about entering this code yet; we'll do it on the next page.

Sharpen your pencil

Assuming the variable process_word already has any punctuation removed from the last character, can you write a couple lines of code (or so) to remove a final *e* character, if it has one? Just write the code fragment here.

A Test Drive

Let's get all these additions based on slicing into the code. You'll find all the new code from the last few pages highlighted here. Go ahead and get it entered and try a test run to see your syllable count change.

```python
def count_syllables_in_word(word):
    count = 0

    endings = '.,;!?:'
    last_char = word[-1]

    if last_char in endings:
        processed_word = word[0:-1]
    else:
        processed_word = word

    if len(processed_word) <= 3:
        return 1

    if processed_word[-1] in 'eE':
        processed_word = processed_word[0:-1]

    vowels = "aeiouAEIOU"
    prev_char_was_vowel = False

    for char in processed_word:
        if char in vowels:
            if not prev_char_was_vowel:
                count = count + 1
            prev_char_was_vowel = True
        else:
            prev_char_was_vowel = False

    return count
```

Make sure you've made these additions we covered on the previous page.

We've put the code to remove silent e characters here, after the test for words that are length three or less.

Notice the number of syllables calcuation has changed with those code changes!

```
Python 3.6.0 Shell
300 words
12 sentences
410 syllables
>>>
```

Finishing off the heuristic code

We're on the last step of implementing the heuristic—all we need to do now is count the *y*'s at the end of words as syllables. At this point we know how to examine the end of a word, and we know that if we see a *y* at the end, we just need to increment our `count` local variable by one. Let's put it all together and test the final version of `count_syllables_in_word`, not to mention `count_syllables`.

☑ If a word has fewer than three characters, then count it as one syllable.

☑ Otherwise, count the number of vowels and let that represent the number of syllables.

☑ To make the previous step more accurate, remove any consecutive vowels in a word.

☑ Remove the final *e* from words, in order to account for silent *e*'s.

☐ Treat the character *y* as a vowel if it's the last character.

A Test Drive

It's time to finish off the `count_syllables_in_word` function. Below you'll find the code to increase the syllable count if there is a *y* at the end of the word. Give it a test run and check out the final syllable number.

```python
def count_syllables_in_word(word):
    count = 0

    endings = '.,;!?:'
    last_char = word[-1]

    if last_char in endings:
        processed_word = word[0:-1]
    else:
        processed_word = word

    if len(processed_word) <= 3:
        return 1

    if processed_word[-1] in 'eE':
        processed_word = processed_word[0:-1]


    vowels = "aeiouAEIOU"
    prev_char_was_vowel = False

    for char in processed_word:
        if char in vowels:
            if not prev_char_was_vowel:
                count = count + 1
            prev_char_was_vowel = True
        else:
            prev_char_was_vowel = False

    if processed_word[-1] in 'yY':
        count = count + 1

    return count
```

Check the word to see if it ends in y or Y, and if so, increase the syllable count.

Looks like we found some words ending in y, so our syllable count increased.

You'll notice we've written quite a long function here, which is perfectly acceptable. A bit like a paragraph, you'll find a function is probably too long when it becomes hard to understand and keep in your head as you study it.

```
Python 3.6.0 Shell
300 words
12 sentences
416 syllables
>>>
```

Implementing the reading ease formula

We're getting near the end; all we have left is to implement the formula to get a reading ease score, and then to provide some output to report the results. In terms of the formula, we have all the pieces we need: a count of words, a count of sentences, and a count of syllables. Let's look at the original formula:

$$206.835 - 1.015 \left(\frac{\text{total words}}{\text{total sentences}} \right) - 84.6 \left(\frac{\text{total syllables}}{\text{total words}} \right)$$

and let's translate it into Python:

```
score = (206.835 - 1.015 * (total_words / total_sentences)
                 - 84.6 * (total_syllables / total_words))
```

Remember we can wrap the formula in parentheses so we can write it across multiple lines.

A Test Drive

And now let's get the formula in our `compute_readability` function. Go ahead and add the formula as well as the new `print` statement and give it a try.

```
def compute_readability(text):
    total_words = 0
    total_sentences = 0
    total_syllables = 0
    score = 0

    words = text.split()
    total_words = len(words)
    total_sentences = count_sentences(text)
    total_syllables = count_syllables(words)

    score = (206.835 - 1.015 * (total_words / total_sentences)
                     - 84.6 * (total_syllables / total_words))

    print(total_words, 'words')
    print(total_sentences, 'sentences')
    print(total_syllables, 'syllables')
    print(score, 'reading ease score')
```

Add the formula below to our word, sentence, and syllable count code.

And add a print statement so you can see the results.

Nice, we have a reading ease score!

```
Python 3.6.0 Shell
300 words
12 sentences
416 syllables
64.14800000000001 reading ease score
>>>
```

Sharpen your pencil

You have the reading ease score, so all you need to do is output the results. Define a function, `output_results`, that takes a score as a parameter and outputs the reading level as specified in the pseudocode. We've reproduced pseudocode below to make things easier.

IF score >= 90.0:
   PRINT 'Reading level of 5th Grade'
ELIF score >= 80.0:
   PRINT 'Reading level of 6th Grade'
ELIF score >= 70.0:
   PRINT 'Reading level of 7th Grade'
ELIF score >= 60.0:
   PRINT 'Reading level of 8-9th Grade'
ELIF score >= 50.0:
   PRINT 'Reading level of 10-12th Grade'
ELIF score >= 30.0:
   PRINT 'Reading level of College Student'
ELSE:
   PRINT 'Reading level of College Graduate'

Here's the pseudocode.

Write your Python code here.

A Test Drive

This is it—we just need to add in the `output_results` function and we should have everything we need to complete the code! Go ahead and make the additions and changes below. You'll find the complete code over the next two pages.

```python
import ch1text

def count_syllables(words):
    count = 0

    for word in words:
        word_count = count_syllables_in_word(word)
        count = count + word_count

    return count

def count_syllables_in_word(word):
    count = 0

    endings = '.,;!?:'
    last_char = word[-1]

    if last_char in endings:
        processed_word = word[0:-1]
    else:
        processed_word = word

    if len(processed_word) <= 3:
        return 1

    if processed_word[-1] in 'eE':
        processed_word = processed_word[0:-1]

    vowels = "aeiouAEIOU"
    prev_char_was_vowel = False

    for char in processed_word:
        if char in vowels:
            if not prev_char_was_vowel:
                count = count + 1
            prev_char_was_vowel = True
        else:
            prev_char_was_vowel = False

    if processed_word[-1] in 'yY':
        count = count + 1

    return count
```

Here's all the code we've already written. This should be in your analyze.py file already.

There's more code on the next page.

```
def count_sentences(text):
    count = 0

    terminals = '.;?!'
    for char in text:
        if char in terminals:
            count = count + 1

    return count

def output_results(score):
    if score >= 90:
        print('Reading level of 5th Grade')
    elif score >= 80:
        print('Reading level of 6th Grade')
    elif score >= 70:
        print('Reading level of 7th Grade')
    elif score >= 60:
        print('Reading level of 8-9th Grade')
    elif score >= 50:
        print('Reading level of 10-12th Grade')
    elif score >= 30:
        print('Reading level of College Student')
    else:
        print('Reading level of College Graduate')

def compute_readability(text):
    total_words = 0
    total_sentences = 0
    total_syllables = 0
    score = 0

    words = text.split()
    total_words = len(words)
    total_sentences = count_sentences(text)
    total_syllables = count_syllables(words)

    score = (206.835 - 1.015 * (total_words / total_sentences)
                     - 84.6 * (total_syllables / total_words))

    print(total_words, 'words')
    print(total_sentences, 'sentences')
    print(total_syllables, 'syllables')
    print(score, 'readability score')
    output_results(score)


compute_readability(ch1text.text)
```

Add the new output_results code.

So our writing is at the 8th- to 9th-grade level. Scores in that range are considered acceptable for most books and articles, so we're not doing too bad!

Python 3.6.0 Shell

Reading level of 8-9th Grade
>>>

And make sure we're calling our new function, passing it the score.

Are you trying to tell me an 8th- or 9th-grade reading level is good? Doesn't the author of this book have a Ph.D. or something?

The goal is not to get a really high or really low score. A low score on Flesch's readability test indicates that the text is quite challenging to read. For example, a score in the 30–50 range would indicate that the text is written like an advanced college textbook or research paper in a scientific field. Not exactly the score you'd want for the opening text of a *Head First* book; in fact, it's just the opposite of what you'd want.

Hopefully this book is accessible to those entering high school, so this score doesn't seem too off the mark. In fact, think of another example: say you wrote a novel for the young adult market. You'd probably want a score that indicates an even lower reading level (say, 7th grade) and higher score (say, 70–80) so that it is accessible to those, say, in junior high school.

Score	School Level	Notes
100.00–90.00	5th grade	Very easy to read. Easily understood by an average 11-year-old student.
90.0–80.0	6th grade	Easy to read. Conversational English for consumers.
80.0–70.0	7th grade	Fairly easy to read.
70.0–60.0	8th & 9th grade	Plain English. Easily understood by 13- to 15-year-olds.
60.0–50.0	10th–12th grade	Fairly difficult to read.
50.0–30.0	College	Difficult to read.
30.0–0.0	College Graduate	Very difficult to read. Best understood by university graduates.

Taking it even further

Are you all ready to test the writing of your favorite author, news sources, or even your own writing? Here's instructions for how to do that:

- Create a new file of your own, with a name ending in *.py*.

  We'll see an even better way in the next chapter.

- Using the three-quote syntax, add your own multiline text and assign it to a variable—we recommend naming it `text` for consistency.

- In your *analyze.py* file, import your new file (otherwise known as a module).

- Call the `compute_readability` function and pass it your module name followed by the variable name `text`.

And don't forget our heuristic code could still be improved. Just take a look at words in the word list; there's still some issues, like the use of double quotes that show up in words, that could be cleaned up. Also, we could still build that special-case word list, right?

As you can see, a coder's job is never truly done. But in terms of this chapter you are done—oh, except for the bullet points and the crossword. Anyway, congrats, this was a tough chapter that really demonstrates the coding chops you're developing!

Nice job!

Coding cross

This was a character-building chapter. Relax with a little crossword.

Across

2. We removed these.
3. What test text was from.
5. The in operator works on these.
6. At the end of some words.
7. Another name for separator.
10. We ignored these vowels.
12. Subset of a string.
13. Heard you on this in 52.
15. Came up with the formula.
16. We needed a heuristic for this.

Down

1. Our new business.
4. A solution that's not 100%.
8. Means you can't change it.
9. May have made computing syllables easier.
11. Python's way to get substrings.
14. Breaking a string apart.

Exercise Solution

We're going to take the text in the *ch6/text.txt* file and get it into a Python file. To do that, in IDLE, create a new file and add the code below. For the Chapter 1 text, you'll want to open the *text.txt* file in IDLE as well, and then copy and paste the text into your new file. When you're done, save your file as *ch1text.py*.

Finally, run your code, and you should see the entire article printed to the shell.

The code printed the entire article; here's the tail end.

```
Python 3.6.0 Shell

into pond", or "pull in the fish." But also notice that other
instructions are a bit different because they depend on a condition,
like "is the bobber above or below water?". Instructions might also
direct the flow of the recipe, like "if you haven't finished fishing,
then cycle back to the beginning and put another worm on the hook."
Or, how about a condition for stopping, as in "if you're done" then go
home.

You're going to find these simple statements or instructions are the
first key to coding, in fact every App or software program you've ever
used has been nothing more than a (sometimes large) set of simple
instructions to the computer that tell it what to do.
>>>
```

Sharpen your pencil Solution

Now that you know how to use the `split` function, let's return to the `compute_readability` function and take it a little further. In our pseudocode we were going to write a function `count_words`, but as it turns out, with `split` we can handle the job of computing the total number of words with only two lines of code, so let's forgo the function. Go ahead and complete that code below.

```
import ch1text

def compute_readability(text):
    total_words = 0
    total_sentences = 0
    total_syllables = 0
    score = 0

    words = text.split()
    total_words = len(words)

    print(words)
    print('total words', total_words)
    print(text)

compute_readability(ch1text.text)
```

To get the total number of words we use the len function on the list of words.

```
Python 3.6.0 Shell

['The', 'first', 'thing', 'that', 'stands', 'between', 'you', 'and', 'writing', 'your',
'first', 'real', 'piece', 'of', 'code', 'is', 'learning', 'the', 'skill', 'of', 'breaking',
'problems', 'down', 'into', 'achievable', 'little', 'actions', 'that', 'a', 'computer',
'can', 'do', 'for', 'you.', 'Of', 'course', 'you', 'and', 'the', 'computer', 'will', 'also',
'need', 'to', 'be', 'speaking', 'a', 'common', 'language,', 'but', "we'll", 'get', 'to',
'that', 'topic', 'in', 'just', 'a', 'bit.', 'Now', 'breaking', 'problems', 'down', 'into',
'a', 'number', 'of', 'steps', 'may', 'sound', 'a', 'new', 'skill,', 'but', 'its', 'actually',
'something', 'you', 'do', 'every', 'day.', "Let's", 'look', 'at', 'an', 'example,', 'a',
'simple', 'one:', 'say', 'you', 'wanted', 'to', 'break', 'the', 'activity', 'of', 'fishing',
'down', 'into', 'a', 'simple', 'set', 'of', 'instructions', 'that', 'you', 'could', 'hand',
'to', 'a', 'robot,', 'who', 'would', 'do', 'your', 'fishing', 'for', 'you.', "Here's",
'our', 'first', 'attempt,', 'to', 'do', 'that,', 'check', 'it', 'out:', 'You', 'can', 'think',
'of', 'these', 'statements', 'as', 'a', 'nice', 'recipe', 'for', 'fishing.', 'Like', 'any',
'recipe,', 'this', 'one', 'provides', 'a', 'set', 'of', 'steps,', 'that', 'when', 'followed',
'in', 'order,', 'will', 'produce', 'some', 'result', 'or', 'outcome', 'in', 'our', 'case,',
'hopefully,', 'catching', 'some', 'fish.', 'Notice', 'that', 'most', 'steps', 'consists',
'of', 'simple', 'instruction,', 'like', '"cast', 'line', 'into', 'pond",', 'or', '"pull',
'in', 'the', 'fish."', 'But', 'also', 'notice', 'that', 'other', 'instructions', 'are',
'a', 'bit', 'different', 'because', 'they', 'depend', 'on', 'a', 'condition,', 'like',
'"is', 'the', 'bobber', 'above', 'or', 'below', 'water?".', 'Instructions', 'might', 'also',
'direct', 'the', 'flow', 'of', 'the', 'recipe,', 'like', '"if', 'you', "haven't", 'finished',
'fishing,', 'then', 'cycle', 'back', 'to', 'the', 'beginning', 'and', 'put', 'another',
'worm', 'on', 'the', 'hook.",', 'Or,', 'how', 'about', 'a', 'condition', 'for', 'stopping,',
'as', 'in', '"if', "you're", 'done"', 'then', 'go', 'home.', "You're", 'going', 'to', 'find',
'these', 'simple', 'statements', 'or', 'instructions', 'are', 'the', 'first', 'key', 'to',
'coding,', 'in', 'fact', 'every', 'App', 'or', 'software', 'program', "you've", 'ever',
'used', 'has', 'been', 'nothing', 'more', 'than', 'a', '(sometimes', 'large)', 'set', 'of',
'simple', 'instructions', 'to', 'the', 'computer', 'that', 'tell', 'it', 'what', 'to', 'do.']
300 words
>>>
```

Sharpen your pencil
Solution

Can you write the code to test each character to see if it is a period, semicolon, question mark, or exclamation point, and then, if so, increase the value of the count variable by one?

```python
def count_sentences(text):
    count = 0

    for char in text:
        if char == '.' or char == ';' or char == '?' or char == '!':
            count = count + 1

    return count
```

Check if char is any of the terminal characters, and if so, increment count by one.

Sharpen your pencil

Let's see if we can make the count_sentences function more concise (and readable) by using the in operator. Below we've removed the existing code that checks for terminal characters. We've also added a new local variable called terminals, which holds a string containing all the terminal characters. Complete the if statement, using the in operator, so that it determines if the current character is a terminal.

```python
def count_sentences(text):
    count = 0

    terminals = '.;?!'

    for char in text:

        if char in terminals:
            count = count + 1

    return count
```

Wow, that is a lot more concise and readable!

BE the Interpreter SOLUTION

Using the count_syllables_in_word function above, your job is to play like you're the interpreter. The function is being called with the argument "roomful".

char	prev_char_was_vowel	count
r	False	0
o	True	1
o	True	
m	False	
f	False	
u	True	2
l	False	

WHO DOES WHAT? SOLUTION

We had our slice operation and substrings all figured out, and then they got all mixed up. Can you help us figure out who does what? Be careful, we're not sure if each slice matches zero, one, or more substrings. We've already figured one out, which is marked below:

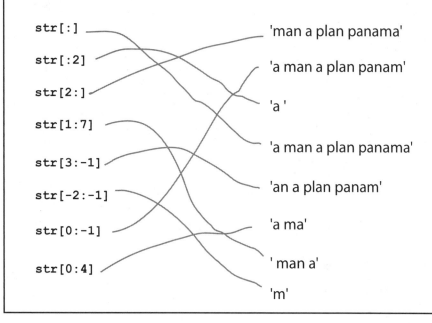

str[:]
str[:2]
str[2:]
str[1:7]
str[3:-1]
str[-2:-1]
str[0:-1]
str[0:4]

'man a plan panama'
'a man a plan panam'
'a '
'a man a plan panama'
'an a plan panam'
'a ma'
'man a'
'm'

Sharpen your pencil

Assuming the variable `process_word` alread has any punctuation removed from the last character, can you write the code to remove a final *e* character, if it has one?

If the last character of process_word is either 'e' or 'E' then...

```python
if processed_word[-1] in 'eE':
    processed_word = processed_word[0:-1]
```

...set processed_word to itself, without the last character.

Sharpen your pencil
Solution

You have the reading ease score, so all you need to do is output the results. Define a function, `output_results`, that takes a score as a parameter and outputs the reading level as specified in the pseudocode.

```python
def output_results(score):
    if score >= 90:
        print('Reading level of 5th Grade')
    elif score >= 80:
        print('Reading level of 6th Grade')
    elif score >= 70:
        print('Reading level of 7th Grade')
    elif score >= 60:
        print('Reading level of 8-9th Grade')
    elif score >= 50:
        print('Reading level of 10-12th Grade')
    elif score >= 30:
        print('Reading level of College Student')
    else:
        print('Reading level of College Graduate')
```

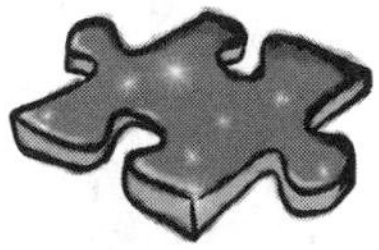

Coding Cross Solution

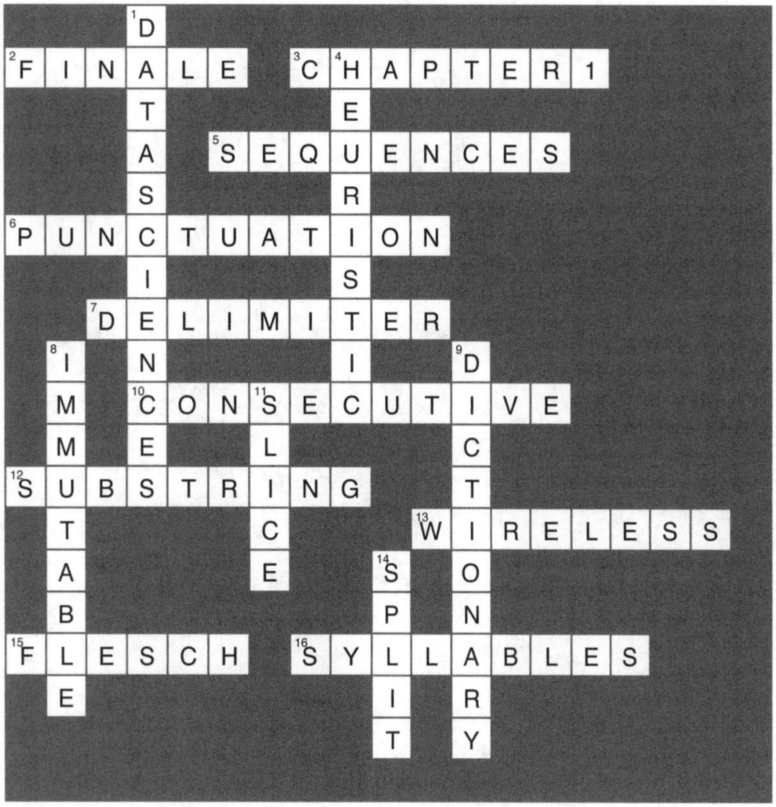
1 D
2 FINALE 3 C 4 HAPTER1
5 SEQUENCES
6 PUNCTUATION
7 DELIMITER
8 I 9 D
10 CON 11 SECUTIVE
12 SUBSTRING
13 WIRELESS
14 S
15 FLESCH 16 SYLLABLES

Getting Modular

Your code is growing in size and complexity. As that happens you need better ways to abstract, to modularize, to organize your code. You've seen that functions can be used to group lines of code together into bundles you can reuse over and over. And you've also seen that collections of functions and variables can be placed into modules so that they can be more easily shared and reused. In this chaper we'll revisit modules and learn how to use them even more effectively (so you're all ready to share your code with others) and then we're going to look at the ultimate in code reuse: *objects*. You're going to see that Python objects are all around you, just waiting to be used.

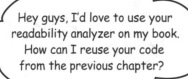

Hey guys, I'd love to use your readability analyzer on my book. How can I reuse your code from the previous chapter?

Cory Doctorow

Text from his book "Little Brother"

it," I said. "You're the best coder I know. genius, Jolu. I would be honored if you'd

ingers some more. "It's just -- You know. an's the smart one. Darryl was... He was your l, the guy who had it all organized, who Being the programmer, that was *my* thing. It lying you didn't need me."

ch an idiot. Jolu, you're the best-qualified this. I'm really, really, really --"

. Stop. Fine. I believe you. We're all really w. So yeah, of course you can help. We can

If you've never programmed a computer, you should. There's nothing like it in the whole world. When you program a computer, it does *exactly* what you tell it to do. It's like designing a machine -- any machine, like a car, like a faucet, like a gas-hinge for a door -- using math and instructions. It's awesome in the truest sense: it can fill you with awe.

A computer is the most complicated machine you'll ever use. It's made of billions of micro-miniaturized transistors that can be configured to run any program you can imagine. But when you sit down at the keyboard and write a line of code, those transistors do what you tell them to.

Most of us will never build a car. Pretty much none of us will ever create an aviation system. Design a building. Lay out a city.

Cubicle conversation

Greg

Frank

Joe

Greg: That's easy; just ship him *analyze.py*. He can just import it and call the `compute_readability` function. Done!

Frank: Totally. Modules are just Python files; just ship it.

Joe: I don't think that is quite right. I know we've said a file is just a module and all that, and we've certainly used `import`, but I think there is more to it than that.

Greg: Like what?

Joe: Well, for instance, right now, if you'll remember, our *analyze.py* file has the code to compute the readability of the Chapter 1 text.

Frank: That was great for testing out the analyzer, but Cory will need to rewrite that to use his text.

Joe: Right, but anyone should be able to use our code without having to open the code and edit it; and I'd love to leave in our test in case we want to improve our heuristic in the future. There's gotta be a better way.

Greg: What do you have in mind?

Joe: I've been doing some research. There's a convention for organizing modules so that we can still have our test code, and Cory can use it for his own analysis.

Greg: I'd love to hear more.

Frank: Wait, is this going to be a lot of work?

Joe: Frank, this isn't difficult, and I think you're going to like the end result. These changes are going to make our code more reusable by other people *and* us.

A quick module review

Now, as you also already know, to import a module, we use the `import` statement, like this:

```
import random
```
← Import the random module.

And then you can refer to any of that module's functions or variables by prepending their name with the module name, like this:

We would like to invoke the randint function, which is found in the random module.

↘

```
num = random.randint(0,9)
```

We start with the module name...

...and then the function or variable name in the module.

...followed by the dot operator...

Notice that we've already used the dot operator quite few times in this book without really talking about it—think of the dot operator as just a way of saying "look for `randint` in the module `random`."

← We're going to see that the dot operator has a few more tricks up its sleeve when it comes to objects; more on that later.

there are no
Dumb Questions

Q: How does Python know where to look for a module when I import it?

A: Good question, because when you import a module you specify only the module's name and not, say, a directory path. So how does Python find modules? Python starts by looking at its internal list of built-in modules (**random** is a built-in module) and if it doesn't find the module in that list, it looks in the local file directory where you ran your code from. There are more advanced ways to tell Python to look in other directories too, should you need that functionality.

Q: I've seen the term "Python library"; is that related to a module?

A: A library is a generic term sometimes used with Python modules (or collections of Python modules). Typically the term *library* just means that the modules have been published for others to use. You'll hear the term *package* too, which often means a set of Python modules that work together.

Q: What happens if I import, say, the random module into my code, but I also import another module that already imports random? Is there going to be a problem or conflict?

A: No, Python keeps track of the modules that have been imported so that it doesn't have to reimport modules over and over. It's also perfectly fine for your code and another module to both import the same module.

Cubicle conversation continued...

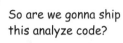

So are we gonna ship this analyze code?

Frank: We are; we just have to make sure we have it in a form that other people can use.

Joe: Right now we still have our test of the Chapter 1 text in the code.

Judy: Can't you just pull it out?

Joe: We could, but we really want to keep it around for testing as we improve our own heuristic.

Judy: Oh, well, how are you going to do that?

Frank: Joe's been studying Python modules. You can structure a module file so that it knows if it is running as the main program, or if it has been imported by another Python file.

Judy: What does that get us?

Joe: Think about it like this, Judy: if someone is running *analyze.py* directly, then it's probably us and we'll want to execute our test code. If not, then someone is importing *analyze.py*, so they'd want to skip the test code.

Judy: Oh, that makes a lot of sense. We can do that?

Joe: Yes, we use a convention that allows us to check if *analyze.py* is being executed directly as the main program, and, if so, we'll invoke the test code; otherwise, we'll ignore it. Let me show you...

The __name__ global variable

Whenever a Python file is executed, behind the scenes the Python interpreter creates a global variable __name__, which consists of two underscores, the word "name," and two more underscores. After it creates the variable, Python then sets this variable to one of two things: if the Python file is being executed directly as the main program, the variable is set to the string "__main__". Otherwise, __name__ is set to the name of your module, like "analyze". Given how __name__ works, there is a long-standing Python convention of using the following code to test if your code is running as the main program:

Serious Coding

Python coders pronounce the __name__ variable as *dunder name*, which is short for "double underscore name, double underscore."

Test to see if this is the main program, and if so, supply whatever code you want here.

```python
if __name__ == '__main__':
    print("Look, I'm the main program y'all.")
```

The important thing to note is this print statement will be ignored if this file is being imported.

A Test Drive

Let's put __name__ to the test. Below you'll find two Python files; type them both into IDLE, *store them in the same folder*, and run them both. Check your output.

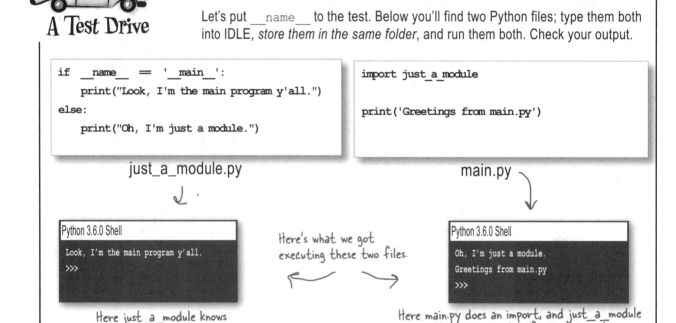

```python
if __name__ == '__main__':
    print("Look, I'm the main program y'all.")
else:
    print("Oh, I'm just a module.")
```

just_a_module.py

```python
import just_a_module

print('Greetings from main.py')
```

main.py

Here's what we got executing these two files.

```
Python 3.6.0 Shell
Look, I'm the main program y'all.
>>>
```

Here just_a_module knows it's the main program.

```
Python 3.6.0 Shell
Oh, I'm just a module.
Greetings from main.py
>>>
```

Here main.py does an import, and just_a_module knows it's being executed from an import.

Cubicle conversation continued...

Okay, I think I got it.

Greg: Yeah, we just need to test to see if the __name__ variable is set to "__main__", and if so, we'll run our test code; otherwise, we'll do nothing. After we've done that, we can give it to Cory.

Frank: Let's do it... Wait, how is Cory going to know *which* functions to use?

Greg: One problem at a time, Frank; we'll come back to that one. Let's get the code in there first.

Frank: Fair enough!

Updating analyze.py

At this point copy the *analyze.py* file from your Chapter 6 folder to your Chapter 7 folder and open it. You'll want to make these changes:

> Go ahead and make a copy of *ch1text.py* from the Chapter 6 folder as well and place it in your Chapter 7 folder.

> Here's the top of your *analyze.py* file.

```
import ch1text

def count_syllables(words):
    count = 0

    for word in words:
        word_count = count_syllables_in_word(word)
        count = count + word_count

    return count

def count_syllables_in_word(word):
    count = 0

    endings = '.,;!?:'
    last_char = word[-1]
```

> At the top of the file, delete the import of the *ch1text* file. We're going to move this to the bottom of the file.

```
def compute_readability(text):
    total_words = 0
    total_sentences = 0
    total_syllables = 0
    score = 0

    words = text.split()
    total_words = len(words)
    total_sentences = count_sentences(text)
    total_syllables = count_syllables(words)

    score = (206.835 - 1.015 * (total_words / total_sentences)
                     - 84.6 * (total_syllables / total_words))


    output_results(score)


if __name__ == "__main__":
    import ch1text
    print('Chapter1 Text:')
    compute_readability(ch1text.text)
```

Here's the bottom of your analyze.py file.

Here's the conditional test for the __main__ value in the __name__ variable.

If true we're going to import the ch1text file, and compute its readability.

We added a print statement too.

Yes, you can use the import statement anywhere in your code!

Don't forget to indent the compute_readability line four spaces under the if statement.

A Test Drive

Get the changes made to *analyze.py* and then give it a test drive. Because we're running it as the main program, you should get the same output you did in Chapter 6. Don't forget to make sure you have a copy of *ch1text.py* in the same folder.

Works as advertised. We're running analyze.py as the main program, so it goes ahead and does a test of the text in ch1text.py.

```
Python 3.6.0 Shell

Chapter 1 Text:
Reading level of 8-9th Grade
>>>
```

Using analyze.py as a module

So how are others going to reuse our code? Well, they're first going to import the
`analyze` module into their own code, and then they'll call `compute_readability`
in the `analyze` module with a text string. Let's create a new file called *cory_analyze.py*
and write the code to do that:

Import the module.

```
import analyze
```

And call analyze.compute_readability with the text.

```
analyze.compute_readability("""
If you've never programmed a computer, you should. There's nothing like it in the
whole world. When you program a computer, it does exactly what you tell it to do.
It's like designing a machine:  any machine, like a car, like a faucet, like a gas
hinge for a door using math and instructions. It's awesome in the truest sense it
can fill you with awe.

A computer is the most complicated machine you'll ever use. It's made of billions
of micro miniaturized transistors that can be configured to run any program you
can imagine. But when you sit down at the keyboard and write a line of code, those
transistors do what you tell them to.

Most of us will never build a car. Pretty much none of us will ever create an
aviation system. Design a building. Lay out a city.""")
```

Remember, you can use
three double quotes to
create a multiline string.

A Test Drive

Get *cory_analyze.py* typed in and then give it a test drive as well. Because we're
running *analyze.py* as a module now, our test code is not going to be run. Give it a try
and see what you get.

You don't actually
have to type in
Cory's text; you
can find it in the
Chapter 7 source
files under cory.txt.

Cory's text gets a 7th-grade
rating. That seems perfect for a
book with teen subject matter!

```
Python 3.6.0 Shell

Reading level of 7th Grade
>>>
```

Frank

> Okay, I'd still love to know how Cory is going to know what functions to call in the analyze module?

That's where Python help comes in.

With Python you can add help documentation right into your source code. Of course, you've already seen how to add comments to your code—those are for the purpose of documenting your low-level code—but Python also allows you to add *docstrings* to provide higher-level documentation for programmers who are using your modules (but aren't interested in digging through your code).

The docstring format is simple: you just add a string at the top of your module as a general description, and a string after each function definition (as well as object definitions, which you haven't learned about yet).

So how do you use these docstrings? Do they require others to open your module file and read them? No, there's a better way: Python provides a `help` function, which anyone can use in the interpreter to see the documentation.

Let's add some docstrings to *analyze.py* and see how this works.

You'll find most modern programming languages provide some form of docstrings.

Adding docstrings to analyze.py

Let's add in some docstrings so other coders can make use of Python's help system to learn how to use our module.

```python
"""The analyze module uses the Flesch-Kincaid readability test to analyze text and
   produce a readability score. This score is then converted into a
   grade-based readability category.

"""

def count_syllables(words):
    """This function takes a list of words and returns a total
       count of syllables across all words in the list.
    """
    count = 0

    for word in words:
        word_count = count_syllables_in_word(word)
        count = count + word_count

    return count

def count_syllables_in_word(word):
    """This function takes a word in the form of a string
       and returns the number of syllables. Note this function is
       a heuristic and may not be 100% accurate.
    """
    count = 0

    endings = '.,;!?:'    # these are the word terminals we care about
    last_char = word[-1]

    if last_char in endings:
        processed_word = word[0:-1]
    else:
        processed_word = word

    if len(processed_word) <= 3:
        return 1

    if processed_word[-1] in 'eE':
        processed_word = processed_word[0:-1]


    vowels = "aeiouAEIOU"
    prev_char_was_vowel = False

    for char in processed_word:
        if char in vowels:
            if not prev_char_was_vowel:
                count = count + 1
            prev_char_was_vowel = True
        else:
            prev_char_was_vowel = False

    if processed_word[-1] in 'yY':
        count = count + 1

    return count
```

You can add a multiline string at the top of your module...

...and below any definition.

Only docstrings are included in Python help. Comments added to the code, like this one, are not included.

Continued on next page...

```python
def count_sentences(text):
    """This function counts the number of sentences in a string of text
       using period, semicolon, question mark and exclamation mark as
       terminals.
    """
    count = 0

    terminals = '.;?!'
    for char in text:
        if char in terminals:
            count = count + 1

    return count

def output_results(score):
    """This function takes a Flesch-Kincaid score and prints the
       corresponding reading level.
    """
    if score >= 90:
        print('Reading level of 5th Grade')
    elif score >= 80:
        print('Reading level of 6th Grade')
    elif score >= 70:
        print('Reading level of 7th Grade')
    elif score >= 60:
        print('Reading level of 8-9th Grade')
    elif score >= 50:
        print('Reading level of 10-12th Grade')
    elif score >= 30:
        print('Reading level of College Student')
    else:
        print('Reading level of College Graduate')

def compute_readability(text):
    """This function takes a text string of any length and prints out a
       grade-based readability score.
    """
    total_words = 0
    total_sentences = 0
    total_syllables = 0
    score = 0

    words = text.split()
    total_words = len(words)
    total_sentences = count_sentences(text)
    total_syllables = count_syllables(words)

    score = (206.835 - 1.015 * (total_words / total_sentences)
                     - 84.6 * (total_syllables / total_words))

    output_results(score)

if __name__ == "__main__":
    import ch1text
    print('Chapter 1 Text:')
    compute_readability(ch1text.text)
```

Even more docstrings!

Note that you can make your documentation as elaborate as you like or as is needed. Python allows you to do this in a free-form manner. Some other programming languages have quite sophisticated systems for specifying docstrings that are more standardized and less free-form.

A Test Drive

Go ahead and document the *analyze.py* file; get creative if you like and expand your documentation. After you've done that, <u>you need to follow some very specific instructions</u>. Remember we said that Python, for efficiency reasons, won't import the same module over and over? Instead, it keeps a cached version around in memory. So you've changed your `analyze` module, but Python is still going to rely on the cached version (the one without docstrings). **To get around that, you need to exit IDLE**. *Quit all the way out*. Then, run IDLE again, open your *cory_analyze.py* file and run it to ensure you didn't introduce any errors when you documented the code. After that, locate IDLE's shell window and follow the instructions below to test your new help documentation:

Depending on your operating system and version of Python

Don't skip running cory_analyze.py, as it imports your new analyze.py file and ensures IDLE is using the right directory paths.

```
Python 3.6.0 Shell

>>> help(analyze)
Help on module analyze:

NAME
    analyze

DESCRIPTION
    The analyze module uses the Flesch-Kincaid readability test to analyze text and
    produce a readability score. This score is then converted into a
    grade-based readability category.

FUNCTIONS
    compute_readability(text)
        This function takes a text string of any length and prints out a
        grade-based readability score.

    count_sentences(text)
        This function counts the number of sentences in a string of text
        using period, semicolon, question mark and exclamation mark as
        terminals.

    count_syllables(words)
        This function takes a list of words and returns a total
        count of syllables across all words in the list.

    count_syllables_in_word(word)
        This function takes a word in the form of a string
        and returns the number of syllables. Note this function is
        a heuristic and may not be 100% accurate.

    output_results(score)
        This function takes a Flesch-Kincaid score and prints the
        corresponding reading level.
```

Here's how you import and call help on the analyze module.

Here we're asking for help on the entire analyze module.

```
Python 3.6.0 Shell

>>> help(analyze.compute_readability)
Help on function compute_readability in module analyze:

compute_readability(text)
    This function takes a text string of any length and prints out a
    grade-based readability score.
```

You can also ask for help on a specific function in a module.

Nice job! I was quickly able to use the analyze module, especially with the help of the great documentation!

BRAIN POWER

If you think about how another programmer might want to use the `analyze` module, are there ways you might restructure it? For instance, might another programmer want to get direct access to the score value? Think through how you might refactor the code.

Exploring other Python modules

Now that you have a better understanding of modules and how to use Python's help system, there are plenty of interesting modules out there for you to explore. We'll be tackling some of the more interesting ones throughout the rest of the book, and you'll find a few discussed in the appendix as well. Here's a few that are popular just to get your creative juices flowing...

We use the **requests** module to connect to and retrieve web pages that we monitor.

We use Python's **datetime** module in everything we do; we're a shipping company, and the datetime module gives us all the tools we need to create, manipulate, and compare dates and times.

In my computational physics group, we rely on the **math** module heavily!

I love Python's **turtle** module. I teach children and beginners, and it gives them a great way to create and play with graphics on the screen. It's inspired by Seymour Papert's work at MIT.

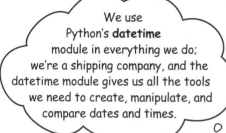

In our health care app, the entire interface is written using the **Tkinter** module, which gives you everything you need to build desktop user interfaces.

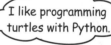

I like programming turtles with Python.

Wait, did someone say "turtles"?!

Ah, one of our favorite topics, because, as you'll see, they're a great way to play with computation, and they are built right into Python. All you need to do is import the `turtle` module and then you're all ready to create your own turtles. But, before you start creating turtles, let's take a look at what a turtle living in Python-land looks like:

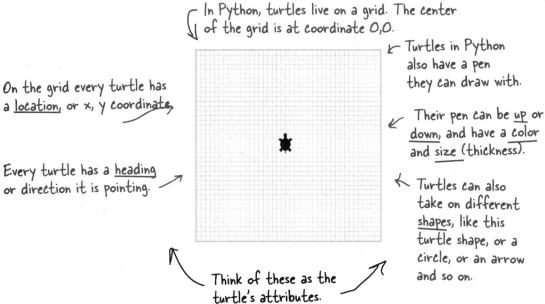

In Python, turtles live on a grid. The center of the grid is at coordinate 0,0.

Turtles in Python also have a pen they can draw with.

On the grid every turtle has a <u>location</u>, or x, y coordinate.

Their pen can be <u>up</u> or <u>down</u>, and have a <u>color</u> and <u>size</u> (thickness).

Every turtle has a <u>heading</u> or direction it is pointing.

Turtles can also take on different <u>shapes</u>, like this turtle shape, or a circle, or an arrow and so on.

Think of these as the turtle's <u>attributes</u>.

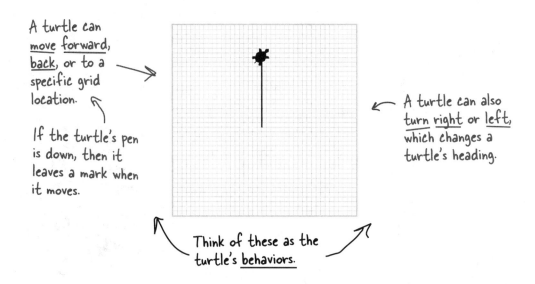

A turtle can <u>move forward</u>, <u>back</u>, or to a specific grid location.

If the turtle's pen is down, then it leaves a mark when it moves.

A turtle can also turn <u>right</u> or <u>left</u>, which changes a turtle's heading.

Think of these as the turtle's <u>behaviors</u>.

Turtles, really? You started the book with recipes and now we're learning about turtles?

Sorry, were you expecting an MIT-level treatment? Well, guess what? That's exactly what you're getting! Turtle graphics were invented at MIT (the Massachusetts Institute of Technology) by pioneering computer scientist Seymour Papert in the 1960s. Since that time, turtle graphics have had a big influence on many programming languages that followed and they've also helped to educate computer scientists and mathematicians alike (not to mention lots of kids). We'll ask you to withhold judgment until you've finished this chapter (and a few other chapters in this book), when we think you'll be quite pleased with what you've accomplished using turtles.

Creating your very own turtle

What are we waiting for? Let's create a turtle (or two). First we're going to need to import the `turtle` module.

`import turtle`

Don't start entering code yet; we'll do that in just a bit.

And then we can create a turtle like this:

turtle module

The dot operator

What looks like a function call, only we usually don't name functions with uppercase letters

When you create a turtle, this window will pop up.

`slowpoke = turtle.Turtle()`

And let's assign the new turtle to the variable slowpoke.

This creates a new turtle.

Now let's make slowpoke do something:

A variable referencing our new turtle

The dot operator

One of the turtle's behaviors

An argument, like when making a function call

`slowpoke.forward(100)`

This is one of slowpoke's behaviors.

This tells our slowpoke turtle to move forward 100 units.

So slowpoke moved straight 100 units and drew a line with its pen as it did. But did you notice slowpoke doesn't look much like a turtle? Let's fix that by setting one of its attributes and rerunning the code.

`slowpoke.shape('turtle')`

This sets the slowpoke turtle's shape attribute to be 'turtle'.

That's better!

Turtle lab

Okay, now it's time for you to join in: let's write a little code to see if we can do something interesting with Python turtles. Go ahead and put this code in a file called *turtle_test.py*:

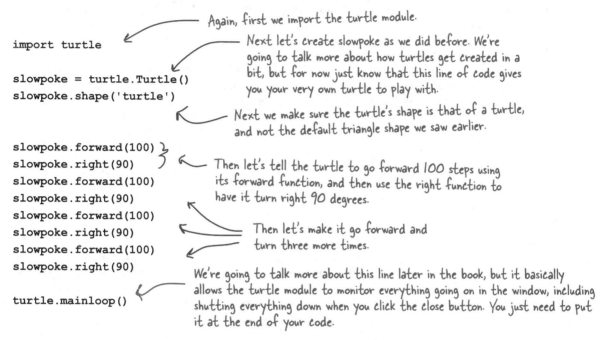

Again, first we import the turtle module.

```
import turtle
```

Next let's create slowpoke as we did before. We're going to talk more about how turtles get created in a bit, but for now just know that this line of code gives you your very own turtle to play with.

```
slowpoke = turtle.Turtle()
slowpoke.shape('turtle')
```

Next we make sure the turtle's shape is that of a turtle, and not the default triangle shape we saw earlier.

```
slowpoke.forward(100)
slowpoke.right(90)
slowpoke.forward(100)
slowpoke.right(90)
slowpoke.forward(100)
slowpoke.right(90)
slowpoke.forward(100)
slowpoke.right(90)

turtle.mainloop()
```

Then let's tell the turtle to go forward 100 steps using its forward function, and then use the right function to have it turn right 90 degrees.

Then let's make it go forward and turn three more times.

We're going to talk more about this line later in the book, but it basically allows the turtle module to monitor everything going on in the window, including shutting everything down when you click the close button. You just need to put it at the end of your code.

With that, go ahead and give this a test run and you'll see your turtle move forward and turn right four times, each time leaving a trail behind it to form the shape of a square.

Here's what we got!

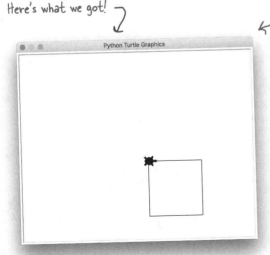

If you're not seeing this window and you have no errors in the shell, look behind your Python windows. On some systems the turtle window does not automatically appear on top of the others.

Watch it!

Don't name your file turtle.py

Careful, if you name your test file the same name as a module you're importing, then you're going to run into trouble: when Python goes looking for the turtle *module it's going to find your file first. So, just make sure you don't name your Python files the same names as common modules, especially ones you're importing.*

there are no
Dumb Questions

Q: So when we tell a turtle to turn, we do it with degrees?

A: Correct. For instance, turning right 360 degrees would mean it would turn all the way around clockwise. Turning 90 degrees would turn a quarter of a turn, and so on.

Q: When the turtle is going forward, what does the argument 100 mean?

A: 100 units. What's a unit? A pixel on your screen. So turtle.forward(50) would move a turtle 50 pixels in the direction it is heading.

Q: Why did we have to set the shape to be a turtle? I thought it *was* a turtle!

A: For historical reasons, by default the turtle displays a shape similar to a triangle. You can also set it to shapes like a square, a circle, an arrow, or even your own images. But what could be more fun than the shape of a real turtle?

 **Sharpen your pencil**

Hey, it's Chapter 7 already, so we're confident you're in good shape to take the turtle square code (on the previous page) and get it wrapped up in a nice function; call it make_square, which will take one parameter, a turtle. Write your code here and see how much you can clean things up by removing any duplicated code. Of course you'll find our version at the end of the chapter if you need any hints.

Make sure you take a look at our version, because that's what we'll work from on the next few pages.

Adding a second turtle

How about we give slowpoke a friend? Let's add another turtle
to our code:

Here's the nice new code
we generalized in the last
Sharpen exercise.

```python
import turtle

slowpoke = turtle.Turtle()
slowpoke.shape('turtle')
pokey = turtle.Turtle()
pokey.shape('turtle')
pokey.color('red')

def make_square(the_turtle):
    for i in range(0,4):
        the_turtle.forward(100)
        the_turtle.right(90)

make_square(slowpoke)
pokey.right(45)
make_square(pokey)

turtle.mainloop()
```

Create a second turtle
and assign it to the
variable pokey. We're
going to set pokey's shape
attribute to a turtle as
well, and also set its color
attribute to red.

Then let's turn pokey slightly, 45
degrees to the right.

And then pass pokey to make_square.

In this code, slowpoke draws a square
as before, but pokey turns slightly
and then draws its own red square.

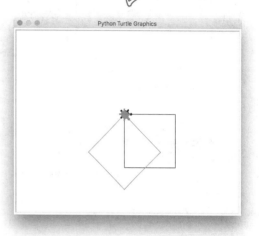

If the make_square function looks
new to you, make sure you go through
the answer to the last Sharpen your
pencil on the previous page.

Let's use your newfound superpower of creating and using
functions to take this further. Let's write a function that uses
`make_square` and see what kind of interesting graphic we can
generate:

```python
import turtle

slowpoke = turtle.Turtle()
slowpoke.shape('turtle')
slowpoke.color('blue')
pokey = turtle.Turtle()
pokey.shape('turtle')
pokey.color('red')
```

To make it interesting, let's change
slowpokes' pen color to blue.

Rest of the code continued
on the next page...

```
def make_square(the_turtle):
    for i in range(0,4):
        the_turtle.forward(100)
        the_turtle.right(90)
```

Let's add a new function called make_spiral.

```
def make_spiral(the_turtle):
    for i in range(0, 36):
        make_square(the_turtle)
        the_turtle.right(10)
```

make_spiral is going to call make_square 36 times, and then, each time, have the turtle turn an additional 10 degrees.

```
make_square(slowpoke)
pokey.right(45)
make_square(pokey)
```

Get rid of these calls to make_square.

Now we're going to call make_spiral instead of make_square.

Notice that each turtle has its own position, heading, color, and so on.

```
make_spiral(slowpoke)
pokey.right(5)
make_spiral(pokey)
```

pokey is going to turn right 5 degrees before making a spiral.

```
turtle.mainloop()
```

A Test Drive

Update *turtle_test.py* and give it a test drive. Is this the output you expected?

Here's what we got! Are you having Spirograph flashbacks?

Feel free to play with all the attributes and parameters and see what you can come up with. We've also got some more turtle experiments for you on the next page.

MORE TURTLE EXPERIMENTS

We've got even more turtle experiments for you below. Take a look at each one, guess what it does, and then run it to see if you were right. Change a few values; how does the output change?

Experiment #1

```
for i in range(5):
    slowpoke.forward(100)
    slowpoke.right(144)
```

What happens if you change this number? Or this one?

Just take your turtle_test.py file and delete everything but the first three lines (and the final mainloop line), then add in this code in the middle.

Draw your output here.

Experiment #2

```
slowpoke.pencolor('blue')
slowpoke.penup()
slowpoke.setposition(-120, 0)
slowpoke.pendown()
slowpoke.circle(50)

slowpoke.pencolor('red')
slowpoke.penup()
slowpoke.setposition(120, 0)
slowpoke.pendown()
slowpoke.circle(50)
```

We're using some new turtle functions here: we're setting the color of the pen, lifting it up, moving to a position, and putting it down before drawing a circle.

What happens if you remove the calls to penup?

Experiment #3

```
def make_shape(t, sides):
    angle = 360/sides
    for i in range(0, sides):
        t.forward(100)
        t.right(angle)

make_shape(slowpoke, 3)
make_shape(slowpoke, 5)
make_shape(slowpoke, 8)
make_shape(slowpoke, 10)
```

Try some more values, like 1, 2? 50?

As usual, you'll find our answers in the back of the chapter.

What are turtles, anyway?

Let's return to the code where we first created our turtle. At first glance it looks like we called a function named `Turtle` that is located in the turtle module:

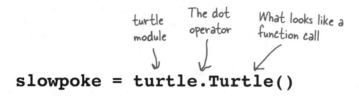

```
slowpoke = turtle.Turtle()
```

So does the `turtle` module have a function that creates turtles? And what is a turtle, anyway? We know about integers and strings and lists and booleans, but what's a turtle? Is it a new type? To dig a little deeper, we could always ask Python for help:

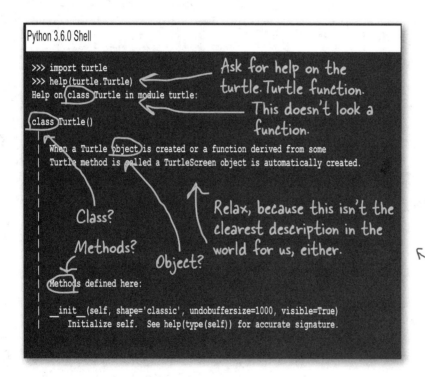

So reading this not-so-clear docstring, you'd think that `Turtle` is either a class or an object, or both (whatever those are), and it has something called *methods*. And you'd be right. But is it a class or an object? Well, although we haven't made much of a point of it yet, we should tell you that Python is a very *object-oriented language*—as are most modern languages—and given how far you've come in your coding, it's about time you learn what objects, classes, and methods are.

What are objects?

Of course you intuitively know about objects; they're all around you. Cars, iPhones, radios, toasters, kitchen appliances, you name it. And one thing that all these objects have in common is they have some *internal state* and they have some *behavior*. Take a car, for example—it has state:

- Make
- Model
- Fuel level
- Speed
- Mileage
- Engine state (on/off)

← *Just a few off the top of our heads; we're sure you can think of even better ones.*

And it has behavior. A car can:

- Start
- Turn Off
- Drive
- Brake

With programming, objects are no different. The whole point of software objects is that we can *bundle state and behavior together*. Think about a Boolean value: it has state but no behavior. Think about a Python function: it has behavior but no state. With Python objects, we can have both working together. For example, when you start the car, the engine state is changed from off to on. Likewise, if the brake behavior is applied, then the speed state will naturally decrease.

So what's the big deal? We could do all that with functions and variables, right? But when you start thinking in terms of objects, you can approach solving computational problems at an even higher level—you can think about programming as composing a set of objects and managing their interactions, instead of herding a large number of variables and functions.

Our turtles are a good example—we could write code to manage locations and colors and coordinates to draw graphics (always a difficult task). Or we can use our turtle objects, which inherently keep track of much of this state internally, freeing us to just think about the larger issues, like how to get two turtles to draw a spiral together. It's a simplistic example, but you have to start somewhere when thinking about objects.

```
make: 'Chevy'
model: 'Bel Air'
fuel: 8
speed: 0
mileage: 1211
engine_on: False
  def start():
  def turn_off():
  def brake():
```

← *State and behavior bundled together in an object* ↓

'57 Chevy

```
make: 'Mini'
model: 'Cooper'
fuel: 2
speed: 14
mileage: 43190
engine_on: True
  def start():
  def turn_off():
  def brake():
```

Mini

Objects aren't unique to Python; practically all modern languages provide objects. ↰

```
make: 'Pontiac'
model: 'Fiero'
fuel: 10
speed: 56
mileage: 196101
engine_on: True
  def start():
  def turn_off():
  def brake():
```

Fiero

```
make: 'DeLorean'
model: 'DMC-12'
fuel: 6
speed: 88
mileage: 10125
engine_on: True
  def start():
  def turn_off():
  def brake():
```

DeLorean

Okay, what's a class then?

If we're going to have lots of objects, say lots of turtles, we want all our turtles to share common behaviors (after all, who wants to reinvent the wheel every time we need a turtle to move forward), but we also want each turtle to have its own state (because if every turtle was in the same location, had the same heading, and had the same color, we couldn't get much interesting work out of them). A class gives us a template or blueprint for creating objects of the same type.

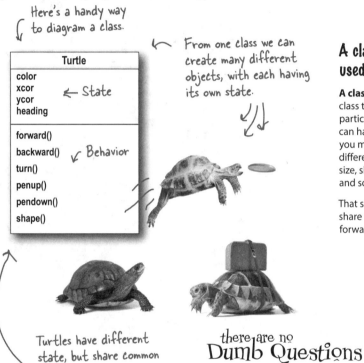

Here's a handy way to diagram a class.

Turtle
color xcor ← State ycor heading
forward() backward() ← Behavior turn() penup() pendown() shape()

From one class we can create many different objects, with each having its own state.

Turtles have different state, but share common behaviors.

A class is not an object, it's used to construct them.

A class is a blueprint for making objects. A class tells Python how to make an object of that particular type. Each object made from that class can have its own values for its state; for example, you might use the Turtle class to make dozens of different turtles, and each turtle has its own color, size, shape, location and pen settings (up or down), and so on.

That said, all turtles created from the same class share the same behaviors, like turning, going forward and backwards, and controlling the pen.

there are no
Dumb Questions

Q: Okay, but what is the point of creating all these objects from classes?

A: Without classes and objects you'll always be stuck solving any problem in terms of the Python basic types, like strings or numbers or lists, and so on. With classes and objects, you can use types that are higher level and closer to the problem you're trying to solve. For example, if you were creating a fishing game, having fish objects and a pond object would be a lot easier than managing a whole collection of variables and functions.

Q: Is a class like a type?

A: Exactly. Think of each class as a Python type, just like the string and list and number types that you already know.

Q: So a class is a blueprint for making many objects. Can I make my own class?

A: You sure can, and that is the beauty of object-oriented programming: you can extend Python (or any language) with your very own classes, or even extend the functionality of anyone else's classes.

In this chapter we'll be looking at how to use pre-existing classes, and in Chapter 12 we'll start making our own.

Q: Objects have a lot in them (data and functions). How does a variable like slowpoke actually hold an object?

A: Remember when we talked about how a variable is assigned to a list? We said that a variable holds a reference to where the list is stored, like a pointer to the list. Objects are assigned to variables in the same way; the variable holds a reference to the object in Python's memory, not the object itself.

A class tells us what an object knows and what an object can do

On the previous page we saw a diagram for sketching out a class. Let's take a little closer look at what it provides. A class diagram tells you two things (for starters): what a object knows and what a object can do.

Here's our Turtle class diagram again.

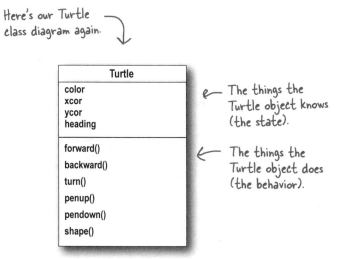

Turtle
color xcor ycor heading
forward() backward() turn() penup() pendown() shape()

← The things the Turtle object knows (the state).

← The things the Turtle object does (the behavior).

The things the object knows about itself are called its:

- **attributes**

The things the object can do are called:

- **methods**

Attributes represent an object's state (its data), and each object has its own attribute values. Attributes are similar to local variables, only they live in an object. Also like variables, attributes can be assigned to any of the Python types you're already familiar with. You'll also hear the term *instance variable* around coding circles. An instance variable is the same as a Python object attribute. In fact, anytime you hear the word *instance*, just substitute the word *object*. So, an instance variable is the same as an object variable, which is the same as a Python attribute.

Things an object can do are called methods. Think of methods as functions that belong to an object. The difference between a method and a function is that methods are typically getting, setting, altering, and making decisions based on an object's attributes.

Sharpen your pencil

Fill in what a radio object might need to know and do.

Radio
attributes
methods

How to use objects and classes

In this chapter we're learning how to *use* objects and classes. As it turns out, there are lots of classes out there, written by other developers, all ready for you to use. To use them all you really have to know is what an object can do (in other words, its methods) along with any attributes you might want to make use of. Of course you also need to know how to create an object (otherwise known as an *instance*) before you can use one. We've created a couple Turtle objects, but let's take another look at how to do this:

In Chapter 12 you're going to learn how to make your own classes and objects.

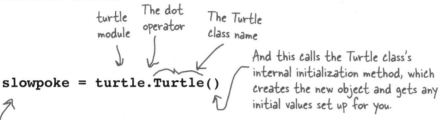

turtle module

The dot operator

The Turtle class name

```
slowpoke = turtle.Turtle()
```

And this calls the Turtle class's internal initialization method, which creates the new object and gets any initial values set up for you.

The result of calling the initialization method is a brand new Turtle object created from the Turtle class blueprint. The new Turtle object is assigned to the variable slowpoke.

In the object-oriented world, we don't just create new objects, we <u>instantiate</u> them. And we call each object an <u>instance</u>.

So there's a lot going on here in this little line of code. Let's talk through it. The first thing to know is that we're accessing the Turtle class from the turtle module. That's the reason for the dot notation here: the dot has nothing to do with attributes or methods in this statement.

```
turtle.Turtle
```

Notice that, by convention, class names start with an uppercase letter. We'll see some exceptions to this later in the chapter.

Here's where we're getting the Turtle CLASS from the turtle module.

Next, we're invoking the class like it was a function. What's going on here?

```
turtle.Turtle()
```
Invoking the class like a function?

In the object-oriented world, we call these initialization methods <u>constructors</u>. Any time you hear "constructor," just think "the method that initializes the object."

Here's what's going on: every class has a special method known as its *constructor*. The constructor gets the object all set up with whatever default attribute values it needs (among other things it might do). The constructor always has another important role: it always returns the newly created object (again, we call it the instance) to you.

So when the object is created, initalized, and returned, it is assigned to the variable slowpoke.

```
slowpoke = turtle.Turtle()
```
Returns a new object that is instantiated from the Turtle blueprint

Constructors can take arguments too, although we'll see these a bit later

What about those methods and attributes?

As you've already seen, once you have an object in hand, you are free to call its methods:

```
slowpoke.turn(90)
```
To call a method, start with the name of an object, followed by a dot, and then the method name—in other words, you call them just like you call functions, only you precede the function with an object name (and a dot).

```
slowpoke.forward(100)
```

You always need an object to call a method on. Calling a method without an object doesn't compute (which object's state is the method supposed to act on?).

So what about attributes? We haven't seen any code where we're getting or setting an attribute's value. To access an attribute in an object, you use dot notation. Say the `Turtle` class had an attribute named `shape` (it doesn't, but hold that thought). Then you'd access or set the value of the `shape` attribute like this:

```
slowpoke.shape = 'turtle'
```
You can set or get the value of an object's attribute using dot notation (it's the same syntax as accessing a variable in a module).

```
print(slowpoke.shape)
```

If this were valid code, this would print 'turtle'.

Okay, but as you've already seen we've been using the `shape` method to set a turtle's shape. So why doesn't the `Turtle` object have a `shape` attribute? Well, it could, but there is a common strategy used in object-oriented programming where we rely on a method to get or set an attribute's value. The reason stems from an idea called *encapsulation* that we'll talk more about in Chapter 12. Encapsulation often gives the object developer more control over an object (than just letting any code change an attribute's value). Again, we'll return to this point in Chapter 12.

For now just know that many of the attributes you'll want to get your hands on are accessed through methods, rather than directly. Here's an example: to get or set the state of the shape attribute, we use a method, `shape`, instead:

```
slowpoke.shape('circle')
```
We can call the shape method to change slowpoke's internal shape attribute to a circle.

```
print(slowpoke.shape())
```

And we can call the shape method without arguments to get its current value.

Seeing classes and objects everywhere

With that background behind us, let's take a new look at the Python world—we did say Python was a very object-oriented language, and in fact objects are all around you. Check this out:

A list is actually a Python class.

Here we're calling the list constructor to instantiate a new, empty list.

```python
my_list = list()
my_list.append('first')
my_list.append('second')
my_list.reverse()
print(my_list)
```

Here we're calling the append method...

...and the reverse method, which you haven't seen before.

All these methods change the list object's internal state.

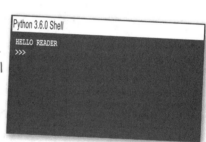

```
Python 3.6.0 Shell
['second', 'first']
>>>
```

Remember we said class names start with an uppercase letter? Unfortunately, this isn't the case for some Python built-in classes (for historical reasons). So just know that some built-in classes start with a lowercase letter, and any other classes you run into should begin with an uppercase letter.

Here's another class that may look familiar. Check this one out:

It turns out strings are really classes. Here's how you'd instantiate one with the constructor.

```python
greeting = str('hello reader')
shout = greeting.upper()
print(shout)
```

Notice this constructor takes an argument; we'll see more as the book progresses.

Calling one of the string methods.

```
Python 3.6.0 Shell
HELLO READER
>>>
```

What about this one?

That's right, another class...

Because lists and strings and floats are built into Python, you don't need to explicitly call the classes' constructor like we're doing here. Python handles it for you behind the scenes.

```python
pi = float(3.1415)
is_int = pi.is_integer()
print(pi, is_int)
```

...and another method.

```
Python 3.6.0 Shell
3.1415 False
>>>
```

Are you telling me we've been using objects the whole time and you're just now telling us?

Pretty much... if you forget about modules for a moment, anytime you see a variable followed by dot notation, you can bet that what follows the dot is either an object attribute or a method. Not only that, but almost everything in Python, including the built-in types, is actually a class. The reason it didn't initially appear so was because Python goes to a lot of trouble to make things easy—for instance, when you type:

```
my_list = []
```

to create an empty list. Behind the scenes, Python is effectively rewriting that as:

```
my_list = list()
```

So until you start using methods on your lists, like:

```
my_list.append(42)
```

you really have no reason to think you're dealing with an object.

But now that you know the truth, objects are all around you in Python. So, it's probably time we get back to using them.

Get ready for some turtle races

We've seen that the selling point of an object is that each object maintains its own state, but objects also benefit from sharing their behavior (their methods) with all other objects of the same class.

You already know that each turtle is its very own object—its very own independent instance, complete with its own set of attributes. That means each turtle has its own color, position, heading, and shape (to name a few attributes). Let's leverage that by creating a little game. Would you believe racing turtles?

> We're going to create a bunch of turtles, each with its own color and position, and then let them duke it out, racing across the screen. Place your bets!

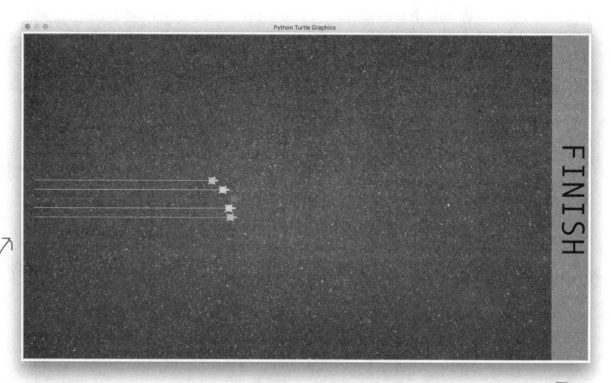

The starting line for the turtles is going to be on the left side the screen.

And they'll race toward the right side of the screen. The first turtle across the finish line wins.

Planning the game

You're going to see that treating our turtles as objects will make this game a lot easier to implement. Without them we'd presumably have to create and update a lot of variables to track the turtles and their positions, which would be messy business. But with turtle objects, we're just going to use the turtle's methods to move them on the screen, relying on each turtle to track its own state.

So, let's hash out a little pseudocode for how this racing game is going to work:

First we need to create our turtles, and assign each one to a different color and position on the starting line. Each turtle is a different instance of a Turtle, so we can do this!

1 **Set up game.**
Create a few turtles, each with its own color and position on the starting line.

We're going to let the race run until a turtle wins by crossing the finish line. But we need a way to know if a turtle has won. Let's create a variable called winner that is initially set to False, and then set it to True when a turtle crosses the line.

2 **Start the race.**
Set a variable **winner** to False.

While **winner** is false:

Now we're just going to cycle over each turtle, over and over, letting it make a move—that is, until one of them wins.

A For each turtle:

i Pick a random amount to move forward, say between 0 and 2 pixels.

Move forward.

To make a move, we'll generate a random number between 0 and 2 and move the turtle by that amount—and we'll do this for each turtle.

ii Check to see if turtle's position is across finish line. If so:

a Set **winner** to True.

Each time we move we need to check to see if the turtle crossed the finish line. And if so, we'll set winner to True.

3 **Game finishes.**
Announce the winner's name!

Once winner is set to True, the loop stops and we'll announce a winner.

Let's start coding

Let's first set up the game board and all the turtles, and then we'll move on to implementing the game logic. And, just to get the coding kicked off, we already know two modules we're going to need, namely the `turtle` module and the `random` module, so let's import those into our code. We're also going to use one global variable to hold the turtle racers, so let's add that too. Go ahead and create a new file called *race.py* and enter this code:

```
import turtle
import random

turtles = list()
```

← We'll need these modules.

And we'll use a list to hold all our turtles. Just to rub in the constructor syntax, we're creating an empty list by calling the list constructor. We could have used the shorthand [] like we have in the past.

Note, xcor and ycor are the x and y coordinates of the turtle in the window.

Setting up the game

Referring to our pseudocode, most of the setup consists of creating the set of turtles, each with its own attributes. To do that we need some idea of the turtles we want to create. How about these turtle objects:

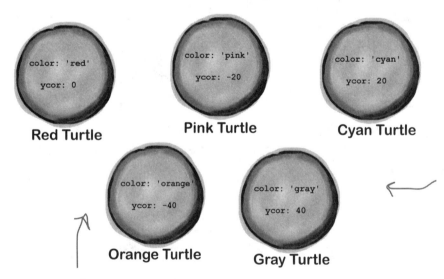

Turtle
color
shape
xcor
ycor
heading
forward()
backward()
turn()
penup()
pendown()

Red Turtle
color: 'red'
ycor: 0

Pink Turtle
color: 'pink'
ycor: -20

Cyan Turtle
color: 'cyan'
ycor: 20

Orange Turtle
color: 'orange'
ycor: -40

Gray Turtle
color: 'gray'
ycor: 40

These are objects instantiated from the Turtle class.

Each turtle has a name, a color, and a ycor, which is its vertical position on the start line. You'll see how this is used in a bit. Of course the turtle has all its other attributes too, but these are the ones we want to set up.

Writing the setup code

Now let's write the code to instantiate and set up those turtles. If you look at the turtle attributes on the previous page, we need a place to store those so we can intialize our turtles with those values. To do that, let's create a list that contains the values of each turtle's attributes—actually we'll need two lists, one for the y positions and one for color. Then we'll instantiate each turtle, and set its attributes to the appropriate values. Of course, let's put all this in a setup function like this:

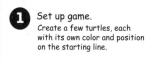

1 Set up game.
Create a few turtles, each with its own color and position on the starting line.

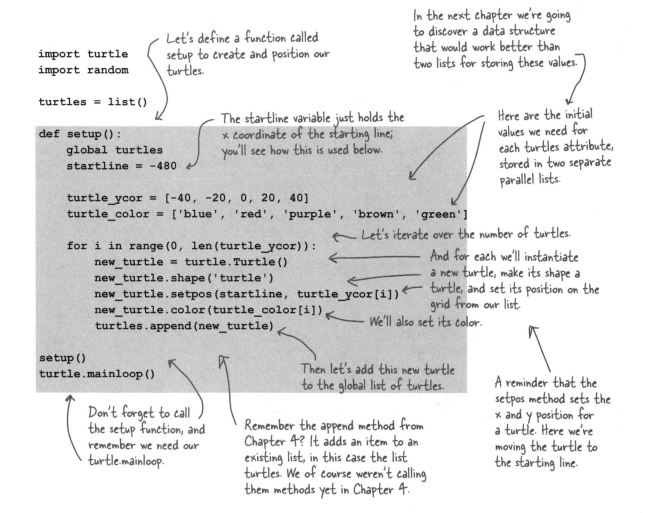

Let's define a function called setup to create and position our turtles.

In the next chapter we're going to discover a data structure that would work better than two lists for storing these values.

```
import turtle
import random

turtles = list()

def setup():
    global turtles
    startline = -480

    turtle_ycor = [-40, -20, 0, 20, 40]
    turtle_color = ['blue', 'red', 'purple', 'brown', 'green']

    for i in range(0, len(turtle_ycor)):
        new_turtle = turtle.Turtle()
        new_turtle.shape('turtle')
        new_turtle.setpos(startline, turtle_ycor[i])
        new_turtle.color(turtle_color[i])
        turtles.append(new_turtle)

setup()
turtle.mainloop()
```

The startline variable just holds the x coordinate of the starting line; you'll see how this is used below.

Here are the initial values we need for each turtles attribute, stored in two separate parallel lists.

Let's iterate over the number of turtles.

And for each we'll instantiate a new turtle, make its shape a turtle, and set its position on the grid from our list.

We'll also set its color.

Then let's add this new turtle to the global list of turtles.

A reminder that the setpos method sets the x and y position for a turtle. Here we're moving the turtle to the starting line.

Don't forget to call the setup function, and remember we need our turtle.mainloop.

Remember the append method from Chapter 4? It adds an item to an existing list, in this case the list turtles. We of course weren't calling them methods yet in Chapter 4.

Not so fast!

It would be easy to blow through that code on the last page. And, on the other hand, we could step you through every single line, but this is Chapter 7, and you're definitely up to the task of studying a little code. So, given there's a lot happening on the previous page, go back and make sure you understand every line until you know exactly what the code does. Then proceed...

A Test Drive

Update your code and let's give this a test drive to see how it is progressing before going further.

You may find the default window size on your machine is smaller than shown here. If you see the turtles fly off the left side of your window, adjust the width of your window until you can see them.

A step in the right direction, but this looks a little weird. What happened?

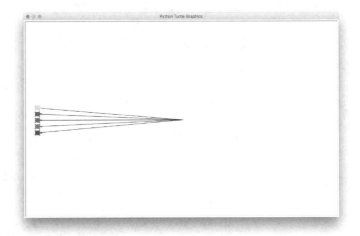

Our turtles are the right color and seem to be in the right position. But remember, they start life at coordinate 0,0, in the center of the window; so it looks like they drew lines on their way from the center to the start position, which isn't what we wanted. Let's add some code to pull their pen up on their way to the new position.

And while we're talking about the look and feel of the game, let's make the window a little bigger and add a nice background too.

A Test Drive

Check out the updated fixes: we're lifting up the turtle pen so it doesn't draw on the way to the starting position; we're also enlarging the window and adding a background image. Make these changes and try again. You'll want to grab the file *pavement.gif* from the chapter source files and place it in the same folder as *race.py*.

```python
import turtle
import random

turtles = list()

def setup():
    global turtles
    startline = -620
    screen = turtle.Screen()
    screen.setup(1290,720)
    screen.bgpic('pavement.gif')

    turtle_ycor = [-40, -20, 0, 20, 40]
    turtle_color = ['blue', 'red', 'purple', 'brown', 'green']

    for i in range(0, len(turtle_ycor)):
        new_turtle = turtle.Turtle()
        new_turtle.shape('turtle')
        new_turtle.penup()
        new_turtle.setpos(startline, turtle_ycor[i])
        new_turtle.color(turtle_color[i])
        new_turtle.pendown()
        turtles.append(new_turtle)

setup()
turtle.mainloop()
```

Don't miss this tiny change; we're going to move the turtles more to the left. Remember the center is at 0,0, so an x coordinate of -620 is far left on the screen.

These three lines use another object we haven't seen yet, the Screen object. With the Screen object we can make the window bigger and add a background image.

Let's pull up the pen before we move.

For now you can probably tell what this code is doing, but we're going to explore the Screen object more in Chapter 11.

And put it back down when we're done moving the turtle to the starting line.

Here's what we got! Now we're talkin'. We've got each turtle lined up on the starting line ready to go. Looks like we're in great shape to start on the actual game now.

Note the finish line is just part of the background image graphic.

Think about what's going on here: you've got five Turtle objects, all with their own internal state, including color and position.

Starting the race

Now it's time to get these turtles racing. We've got some nice pseudocode to guide us, so let's just work through it:

2 Start the race.
Set a variable **winner** to False.
While **winner** is false:

A For each turtle:

i Pick a random amount to move forward, say between 0 and 2 pixels.

Move forward.

ii Check to see if turtle's position is across finish line. If so:

a Set **winner** to True.

 First we need to get the winner variable set up. To do that let's create a new function called race. The winner variable is easily implemented as a Boolean initially set to False. We'll also be using the global turtles variable in this function too, so let's remember that in this code.

```
def race():
    global turtles
    winner = False
```

We're also going to add a local variable that holds the x position of the finish line:

The x value of 590 is located about here on the grid.

```
def race():
    global turtles
    winner = False
    finishline = 590
```

Now we are going to keep the game going until there is a winner. To do that we're going to start with a while statement, which will loop until the variable winner is set to True.

```
def race():
    global turtles
    winner = False
    finishline = 590

    while not winner:
```

We're going to endlessly loop until the winner variable is set to True.

A **Next we need to give the turtles a chance to move forward.** To do that we simply use a for/in statement over our global turtles lists.

```
def race():
    global turtles
    winner = False
    finishline = 590

    while not winner:
        for current_turtle in turtles:
```

And each time through the while loop we're going to iterate through every turtle, giving it a chance to move forward across the screen.

Now we use random numbers to move the turtles forward. So let's compute a number between 0 and 2 and move the turtle forward that many units.

```
def race():
    global turtles
    winner = False
    finishline = 590

    while not winner:
        for current_turtle in turtles:
            move = random.randint(0,2)
            current_turtle.forward(move)
```

Compute a random number between 0 and 2 and move the turtle forward that many units.

Finally we just need to check for a winner. Note that we have a winner if a turtle's xcor attribute is greater than or equal to finishline, which is set to 590. So, let's get the turtle's xcor attribute and do the comparison. If the turtle is over the finish line, we set winner to True and announce the winner.

```
def race():
    global turtles
    winner = False
    finishline = 590

    while not winner:
        for current_turtle in turtles:
            move = random.randint(0,2)
            current_turtle.forward(move)

            xcor = current_turtle.xcor()
            if (xcor >= finishline):
                winner = True
                winner_color = current_turtle.color()
                print('The winner is', winner_color[0])
```

Let's get the turtle's x coordinate to see if it's crossed the finish line. To do that, we use the xcor method, which returns a turtle's x coordinate.

Compare it to the finish line.

And if greater we have a winner.

Set the winner to True.

Note the color method returns two values, a pen color and a fill color. We're interested in the first one, the pen color, so we use the index 0 to get it.

Use the color method to get the winning turtle's color.

3 Game finishes
Announce the winner's name!

A Test Drive

We should be ready to race now. Get all the code additions made to your *race.py* file. You'll find the complete code below. So, place your bets and give it a true test drive.

```python
import turtle
import random

turtles = list()

def setup():
    global turtles
    startline = -620
    screen = turtle.Screen()
    screen.setup(1290,720)
    screen.bgpic('pavement.gif')

    turtle_ycor = [-40, -20, 0, 20, 40]
    turtle_color = ['blue', 'red', 'purple', 'brown', 'green']

    for i in range(0, len(turtle_ycor)):
        new_turtle = turtle.Turtle()
        new_turtle.shape('turtle')
        new_turtle.penup()
        new_turtle.setpos(startline, turtle_ycor[i])
        new_turtle.color(turtle_color[i])
        new_turtle.pendown()
        turtles.append(new_turtle)

def race():
    global turtles
    winner = False
    finishline = 590

    while not winner:
        for current_turtle in turtles:
            move = random.randint(0,2)
            current_turtle.forward(move)

            xcor = current_turtle.xcor()
            if (xcor >= finishline):
                winner = True
                winner_color = current_turtle.color()
                print('The winner is', winner_color[0])

setup()
race()
turtle.mainloop()
```

Remember the amount each turtle moves is random, so your mileage may vary.

Brown wins!

Don't forget to call race!

```
Python 3.6.0 Shell
The winner is brown
>>>
```

BRAIN POWER

Look at the code on the previous page. Say there is a photo finish and two or more turtles cross the finish line during the same iteration of the `while` loop. What happens? Who wins? Do you think this is the correct behavior?

WHO DOES WHAT?

With object-oriented programming there's a lot of new jargon flying around. In this game of who does what, match each piece of jargon to its description.

class   Things an object knows about.

object   Blueprint for an object.

methods   Act of creating an object from a class.

instantiate   The behavior an object can do.

attributes   Created from the blueprint.

instance   Another name for an object.

I feel like we've just only started and the chapter's already over.

Remember you can use Python's help on a class, like help(Turtle). Or even on a module, like help(turtle). Don't forget to import the turtle module first! We'll be getting experience with more classes and objects ahead in the book as well.

Don't worry, this isn't the end of objects.

You're right, we've barely scratched the surface. Object-oriented programming is a huge topic, one that would fill this entire book, and this chapter is just the beginning. Next time you encounter a **class** in a module you're going to know that you can **instantiate** it using its **constructor**. You're going to know it has **methods** and **attributes** that are accessible to you. And you're going to understand that each **instance** of any object you create has its own attributes.

You've also gained a general awareness now that all Python types are, in fact, classes, which is great because in the remaining chapters we're going to meet a lot of new classes and objects. And in Chapter 12 we'll break the surface and explore object-oriented programming, including topics like how to create your own classes. We'll see you when you get there.

Oh, and this chapter's not really over, anyway. You've got a mystery to solve, some bullet points to read, a crossword to do. But then you really should move on—we don't want things to get awkward.

Odd goings-on at the turtle races.

Since you've released your turtle racing code, something strange has started to happen: the green turtle is always winning, and by a large margin. The police are thinking someone has hacked the code. Can you take a look and see what is going on?

```python
import turtle
import random

turtles = list()

class SuperTurtle(turtle.Turtle):
    def forward(self, distance):
        cheat_distance = distance + 5
        turtle.Turtle.forward(self, cheat_distance)

def setup():
    global turtles
    startline = -620
    screen = turtle.Screen()
    screen.setup(1290,720)
    screen.bgpic('pavement.gif')

    turtle_ycor = [-40, -20, 0, 20, 40]
    turtle_color = ['blue', 'red', 'purple', 'brown', 'green']

    for i in range(0, len(turtle_ycor)):
        if i == 4:
            new_turtle = SuperTurtle()
        else:
            new_turtle = turtle.Turtle()
        new_turtle.shape('turtle')
        new_turtle.penup()
        new_turtle.setpos(startline, turtle_ycor[i])
        new_turtle.color(turtle_color[i])
        new_turtle.pendown()
        turtles.append(new_turtle)

def race():
    global turtles
    winner = False
    finishline = 590

    while not winner:
        for current_turtle in turtles:
            move = random.randint(0,2)
            current_turtle.forward(move)

            xcor = current_turtle.xcor()
            if (xcor >= finishline):
                winner = True
                winner_color = current_turtle.color()
                print("The winner is", winner_color[0])
setup()
race()

turtle.mainloop()
```

Whoa! Green is really fast!

FINISH

Study the code carefully; what has changed? What does this new code do? You won't be able to fully solve this mystery until Chapter 12, but do your best and think through what this code might be doing.

CRIME SCENE DO NOT ENTER   CRIME SCENE DO NOT ENTER   CRIME SCENE DO NOT ENTER

BULLET POINTS

- Modules are collections of Python variables, functions, and classes.

- Using the __name__ variable you can determine if your code is being imported or being run as the main program (by looking for a value of "__main__").

- In the Python Shell you can use the `help` function to see documentation on functions, modules, and classes.

- In your own code, add docstrings to supply help for programmers using your code.

- You'll find plenty of Python modules to explore in the areas of math, user interfaces, interacting with web services, dates and time, and pedagogy, to name a few.

- The turtle module provides an implementation of a turtle graphics system, originally developed at MIT for teaching.

- With turtle graphics, turtle objects live on a grid and can move and draw.

- Turtles are Python objects and include data and behavior.

- We call the data in Python objects attributes.

- Some languages use the name instance variables or properties for object attributes.

- An attribute can be assigned any valid Python value.

- The behavior in Python objects is known as methods.

- A method is a Python function that belongs to an object.

- You can access attributes and methods by using the dot notation on an object.

- Objects are created from classes. Classes supply a blueprint to create objects from.

- When we create a new object, we say that we instantiate it.

- An object instantiated from a class is known as an instance.

- An object is instantiated using a constructor method, defined in the class.

- Constructors do all the setup and initialization needed for an object.

- All types in Python are classes, including numbers, strings, lists, and so on.

Mod coding cross

Get more modular as you do the crossword.

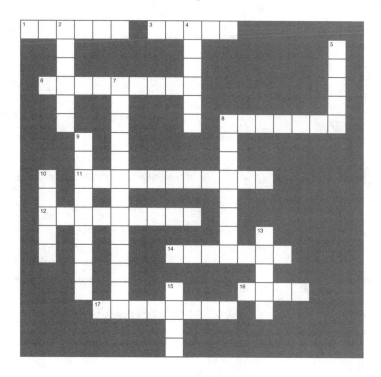

Across

1. Behavior of object.
3. Who won the first race?
6. Another name for instance variable.
8. Unit of turning a turtle.
11. Method that sets up object.
12. Data of object.
14. Command to move ahead.
16. Function to get documentation.
17. Another word for object.

Down

2. Graphics system from MIT.
4. Another word for instance.
5. Every type in Python is one.
7. Creating an object.
8. Famous science fiction author.
9. Type of string used in help.
10. Blueprint.
13. Which turtle did the hacker hack?
15. Value of __name__ when main program is run (excluding underscores).

Sharpen your pencil Solution

Hey, it's Chapter 7 already, so we're confident you're in good shape to take the turtle square code (on the previous page) and get it wrapped up in a nice function; call it `make_square`, which will take one parameter, a turtle. Write your code here and see how much you can clean things up by removing any duplicated code.

Notice we can pass any turtle into make_square, not just slow_poke.

```
import turtle

slowpoke = turtle.Turtle()
slowpoke.shape('turtle')

def make_square(the_turtle):
    the_turtle.forward(100)
    the_turtle.right(90)
    the_turtle.forward(100)
    the_turtle.right(90)
    the_turtle.forward(100)
    the_turtle.right(90)
    the_turtle.forward(100)
    the_turtle.right(90)

make_square(slowpoke)

turtle.mainloop()
```

← *Define a make_square function.*

← *And make sure you call the function.*

↖ *Step 1: get the code in a function and use it.*

```
import turtle

slowpoke = turtle.Turtle()
slowpoke.shape('turtle')

def make_square(the_turtle):
    for i in range(0,4):
        the_turtle.forward(100)
        the_turtle.right(90)

make_square(slowpoke)

turtle.mainloop()
```

We don't need all that duplicate code, we can just iterate over it four times.

Step 2: look at all that duplicated code in our function let's just iterate over the forward/right calls four times.

MORE TURTLE EXPERIMENTS SOLUTIONS

We've got even more turtle experiments for you below. Take a look at each one, guess what it does, and then run it to see if you were right. Change a few values; how does the output change?

Experiment #1

```
for i in range(5):
    slowpoke.forward(100)
    slowpoke.right(144)
```

Here's what we got. Did you get anything cool by tweaking the various variable values?

Experiment #2

```
slowpoke.pencolor('blue')
slowpoke.penup()
slowpoke.setposition(-120, 0)
slowpoke.pendown()
slowpoke.circle(50)

slowpoke.pencolor('red')
slowpoke.penup()
slowpoke.setposition(120, 0)
slowpoke.pendown()
slowpoke.circle(50)
```

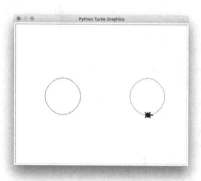

Experiment #3

```
def make_shape(t, sides):
    angle = 360/sides
    for i in range(0, sides):
        t.forward(100)
        t.right(angle)

make_shape(slowpoke, 3)
make_shape(slowpoke, 5)
make_shape(slowpoke, 8)
make_shape(slowpoke, 10)
```

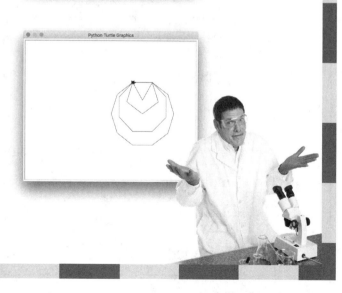

Sharpen your pencil
Solution

Fill in what a radio object might need to know and do.

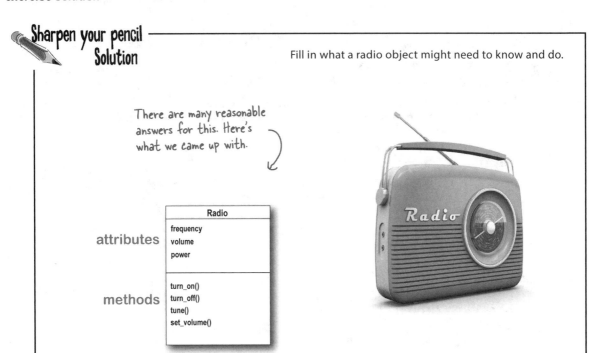

There are many reasonable answers for this. Here's what we came up with.

Radio
frequency
volume
power
turn_on()
turn_off()
tune()
set_volume()

attributes

methods

WHO DOES WHAT? SOLUTION

With object-oriented programming, there's a lot of new jargon flying around. In this game of who does what, match each piece of jargon to its description.

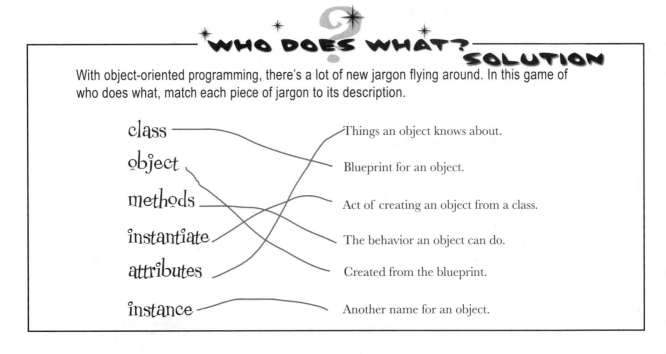

class — Things an object knows about.

object — Blueprint for an object.

methods — Act of creating an object from a class.

instantiate — The behavior an object can do.

attributes — Created from the blueprint.

instance — Another name for an object.

Mod cross Solution

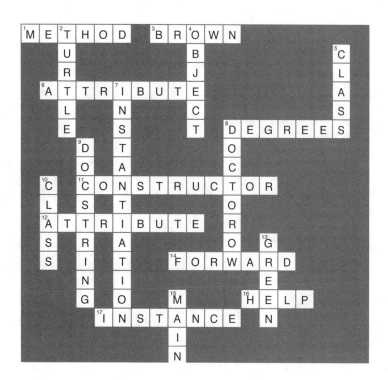

8 recursion and dictionaries

Beyond Iteration and Indices

It's time for a few new tools in that toolbelt.

It's time to take your computational thinking up a notch.

And this is the chapter to do it: we've been happily coding along with an iterative style of programming—we've created data structures like lists and strings and ranges of numbers, and we've written code to compute by iterating over them. In this chapter we're going to look at the world differently, first in terms of computation, and then in terms of data structures. Computationally we'll look at a style of computing that involves writing code that *recurs*, or calls itself. We'll expand the kinds of data structures we can work with by looking at a dictionary-like data type that is more like an *associative map* than a list. We'll then put them together and cause all kinds of trouble. Be forewarned: these topics take a while to settle into your brain, but the effort is going to pay off in spades.

A different way to compute

It's time for some mind-bending activity—you've been thinking about the same, iterative style of programming for too long. So let's expose your brain to a totally different way of thinking about solving problems.

Before we get there, though, let's take a simple problem and think it through the way we have throughout this book. For instance, take a handy list of numbers you want to sum up; it could be any numbers, say the number of marbles you and each of your friends has in his or her pockets. Now, Python does have a sum function that can be used to sum a list of numbers:

> We've got a list with each friend's count of marbles.

```python
marbles = [10, 13, 39, 14, 41, 9, 3]

print('The total is', sum(marbles))
```

Here we use Python's built-in sum function to tally up the marbles.

```
Python 3.6.0 Shell
The total is 129
>>>
```

But we're still learning about computation, so let's compute the sum the old-fashioned way (again, using what we've learned so far in this book) by writing code that uses iteration to tally the list. Like this:

> Let's define a function to compute a sum of numbers.

```python
def compute_sum(list):
    sum = 0

    for number in list:
        sum = sum + number

    return sum

print('The total is', compute_sum(marbles))
```

To compute the sum of a list of numbers, we start with a local variable, sum, set to zero, which will hold the running total.

Then we iterate through the list, and add each number to sum.

Finally, we return the sum.

Good, we got the same result.

Let's test this by calling compute_sum on our marbles list.

```
Python 3.6.0 Shell
The total is 129
>>>
```

BRAIN POWER

Pretend the folks who developed the Python language decided to remove any form of iteration (like the `for` and `while` loops). But you still needed to sum a list of numbers, so could you do it without iteration?

No! You can't use the built-in sum function either.

And now the different way...

There's another approach that computer scientists (and some in-the-know coders) use to break down problems. At first, this approach may seem a little like magic (or sleight of hand), but let's get a feel for it by revisiting our problem of summing our marbles. Here's how the approach works: we come up with two cases for summing our list of numbers: a *base case*, and a *recursive case*.

The base case is the simplest case you can think of. So what is the simplest list of numbers you can take the sum of? How about an empty list? What is its sum? Zero, of course!

An empty list
↓

```
compute_sum([])
```

Here's the simplest case: if we have an empty list, then we know the sum is going to be 0.

Now for the recursive case. With the recursive case we're going to solve a smaller version of the same problem. Here's how: we take the first item in the list, and add it to the sum of the rest of the list...

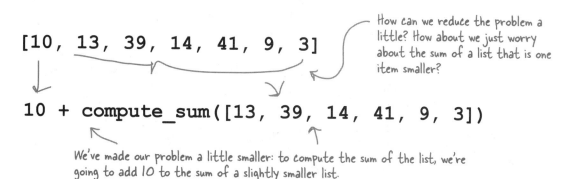

```
[10, 13, 39, 14, 41, 9, 3]
```

How can we reduce the problem a little? How about we just worry about the sum of a list that is one item smaller?

```
10 + compute_sum([13, 39, 14, 41, 9, 3])
```

We've made our problem a little smaller: to compute the sum of the list, we're going to add 10 to the sum of a slightly smaller list.

Now let's write some code for our two cases

Now that we have our base case and our recursive case, we're ready to code this new way of computing a sum. As we said up front, doing so is a little mind-bending for most, at least at first. So let's very slowly step through coding our new recursive sum function.

 For the base case our job is easy: we just need to see if the list is empty, and if so, return 0 as the sum of the list:

```
def recursive_compute_sum(list):
    if len(list) == 0:
        return 0
```

Here we check to see if the list is empty (in other words, if its size is 0), and if so, we return 0.

 The recursive case is less obvious. Let's take it a step at a time. We know that we're going to take the first item of the list and add it to the sum of the rest of the list. For clarity, let's first set up some variables to hold the first item and the remainder of the list (without the first item):

```
def recursive_compute_sum(list):
    if len(list) == 0:
        return 0
    else:
        first = list[0]
        rest = list[1:]
```

Here's our base case again.

Let's set a variable to the first item in the list, and another one to the rest of the list.

Remember your list notation? This returns a list starting at index 1 through the last element in the list.

What is the value of rest if the list only has one item? It's the empty list.

Now we need to add the first item to the sum of the remainder of the list:

```
def recursive_compute_sum(list):
    if len(list) == 0:
        return 0
    else:
        first = list[0]
        rest = list[1:]
        sum = first + Sum of rest of list
```

We need to sum the rest of the list, but isn't that exactly what we're coding? A way to sum lists? It feels like a conundrum.

The sum is the first item plus the sum of the rest of the list.

But how do we code this?

If only we knew how to compute the sum of the rest of the list, we'd be set. But how? Well, do you know of any good functions sitting around ready to compute the sum of a list? How about `recursive_compute_sum`?

```python
def recursive_compute_sum(list):
    if len(list) == 0:
        return 0
    else:
        first = list[0]
        rest = list[1:]
        sum = first + recursive_compute_sum(rest)
        return sum
```

Let's not forget to return the sum after we've computed it!

Our assumption up front was that the recursive_compute_sum computes the sum of lists, so let's call it to finish the job on the slightly smaller list.

A Test Drive

Whether you believe this code will work or not, go ahead and get the `recursive_compute_sum` code (repeated below, including some test code) into a file called *sum.py*. Save your code and choose the **Run > Run Module** menu item. After that, head to the console to see the sum magically computed.

```python
marbles = [10, 13, 39, 14, 41, 9, 3]

def recursive_compute_sum(list):
    if len(list) == 0:
        return 0
    else:
        first = list[0]
        rest = list[1:]
        sum = first + recursive_compute_sum(rest)
        return sum

sum = recursive_compute_sum(marbles)
print('The total is', sum)
```

We got the same result we did from iteration!

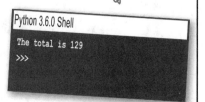

Python 3.6.0 Shell
The total is 129
>>>

Aren't we violating that "define your functions before you call them" rule we talked about? After all, the recursive_compute_sum function is called from within its own definition!

No. Remember a function body is not evaluated until the function is called. So, in this code, the function `recursive_compute_sum` is first defined. Then, when the `recursive_compute_sum` function is called with:

```
sum = recursive_compute_sum(marbles)
```

the function's body is then evaluated and calls itself to recur. When that happens, the `recursive_compute_sum` function is already defined, so we are not violating that rule.

If you're finding this takes a bit to wrap your head around, that's normal. The trick is deliberate practice: write as many recursive functions as you can. Trace through the execution and understand how and why recursive functions work.

We'll be tracing through some recursive code in just a bit.

On that topic, let's get some more practice...

Let's get some more practice

Have no fear: getting your brain to think recursively takes a little extra effort, but it's well worth the blood, sweat, and tears (you think we're kidding). Now, we could stop at this point and analyze the `recursive_compute_sum` to death, but the best way to get your brain thinking more recursively is deliberate practice: take problems and solve them recursively, and, of course, write the code.

Let's practice on another problem. Remember those palindromes from Chapter 4? You'll recall that palindromes are words that read the same forward as they do backward, like "tacocat":

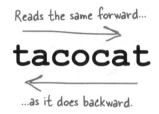

Reads the same forward...

tacocat

...as it does backward.

Want some more examples? How about "madam" or "radar" or "kayak," or there are even whole phrases (assuming you remove the punctutation and whitespace), like "a nut for a jar of tuna" or "a man, a plan, a canal: panama" or even more impressive, "a man, a plan, a cat, a ham, a yak, a yam, a hat, a canal: panama." Don't believe the last few? Try them; they're palindromes, alright.

Sharpen your pencil

Forget recursion for a bit, and think through how you might write a function to check if a word is a palindrome. Do that using the skills you learned in Chapters 1 through 7. Write some simple pseudocode to summarize your thoughts. Or, if you just had that cup of java and feel like writing some code, don't let us get in your way.

Using recursion to detect palindromes

So can we write a recursive function to detect palindromes? And if so, will we have gained anything? Let's give it a try and find out. Do you remember what to do? To write a recursive function we need a base case, and then we need a case that recurs by reducing the problem and then calling the same function recursively. Let's figure out the base and recursive cases:

The base case is the simplest case we can think of. We can actually think of two simple cases. First, how about an empty string? Is the empty string a palindrome? It reads the same front and backward, so yes.

The empty string

↓

`is_palindrome('')` ← Here's the simplest case: if we have an empty string, then we know it's a palindrome.

But there's another really simple case to consider: the case of a single letter. Is a single letter a palindrome? It's the same forward and backward, so yes.

`is_palindrome('a')` ← A single letter is a palindrome too; after all, it is the same read forward and backward.

Now for the recursive case. This is where things always get interesting. Remember, we want to reduce the problem size a little before asking our `is_palindrome` function to finish the job for us. How about we compare the outer two characters and if they are the same, we can then check to see if the middle of the word (which is a little smaller) is a palindrome?

Check the outermost characters to see if they are the same.

`'tacocat'`

`'acoca'`

And let our is_palindrome function worry about whether the middle is a palindrome.

Writing a recursive palindrome detector

We've got our base case and our recursive case, so once again we're ready to write our recursive code. As is typical, our base case is going to be fairly trivial to implement. Then we just need to wrap our minds around the recursive case. As with computing sums, the trick is always to reduce the problem a little and to rely on a recursive call to solve the problem.

 base case For the base case our job is easy: we just need to see if the word is the empty string or has one character:

```
def is_palindrome(word):
    if len(word) <= 1:
        return True
```

Let's check our base case to see if the word is the empty string (len is 0) or has one character (len is 1), and if so, return True.

 recursive case Now for the recursive case. First we're going reduce the problem by checking the outer two characters. If they match, we have a palindrome if all the rest of the letters (inside the two characters) make a word that is a palindrome. If not, we're going to return `False`:

```
def is_palindrome(word):
    if len(word) <= 1:
        return True
    else:
        if word[0] == word[-1]:


        else:
            return False
```

Here's our base case again.

Compare the first character to the last character to make sure they are equal. If not, we'll return False.

We'll think through the recursive call in the next step.

Now we need to finish the recursive case. At this point the code has determined the two outer characters are equal, so we have a palindrome *if the middle of the word is a palindrome,* and that's exactly what we need to code.

```
def is_palindrome(word):
    if len(word) <= 1:
        return True
    else:
        if word[0] == word[-1]:
            return is_palindrome(word[1:-1])
        else:
            return False
```

If the two ends match, then we need to see if the middle of the word is a palindrome. Good thing we have a function to do that—let's call it.

Note that we need to return the result of calling is_palindrome, which will ultimately return True or False.

A Test Drive

Go ahead and get the `is_palindrome` code (repeated below, including some test code) into a file called *palindrome.py*; save your code and choose the **Run > Run Module** menu item. After that head to the console to see if it is correctly detecting palindromes. Feel free to add your own palindrome candidates to the test as well.

```python
def is_palindrome(word):
    if len(word) <= 1:
        return True
    else:
        if word[0] == word[-1]:
            return is_palindrome(word[1:-1])
        else:
            return False
```

Take a look through the code again. Is this clearer than the iterative version? What do you think?

Looks like it works!

```python
words = ['tacocat', 'radar', 'yak', 'rader', 'kayjak']
for word in words:
    print(word, is_palindrome(word))
```

```
Python 3.6.0 Shell

tacocat True
radar True
yak False
rader False
kayjak False
>>>
```

there are no
Dumb Questions

Q: How do you know a recursive function will ever end?

A: In other words, if a function keeps calling itself, over and over, how does it ever stop? That's where the base condition comes in. The base condition acts as a piece of the problem we know we can solve directly, without the help of recursively calling the function again. So, when we hit the base condition, we know we've reached the point where the recursive calls stop.

Q: Okay, but how do we know if we'll ever get to the base case?

A: Remember each time we call the recursive case, we make the problem a little smaller before calling the function again. So, if you designed your code correctly, you can see that at some point, by making the problem repeatedly smaller, you will eventually reach the base case.

Q: I kinda get how we could call a function from itself—after all, it is just like any other function call—but how do all the parameters not get messed up? That is, each time I recursively call the function, the parameters are reassigned to a new set of arguments, right?

A: This is a very good question. You are right; each time you call a function, the parameters are bound to a set of arguments. To make matters worse, if it is a recursive call, we're calling the *same function*, and so those parameters are going to get rebound to other arguments—you'd think the whole thing would go haywire when those parameter values get overridden, right? Ah, but that isn't what happens. You see, Python and all modern languages keep track of every call to a function along with its corresponding set of parameters (and local variables). Hang tight; we're going to look at this in a sec.

Behind the Scenes

How is Python handling recursion and keeping track of all those calls to the same function? Let's take a look behind the scenes and see how `is_palindrome` is being computed by the Python interpreter.

```python
def is_palindrome(word):    ❶
    if len(word) <= 1:    ❷
        return True
    else:
        first = word[0]    ❸
        last = word[-1]
        middle = word[1:-1]
        if first == last:    ❹
            return is_palindrome(middle)❺
        else:
            return False
```

Here's the code again. Notice that we added some local variables that make the code a bit clearer. It also allows us to see how the variables work behind the scenes.

Let's evaluate this statement.

```
is_palindrome('radar')
```

❶ The first thing Python (or practically any language) does when it sees a function call is to create a data structure to hold its parameters and local variables. This is typically called a *frame*. Python first puts the value for the parameter `word` in the frame.

```
frame 1
  word = 'radar'
```

❷ Next we see if the word has a length of 1 or less, which it doesn't.

❸ Next we have three local variables that are created and set to the first, last, and middle portions of the word passed in. These values are added to the frame as well.

```
frame 1
  word = 'radar'
  first = 'r'
  last = 'r'
  middle = 'ada'
```

❹ Next we check to make sure the first and last characters are equal, which they are, so we then recursively call `is_palindrome`:

```
    return is_palindrome(middle)
```

Referring to frame 1, middle is 'ada'.

---

❶ We're back to another function call, so we need a new frame to hold the parameters and local variables. Python stores the multiple frames like a stack of plates, putting one on top of the other. We refer to the set of frames as a stack or *call stack*. That name kinda makes sense, doesn't it?

❷ Okay, next we can see this word is not <= 1 characters, so we move on to the `else` statement.

```
frame 2
  word = 'ada'

frame 1
  word = 'radar'
  first = 'r'
  last = 'r'
  middle = 'ada'
```

❸ Once again, we compute our local variables and
add them to the frame.

❹ And we can see that the first and last characters
are equal.

So, all that remains is to call `is_palindrome`
again.
```
return is_palindrome(middle)
```

Referring to frame 2,
middle is 'd'.

```
frame 2
  word = 'ada'
  first = 'a'
  last = 'a'
  middle = 'd'
frame 1
  word = 'radar'
  first = 'r'
  last = 'r'
  middle = 'ada'
```

---

❶ We're back to another function call, so we need
a new frame to hold the parameters and local
variables. At this point the `word` parameter is just
the string `'d'`.

❷ Finally, the length of the `word` parameter is finally
less than or equal to 1, meaning we return `True`.
When the call returns, we remove, or *pop*, the top
frame off the stack.

```
frame 3
  word = 'd'

frame 2
  word = 'ada'
  first = 'a'
  last = 'a'
  middle = 'd'
frame 1
  word = 'radar'
  first = 'r'
  last = 'r'
  middle = 'ada'
```

When we
return from
the function
its frame is
popped off
the stack.

---

❺ Now we need to return the result of calling
`is_palindrome`, which is `True`. So we pop
another frame off the stack as we return `True`.

```
frame 2
  word = 'ada'
  first = 'a'
  last = 'a'
  middle = 'd'
frame 1
  word = 'radar'
  first = 'r'
  last = 'r'
  middle = 'ada'
```

When we
return from
the function
its frame is
popped off
the stack.

---

❺ Again, now we need to return the result of calling
`is_palindrome`, which is `True`. Note this is the only
remaining frame that resulted from calls to `is_
palindrome`, so we're done (again, with a result of `True`).

```
frame 1
  word = 'radar'
  first = 'r'
  last = 'r'
  middle = 'ada'
```

Again, we pop
a frame off
the stack.

When we return from the initial call to `is_
palindrome`, we return the value `True`.

```
is_palindrome('radar')
```

Evaluates to True!

The stack is
now clear of
all calls to
is_palindrome.

Sharpen your pencil

Try evaluating some recursive code yourself. How about using our
`recursive_compute_sum` function?

```python
def recursive_compute_sum(list):
    if len(list) == 0:
        return 0
    else:
        first = list[0]
        rest = list[1:]
        sum = first + recursive_compute_sum(rest)
        return sum

recursive_compute_sum([1, 2, 3])
```

← Here's the code again.

And here we're calling the function.

`recursive_compute_sum([1, 2, 3])`

frame 1
list = [1, 2, 3]
first = 1
rest = [2, 3]

← We did the first one for you. The parameter list is bound to the list [1,2,3] and then the local variables first and rest get computed and added to the frame.

`recursive_compute_sum([2, 3])`

frame 2
list =
first =
rest =

frame 1
list = [1, 2, 3]
first = 1
rest = [2, 3]

Trace through the rest of the computation and fill in the stack details.

`recursive_compute_sum([3])`

frame 3
list =
first =
rest =

frame 2
list =
first =
rest =

frame 1
list = [1, 2, 3]
first = 1
rest = [2, 3]

`recursive_compute_sum([])`

```
frame 4
 list =
```
```
frame 3
 list =
 first =
 rest =
```
```
frame 2
 list =
 first =
 rest =
```
```
frame 1
 list = [1, 2, 3]
 first = 1
 rest = [2, 3]
```

`recursive_compute_sum([3])`

```
frame 3
 list =
 first =
 rest =
 sum =
```
```
frame 2
 list =
 first =
 rest =
```
```
frame 1
 list = [1, 2, 3]
 first = 1
 rest = [2, 3]
```

`recursive_compute_sum([2, 3])`

```
frame 2
 list =
 first =
 rest =
 sum =
```
```
frame 1
 list = [1, 2, 3]
 first = 1
 rest = [2, 3]
```

`recursive_compute_sum([1, 2, 3])`

```
frame 1
 list = [1, 2, 3]
 first = 1
 rest = [2, 3]
 sum =
```

Fireside Chats

Tonight's talk: **Iteration and Recursion answer the question "Who's better?"**

Iteration

To know I'm better, all you have to do is look at how many times coders use iteration over recursion.

What do you mean? Any modern language supports recursion, and yet coders opt to use me.

Last time I looked, this book was in Python.

Hah! Efficient? Ever heard of a call stack?

Every time a function calls itself, the Python interpreter has to create a little data structure to hold all the parameters and local variables of the current function. As the function gets called recursively, it has to maintain a whole stack of those data structures, which goes on and on as you keep calling the function over and over. Call it enough times and that adds up to a lot of memory, and then BOOM, your program goes bye bye.

Recursion

I think that depends on the language you're talking about.

Take a language like LISP or Scheme or Clojure, for instance—way more recursion is used than iteration.

That's not the point. The point is, some programmers know and understand recursion very well, and see the beauty and efficiency of using it.

Well, yes, and so have the readers, but please, do educate us.

Iteration

Right, but as I said, when you do it recursively, it's like abusing the system, and sooner or later there's going to be trouble.

Hasn't stopped millions of coders from writing palindromes iteratively.

Sure, for those brainiacs who get recursion.

You have to admit, for a lot of problems, iterative solutions are better.

I say why bother for a little clarity?

Oh, you mean for those Earth-Shattering-Grand-Challenge-type problems like finding palindromes?

You think talking about talking about the book in the book is...oh dear.

Recursion

That's actually the way any modern (or ancient, for that matter) language, including Python, works. Anytime you call a function, that is happening.

Not true. For many recursive algorithms, that isn't an issue and there are techniques for dealing with that, anyway. The point is, look at the clarity of using a recursive solution. Palindromes were a good example; look how ugly and unclear the iterative code was.

My point is, for some algorithms the recursive one is easier to think about and code.

Oh please, as we've seen it just takes a little practice.

I wouldn't say better, I'd say more natural, but I'd also say for some problems recursion is more natural.

It's not just that the code is more readable, it's that there are algorithms that are downright hard to code iteratively, but that work out easily and naturally with recursion.

Of course not; however, maybe we'll see one before the end of this book.

By the way, you don't find the fact we're talking about the book *in the book* slightly recursive? Recursion is everywhere.

RECURSION LAB

Today we're testing the code for a recursive algorithm that computes the *Fibonacci sequence*. The sequence produces a set of numbers that appear often in nature and can describe shapes, like the pattern of seeds in a sunflower or the shape of galaxies.

It works like this:

fibonacci(0) = 0
fibonacci(1) = 1

If you evaluate the function with 0 you get 0, and if you evaluate it with 1 you get 1.

fibonacci(n) = fibonacci(n-1) + fibonacci(n-2)

And for any other number, n, we produce the Fibonacci number by adding fibonacci(n-1) to fibonacci(n-2).

The Fibonacci sequence is related to the Golden Ratio, which appears often in nature and is considered by many artists to be related to good design.

Here are a few values from the sequence:

fibonacci(0) is 0
fibonacci(1) is 1
fibonacci(2) is 1
fibonacci(3) is 2
fibonacci(4) is 3
fibonacci(5) is 5
fibonacci(6) is 8

Every number in the sequence is computed by adding the two Fibonacci numbers before it.

and continuing from there... 13, 21, 34, 55, 89, 144, 233, 377, 610, 987, 1597, 2584, 4181...and so on.

In the lab we've developed an algorithm to compute Fibonacci numbers. Let's take a look:

Working from the definition above...

```
def fibonacci(n):
    if n == 0:
        return 0
    elif n == 1:
        return 1
    else:
        return fibonacci(n-1) + fibonacci(n-2)
```

base case

recursive case

If n is 0 or 1, we just return that number.

Otherwise, we return the sum of the two previous Fibonacci numbers in the sequence, by recursively calling fibonacci.

Did you notice the recursive case calls fibonacci not once but twice!

Now it's time to test the code. Here in the Recursion Lab we need it to be correct and fast. To do that we've developed a little test code using a new module, `time`, which is going to help us time our code's execution.

```
import time
```
← We're going to use Python's time module to time our code execution; see below.

```
def fibonacci(n):
    if n == 0:
        return 0
    elif n == 1:
        return 1
    else:
        return fibonacci(n-1) + fibonacci(n-2)
```
← Here's the recursive Fibonacci code.

Test code. ↘

```
for i in range(20, 55, 5):
    start = time.time()      ← Start timer.
    result = fibonacci(i)    ← Compute the Fibonacci.
    end = time.time()        ← End timer.
    duration = end - start   ← Compute duration.
    print(i, result, duration)  ← Print results.
```

As a test we're going to compute the Fibonacci numbers 20 through 50, counting by fives. If that goes well, we'll compute all 100.

We're also going to time each computation of Fibonacci. To do that we're going to use a module called time. See Appendix A for more on date and time modules.

You job is to get this code entered and to perform the test run. When you get the data, record it below, including the value of n, the Fibonacci number, and how long it took to compute, in seconds. **For this code to be used in production, it has to compute the first 100 Fibonacci numbers in less than 5 seconds. Based on this test run, would we pass?**

If this program is taking too long to execute, you can always stop it by closing the shell window it's running in.

Here's what we got for the first test, n=20. Your timings may differ depending on the speed of your computer.

Fibonacci Test Data

Number	Answer	Time to compute
20	6765	.002 seconds

Our results are on the next page; compare them with yours!

So far it looks nice and fast!

RECURSION LAB FAIL

To meet Recusion Lab standards, this code has to compute the first 100 Fibonacci numbers in less than 5 seconds. How did you do? What? You had lunch and they are still computing? No worries—we went ahead and computed the results. Our numbers are below, but they don't look encouraging at all.

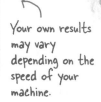

The code is working great in that we're getting the right answers.

Fibonacci Test Data

Number	Answer	Time to compute
20	6765	0.002 seconds
25	75025	0.04 seconds
30	832040	0.4 seconds
35	9227465	4.8 seconds
40	102334155	56.7 seconds
45	1134903170	10.5 minutes
50	12586269025	1.85 hours

Your own results may vary depending on the speed of your machine.

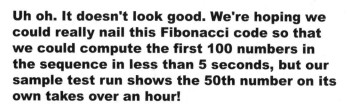

But while the execution time started very fast, it is getting slower and slower the larger n is. At 50 we're taking almost 111 minutes to compute just that one Fibonacci number!

Uh oh. It doesn't look good. We're hoping we could really nail this Fibonacci code so that we could compute the first 100 numbers in the sequence in less than 5 seconds, but our sample test run shows the 50th number on its own takes over an hour!

Are we doomed? What on earth is taking so long? Give it some thought, and we'll come back to this after learning about an interesting data structure (maybe it will help us?).

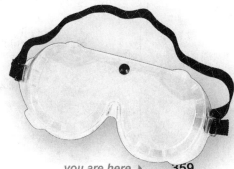

The Anti-Social Network

You've really started to develop some coding chops. In fact, we think you've got the skills to create a prototype to launch your first startup. And we even have an idea for the startup: *a new social network*. Wait, what? Oh, you've had quite enough of Facebook and its competitors? No worries—actually the *Anti-Social Network* is just what you've been looking for. With the Anti-Social Network it's easy to communicate sentiments like "turn that smile upside down" or "if you're happy and you know it, then get away from me" to your network of, umm, friends. The Anti-Social Network also has this killer feature where you can see the top anti-social user at any time. Sounds like a billion-dollar idea to us; all you need to do is get started.

Let's start simple: the first thing we need is to maintain a list of users. For each user we'll store a name and an email address.

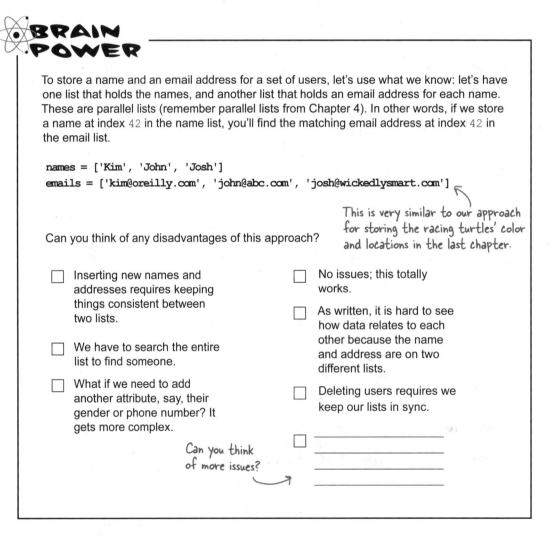

BRAIN POWER

To store a name and an email address for a set of users, let's use what we know: let's have one list that holds the names, and another list that holds an email address for each name. These are parallel lists (remember parallel lists from Chapter 4). In other words, if we store a name at index `42` in the name list, you'll find the matching email address at index `42` in the email list.

```
names = ['Kim', 'John', 'Josh']
emails = ['kim@oreilly.com', 'john@abc.com', 'josh@wickedlysmart.com']
```

This is very similar to our approach for storing the racing turtles' color and locations in the last chapter.

Can you think of any disadvantages of this approach?

☐ Inserting new names and addresses requires keeping things consistent between two lists.

☐ We have to search the entire list to find someone.

☐ What if we need to add another attribute, say, their gender or phone number? It gets more complex.

Can you think of more issues?

☐ No issues; this totally works.

☐ As written, it is hard to see how data relates to each other because the name and address are on two different lists.

☐ Deleting users requires we keep our lists in sync.

☐ _____
  _____
  _____

If only I could find a data
structure that actually allowed me to give
each item a nice memorable name without having to
deal with indices in a list. And a data structure I could
just add to without having to worry about where in
a list I'm putting it. And a data structure in which I
could look up values quickly, without having to search the
whole list. That would be dreamy. But I know it's just a
fantasy...

Introducing the dictionary

Meet Python's *dictionary* data type. A dictionary, often called a *map* or an *associative array* (by those computer science types), is a powerful and versatile data structure. Given its versatility, we're going to cover a few different ways you can use one, including using one to solve our Anti-Social Network problems (that is, finding a better way to store and retrieve our users). Before that, though, let's first get acquainted with the dictionary and how it works.

The first thing to know is that, unlike Python lists, dictionaries are an *unordered* data type. With a list each value is stored in order according to its index. If we want the third value in the list, we can ask for it by its index. Dictionary items don't have an inherent order; rather, each *value* stored in a dictionary is accessed by a *key*. To access a value in a dictionary, we present its key.

Let's see how to create a dictionary

```
my_dictionary = {}
```

Use two curly braces to create an empty dictionary that is all ready to hold keys and values.

Remember, use curly braces for dictionaries and square brackets for lists.

And then add items

A dictionary stores items as key/value pairs. Say we have a phone number 867-5309 that we need to store for our friend Jenny:

```
my_dictionary['jenny'] = '867-5309'
```

Here we're storing this value, a phone number in the form of a string, under the key 'jenny', also a string.

And you can store any number of key/value pairs. Let's store a few more:

```
my_dictionary['paul'] = '555-1201'
my_dictionary['david'] = '321-6617'
my_dictionary['jamie'] = '771-0091'

my_dictionary['paul'] = '443-0000'
```

We can store as many key/value pairs as we like.

Storing a value at a key that already exist, overwrites its previous value.

And then retrieve values by their keys

To retrieve a value from a dictionary, we just use the key:

```
phone_number = my_dictionary['jenny']
print("Jenny's number is", phone_number)
```

Python 3.6.0 Shell

Jenny's number is 867-5309
>>>

Keys and values do not have to be strings

For keys you can use numbers, strings, or Booleans. For dictionary values you can use any valid Python value. Here are some examples:

```
my_dictionary['age'] = 27
my_dictionary[42] = 'answer'
my_dictionary['scores'] = [92, 87, 99]
```

We can have a string key and an integer value, an integer key and a string value, a string key and a list value, and so on, using any of Python's data types as a value.

There are a few other types that can act as keys as well, but we haven't covered them yet.

Of course you can remove keys as well

```
del my_dictionary['david']
```

This removes the key 'david' along with its value from the dictionary.

Remember, we can use the del statement on other things too, like Python lists.

But you might want to test to see if it exists first

Python is quite consistent in how you test to see if an item is part of a set of things (which coders often call a *collection*), like a list or string, and the same holds for dictionaries. You can test to see if a key is in a dictionary like this:

You can also use the pop method on a dictionary, which removes the key and returns the value to you.

```
if 'jenny' in my_dictionary:
    print('Found her', my_dictionary['jenny'])
else:
    print('I need to get her number')
```

Use the in operator to check to see if the key exists in the dictionary.

So we should have written the code to delete an item above as:

```
if 'david' in my_dictionary:
    del(my_dictionary['david'])
```

there are no Dumb Questions

Q: What happens if I try to delete a key that doesn't exist??

A: Python will raise a runtime exception known as a KeyError. We'll be talking about how to handle exceptions later in the book, but you can avoid them by testing to see if the key exists first.

Q: So there's only one of every key in a dictionary?

A: Right. In other words, each key is unique within a dictionary. For instance, there is only one key 'Kim' in my_dictionary; if you were to assign a value to that key a second time, it would overwrite the previous value.

Q: I can see the convenience of using a dictionary, but I'm guessing that not having indices is going to make things less efficient. Am I going to have to worry about performance when I use dictionaries for a lot of data?

A: Remember how we promised this chapter would be a little mind-bending? Well, as it turns out, for many applications, dictionaries are way more efficient than using a list to store the same data. Hold on to that thought; we're going to get to it soon.

Q: Given we can use the built-in operator del on a dictionary, can we use len too?

A: You sure can. The **len** operator will tell you the total number of keys in the dictionary.

What about iterating through a dictionary?

The one thing to remember about dictionaries is they are unordered.
You can iterate through the keys, just don't expect them to be in any
particular order.

 As with lists and strings, use
the for/in statement to iterate
through the keys of a dictionary.

```
for key in my_dictionary:
    print(key, ':', my_dictionary[key])
```

Let's print the key...

...followed by its value
in the dictionary.

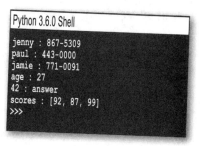

```
Python 3.6.0 Shell

jenny : 867-5309
paul : 443-0000
jamie : 771-0091
age : 27
42 : answer
scores : [92, 87, 99]
>>>
```

Your order may be different
and that's just fine.

Okay, but can we get literal for a sec?

As with lists, there's also a literal notation for creating dictionaries,
which looks like this:

```
harry = {'firstname': 'Harry',
         'lastname': 'Potter',
         'house': 'Gryffindor',
         'friends': ['Ron', 'Hermione'],
         'born': 1980}
```

Each key/value is separated by a colon,
and followed by a comma (except for the
final pair).

This creates a full-fledged
dictionary.

You can also print a dictionary to see its literal form:

```
print(my_dictionary)
```

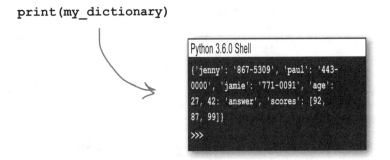

```
Python 3.6.0 Shell

{'jenny': '867-5309', 'paul': '443-
0000', 'jamie': '771-0091', 'age':
27, 42: 'answer', 'scores': [92,
87, 99]}

>>>
```

Watch it!

Never count on dictionary order

Even if you find the keys in your dictionary are always in the same order, you won't be able to count on that fact across different operating systems and implementations of Python. Just remember, if you're counting on the order of a dictionary, you're going to run into trouble sooner or later.

Sharpen your pencil

Now that you've got some book
knowledge of dictionaries, it's time
to put that knowledge to work. Work
through the code below to see what it
computes.

```
movies = []         ← List
movie = {}          ← Dictionary

movie['name'] = 'Forbidden Planet'
movie['year'] = 1957
movie['rating'] = '*****'
movie['year'] = 1956

movies.append(movie)

movie2 = {'name': 'I Was a Teenage Werewolf',
          'year': 1957, 'rating': '****'}
movie2['rating'] = '***'

movies.append(movie2)

movies.append({'name': 'Viking Women and the Sea Serpent',
               'year': 1957,
               'rating': '**'})

movies.append({'name': 'Vertigo',
               'year': 1958,
               'rating': '*****'})

print('Head First Movie Recommendations')
print('------------------------------')
for movie in movies:
    if len(movie['rating']) >= 4:
        print(movie['name'], '(' + movie['rating'] + ')',  movie['year'])
```

Leveraging dictionaries at the Anti-Social Network

Having read the last few pages, you know 95% of everything there is to know about using Python dictionaries, except, well, *how to* actually use them. Sure, you can store and retrieve values, but there has to be more to it than that, right? Yes, simplicity can be deceptive. Let's look at how you might use dictionaries at the Anti-Social Network.

Recall that when we last left off, we needed to store a set of names with email addresses. We started by using two lists, which turned out to be rather clumsy because adding new names required adding to both lists, as did deleting names; looking up a name meant we had to search over the entire list; and adding more properties, like say the user's gender, was going to require an entirely new list to manage. Yuck. Well, let's see if we can do better with dictionaries.

Here are some users and their emails stored in two lists.

```python
names = ['Kim', 'John', 'Josh']
emails = ['kim@oreilly.com', 'john@abc.com', 'josh@wickedlysmart.com']
```

Let's see if a dictionary can help us.

Well, that is certainly more readable!

```python
users = {'Kim' : 'kim@oreilly.com',
         'John': 'john@abc.com',
         'Josh': 'josh@wickedlysmart.com'}
```

What about adding new users, or removing them?

```python
users['Avary'] = 'avary@gmail.com'
del users['John']
```

Adding

Removing

Okay, that was easy—no worrying about having two lists to keep in sync.

What about quickly getting a user's email address? Let's say we're after Josh's email address:

```python
if 'Josh' in users:
    print("Josh's email address is:", users['Josh'])
```

Let's first check to make sure the key 'Josh' exists, and if it does, we grab the email address.

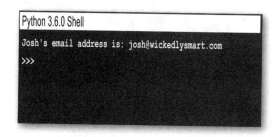

```
Python 3.6.0 Shell
Josh's email address is: josh@wickedlysmart.com
>>>
```

I've gotta admit, from a coding perspective this is so much nicer than dealing with two lists. But is this really as efficient as using explicit indices?

The dictionary is more efficient, by a long shot.

To understand why, you have to understand how dictionaries actually work behind the scenes. Let's start with a list as an example: if you looked up "Josh" in a list of users, you'd have to go through every single user in the list until you found Josh. In the worst case, that means you'd have to go through the entire list.

Dictionaries use a data structure behind the scenes that's known as a *hash map*. With a hash map the dictionary stores all the values in a list or array-like data structure, but it uses a special function, known as a *hash function*, to compute where the value is in that list, based on the key. So, rather than brute-force searching the entire list, a dictionary, by way of the hash function, can go right to the index where the value is located. Lucky for you, the dictionary does all this for you.

Now hash functions aren't perfect, and sometimes multiple values may be mapped to one location (the dictionary knows how to deal with this case), but this isn't likely to happen often, so the average time to look up a value based on a key is *constant time* (you can think of constant time as the time it takes to perform a single operation). So, when searching for keys, dictionaries are blindingly fast.

A computer science term

But how do we add more attributes?

Managing the Anti-Social Network usernames and email addresses with a dictionary seems like a real win, but remember we also wanted to potentially add some attributes, like a user's gender. Now, we know if we're using parallel lists then we'd need another list to hold the genders, but with dictionaries, don't we need to use another dictionary too? Something like:

```
email = {'Kim' : 'kim@oreilly.com',
         'John': 'john@abc.com',
         'Josh': 'josh@wickedlysmart.com'}

genders = {'Kim' : 'f',
           'John': 'm',
           'Josh': 'm'}
```

We could do it this way, but now we're back to managing two data structures anytime we add, delete, or look up a user. Yuck again.

Sure, that would work, but then we're back to managing two data structures—that's obviously not what we want. To solve this problem, we need to think a little deeper about how to use dictionaries. What if we use a dictionary to hold all the attributes for each user, like this:

```
attributes = {
        'email' : 'kim@oreilly.com',
        'gender': 'f',
        'age': 27,
        'friends': ['John', 'Josh']
}
```

Here's a dictionary holding the attributes for Kim. We can create a dictionary like this for every user.

Notice we've added a new list to each user as well, a list of friends. This will play into our killer feature.

With this new scheme, let's start over, create a brand new users dictionary, and store Kim's attributes:

```
users = {}
users['Kim'] = attributes
```

We're setting the users variable to an empty dictionary, and then adding the attributes dictionary under the key 'Kim'.

Don't move too quickly and overlook what is going on in this code. We're making the value of the 'Kim' key another dictionary, the attributes dictionary.

Let's add John and Josh too:

```
users['John'] = {'email' : 'john@abc.com','gender': 'm', 'age': 24, 'friends': ['Kim', 'Josh']}
users['Josh'] = {'email' : 'josh@wickedlysmart.com','gender': 'm', 'age': 32, 'friends': ['Kim']}
```

Same here: don't move too quickly and overlook what is going on in this code. We're assigning dictionaries to 'John' and 'Josh' as well.

We're assigning dictionaries to the keys 'John' and 'Josh'. We're specifying those dictionaries with the literal syntax.

Sharpen your pencil

Dictionaries in dictionaries—it's a common arrangement. See how it plays out at the cinema by using your brain to execute the code below.

```
movies = {}
movie = {}

movie['name'] = 'Forbidden Planet'
movie['year'] = 1957
movie['rating'] = '*****'
movie['year'] = 1956

movies['Forbidden Planet'] = movie

movie2 = {'name': 'I Was a Teenage Werewolf',
          'year': 1957, 'rating': '****'}
movie2['rating'] = '***'
movies[movie2['name']] = movie2

movies['Viking Women and the Sea Serpent'] = {'name': 'Viking Women and the Sea Serpent',
                                              'year': 1957,
                                              'rating': '**'}

movies['Vertigo'] =  {'name': 'Vertigo',
                      'year': 1958,
                      'rating': '*****'}

print('Head First Movie Recommendations')
print('--------------------------------')
for name in movies:
    movie = movies[name]
    if len(movie['rating']) >= 4:
        print(movie['name'], '(' + movie['rating'] + ')',  movie['year'])

print('Head First Movie Staff Pick')
print('---------------------------')
movie = movies['I Was a Teenage Werewolf']
print(movie['name'], '(' + movie['rating'] + ')',  movie['year'])
```

Brain Building

Now that we know how we're going to store our users on the Anti-Social Network, it's time to write a little code. Let's create a function we might need for the startup, called `average_age`, that takes a name and returns the average age of that user's friends. We're letting you tackle this on your own—after all, it is Chapter 8—although don't forget to write some some pseudocode or do similar planning, as it goes a long ways toward writing correct code the first time.

```python
users = {}
users['Kim'] = {'email' : 'kim@oreilly.com','gender': 'f', 'age': 27, 'friends': ['John', 'Josh']}
users['John'] = {'email' : 'john@abc.com','gender': 'm', 'age': 24, 'friends': ['Kim', 'Josh']}
users['Josh'] = {'email' : 'josh@wickedlysmart.com','gender': 'm', 'age': 32, 'friends': ['Kim']}
```

← *Write your average_age function here.*

```python
average_age('Kim')
average_age('John')
average_age('Josh')
```

Here's the output you should get with this test code.

```
Python 3.6.0 Shell
Kim's friends have an average age of 28.0
John's friends have an average age of 29.5
Josh's friends have an average age of 27.0
>>>
```

Remember the Anti-Social Network's killer feature?

You didn't forget, did you? It's going to be the crucial feature to demo when raising your seed round of investor cash. The killer feature for the Anti-Social Network is finding the least social person at any time—that is, the user with the fewest friends. All we need to do is write the code.

So let's take stock: we've got a dictionary of users, and each entry in that dictionary consists of a key, which is the user's name, and a value, which is another dictionary full of the user's attributes. One of those attributes is a list of friends. So, we're going to have to iterate through all the users and keep track of who has the least friends. Let's give it a shot.

Who will it be?

Exercise

Finding the most anti-social user

The code for finding the most anti-social user isn't going to be the most complex we've written, but let's just hash it out in a little pseudocode so we have a clear picture of what we're doing:

1 Set max to large number ⟵ We're going to create a variable to hold the current most anti-social count. We'll call it max and initialize it to something large for starters.

2 For each name in users ⟵ Iterate through every key in the users dictionary.

   A Get the user attribute dictionary. ⟵ For each user, grab the dictionary of attributes associated with the name.

   B Get the list of friends from the attribute dictionary. ⟵ Use the 'friends' key to grab the list of friends.

   C If number of friends is less than max ⟵ If the number of friends is less than any we've seen so far (max), then that's our current least candidate.

      i set variable most_anti_social to name. ⟵ Set a variable most_anti_social to the name...

      ii set variable max to number of friends ...and max to the new number of friends.

3 Print user with key most_anti_social ⟵ When we've been through all the keys in names, we then have the most_anti_social user. Let's print it, and so on.

Sharpen your pencil

Now that we have some pseudocode, use your new knowledge of dictionaries to complete this code. After that we'll get it running.

```
max = 1000
for name in _____:
    user = _____[_____]
    friends = user[_____]
    if len(_____) < max:
        most_anti_social = _____
        max = len(_____)

print('The most_anti_social user is', _____)
```

A Test Drive

Let's get this code in and test it (it's been a few pages since we ran real code). Put the code below in a file called *antisocial.py*. Give it a run, and double-check your output.

```python
users = {}
users['Kim'] = {'email' : 'kim@oreilly.com','gender': 'f', 'age': 27, 'friends': ['John', 'Josh']}
users['John'] = {'email' : 'john@abc.com','gender': 'm', 'age': 24, 'friends': ['Kim', 'Josh']}
users['Josh'] = {'email' : 'josh@wickedlysmart.com','gender': 'm', 'age': 32, 'friends': ['Kim']}

max = 1000
for name in users:
    user = users[name]
    friends = user['friends']
    if len(friends) < max:
        most_anti_social = name
        max = len(friends)

print('The most_anti_social user is', most_anti_social)
```

```
Python 3.6.0 Shell

The most_anti_social user is Josh
>>>
```

That Josh! →

Now, it's all you!

That's about as far as we're going to take the Anti-Social Network because we think you're in a good position to take it forward on your own. The idea and the code are yours, so run with it and send us a postcard when you're rich and famous (although maybe postcard is a little too social for the founders of the Anti-Social Network).

We're not quite done with dictionaries, though, as we've got another hoop we're going to make them jump through...

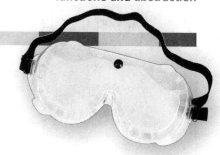

Meanwhile, back at the...
RECURSION LAB

We last left the Recursion Lab in a bit of a demoralized state. While we needed to compute the first 100 Fibonacci numbers in less than 5 seconds, it took us much longer. So long, in fact, that the 50th alone took over an hour. Given that, is there any hope? Of course.

But we can't make progress if we don't figure out why our computation is so slow. Let's start by looking at the recursive calls that are made when we compute, say, `fibonacci(50)`:

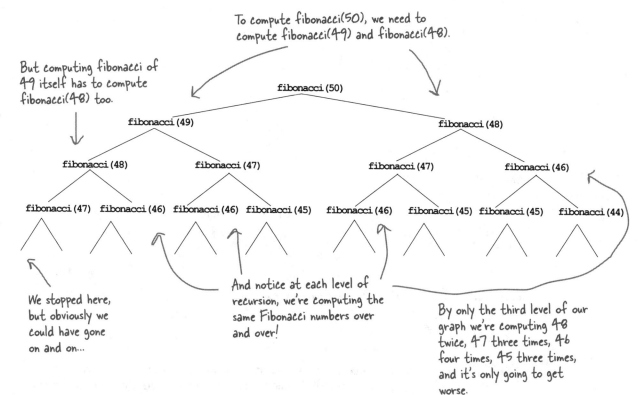

So while our code is logically correct and clear, it is very inefficient. For any number, the algorithm has to compute all the Fibonacci numbers less than that number. That leads to a lot of unnecessary computation because we're repeatedly computing the same Fibonacci numbers over and over again. Every time we need `fibonacci(5)`, we have to recompute `fibonacci(4)`, `fibonacci(3)`, and `fibonacci(2)` as well.

Sharpen your pencil

Try drawing a graph of all the function calls it takes to compute `fibonacci(7)`. When you're done, total up how many duplicated calls you find for each value 0 through 7.

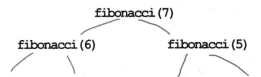

Put your totals here. We've already filled in the answer to fibonacci(7), which is called one time, as is fibonacci(6).

fibonacci(7): <u>1 time</u>   **fibonacci(6):** <u>1 time</u> **fibonacci(5):** _____

fibonacci(4): _____   **fibonacci(3):** _____   **fibonacci(2):** _____

fibonacci(1): _____   **fibonacci(0):** _____

Warning: you may find the answer shocking.

Any guess how many times `fibonacci(50)` has to compute `fibonacci(3)`? _____

BRAIN POWER

We're computing the same Fibonacci numbers over and over again. Without drastically changing the code, think about how we might make this code way more efficient. Put your ideas here.

If only there was a way to store previous function call results so that if the function gets called with the same value again, we just remember its previous result rather than having to recompute it every time. I know it's just a fantasy...

Can we just remember function call results?

It's not a bad idea. So, for instance, if fibonacci is called with the argument 49, the result is computed and stored, so the next time fibonacci is called with 49, the function can look up the result, rather than recomputing it.

With the Fibonacci code recomputing so many function calls, if we could just store the results rather than recomputing them, we'd probably shave a lot of time off the execution. But can we really save hours of computation time? We shall see.

So what would we need to store the results of the calls to the fibonacci function? We need a way to store the value of the n argument, and also the result that gets computed for fibonacci(n). Oh, and we'd need to be able to access the computed result quickly, for a given value of n.

Any ideas? Is this sounding familiar?

Using a dictionary to remember our Fibonacci results

Does this sound like a job made for a dictionary? Let's take a look at how it might work.

> A cache is a common name for a place to store data you need quick access to.

1 Create a dictionary, and name it cache.

2 Every time fibonacci is called with a number n:

   A Check if there is a key, n, in the cache.

      i If so, return the value of key n.

   B Otherwise, compute the Fibonacci number of n.

   C Store the result in the cache under the key n.

   D Return the value of the Fibonacci number.

So each time the Fibonacci code function is called with a value n, we first check our dictionary, cache, to see if a key n is already in the cache. If it is, great, that's the Fibonacci number for n, so just return it as the result of calling the function.

If not, we compute the Fibonacci number as we always do, but before we return the result, we first stash it in the cache for the key n.

We might as well use the $5 words: memoization

If you thought we just made up this brilliant idea of storing function call results, well, we wish we did, but we didn't. In fact, it's a simple but powerful technique called *memoization*. Memoization can be thought of as a way to optimize a program by storing the results of expensive function calls. What's expensive? Well, how much you got? Just kidding. In computer science terms, expensive typically means a computation takes a lot of time or consumes a lot of space (typically memory). Whether you're trying to optimize time or space really depends on what your code does, but in our case it's mostly time we're trying to optimize.

So how does memoization work? You already know, becasue the pseudocode we wrote on the previous page is an implementation of memoization.

To understand it better, let's rework our existing code using the pseudocode as a guide. Doing so is pretty straightforward:

```python
import time

cache = {}

def fibonacci(n):
    global cache
    if n in cache:
        return cache[n]

    if n == 0:
        result = 0
    elif n == 1:
        result = 1
    else:
        result = fibonacci(n-1) + fibonacci(n-2)
    cache[n] = result
    return result

start = time.time()

for i in range(0, 101):
    result = fibonacci(i)
    print(i, result)

finish = time.time()
duration = finish - start
print('Computed all 100 in', duration, 'seconds')
```

Here's the dictionary we're going to use as a cache.

Now the first thing we do is check to see if n is a key in the cache dictionary. If it is, then we return the value stored for that key.

Now rather than returning immediately if n equals 0 or 1, we assign n to a local variable named result.

If we end up recursively computing the result, we then assign that to the result local variable as well.

Before we return the result, we store it in the cache under the key n. Remember in Python a dictionary key can be any value, including integers.

We must be confident because we've changed the timing code to capture the duration of computing the entire first 100 Fibonacci numbers.

RECURSION LAB SUCCESS

What are you waiting for? Are you skeptical a couple lines of code using a dictionary could cut hours of computation down to less than 5 seconds? Well, get these code updates made and give it a run!

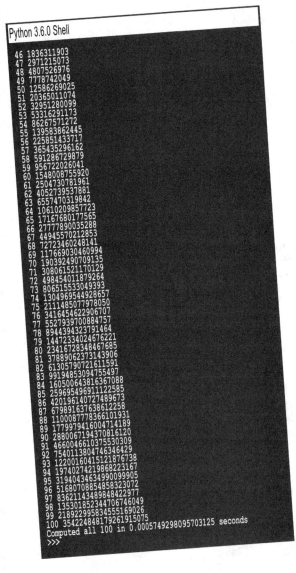

```
Python 3.6.0 Shell
46  1836311903
47  2971215073
48  4807526976
49  7778742049
50  12586269025
51  20365011074
52  32951280099
53  53316291173
54  86267571272
55  139583862445
56  225851433717
57  365435296162
58  591286729879
59  956722026041
60  1548008755920
61  2504730781961
62  4052739537881
63  6557470319842
64  10610209857723
65  17167680177565
66  27777890035288
67  44945570212853
68  72723460248141
69  117669030460994
70  190392490709135
71  308061521170129
72  498454011879264
73  806515533049393
74  1304969544928657
75  2111485077978050
76  3416454622906707
77  5527939700884757
78  8944394323791464
79  14472334024676221
80  23416728348467685
81  37889062373143906
82  61305790721611591
83  99194853094755497
84  160500643816367088
85  259695496911122585
86  420196140727489673
87  679891637638612258
88  1100087778366101931
89  1779979416004714189
90  2880067194370816120
91  4660046610375530309
92  7540113804746346429
93  12200160415121876738
94  19740274219868223167
95  31940434634990099905
96  51680708854858323072
97  83621143489848422977
98  135301852344706746049
99  218922995834555169026
100 354224848179261915075
Computed all 100 in 0.0005749298095703125 seconds
>>>
```

Impressive! You got it computed in way under 1 second!

Optimizing your code can affect its runtime behavior in a HUGE way.

Some more brain building

Hopefully this has been the mind-bending chapter we promised, but before you go we wanted to show you that recursive code isn't just for computing Fibonacci numbers and palindromes. In fact, we're going to apply recursion to generating some computer graphics, more specifically *fractals*. Now everyone's familiar with the term, but what does it actually mean? Think of a fractal as a geometry shape that is similar at any scale. So if you zoom out and look at a fractal, you see the same general shape as when you zoom way in. The best way to get the feel for fractals is to make some. To do that let's look at some code.

```python
import turtle

def setup(pencil):
    pencil.color('blue')
    pencil.penup()
    pencil.goto(-200,100)
    pencil.pendown()

def koch(pencil, size, order):
    if order == 0:
        pencil.forward(size)
    else:
        for angle in [60, -120, 60, 0]:
            koch(pencil, size/3, order-1)
            pencil.left(angle)

def main():
    pencil = turtle.Turtle()
    setup(pencil)

    order = 0
    size = 400
    koch(pencil, size, order)

if __name__ == '__main__':
    main()
    turtle.tracer(100)
    turtle.mainloop()
```

Our turtles are back.

All this setup function does is set the turtle (we're calling it a pencil in this code) color and move it to a location that will make the drawing more centered.

This is the recursive function; we'll come back to this and study it.

The main function creates a turtle (the pencil); defines two variables, order and size; and then calls the recursive function, sending it all three arguments.

Notice the order starts at 0, and size starts at 400. You'll see how these are used in a bit.

About what we'd expect in this bit of code. We call main and then make sure the turtle mainloop is running. We also use a function we haven't seen before, tracer, which accelerates the speed on the turtle.

A closer look at the koch function

Our code (on the previous page) is pretty basic: it creates a turtle, repositions it, and sets its color. Other than that, it just calls the koch function. But what does this koch function do? Let's look at it again, here:

We've pulled out the koch function to take a look, so for the entire context refer to the previous page.

koch takes a pencil, a size, and an order.

base case

recursive case

```
def koch(pencil, size, order):
    if order == 0:
        pencil.forward(size)
    else:
        for angle in [60, -120, 60, 0]:
            koch(pencil, size/3, order-1)
            pencil.left(angle)
```

Our base case: if order equals 0 we draw a straight line of length size.

Otherwise, call koch four times, passing it the size parameter divided by three and reducing order by one.

After each call to koch, we adjust the angle of the turtle.

Niels Fabian Helge von Koch was a Swedish mathematician who gave his name to the fractal known as the Koch snowflake. See more at: https://en.wikipedia.org/wiki/Helge_von_Koch.

The best way to understand this is to see some examples.

We have some abstract idea of what this function does, but we have no idea what it really does. We do know that the order parameter seems to play a big role. Let's start with order equal to 0 and see what this draws. Given 0 is the base case, it should just draw a line.

Type in the code and give it a test drive. Here's what we got:

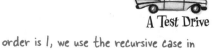

A Test Drive

The base case, a line of 400 pixels (because we're passing it a size of 400)

If we increase order to 1, then we should see the recursive case used. Just change the order local variable to 1 and test it again.

A Test Drive

When order is 1, we use the recursive case in the code. In the recursive case we draw four segments at different angles. The drawing is actually done calling the koch function recursively, where for each segment koch hits the base case and draws a line of size 400/3

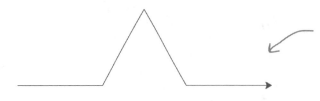

Sharpen your pencil

If you can see what koch does from order 0 to order 1, can you imagine what it might do when we increase the order to 2? Or 3? Remember, at every scale a fractal is the same. See if you can try to work out how the graphic at order 1 will change for order 2, and order 3. We didn't say it was easy to think about, but it's great brain building.

Order 0:

Order 1:

Draw your best guesses here.

Order 2:

Hint: look at what happened between order 0 and 1. What if you did that to each small segment of order 1 to get order 2?

Order 3:

Hint: can you take that one step further on order 3?

Truly exploring the koch fractal

Did that exercise help you think a little more recursively, or fractally? Let's take this all the way and run the code at orders 4 and 5. Go ahead and change your order and do a test drive for each.

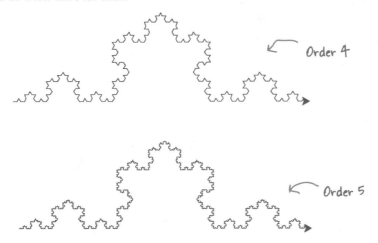

← Order 4

← Order 5

Learn more about the Koch snowflake at https://en.wikipedia.org/wiki/Koch_snowflake.

They don't call it the Koch snowflake for nothin'

Here's one last tweak for you. Edit your `main` function to call the `koch` function three times, rotating 120 degrees between each call.

```python
def main():
    pencil = turtle.Turtle()
    setup(pencil)
    turtle.tracer(100)

    order = 5
    size = 400
    koch(pencil, size, order)

    for i in range(3):
        koch(pencil, size, order)
        pencil.right(120)
```

Not bad for a six-line recursive function. That's a superpower!

Call koch three times, and rotate 120 degrees in between.

With that we'll leave you to ponder the power of recursion and fractals, not to mention dictionaries. Great job— you've done some mind bending and growing in this chapter. Now it's time to go let your brain do something else for a while, but only after the bullets and crossword.

BULLET POINTS

- Iteration and recursion can both be used to solve problems.

- Recursion defines a solution in terms of itself.

- Recursion typically consists of a base case and a recursive case.

- With the recursive case we make the problem a little smaller and then make a recursive function call.

- Programming languages handle recursive calls by putting parameters and local variables on a call stack.

- Recursion can sometimes lead to problems with the size of the call stack growing too large.

- Some solutions are more natural using a recursive style, and some solutions are more natural with iteration.

- For some problems recursion can produce very clear and straightforward solutions.

- Python dictionaries are a type of associative array or map.

- Dictionaries store key/value pairs.

- In Python, dictionary keys can be strings, numbers, or Booleans; dictionary values can be any type of Python value.

- Keys within a dictionary are unique.

- Assigning a value to an existing key overwrites the previous value.

- You can programmatically create dictionaries or specify them with a literal syntax.

- Keys and their associated values may be deleted from a dictionary.

- Key lookup in a dictionary happens in constant time.

- Dictionaries can be used with memoization as an optimization technique.

- Memoization is a technique used to remember previous function calls.

- By not recomputing expensive function calls, we can sometimes significantly speed up computations.

- Fractals are shapes that have similar structure at every scale.

Coding cross

Don't worry: it's not a recursive crossword,
just a normal one.

Across

1. And another name for a dictionary.
4. Snowflake.
5. Functions calling themselves.
6. Another name for dictionary.
8. Just typing a dictionary in.
9. Shape same at every level of scale.
10. Our idea is this kind of social.
11. Keys are this.
12. Makes a dictionary lookup fast.
14. Tacocat is one.
15. Easiest case.
16. Call stack is made up of _____.
17. Computes a sequence seen in nature.

Down

2. Dictionaries store key/value _____.
3. Remembering function calls.
4. Used to look up a value.
7. Alternative to recursion.
11. Dictionaries are _____.
13. Parameters are stored on it.

Sharpen your pencil
Solution

Forget recursion for a bit, and think through how you might write a function to check if a word is a palindrome. Do that using the skills you learned in Chapters 1 through 7. Write some simple pseudocode to summarize your thoughts. Or, if you just had that cup of java and feel like writing some code, don't let us get in your way.

In general we'd want to compare the outside characters and move inward until we find a character that doesn't match, or if we get to the middle and they all match, then we have a palindrome.

We could have an index called i that starts at position 0...

...and another called j that starts at the end.

tacocat

We start at each end of the word and compare pairs of letters from the outside in.

is_palindrome(word):
   set i to 0
   set j to length of word (minus 1) ← When i >= j, then we've reached the middle of the string and we've compared everything.
   while i < j:
      if characters at i and j are not equal then return False
      increment i
      decrement j
   if the loop completes, return True

If at any point our outer characters aren't equal, then the word is not a palindrome.

```python
def is_palindrome(word):
    i = 0
    j = len(word) - 1
    while i < j:
        if word[i] != word[j]:
            return False
        i = i + 1
        j = j - 1
    return True
```

Okay, we just had to write the code. Did you?

This probably works great, but it requires a lot of thinking about indices. It's also not the clearest code in the world. We can probably do better.

Study this until you've convinced yourself it works.

Sharpen your pencil
Solution

Try evaluting some recursive code yourself. How about using our
`recursive_compute_sum` function?

```
def recursive_compute_sum(list):
    if len(list) == 0:
        return 0
    else:
        first = list[0]
        rest = list[1:]
        sum = first + recursive_compute_sum(rest)
        return sum

recursive_compute_sum([1, 2, 3])
```

← Here's the code again.

And here we're calling
the function.

`recursive_compute_sum([1, 2, 3])`

frame 1
```
list = [1, 2, 3]
first = 1
rest = [2, 3]
```

We did the first one for you. The
parameter list is bound to the list
[1,2,3] and then the local variables
first and rest get computed and
added to the frame.

`recursive_compute_sum([2, 3])`

frame 2
```
list = [2, 3]
first = 2
rest = [3]
```

frame 1
```
list = [1, 2, 3]
first = 1
rest = [2, 3]
```

Now we're recursing by calling
recursive_compute_sum again, so we
add a new frame and add list as a
parameter. This time it has the value
[2, 3].

Like before, we have to compute first
and rest.

`recursive_compute_sum([3])`

frame 3
```
list = [3]
first = 3
rest = []
```

frame 2
```
list = [2, 3]
first = 2
rest = [3]
```

frame 1
```
list = [1, 2, 3]
first = 1
rest = [2, 3]
```

Again, we're recursing by calling
recursive_compute_sum, so we add
a third frame and add list as a
parameter. This time it has the value
[3].

Like before, we have to compute first
and rest.

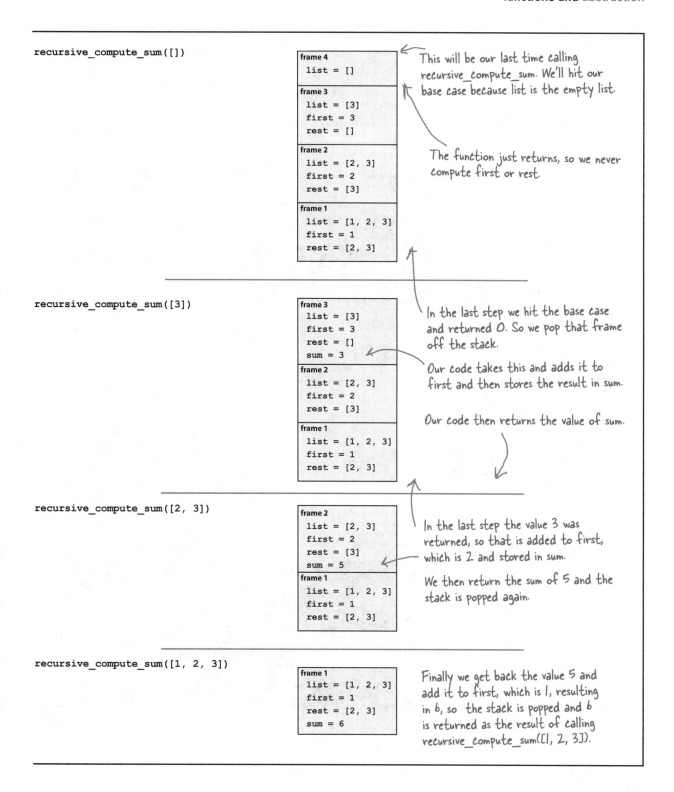

recursive_compute_sum([])

frame 4
list = []

frame 3
list = [3]
first = 3
rest = []

frame 2
list = [2, 3]
first = 2
rest = [3]

frame 1
list = [1, 2, 3]
first = 1
rest = [2, 3]

This will be our last time calling recursive_compute_sum. We'll hit our base case because list is the empty list.

The function just returns, so we never compute first or rest.

recursive_compute_sum([3])

frame 3
list = [3]
first = 3
rest = []
sum = 3

frame 2
list = [2, 3]
first = 2
rest = [3]

frame 1
list = [1, 2, 3]
first = 1
rest = [2, 3]

In the last step we hit the base case and returned 0. So we pop that frame off the stack.

Our code takes this and adds it to first and then stores the result in sum.

Our code then returns the value of sum.

recursive_compute_sum([2, 3])

frame 2
list = [2, 3]
first = 2
rest = [3]
sum = 5

frame 1
list = [1, 2, 3]
first = 1
rest = [2, 3]

In the last step the value 3 was returned, so that is added to first, which is 2 and stored in sum.

We then return the sum of 5 and the stack is popped again.

recursive_compute_sum([1, 2, 3])

frame 1
list = [1, 2, 3]
first = 1
rest = [2, 3]
sum = 6

Finally we get back the value 5 and add it to first, which is 1, resulting in 6, so the stack is popped and 6 is returned as the result of calling recursive_compute_sum([1, 2, 3]).

Sharpen your pencil
Solution

Now that you've got some book
knowledge of dictionaries, it's time
to put that knowledge to work. Work
through the code below to see what it
computes.

Is this what you got?

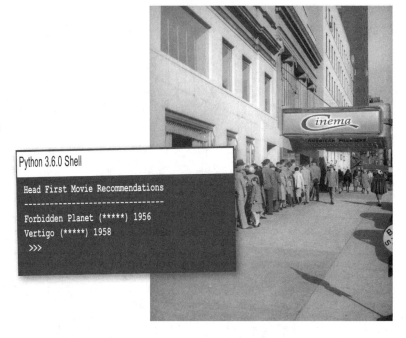

```
Python 3.6.0 Shell

Head First Movie Recommendations
--------------------------------
Forbidden Planet (*****) 1956
Vertigo (*****) 1958
>>>
```

Sharpen your pencil
Solution

Dictionaries in dictionaries—it's a
common arrangement. See how it plays
out at the cinema by using your brain to
execute the code below.

A little trickier with
two dictionaries?

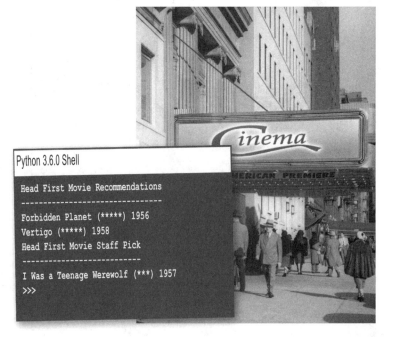

```
Python 3.6.0 Shell

Head First Movie Recommendations
--------------------------------
Forbidden Planet (*****) 1956
Vertigo (*****) 1958
Head First Movie Staff Pick
--------------------------------
I Was a Teenage Werewolf (***) 1957
>>>
```

Brain Building Solution

Now that we know how we're going to store our users on the Anti-Social Network, it's time to write a little code. Let's create a function we might need for the startup, called `average_age`, that takes a name and returns the average age of that user's friends.

```
users = {}
users['Kim'] = {'email' : 'kim@oreilly.com','gender': 'f', 'age': 27, 'friends': ['John', 'Josh']}
users['John'] = {'email' : 'john@abc.com','gender': 'm', 'age': 24, 'friends': ['Kim', 'Josh']}
users['Josh'] = {'email' : 'josh@wickedlysmart.com','gender': 'm', 'age': 32, 'friends': ['Kim']}
```

Here's our function, which takes a username in the form of a string.

```
def average_age(username):
    global users
```

Let's grab the user's attributes dictionary from the users dictionary.

```
    user = users[username]
    friends = user['friends']
```

And then let's grab the friends list from the user's attributes dictionary.

Here's a local variable to keep track of the sum of the friend's ages.

```
    sum = 0
```

Now let's iterate through all the friends.

```
    for name in friends:
        friend = users[name]
```

Now we need to take the friend's name and grab their attributes dictionary out of the users dictionary.

```
        sum = sum + friend['age']
```

And then we can get their age from the attributes dictionary. Here we add it to the sum.

With the ages totaled up, let's compute the average...

```
    average = sum/len(friends)
    print(username + "'s friends have an average age of", average)
```

...and print the result.

```
average_age('Kim')
average_age('John')
average_age('Josh')
```

And here's our test code again.

Here's the output you should get with this test code.

```
Python 3.6.0 Shell
Kim's friends have an average age of 28.0
John's friends have an average age of 29.5
Josh's friends have an average age of 27.0
>>>
```

Sharpen your pencil Solution

Now that we have some pseudocode, use your new knowledge of dictionaries to complete this code. After that we'll get it running.

```
max = 1000
for name in    users    :
    user = users [ name ]
    friends = user[ 'friends' ]
    if len( friends ) < max:
        most_anti_social = name
        max = len(friends )

print('The most_anti_social user is', most_anti_social)
```

Sharpen your pencil Solution

Try drawing a graph of all the function calls it takes to compute fibonacci(7). When you're done, total up how many duplicated calls you find for each value 0 through 7.

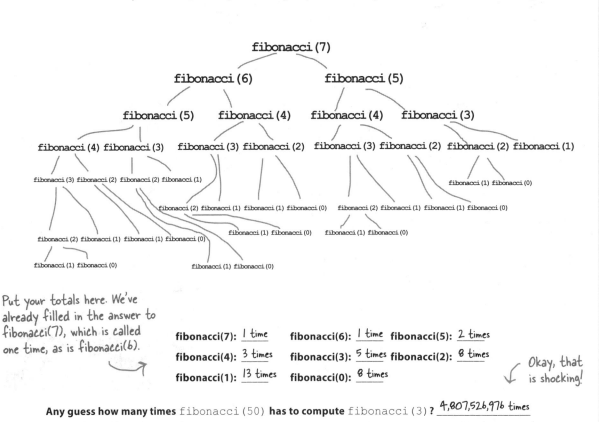

Put your totals here. We've already filled in the answer to fibonacci(7), which is called one time, as is fibonacci(6).

fibonacci(7): 1 time   **fibonacci(6):** 1 time **fibonacci(5):** 2 times

fibonacci(4): 3 times   **fibonacci(3):** 5 times **fibonacci(2):** 8 times

fibonacci(1): 13 times   **fibonacci(0):** 8 times

Okay, that is shocking!

Any guess how many times fibonacci(50) **has to compute** fibonacci(3)? 4,807,526,976 times

Sharpen your pencil
Solution

If you can see what koch does from order 0 to order 1, can you imagine what it might do when we increase the order to 2? Or 3? Remember, at every scale a fractal is the same. See if you can try to work out how the graphic at order 1 will change for order 2, and order 3. We didn't say it was easy to think about, but it's great brain building.

Order 0:

Order 1:

In this step we drew a shape like this...

...to each side (there was only one side).

Order 2:

Same thing; for each straight side in the previous round, we added another.

Order 3:

And as the sides get smaller, we keep adding...

...reducing the scale each time.

Coding Cross Solution

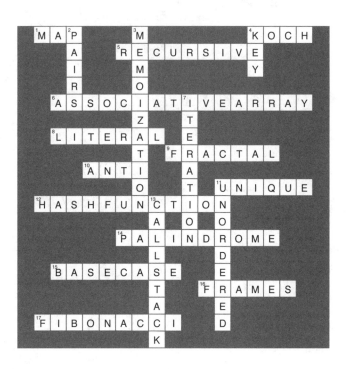

9 saving and retrieving files

Persistence

He was right behind me and then poof!—he was gone. If we'd only saved him out to storage before everything ended.

You know you can save values in variables, but once your program ends poof!—they're gone forever. That's where *persistent* storage comes in—storage that allows your values and data to stick around a while. Most of the devices you're going to run Python on also have persistent storage, like hard drives and flash cards, or they may have access to storage in the cloud as well. In this chapter you'll see how to write code to store and retrieve data from files. What good is that? Oh, anytime you want to save a user's configuration, store the results of your big analysis for the boss, read an image into your code to process it, write some code to search a decade's worth of email messages, reformat some data to be used in your spreadsheet app—we could go on and on, but we should probably start the chapter now.

Ready for some Crazy Libs?

No, that's not a political statement! We're being serious here. We're talking about creating our own version of a game that is in the spirit of the popular Mad Libs™ games—we'll call our version *Crazy Libs*.

If you didn't play a Mad Libs–style game as a kid, here's how it works:

You can create a Crazy Lib from any text story you want. We used some text we just had lying around.

To create a Crazy Lib, just remove arbitrary words and replace them with blanks that indicate their parts of speech (noun, verb, etc.).

How to Play

1. Ask a friend to give you a word for each blank noun, verb, and adjective, but don't show your friend the story.

2. Read the story back to your friend, adding in your friend's words.

3. Hilarity ensues.

Crazy Libs

The first thing that stands between you and _____ your
                                              VERB ENDING IN 'ING'

first, real, piece of _____, is _____ the skill of
                        NOUN   **VERB ENDING IN 'ING'**

breaking problems down into achievable _____ actions that a
                                        ADJECTIVE

_____ can do for you. Of course, you and the computer will
NOUN

also need to be _____ a common _____, but
                 VERB ENDING IN 'ING'   **NOUN**

we'll get to that topic in just a bit.

The text from the first paragraph of Chapter 1

Okay, I'm going with
VERB ENDING IN ING: buying, NOUN:
pudding, VERB ENDING IN ING: forgetting,
ADJECTIVE: crazy, NOUN: monkey, VERB
ENDING IN ING: eating, NOUN: pizza.

So, "The first thing that stands
between you and **buying** your first real piece of
pudding is **forgetting** the skill of breaking problems down
into achievable **crazy** actions that a **monkey** can do for you. Of
course, you and the computer will also need to be **eating** a common
pizza, but we'll get to that topic in just a bit."
Nice!

How Crazy Libs is going to work

To turn Crazy Libs into a computer game, we're going to have the computer retrieve a story stored in a text file, prompt the user for all the missing words, and then create a new text file that contains the completed Crazy Libs. Let's go through that in a little more detail:

By text file, we just mean a file containing text that is stored on your device.

1 **Let's start with a template**

We need a template that has all the text of the story, with placeholders for the words that need to be provided by the user; we also need some indication of each placeholder's part of speech. To signify a placeholder, we'll just use uppercase words like NOUN, VERB, and ADJECTIVE right in the text.

Game code

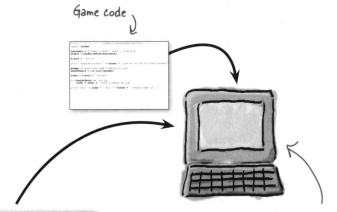

The Python intepreter

Here's an example template.

1
The first thing that stands between you and **VERB_ING** your first, real, piece of **NOUN**, is **VERB_ING** the skill of breaking problems down into achievable **ADJECTIVE** actions that a **NOUN** can do for you. Of course, you and the computer will also need to be **VERB_ING** a common **NOUN**, but we'll get to that topic in just a bit.

lib.txt

A template is just a text file on your computer that contains a story along with placeholders for nouns, verbs, verbs with 'ing' endings, adjectives, and so on.

Feel free to take your favorite story and create your own!

You'll find lib.txt in the ch9 folder in the book's source code.

❷ Reading the template

Next, when you run the game, the code is going to read in the template from the disk and then locate all the placeholders—remember the placeholders are just the uppercase words, like NOUN, VERB, and so on, embedded in the text.

❷

The first thing that stands between you and **VERB_ING** your first, real, piece of **NOUN**, is **VERB_ING** the skill of breaking problems down into achievable **ADJECTIVE** actions that a **NOUN** can do for you. Of course, you and the computer will also need to be **VERB_ING** a common NOUN, but we'll get to that topic in just a bit.

lib.txt

❸ Prompting the user

For each placeholder your code is going to prompt the user to provide a word that matches the needed part of speech. Your code will then take their word, and substitute it into the text in place of the placeholder.

Give me a VERB: buying
Give me a NOUN: pudding
Give me a VERB_WITH_ING
Give me a ADJECTIVE: cr
Give me a NOUN: monkey
Giveme a VERB_WITH_ING:

❸

↙ After getting all the user input, our code creates a new file and writes out the updated crazy version of the story.

❹ Finally, we'll write out a new file that contains the completed Crazy Lib.

After all the placeholders have been collected from the user, we're going to create a new file and then write the completed Crazy Lib to it.

❹

Here's the completed Crazy Lib, which has each placeholder replaced by the user's input.

The first thing that stands between you and **buying** your first, real, piece of **pudding**, is **forgetting** the skill of breaking problems down into achievable **crazy** actions that a **monkey** can do for you. Of course, you and the computer will also need to be **eating** a common **pizza**, but we'll get to that topic in just a bit.

For the output filename, we'll just prepend "crazy_" to the original filename.

crazy_lib.txt

Hey, it's Chapter 9 already, so we have no doubt you can tackle the task of creating a little pseudocode based on the previous two pages. Writing up a little pseudocode now is going to give you a clearer idea of how to approach writing the Crazy Libs game. Don't skip this! But of course you'll find our version at the end of the chapter.

Write your pseudocode here. Remember the story is in a file, so you'll need to read it, figure out where the placeholders are, prompt the user for the placeholder replacements, and then write it all out to a new file.

P.S. We know you don't know how to read or write data from files yet, so just focus on the logic of the code, and don't worry about the specifics (which is the point of pseudocode!).

Step 1: Read the text of the story from a file

The first thing you need to do is get your hands on the text file that contains the example story. You'll find this file, *lib.txt*, in the book source files under the *ch9* folder. Take a quick look at it. We also encourage you to create your own story files, but for testing let's use *lib.txt* so we're testing the same thing.

```
The first thing that stands between you
and VERB_ING your first, real, piece of NOUN,
is VERB_ING the skill of breaking
problems down into achievable ADJECTIVE
actions that a NOUN can do for you. Of
course, you and the computer will also
need to be VERB_ING a common NOUN, but
we'll get to that topic in just a bit.
```

lib.txt

Our test story file, complete with placeholders

1 Read the text for the story from file.

2 Process text.
For each word in text

A If word is a placeholder (NOUN or VERB or VERB_WITH_ING or ADJECTIVE):

  1 Prompt user for placeholder part of speech.

  2 Substitute user's word for the placeholder.

B Otherwise, the word is fine; keep it in the story.

3 Store results.
Take the processed text with the placeholders filled, and write it out to a file with the filename prepended by "crazy_".

To read a file in Python, you first have to open it

If we're going to grab the data out of a file, we first need to *open it*. What does opening a file actually do? From your perspective, not much, but behind the scenes, Python has to locate your file, make sure it exists, and ask the operating system for access to the file—after all, you might not have permission to access it.

You'll find this is the case with practically every programming language—to read or write to a file, you have to open it first.

To open a file you use Python's built-in `open` function, which takes a filename and a *mode* as arguments.

We use the Python's open function to open a file.

It takes a filename to be opened...

...and a mode.

```
my_file = open('lib.txt', 'r')
```

The mode can either be 'r' for reading or 'w' for writing to the file.

The open function returns a file object, which we're assigning to the variable my_file.

The filename can be a simple filename in the same directory as your code, or a more explicit path to a file. Right now we're using a simple filename. More on paths on the next page.

We use the terms "folder" and "directory" interchangeably in this chapter, although when we're talking about files and file paths, we tend to use the word "directory."

How to use file paths

When we used the open function on the previous page, we specified a filename of `'lib.txt'`, and, because we didn't indicate where the file was located, we were assuming the file was located in the current directory. But what if the file you want to open is located somewhere else? How do you then open it? To do that we add a *path* to our filename, which tells open where to look for the file. There are actually two kinds of paths: a *relative path* or an *absolute* one. A relative path is a description of the file's location that is relative to the folder (we usually say directory instead when we talk about paths) you ran your Python code from.

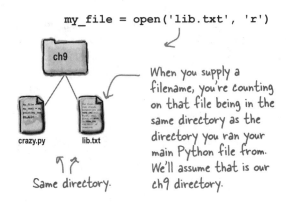

```
my_file = open('lib.txt', 'r')
```

When you supply a filename, you're counting on that file being in the same directory as the directory you ran your main Python file from. We'll assume that is our ch9 directory.

Same directory.

Relative paths

Let's look at relative paths first, which are always specified in relation to your current directory (the directory you ran your program from). Let's say you put the file *lib.txt* in a subfolder (again, we typically say subdirectory) called *libs*; well, you can prepend your filename with the path to the file, like this: `'libs/lib.txt'`. So the open function will first go to the *libs* subdirectory before looking for the file *lib.txt*.

You can list as many subdirectories as you need, separating each one with a path separator, otherwise known as the forward slash character, /.

Windows users, check out the Watch it! below.

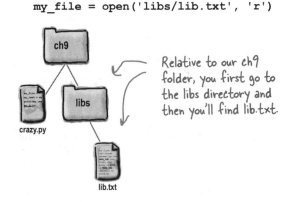

```
my_file = open('libs/lib.txt', 'r')
```

Relative to our ch9 folder, you first go to the libs directory and then you'll find lib.txt.

Mac and Windows use different separators.

Mac (and Linux) machines use a forward slash / as a separator, while Windows uses a backslash, \. That said, Python allows you to enter path separators uniformly using a forward slash. So if you have a Windows path of:

```
C:\Users\eric\code\hfcode\ch9\lib.txt
```

then, instead, use:

```
C:/Users/eric/code/hfcode/ch9/lib.txt
```

So, what if you want to open a file in a directory that's in an adjacent folder (like *ch9* and *libs* are adjacent folders), or a directory higher in your filesystem (like *hfcode* is higher than *libs* in the filesystem)? No problem. You can use the .. (two periods) notation to specify a directory one level higher. If you're running your code from the *ch9* directory and you want to get to the *lib.txt* file in the adjacent *libs* directory, then you can use a path of `'../libs/lib.txt'`. So we go up one directory and then down in to the *libs* directory before finding *lib.txt*.

Or, if you're after the *lib.txt* in the directory *oldlibs*, you can use the path `'../../oldlibs/lib.txt'`.

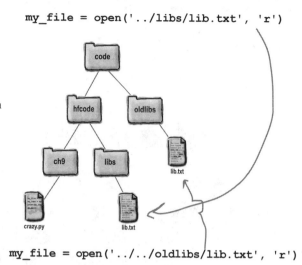

```
my_file = open('../libs/lib.txt', 'r')
```

```
my_file = open('../../oldlibs/lib.txt', 'r')
```

Here we go up two directories, before going down into the oldlibs directory and finally, finding the lib.txt we're after.

Absolute paths

The root of a filesystem is, perhaps counterintuitively, the very top level of your filesystem.

An absolute path is a path that always starts from the root of your filesystem. Absolute paths tell you exactly where a file is in a filesystem. Now, while that may sound like a more definitive way to identify your files, and it is, often absolute paths are less flexible because if you move all your code and files to another machine, you have to update the absolute paths in your code. That said, you'll find times when using an absolute path is more convenient than a relative path.

Let's say we want to specify an absolute path to the *lib.txt* file. That looks like this on our machine:

```
my_file = open('/usr/eric/code/hfcode/ch9/lib.txt', 'r')
```

Here's my top-level folder. Note this is on a macOS X filesystem.

On the Mac and Linux systems, start at the root with a forward slash, and then add the rest of the file path separated by forward slashes.

And on a Windows machine, assuming you have your code on the *C:* drive, your path would look like this:

```
my_file = open('C:/Users/eric/code/hfcode/ch9/lib.txt', 'r')
```

On Windows systems, start with the drive and then a colon and then a forward slash. Then add the rest of the file path separated by forward slashes.

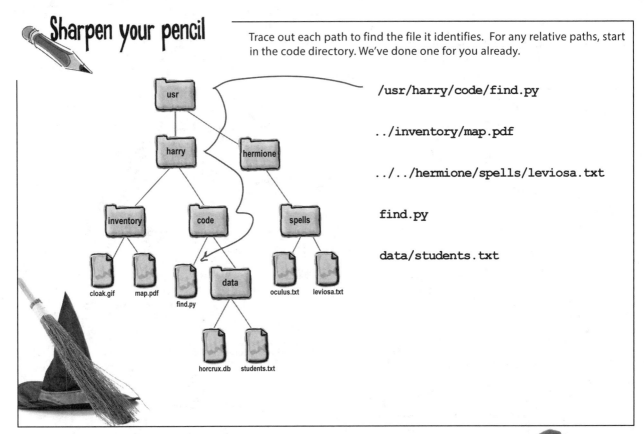

Sharpen your pencil

Trace out each path to find the file it identifies. For any relative paths, start in the code directory. We've done one for you already.

```
/usr/harry/code/find.py

../inventory/map.pdf

../../hermione/spells/leviosa.txt

find.py

data/students.txt
```

Oh, and don't forget to clean up when you're done!

Before we go on, one point of etiquette: if you're going to open a file, when you're done with it, you need to *close* it. Why? Open files take up resources in your machine's operating system, and, especially for long-running programs, leaving files open that you aren't using can lead to code that eventually crashes and burns. So, if you're going to open a file, just make sure you close it too. Here's how:

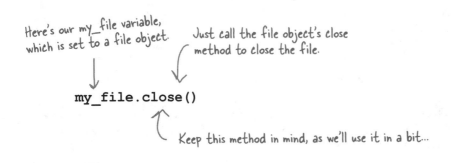

Here's our my_file variable, which is set to a file object.

Just call the file object's close method to close the file.

```
my_file.close()
```

Keep this method in mind, as we'll use it in a bit...

Reading a file into your Python code

First of all, what does it mean to read a file into Python? Well, with Python, the contents of the file are taken and placed into a Python string, which you can examine or process as you wish using standard Python string operations.

> We couldn't fit the whole thing on the page: but you get the point, this string contains all the text in lib.txt.

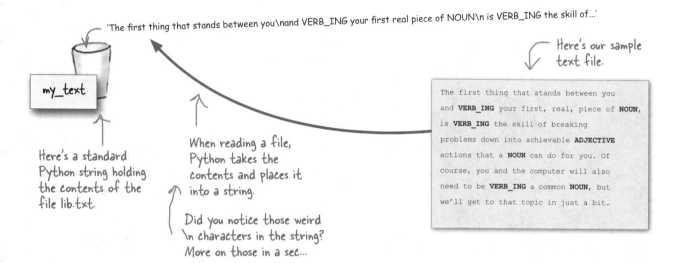

'The first thing that stands between you\nand VERB_ING your first real piece of NOUN\n is VERB_ING the skill of...'

> Here's our sample text file.

`my_text`

Here's a standard Python string holding the contents of the file lib.txt.

When reading a file, Python takes the contents and places it into a string.

Did you notice those weird \n characters in the string? More on those in a sec...

The first thing that stands between you and **VERB_ING** your first, real, piece of **NOUN**, is **VERB_ING** the skill of breaking problems down into achievable **ADJECTIVE** actions that a **NOUN** can do for you. Of course, you and the computer will also need to be **VERB_ING** a common **NOUN**, but we'll get to that topic in just a bit.

Using the file object to read a file

> Technically there are a few other ways too, but we're going to focus on the most common methods of reading files.

There are actually two ways to read the contents of your file into a string: you can read the entire file all at once, or you can read the file a line at a time. Let's start by reading the entire file all at once; to do that we're going to use the file object's `read` method:

Let's use the read method to get the entire contents of the lib file...

...which we'll assign to the string my_text.

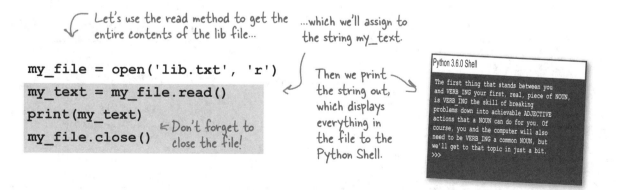

```
my_file = open('lib.txt', 'r')
my_text = my_file.read()
print(my_text)
my_file.close()
```

⟵ Don't forget to close the file!

Then we print the string out, which displays everything in the file to the Python Shell.

Python 3.6.0 Shell

The first thing that stands between you and VERB_ING your first, real, piece of NOUN, is VERB_ING the skill of breaking problems down into achievable ADJECTIVE actions that a NOUN can do for you. Of course, you and the computer will also need to be VERB_ING a common NOUN, but we'll get to that topic in just a bit.
>>>

Code Magnets

Can you help find the needle in the haystack? We've been given a directory of 1,000 files with the filenames *0.txt* through *999.txt*, and only one has the word *needle* in it. We had the code to find the needle all written on the refrigerator, but then someone came along and messed it all up. Can you help us put it back together? Notice, there may be some extra code magnets, so you may not use all of them. Check your answer at the end of the chapter.

```
for i in range(0, 1000):
```

```
file.close()
```

```
if 'needle' in text:
```

```
print('Found needle in file ' + str(i) + '.txt')
```

```
filename = str(i) + '.txt'
```

```
for i in range(0, 999):
```

```
text = file.read()
```

```
file = open(filename, 'r')
```

Rearrange the
magnets here.

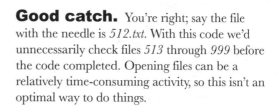

I was looking at the code in the previous exercise and something is bothering me. Even when we find a file with the needle string in it, the code continues on, reading every remaining file. I guess that would be good if we wanted to check every file, but we said it was only in one file.

Good catch. You're right; say the file with the needle is *512.txt*. With this code we'd unnecessarily check files *513* through *999* before the code completed. Opening files can be a relatively time-consuming activity, so this isn't an optimal way to do things.

The problem is, if you look at the code again, we're iterating with a `for` loop, so we can't just stop checking files in the middle. Or can we?

This does bring up something we haven't discussed yet, which is a way to break out of an iteration, in the middle, if we decide we don't need to complete it. If we had something like that, we could easily fix this code so that it stopped the search after finding the needle. Of course we do have something: Python and most programming languages have a `break` statement for just this purpose. Let's take a look at how it works...

Oh, give it a break already...

When we use a `for` statement, say a `for` statement that is iterating over a range of numbers, we know that the `for` statement will iterate over every number in the range before it completes. But there are times when in a computation you'll decide partway through that continuing is pointless, and there is no reason to complete the iteration—our needle in a haystack code is a good example, because once we find the needle, there is no reason to continue the `for` loop to open the remaining files.

The `break` statement gives you a way out. With the `break` statement we can push the eject button and stop the `for` loop at any time. Let's have a look:

> Don't forget us while loops! The break statement works with us too!

while loop

```
for i in range(0, 1000):
    filename = str(i) + '.txt'
    file = open(filename, 'r')
    text = file.read()
    if 'needle' in text:
        print('Found needle in file ' + str(i) + '.txt')
        break
    file.close()
print('Scan complete')
```

Here's our code to find the needle again.

When we hit the break statement we immediately jump out of the for loop.

So now, when we find the needle, we're going to use the break statement and bypass the rest of the code block as well as breaking out of the loop altogether.

BRAIN POWER

Uh oh. By adding the `break` statement to the code above we actually introduced a small bug. Can you find it? Can you determine what it is? How would you fix it?

Hint: is every file still being closed?

Hey, we've got a Crazy Lib game to finish!

Short excursions are great for learning new things about coding, but we've got a game to finish here. When we last left off, we were reading the entire contents of a file at once, which is certainly easy, but it has a drawback: for large files it can consume significant resources. Think about processing a file with, say, hundreds of thousands of lines—you probably don't want to read all that into memory at once, or the result could be out-of-memory errors for your program or even your operating system.

Think of an old-style typewriter with a carriage return. Every time you hit the carriage return, that's like a new line.

A more common approach is to read the contents *one line at a time*. But what is a line? Exactly what you'd think: it is all the text on each line, up until you encounter a new line. In fact, if we could open our *lib.txt* file in a special editor that showed us all the characters in the file, we'd see something like this:

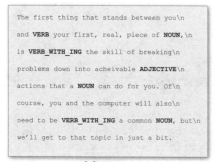

```
The first thing that stands between you\n
and VERB your first, real, piece of NOUN,\n
is VERB_WITH_ING the skill of breaking\n
problems down into acheivable ADJECTIVE\n
actions that a NOUN can do for you. Of\n
course, you and the computer will also\n
need to be VERB_WITH_ING a common NOUN, but\n
we'll get to that topic in just a bit.
```

lib.txt

Each line ends with an actual new line character, otherwise known as a newline, which is represented by the escape character sequence '\n'.

You never see newlines in editors because rather than show them, editors just treat them as a directive to display the next bit of text on the next line.

Using the readline method of the file object

To read one line from a file, we use the `readline` method of the file object. Let's try reading the *lib.txt* file again using `readline`:

```python
my_file = open('lib.txt', 'r')
line1 = my_file.readline()
print(line1)
line2 = my_file.readline()
print(line2)
```

This time we're using the readline method and reading the first two lines into the variables line1 and line2, respectively.

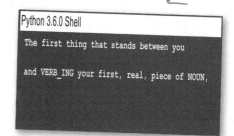

```
Python 3.6.0 Shell

The first thing that stands between you

and VERB_ING your first, real, piece of NOUN,
```

The file object tracks its position as it reads the file. So each time you call the readline method, it picks up where it last left off.

BRAIN POWER

Why do you think the output from the code on the previous page has an extra newline between the two lines "The first thing that stands between you" and "and VERB your first, real, piece of NOUN,"?

Do you see the extra newline?

```
Python 3.6.0 Shell
The first thing that stands between you

and VERB_ING your first, real, piece of NOUN,
```

Back up the bus. A page back you used the term "escape sequence." Excuse me? You didn't really define it.

Fancy name, simple concept.

When you want to create a string with a newline in it, there's no way to directly type in that newline character. Think about it: when you're typing in a string, you type a quote and then some text and if you typed a newline by hitting the Return key, the editor would just go to the next line. So, instead we use a sequence of characters that represents a newline character, and those characters happen to be \n. So when you see the characters \n don't think of them as two characters, a backslash and the letter n, but rather as a way to represent a newline character. So, for example, if you want to print some text followed by five new lines, you'd do this:

```python
print('Get ready for new lines:\n\n\n\n\n')
```

Newlines, of course, aren't the only escape sequence. There's \t for tabs, \b for backspace, and \v for a vertical tab.

You might also hear some coders refer to '\n' as a line feed.

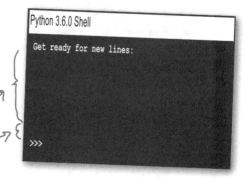

Here we have the text "Get ready for new lines:" followed by how many new lines? Five? Nope! Six! We get five from the string, but, as it turns out, the print function adds a newline to its output by default.

This explains the answer to the Brain Power above.

How do we know when we've read the last line?

Think of `readline` as keeping a pointer to the position it last read. Each time you read another line, `readline` picks up where it last left off, and then reads the next line. When there are no more lines to read, `readline` then returns the empty string. Here's how you can use that to read all the lines in a file a line at a time:

```python
my_file = open('lib.txt', 'r')
while True:
    line = my_file.readline()
    if line != '':
        print(line)
    else:
        break
my_file.close()
```

When we use a while True, that means we're iterating FOREVER.

Note a blank line would have a newline character in it, while the end of file sets line to an empty string.

Each time we loop we read the next line, and if it isn't the end of the file (signified by an empty string), then we print it.

If it is the end of the file, well, then we use our handy break statement to break out of the while loop. Thank goodness—forever is a long time.

Ah, but there's a easier way using the power of Python sequences

We're glad you've adapted so quickly to using the `break` statement, but in this case there's a nicer and cleaner way to iterate over the lines in a file. Remember how we've used the `for` statement to iterate over sequences? We've used it to iterate over the items in a list, and we've used it to iterate over the items in a string. Well, isn't a file just a sequence of lines? Ah, so can we use `for` to iterate over the lines of a file as well? You bet. Let's rewrite the code above using `for`:

```python
my_file = open('lib.txt', 'r')
for line in my_file:
    print(line)
my_file.close()
```

Wow, not only shorter, but much more readable!

Serious Coding

Anytime you're using `for` with the `in` keyword, whether it's on a list or a string or a file or a dictionary, we're using a concept called an *iterator*.

With an iterator we assume the data type we're iterating over gives us a standard way to iterate through its sequence of values. We don't worry about how—the `for` loop does that—we just know we can step through each value until we're out of values.

You'll find iterators in many modern languages—they're based on a high-level software design practice called *Design Patterns*.

Reading in a Crazy Lib template

You now know just about everything there is to know about opening and reading a text file, line by line. Let's put that knowledge to use to write the first part of our Crazy Lib code. Let's start by defining a function, `make_crazy_lib`, that is going to take a filename and return the text of the Crazy Lib in a string, complete with the user's word choices already substituted.

We're also going to create a helper function, `process_line`, which is going to process each line for any placeholders. The `process_line` function will also be responsible for getting each replacement word from the user, and substituting it into the text.

> A helper function is just a common name for a function that takes on a subtask for another function. In this case our make_crazy_lib function is going to rely on process_line to look at a single line and process it for placeholders.

> Here's our function; it takes a filename and then opens it for reading.

> We're going to use a variable, text, to build up the text as we process it.

```python
def make_crazy_lib(filename):
    file = open(filename, 'r')

    text = ''

    for line in file:
        text = text + process_line(line)

    file.close()

    return text

def process_line(line):
    return line

def main():
    lib = make_crazy_lib('lib.txt')
    print(lib)

if __name__ == '__main__':
    main()
```

> For each line in the file we're going to process it with the process_line function, and then add it to the text we're building up.

> After we've gone through each line of the file, we just need to close the file and return the text.

> For testing, let's have process_line return the text we pass it. That way we can test that all the file reading and string concatenation is working correctly in make_crazy_lib.

> And of course we need to call the make_crazy_lib function. Let's add the main function to do that.

> Make sure the file "lib.txt" is in the same directory as your code.

A Test Drive

Get the code above into a file called *crazy.py*, save your code and choose the **Run > Run Module** menu item. Double-check your output.

> Once again you should just see the entire file, complete with placeholders. Remember, all we did was process the entire file, line by line, putting everything back together into the variable, text, but without any real processing.

```
Python 3.6.0 Shell

The first thing that stands between you
and VERB_ING your first, real, piece of NOUN,
is VERB_ING the skill of breaking
problems down into achievable ADJECTIVE
actions that a NOUN can do for you. Of
course, you and the computer will also
need to be VERB_ING a common NOUN, but
we'll get to that topic in just a bit.
>>>
```

Processing the template text

So, moving on in our pseudocode, we now need to process the text, which means we need to get the `process_line` function actually doing something. For starters, in step 2A, we need to iterate through each word in each line. Luckily we learned how to do that back in Chapter 6, when implementing the readability app. Let's give the same technique a try; here's a first cut at the structure of the `process_line` function:

1. Read the text for the story from file.
2. Process text.
   For each word in text
   - A. If word is a placeholder (NOUN or VERB or VERB_WITH_ING or ADJECTIVE):
     1. Prompt user for placeholder part of speech.
     2. Substitute user's word for the placeholder.
   - B. Otherwise, the word is fine; keep it in the story.
3. Store results.
   Take the processed text with the placeholders filled, and write it out to a file with the filename prepended by "crazy_".

```
def process_line(line):
    processed_line = ''

    words = line.split()

    for word in words:



    return processed_line
```

Okay, the processed line takes a line of the text.

And we'll probably need another string to hold the processed version of the line.

Let's split the line into a list of words...

...and then iterate over the list.

All our processing code is going to go here.

And when we're all done, we'll return the processed line.

Now let's process the text

Okay, that's some good skeleton code, but now what? Following on with our pseudocode, now we need to check for our placeholders, and if we have one prompt the user for a replacement word.

```
placeholders = ['NOUN', 'ADJECTIVE', 'VERB_ING', 'VERB']

def process_line(line):
    global placeholders
    processed_line = ''

    words = line.split()

    for word in words:
        if word in placeholders:
            answer = input('Enter a ' + word + ":")
            processed_line = processed_line + answer + ' '
        else:
            processed_line = processed_line + word + ' '
    return processed_line + '\n'
```

Let's just make a list of the placeholders. We will make it global in case it is needed in more than one function.

Then we can check each word to see if it is a placeholder.

If it is, let's prompt the user.

And add their answer to the processed line.

Otherwise, just add the word (which isn't a placeholder) to the processed line.

We also need to put a newline back on the line because split removes them.

A Test Drive

It's time to test Crazy Libs. Other than writing the text back to a file, we should almost have everything working. Get the changes to the code in *crazy. py* and choose the **Run > Run Module** menu item. We've reproduced all the code below. Double-check your output.

```python
def make_crazy_lib(filename):
    file = open(filename, 'r')

    text = ''

    for line in file:
        text = text + process_line(line) + '\n'

    file.close()

    return text
```

```python
placeholders = ['NOUN', 'ADJECTIVE', 'VERB_ING', 'VERB']

def process_line(line):
    global placeholders
    processed_line = ''

    words = line.split()

    for word in words:
        if word in placeholders:
            answer = input('Enter a ' + word + ":")
            processed_line = processed_line + answer + ' '
        else:
            processed_line = processed_line + word + ' '

    return processed_line + '\n'
```

It's worth one more look at the structure of this code. The for loop is stepping through every word in a single line. And for each word we see if the word is a placeholder, and if so, ask the user for a word to substitute in the processed line.

```python
def main():
    lib = make_crazy_lib('lib.txt')
    print(lib)

if __name__ == '__main__':
    main()
```

Here's what we got. Hmm, the code seems to be skipping some of our placeholders.

We have a problem!

```
Python 3.6.0 Shell

Enter a VERB_ING:buying
Enter a VERB_ING:pudding
Enter a ADJECTIVE:forgetting
Enter a NOUN:monkey
Enter a VERB_ING:eating
The first thing that stands between you
and buying your first, real, piece of NOUN,
is pudding the skill of breaking
problems down into achievable forgetting
actions that a monkey can do for you. Of
course, you and the computer will also
need to be eating a common NOUN, but
we'll get to that topic in just a bit.
>>>
```

Sharpen your pencil

Why is the code mysteriously skipping some of the nouns? Is it something to do with the nouns or something more systemic? Take a look at the input and output (and of course the code) and see if you can figure out the problem. Write your observations here.

We have three noun placeholders, but we're only being asked for one.

Is there anything different about the noun placeholders?

Or is something wrong in the code?

```
Python 3.6.0 Shell

Enter a VERB_ING:buying
Enter a VERB_ING:pudding
Enter a ADJECTIVE:forgetting
Enter a NOUN:monkey
Enter a VERB_ING:eating
The first thing that stands between you
and buying your first, real, piece of NOUN,
is pudding the skill of breaking
problems down into achievable forgetting
actions that a monkey can do for you. Of
course, you and the computer will also
need to be eating a common NOUN, but
we'll get to that topic in just a bit.
>>>
```

Using a new string method to fix the bug

We're going to solve this problem a bit differently than we did in Chapter 6 by making use of a string method: `strip`. The `strip` method returns a new string that has characters stripped off the beginning and ending of the string. Let's see how the `strip` method works:

Let's create a couple strings.

```python
hello = '!?are you there?!'
goodbye = '?fine be that !way!?!!'

hello = hello.strip('!?')
goodbye = goodbye.strip('!?')

print(hello)
print(goodbye)
```

The strip method takes a string of characters, and removes any occurrence of each character from the beginning and ending of the string.

All occurrences of ! and ? are stripped from the beginning and ending of the strings hello and goodbye.

```
Python 3.6.0 Shell

are you there
fine be that !way
```

Note that goodbye still has a ! character in it because it wasn't at the end of the string, so it wasn't stripped.

Using the `strip` method, spend some time reworking the `process_line` function to correctly handle placeholders that end in punctuation (commas, periods, semicolons, question marks, and so on). You not only need to recognize placeholders correctly, but you also need to preserve the punctuation in the output. Give your brain a real chance to work on this, and then we'll solve it together. No peeking ahead!

```
def process_line(line):
    global placeholders
    processed_line = ''
    words = line.split()
    for word in words:
        if word in placeholders:
            answer = input('Enter a ' + word + ":")
            processed_line = processed_line + answer + ' '
        else:
            processed_line = processed_line + word + ' '
    return processed_line + '\n'
```

← Here's the code we need to improve.

Actually fixing the bug

Fixing this bug requires a few tweaks to our code. This is a great example of how a small change to the functionality of your code, whether that is fixing a bug or adding a new feature, can introduce a lot of changes to your code. We would have been more effective if we'd caught this issue when we were writing our pseudocode.

You'll find anytime you are making lots of changes to existing code, you're introducing the possibility of even more bugs.

In terms of tweaks, we're going to strip each word of all punctuation, and then compare the stripped version of the word against the placeholder. We also have to be careful to add any punctuation back on to the user's chosen word when we're done. Here's how you do that:

```
def process_line(line):
    global placeholders
    processed_line = ''
    words = line.split()
    for word in words:
        stripped = word.strip('.,;?!')
        if stripped in placeholders:
            answer = input('Enter a ' + stripped + ":")
            processed_line = processed_line + answer
            if word[-1] in '.,;?!':
                processed_line = processed_line + word[-1] + ' '
            else:
                processed_line = processed_line + ' '
        else:
            processed_line = processed_line + word + ' '
    return processed_line + '\n'
```

⌐ First let's strip the word of all periods, commas, semicolons, and so on.

← We'll test the stripped version against the placeholders.

← We want to display the stripped placeholder text, not the one with punctuation.

↰ If there was punctuation, add it back, and then add the space. Otherwise, just add the space.

A Test Drive

Make the changes from the previous page to your *crazy.py* file and then choose the **Run > Run Module** menu item. Double-check your output.

To test your own story, just call make_crazy_lib and pass it the name of your story's file.

Finally, this is what we're looking for! We hope you tried your own set of verbs, nouns, and adjectives.

Try your own story now and see how it works as well.

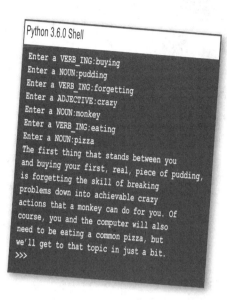

```
Python 3.6.0 Shell

Enter a VERB_ING:buying
Enter a NOUN:pudding
Enter a VERB_ING:forgetting
Enter a ADJECTIVE:crazy
Enter a NOUN:monkey
Enter a VERB_ING:eating
Enter a NOUN:pizza
The first thing that stands between you
and buying your first, real, piece of pudding,
is forgetting the skill of breaking
problems down into achievable crazy
actions that a monkey can do for you. Of
course, you and the computer will also
need to be eating a common pizza, but
we'll get to that topic in just a bit.
>>>
```

Some code has real problems

Give this a try: open your *crazy.py* file and change the filename from `'lib.txt'` to `'lib2.txt'`, and then execute your code.

If you try to open a file for reading and it doesn't exist, you'll get a FileNotFoundError exception.

```
Python 3.6.0 Shell

Traceback (most recent call last):
  File "crazy.py", line 45, in <module>
    main()
  File "crazy.py", line 41, in main
    crazy_lib = make_crazy_lib(filename)
  File "crazy.py", line 2, in make_crazy_lib
    file = open(filename, 'r')
FileNotFoundError: [Errno 2] No such file or directory: 'lib2.txt'
>>>
```

BRAIN POWER

Did our last bug fixes *really* take care of all issues we might encounter with punctuation? Or can you think of other ways the code still is a bit buggy?

Hint: One issue—would 'VERB!ii' be handled correctly in the output, or would only one ! be added? How would you fix that?

Let's take a moment for a little exercise that is going to show you some of the problems the Python interpreter has to deal with on a daily basis. Then we'll see what we can do about them with code. Your job is to act like you're the Python interpreter. You need to parse each piece of code and execute it. Write any output or errors in the Python Shell window.

Actually executing the code might help too. A lot.

```
list = [1, 2, 3, 4]
item = list[5]
```

Python 3.6.0 Shell

Write your results here.

Be the Python Interpreter

```
filename = 'document' + 1 + '.txt'
```

Python 3.6.0 Shell

```
int('1')
int('2')
int('E')
int('4')
int('5')
int('6')
```

Python 3.6.0 Shell

```
msg = 'hello'

def hi():
    print(msg)
    msg = 'hi'

hi()
```

Python 3.6.0 Shell

```
firstname = 'Beethoven'
print('First name: ' + name)
```

Python 3.6.0 Shell

Handling exceptions

We've discussed errors before: they can be syntax errors (essentially, typos in your code), semantic errors (logic problems with your code), or runtime errors (things that go wrong during the execution of your code). For runtime errors, so far we've just let them fall on the floor with the Python interpreter spitting out an error and your program coming to a grinding halt. But it doesn't have to end this way, especially when a runtime error occurs naturally in the course of running your code—say that file you're trying to open for reading just isn't there anymore. We'll see how we can handle that in a sec.

Let's talk a little more about what a runtime error, or *exception*, actually is. An exception is an event that occurs during the execution of your code when the Python interpreter encounters something it can't handle. When that happens, the interpreter stops the execution of your code and creates an exception object that has information about the error that occurred. By default this information is then displayed in the form of a traceback error message, which you're already familiar with from the Python Shell.

As we said, there is a way to deal with these errors when they arise without having the interepter just give up; in fact, in your code you can tell the interpreter you'd like to take over when certain exceptions occur, and handle them your own way. To do this wrap any code at risk in a `try/except` block, like this:

Start with a try keyword...

...then the block of code where the error could occur...

...then the except keyword.

```
try:
    filename = 'notthere.txt'
    file = open(filename, 'r')
except:
    print('Sorry, an error occured opening', filename)
else:
    print('Glad we got that file open')
    file.close()
```

Next, add a block of code to execute if an exception occurs.

And then add an optional else block, with code that will execute only if no exceptions occurred.

You can also add an optional finally block that runs whether an exception occurs or not. More on that in a sec.

Explicitly handling exceptions

When we use the `except` keyword followed by a code block, you get a exception catch-all—that is, the `except` code block will catch any exception that occurs in the `try` block. You can be more precise by giving a specific exception name, like this:

```python
try:
    filename = 'notthere.txt'
    file = open(filename, 'r')
except FileNotFoundError:
    print('Sorry,', filename, 'could not be found.')
except IsADirectoryError:
    print("That's a directory not a file!")
else:
    print("It's a good thing we could open that file.")
    file.close()
finally:
    print("I'm running no matter what happens")
```

Here's our try block again.

This time we've added a specific exception to the except statement.

So this block will execute only if a FileNotFoundError occurs.

We can add more exceptions too; this one executes only if you try to open a directory instead of a file.

As before, if all is good, this block will execute.

Here's where you can add a finally block; this block will execute whether there is an exception or not!

there are no Dumb Questions

Q: Is there a limit on the number of open files I can have?

A: Python does not place a limit on the number of open files, but your operating system does—that's another reason you should close files as you finish with them. If is often possible to increase this limit, although you'll need to reconfigure your operating system's process limits to do so (and you should ask yourself if you *really* need to).

Q: Is there a list of all the exceptions I can get?

A: Of course. As always, check out python.org. Or, more specifically, *https://docs.python.org/3/library/exceptions.html*.

Q: Is it possible to create your own exception types?

A: Yes. Exceptions are just objects, so you can extend Python by creating your own, new exception objects. That's a little beyond the scope of this chapter, but you'll find plenty on this online and at python.org. You'll want to read Chapter 11 too.

Q: Can I catch multiple exceptions using a single block? How do I do that?

A: After your except keyword, you can have one or more exceptions separated by commas within parentheses, like:

```python
except (FileNotFoundError, IOError):
```

As you already know, you can also omit the exception name and your except clause will catch any exception that occurs.

Sharpen your pencil

Trace through the code below three times. The first time enter any number except 0. The next time, enter 0. The last time, enter the string "zero". Write in the output you expect.

```python
try:
    num = input('Got a number? ')
    result = 42 / int(num)
except ZeroDivisionError:
    print("You can't divide by zero!")
except ValueError:
    print("Excuse me, we asked for a number.")
else:
    print('Your answer is', result)
finally:
    print('Thanks for stopping by.')
```

Input a number other than 0

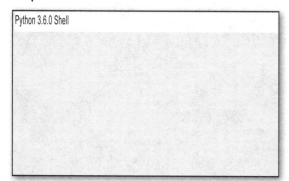

Input 0

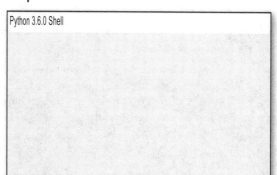

Input the string "zero"

Updating Crazy Libs to handle exceptions

With your new knowledge of exceptions, let's update the code that opens a file to handle some file exceptions:

```python
def make_crazy_lib(filename):
    try:
        file = open(filename, 'r')
        text = ''

        for line in file:
            text = text + process_line(line)
        file.close()

        return text

    except FileNotFoundError:
        print("Sorry, couldn't find", filename + '.')
    except IsADirectoryError:
        print("Sorry", filename, 'is a directory.')
    except:
        print("Sorry, could not read", filename)
```

← Most of this code is making use of a file, so let's put it all in a try block.

← Let's see if we have a file not found error or if the user tried to open a directory (assuming they changed the filename in the code).

And then let's catch any other exceptions that happen when processing the file.

⌐ Notice we don't have an else or finally clause.

That takes care of the `make_crazy_lib` function, but there's something important to notice in this code: what gets returned from the function if we get an exception? Because we are not explicitly returning anything, the value `None` will get returned. Keep this in mind, because *you're going to need to remember this* when we write the code to save the Crazy Libs.

We told you we'd be bumping into the None value now and then.

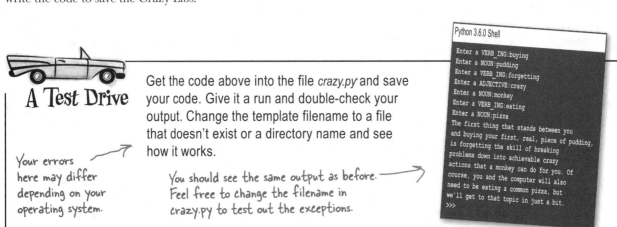

A Test Drive

Get the code above into the file *crazy.py* and save your code. Give it a run and double-check your output. Change the template filename to a file that doesn't exist or a directory name and see how it works.

Your errors here may differ depending on your operating system.

You should see the same output as before. Feel free to change the filename in *crazy.py* to test out the exceptions.

```
Python 3.6.0 Shell

Enter a VERB_ING:buying
Enter a NOUN:pudding
Enter a VERB_ING:forgetting
Enter a ADJECTIVE:crazy
Enter a NOUN:monkey
Enter a VERB_ING:eating
Enter a NOUN:pizza
The first thing that stands between you
and buying your first, real, piece of pudding,
is forgetting the skill of breaking
problems down into achievable crazy
actions that a monkey can do for you. Of
course, you and the computer will also
need to be eating a common pizza, but
we'll get to that topic in just a bit.
>>>
```

Our last step: storing the Crazy Lib

Saving your Crazy Lib or any text to a file is straightforward with the file object's `write` method. To use it we need to first open a file *in write mode*. Let's write a function `save_crazy_lib`, which takes a filename and a string as parameters. When called, `save_crazy_lib` will create the file, save the string to it, and then close the file. Check out this code:

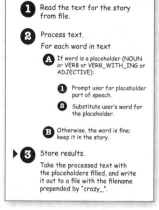

1. Read the text for the story from file.

2. Process text.
   For each word in text

   A. If word is a placeholder (NOUN or VERB or VERB_WITH_ING or ADJECTIVE):
      1. Prompt user for placeholder part of speech.
      2. Substitute user's word for the placeholder.

   B. Otherwise, the word is fine; keep it in the story.

▶ 3. Store results.
   Take the processed text with the placeholders filled, and write it out to a file with the filename prepended by "crazy_".

Our save function expects a filename and some text in the form of a string.

```python
def save_crazy_lib(filename, text):
    file = open(filename, "w")

    file.write(text)
    file.close()
```

First we open the file in 'w' mode so we can write to it. Python will create this file if it doesn't already exist.

Then we use the file object write method, and pass it the text string to save to the file.

Finally, we close the file.

With a lot of programming languages, if you don't close a file you've written to, then you can't guarantee that the data will be fully written to the file.

Watch it!

Be careful opening files in 'w' mode.

When you open an existing file using 'w' mode, its contents will be erased and replaced by whatever you write to the file. So be careful!

Updating the rest of the code

Now that we have `save_crazy_lib` written, we need to call it from the `main` function, and to do that we need to check to make sure `make_crazy_lib` returned a Crazy Lib—remember, if it encounters a file exception it will return `None`.

Let's store the crazy lib filename in a variable to make things more convenient.

If an exception occurs when opening or reading the file, then lib will have the value None. So, we need to test lib to see if it has a value before passing it to save_crazy_lib.

```python
def main():
    filename = 'lib.txt'
    lib = make_crazy_lib(filename)
    print(lib)
    if (lib != None):
        save_crazy_lib('crazy_' + filename, lib)
```

The filename we're going to save the lib under is going to be "crazy_" prepended to the original filename.

A Test Drive

It's time to get a little crazy with
Crazy Libs, because we're all
done; we just need to get these
last changes into the *crazy.py* file.
We've reproduced the entire game
on this page, and we've even
added in some exception code for
you as well. Go ahead and update
your code and give Crazy Libs a
try.

```python
def make_crazy_lib(filename):
    try:
        file = open(filename, 'r')

        text = ''

        for line in file:
            text = text + process_line(line)

        file.close()

        return text

    except FileNotFoundError:
        print("Sorry, couldn't find", filename + '.')
    except IsADirectoryError:
        print("Sorry", filename, 'is a directory.')
    except:
        print("Sorry, could not read", filename)

placeholders = ['NOUN', 'ADJECTIVE', 'VERB_ING', 'VERB']

def process_line(line):
    global placeholders
    processed_line = ''

    words = line.split()

    for word in words:
        stripped = word.strip('.,;?!')
        if stripped in placeholders:
            answer = input('Enter a ' + stripped + ":")
            processed_line = processed_line + answer
            if word[-1] in '.,;?!':
                processed_line = processed_line + word[-1] +
            else:
                processed_line = processed_line + ' '
        else:
            processed_line = processed_line + word + ' '
    return processed_line + '\n'
```

We went ahead and added the
exception code to the save_crazy_
lib for you. Check it out.

```python
def save_crazy_lib(filename, text):
    try:
        file = open(filename, 'w')
        file.write(text)
        file.close()
    except:
        print("Sorry, couldn't write file.", filename)

def main():
    filename = 'lib.txt'
    lib = make_crazy_lib(filename)
    print(lib)
    if (lib != None):
        save_crazy_lib('crazy_' + filename, lib)

if __name__ == '__main__':
    main()
```

I'd love to use this on different templates without having to open the Python source file to change the filename. Could I supply a template filename using my command line?

Ah, yes, that would polish this off nicely.

We haven't used Python on the command line, but if you open your command line and change your directory to the location of your *crazy.py* file, then you can run your code like this on the Mac:

```
python3 crazy.py
```

and like this on your Windows machine:

```
python crazy.py
```

Let's add a command-line argument to specify the Crazy Libs template, like this:

```
python3 crazy.py lib.txt
```

Run the program crazy.py and use the lib.txt template.

To get the *lib.txt* argument from the command line, we'll use Python's `sys` module that includes an attribute called `argv`. The `argv` attribute is a list that holds the terms you typed into the command line (excluding the Python command). For instance, if you type:

```
python3 crazy.py lib.txt
```

then item 0 of `argv` will hold *crazy.py* and item 1 will hold *lib.txt*. Let's see if we can use this, and polish off our Crazy Lib game.

A Test Drive

Let's add that final piece of polish and allow your user to specify a filename on the command line. You'll do that with two simple additions; go ahead and work through the two additions and then give your code another, final, test drive.

1 First import the `sys` module by adding an `import sys` to the top of your *crazy.py* file.

```
import sys
```
← Add this to the top of your file.

2 Then let's make a few changes to the main function in *crazy.py*.

> We want there to be two arguments or the user hasn't provided a filename. So let them know if there aren't two arguments.

```
def main():
    if len(sys.argv) != 2:
        print("crazy.py <filename>")
    else:
        filename = sys.argv[1]
        lib = make_crazy_lib(filename)
        if (lib != None):
            save_crazy_lib('crazy_' + filename, lib)
```

> Otherwise, the filename is the command-line argument at item index 1.

This time we'll need to run our Python from the command line. If you're using a Mac, it's called the Terminal, which you can find in the Applications > Utilities folder.

If you're on a PC, it's called the command prompt, which you can find by clicking the Start button, typing "cmd", and then choosing Command Prompt.

```
Terminal
$ cd /Users/eric/code/ch9
$ python3 crazy.py lib.txt
Enter a VERB_ING:running
Enter a NOUN:hotdog
Enter a VERB_ING:eating
Enter a ADJECTIVE:spicy
Enter a NOUN:taco
Enter a VERB_ING:breaking
Enter a NOUN:glass
$ cat lib.txt
The first thing that stands between you
and running your first, real, piece of hotdog,
is eating the skill of breaking
problems down into achievable spicy
actions that a taco can do for you. Of
course, you and the computer will also
need to be breaking a common glass, but
we'll get to that topic in just a bit.
$
```

You'll need to navigate to the correct directory that contains your crazy.py file using your operating system's cd (short for change directory) command.

Here's our command line on a Mac.

On Windows you'll need to run python, not python3.

Remember to use the "python" command on a Windows machine.

Here's what's in the file crazy_lib.txt.

BULLET POINTS

- You have to open a file to access it from Python.

- To open a file use Python's **open** function.

- When you open a file you supply a mode: **'r'** for reading or **'w'** for writing.

- The **open** function can take either a relative path or an absolute one.

- Call the file object's **close** method when you are done reading it or writing to it.

- The **open** function supports several forms of reading standard text files.

- Use the **read** method to read the entire contents of the file at once.

- Reading an entire file may be resource intensive for large files.

- Use the **readline** method to read a single line at a time.

- The empty string signifies when **readline** has read the last line.

- Or you can treat the file as a sequence and use it in a **for** statement, as in **for line in file:**

- An iterator lets us iterate over a sequence with the **for/in** statement.

- The **break** statement prematurely stops the execution of a **for** or **while** loop.

- Most text files have a newline character between lines of text.

- The escape sequence \n represents a newline character.

- The **strip** method removes zero or more occurrences of the specified characters from the beginning and end of a string. If no character is specified, **strip** defaults to removing whitespace.

- Use **try/except** to capture exceptions. Place the code that may generate an error in the **try** block and then one or more **except** statements to catch the exceptions.

- An **except** without an explicit exception acts as a catch-all.

- The **finally** statement is always executed, whether or not an exception occurs.

- The **sys** module has an attribute **argv** that contains your program's command-line arguments.

- The **argv** attribute holds a list that contains each word used on the command line.

Coding cross

Let files sink into your brain as you do the crossword.

Across

3. Gets you the entire file.
4. Use try/except to catch these.
9. Windows and Mac disagree.
10. If your path isn't relative it must be.
11. A huge file might lead to these errors.
12. End of file when you hit this.
13. Holds your command line arguments.
14. Another name for \n.
15. How to access a file.
17. Our new game.
18. You can 'r' or 'w'.
19. Cleans up the ends of strings.

Down

1. Type of argv
2. An except without an explicit exception.
5. What's \n?
6. Always do this when you're done.
7. A design pattern.
8. Just need one line?
9. Module with argv.
13. When a finally statement is executed.
16. When you're done.

Sharpen your pencil
Solution

Hey, it's Chapter 9 already, so we have no doubt you can tackle the task of creating a little pseudocode based on the previous two pages. Writing up a little pseudocode now is going to give you a clearer idea of how to approach writing the Crazy Libs game.

Here's what we came up with; depending on the level of detail you went into, your pseudocode may differ, but just make sure we're aligned on the general logic before moving on.

1 Read the text for the story from file.

Somehow we're going to read the contents of the story into Python.

2 Process text.

Then we're going to start processing the text by examining each word.

For each word in text

A If word is a placeholder (NOUN or VERB or VERB_ING or ADJECTIVE):

If we find a word that is a placeholder, we need to ask the user for a word to replace it with.

1 Prompt user for placeholder part of speech.

2 Substitute user's word for the placeholder in text.

And then we need to substitute that word for the placeholder in the story text.

B Otherwise, the word is fine; keep it in the story.

And if the word isn't a placeholder, then we just keep the original word.

3 Store results.

Take the processed text with the placeholders filled, and write it out to a file with the filename prepended by "crazy_".

Finally, when we're done processing every word, we write all the text of the story into a new file.

Sharpen your pencil
Solution

Draw a line from each file path to the file it identifies. For any relative paths, all code is run from the code directory.

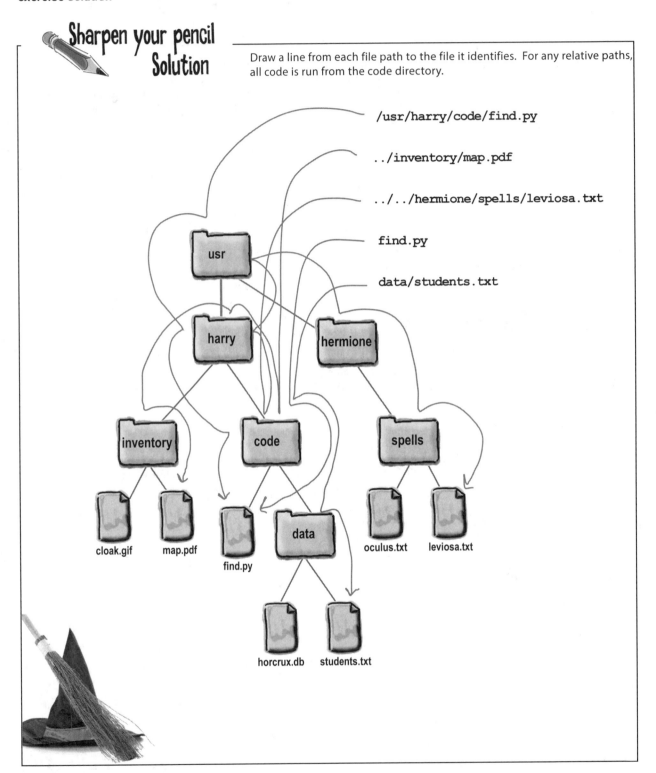

/usr/harry/code/find.py

../inventory/map.pdf

../../hermione/spells/leviosa.txt

find.py

data/students.txt

Code Magnets Solution

Can you help find the needle in the haystack? You've been given a directory of 1,000 files with the filenames *0.txt* through *999.txt*, and only one has the word *needle* in it. Can you find the needle? We had the code all written and on the refrigerator, but then someone came along and messed it all up. Can you help us put it back together? Notice, there may be some extra code magnets, so you may not use all of them.

Rearrange the magnets here. ↓

```python
for i in range(0, 1000):
```
Iterate over all 1,000 files, constructing a filename for each one of 0.txt, 1.txt, 2.txt...

```python
filename = str(i) + '.txt'
```

```python
file = open(filename, 'r')
```
Open the file for reading.

```python
text = file.read()
```
Read in the entire file, which returns a string, assigned to text.

```python
if 'needle' in text:
```
Check to see if the needle in the string, and...

```python
print('Found needle in file ' + str(i) + '.txt')
```

```python
file.close()
```
And don't forget to close each file.

...if found, print out the filename.

Give it a try; look at the needle directory in the ch9 source code directory for the files 0.txt through 999.txt. Which file has the needle?

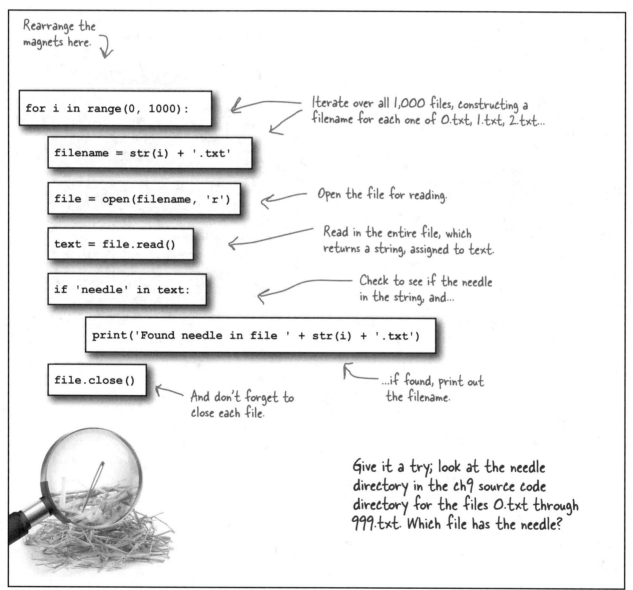

Sharpen your pencil
Solution

Why is the code mysteriously skipping some of the nouns? Is it something to do with the nouns or something more systemic? Take a look at the input and output (and of course the code) and see if you can figure out the problem.

It looks like we're skipping the first noun, and the last.

```
The first thing that stands between you
and VERB_ING your first, real, piece of NOUN,
is VERB_ING the skill of breaking
problems down into achievable ADJECTIVE
actions that a NOUN can do for you. Of
course, you and the computer will also
need to be VERB_ING a common NOUN, but
we'll get to that topic in just a bit.
```

Python 3.6.0 Shell

```
Enter a VERB_ING:buying
Enter a VERB_ING:pudding
Enter a ADJECTIVE:forgetting
Enter a NOUN:monkey
Enter a VERB_ING:eating
The first thing that stands between you
and buying your first, real, piece of NOUN,
is pudding the skill of breaking
problems down into achievable forgetting
actions that a monkey can do for you. Of
course, you and the computer will also
need to be eating a common NOUN, but
we'll get to that topic in just a bit.
>>>
```

If we look at the skipped noun placeholders in the input (or output) file, we can see what is different is that they have punctuation at the end of them.

Argh! It's the same old bug we saw in Chapter 6 with the text analysis. We need to account for the comma (and we'll assume period as well) when comparing text against these placeholders.

Let's take a moment for a little exercise that is going to show you some of the problems the Python interpreter has to deal with on a daily basis. Then we'll see what we can do about them with code. Your job is to act like you're the Python interpreter. You need to parse each piece of code and execute it. Write any output or errors in the Python Shell window.

```python
list = [1, 2, 3, 4]
item = list[5]
```

Be the Python Interpreter Solution

```
Python 3.6.0 Shell
Traceback (most recent call last):
  File "/Users/eric/code/ch8/errors/list.py", line 2, in <module>
    item = list[5]
IndexError: list index out of range
>>>
```

```python
filename = 'document' + 1 + '.txt'
```

```
Python 3.6.0 Shell
Traceback (most recent call last):
  File "/Users/eric/code/ch8/errors/filename.py", line 1, in <module>
    filename = "document" + 1 + ".txt"
TypeError: must be str, not int
>>>
```

```python
int('1')
int('2')
int('E')
int('4')
int('5')
int('6')
```

```
Python 3.6.0 Shell
Traceback (most recent call last):
  File "/Users/eric/code/ch8/errors/ints.py", line 3, in <module>
    int('E')
ValueError: invalid literal for int() with base 10: 'E'
>>>
```

```python
msg = 'hello'

def hi():
    print(msg)
    msg = 'hi'

hi()
```

```
Python 3.6.0 Shell
Traceback (most recent call last):
  File "/Users/eric/code/ch8/errors/function.py", line 7, in <module>
    hi()
  File "/Users/eric/Documents/code/ch8/errors/function.py", line 4, in hi
    print(msg)
UnboundLocalError: local variable 'msg' referenced before assignment
>>>
```

```python
firstname = 'Beethoven'
print('First name: ' + name)
```

```
Python 3.6.0 Shell
Traceback (most recent call last):
  File "/Users/eric/code/ch8/errors/print.py", line 2, in <module>
    print('First name: ' + name)
NameError: name 'name' is not defined
>>>
```

Sharpen your pencil
Solution

Trace through the code below three times. The first time, enter any number except 0. The next time, enter 0. The last time, enter the string `"zero"`. Write in the output you expect.

```python
try:
    num = input('Got a number? ')
    result = 42 / int(num)
except ZeroDivisionError:
    print("You can't divide by zero!")
except ValueError:
    print("Excuse me, we asked for a number.")
else:
    print('Your answer is', result)
finally:
    print('Thanks for stopping by.')
```

Input a number other than 0

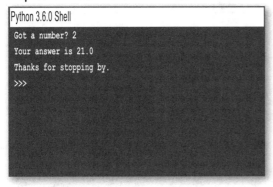

```
Python 3.6.0 Shell
Got a number? 2
Your answer is 21.0
Thanks for stopping by.
>>>
```

Input 0

```
Python 3.6.0 Shell
Got a number? 0
You can't divide by zero!
Thanks for stopping by.
>>>
```

Input the string "zero"

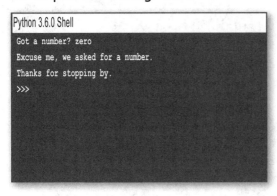

```
Python 3.6.0 Shell
Got a number? zero
Excuse me, we asked for a number.
Thanks for stopping by.
>>>
```

 # File i/o cross Solution

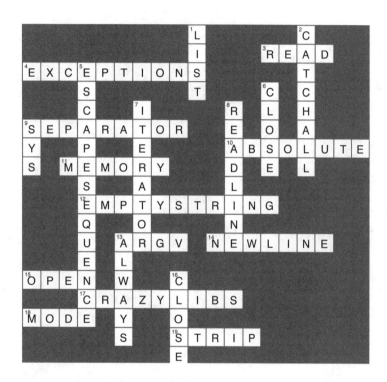

You Really Should Get Out More

Yes, please do bring the car around; we really should get out and see some of these Web APIs we've been hearing so much about.

You've been writing some great code, but you really need to get out more. There's a whole world of **data** just waiting for you on the web: Need weather data? Or how about access to a huge database of recipes? Or are sports scores more your thing? Maybe a music database of artists, albums, and songs? They're all out there for the taking from **Web APIs**. To use them all you need is to learn a bit more about how the web works, how to speak the local web lingo, and how to use a couple of new Python modules: `requests` and `json`. In this chapter we're going to explore Web APIs and take your Python skills to new heights; in fact, we're going to take them all the way to outer space and back.

You think we're kidding!

Extending your reach with Web APIs

You've seen a recurring pattern in this book: first you took your code and abstracted it away into functions. Once you did that, you could make use of the functionality in a function without having to worry about all the details of how the function does what it does. This allowed you to elevate your thinking above the level of simple statements.

Next you packaged things up into modules that contained a whole set of functions and values. Remember the code you handed to Cory? He was able to quickly look at your documentation, see what functions were available, and make use of them. *That's an API.* Think of an API, otherwise known as an *application programming interface*, as a set of documented functions that anyone can use in their code.

You've also seen there are modules created by other developers, which you can think of as APIs, available to you in Python. These modules—modules for math and random numbers and graphics and turtles and a lot more—really allow you to expand the capabilities of your own code.

And now we're going to take abstraction one step further by considering code on the internet that you can use to extend the capabilities of your code. Only this code isn't necessarily written in Python, it's code that runs on the web and it's accessible through a Web API.

You might be asking, though, what kind of API would we find on the web? How about an API that computes and returns weather current conditions, or information about songs and music artists? Or how about an API that gives you the actual location of objects in outer space?

Though are all actual Web APIs and they're just a few examples from a vast catalog of information available *to your code* over the internet.

> We've seen another example of abstraction with object-oriented programming. We'll be seeing even more of that coming up in Chapter 12 when we learn how to create our own objects.

BRAIN POWER

Pretend your boss just walked in and asked you to quickly write an application that shows the current local weather conditions—and he needs it for a demo tomorrow. How much would it help to use a Web API that gives you the actual current weather conditions? How would you write the app without such a service? How long do you think it would take to write your app in each case?

How Web APIs work

With Web APIs we don't call a function in a module or library; instead, we issue a request over the web. So, rather than looking at a set of *functions* that a module provides, we look at the different *web requests* we can issue to a web server to understand its Web API.

Issuing a web request is something you already know how to do if you know how to use a web browser. And who doesn't? You do it every time you request a web page. The main difference with a Web API is that *your code* makes the request to a web server, and that server sends back *data*, rather than a page, to your code.

In this chapter we're going to take a close look at how all this works, and where Python fits into it—but for now, let's take a look at how an actual Web API request works:

To use a Web API, send it a request

Think of a Web API as just a web server, only it serves up *data* rather than pages. To make use of a Web API, your code sends a **request** to a web server. The web server in turn generates a **response**, and sends it back to your code.

> Sure!
> 67.2 degrees with
> a 40% chance of rain

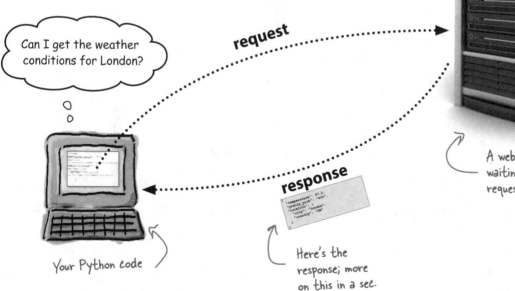

> Can I get the weather
> conditions for London?

request

response

A web server, waiting for API requests

Your Python code

Here's the response; more on this in a sec.

All Web APIs have a web address

With Web APIs we use web addresses similar to the ones you type into your browser—they contain a server name along with a description of a resource. With a web browser, that resource is typically a web page. With a Web API, the resource is data, which can vary greatly. The way we specify the resource for a Web API can also vary quite a bit, depending on the Web API. Let's take a look at a few examples:

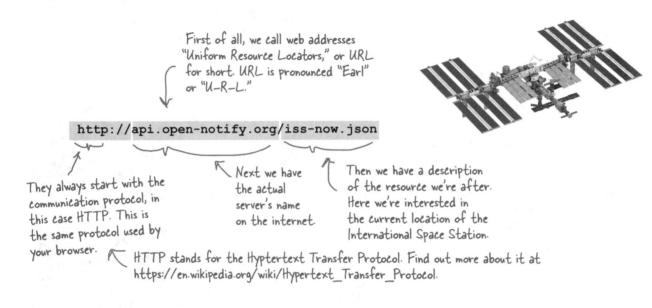

First of all, we call web addresses "Uniform Resource Locators," or URL for short. URL is pronounced "Earl" or "U–R–L."

`http://api.open-notify.org/iss-now.json`

They always start with the communication protocol, in this case HTTP. This is the same protocol used by your browser.

Next we have the actual server's name on the internet.

Then we have a description of the resource we're after. Here we're interested in the current location of the International Space Station.

HTTP stands for the Hyptertext Transfer Protocol. Find out more about it at https://en.wikipedia.org/wiki/Hypertext_Transfer_Protocol.

Let's look at another example, this time weather data for the city of London from the Open Weather Map organization:

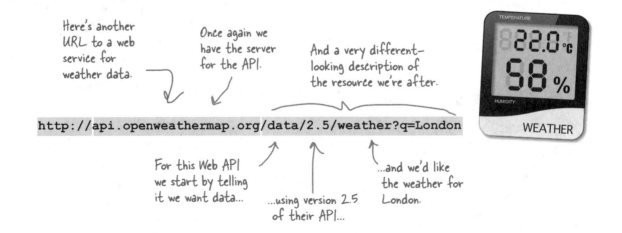

Here's another URL to a web service for weather data.

Once again we have the server for the API.

And a very different-looking description of the resource we're after.

`http://api.openweathermap.org/data/2.5/weather?q=London`

For this Web API we start by telling it we want data...

...using version 2.5 of their API...

...and we'd like the weather for London.

And one more example: how about looking up some
related artist information on Spotify?

Here we're using version 1
of the API.

We're asking for data for
a particular artist.

Here's the ID of
the artist we're
interested in.

`http://api.spotify.com/v1/artists/43ZHCT0cAZBISjO8DG9PnE/related-artists`

As always we have our
server name.

Any idea what
artist this
is? Would the
nickname "The
King" help?

And we'd like data
on related artists.

All of those
web addresses look
completely different, so how
are we supposed to know how
to make a request?

Consult the API documentation.

We're serious. And it's not as bad as it sounds. All Web APIs follow the
standard syntax for a web URL (and you can look that up if you're
interested), but they expose very different APIs for very different types
of data. So, the way you request that data often looks quite different.
Look at our examples: the Open Notify URL is quite simple, while the
Spotify URL is more complex.

You'll find that most Web APIs provide adequate documentation
for knowing how to form a request URL to access whatever type of
information you're looking for. Hang tight, because we're going to
explore Open Notify API in just a bit.

I typed the Spotify URL into my browser and I got a "no token" error.

Good point.

Making a Web API request through a browser is often a great way to explore an API firsthand. That said, many Web APIs require that you register (usually free) as a developer before using their services. Registering usually gets you an authorization token or an access key, which you pass along when you're making your requests. Without the access token, many of these APIs will send back an error, such as your "no token" error.

So, the best thing to do is to review the Web API's documentation for any access tokens it requires.

In our examples so far, the Spotify and Open Weather Web APIs require access tokens. The Open Notify API, however, doesn't currently require a token.

Exercise

Enter the following URL in your browser. What do you get?

```
http://api.open-notify.org/iss-now.json
```

Try retrieving this URL multiple times. You can also try entering the longitude and latitude, like "−0.2609, 118.8982," directly into Google Maps (latitude first).

Time for a quick upgrade

Before we start making requests to Web APIs, we're going to quickly add a *new package* to Python that will help us make those requests. What's a Python package? As we mentioned in Chapter 7, a package is just a formal name for a set of related Python modules—you could also informally call it a library.

To add a new package we're going to use the `pip` utility, which is an acronym for "Pip Installs Packages." Using `pip`, you can add packages (or remove them later) to your local installation.

With `pip`, we're going to add a handy package called `requests`, which allows us to make requests to Web APIs. More specifically, we'll be using the `requests` module, which comes as part of the `requests` package (not to be too confusing). Now we should tell you that Python does have its own built-in module for making web requests, but a lot of coders find `requests` easier to use and more functional than the built-in module. Using the `requests` package also gives us an excuse to gain some experience using `pip`.

Let's get `requests` installed and then we'll see what this package is all about.

Can you say "recursive acronym"?

Who might we be referring to? Oh, just Twitter, Spotify, Microsoft, Amazon, Lyft, BuzzFeed, Reddit, the NSA, and we could go on, and on, and on...

You can read more about the requests package and module at: http://docs.python-requests.org.

We often call packages written by other developers and organizations (outside of Python's core development team) third-party packages.

Doing the upgrade

The `pip` utility is built into Python, so get yourself into the appropriate command line for your operating system and let's get the `requests` package installed.

Use your operating system's command line like we did in Chapter 9. If you're using a Mac you'll want the terminal app, on a Windows machine use the command prompt, and on Linux—oh, who are we kidding? If you are using Linux, you live in the command line.

[Note from editor: apparently, you love this Linux joke.]

```
Terminal
$ python3 -m pip install requests
```

Windows users should use "python" and not "python3".

Go ahead and enter the command above to start the installation. Note, you need to be connected to the internet for pip to retrieve and install packages. Also note this is installing in Python's library directory, not your current working directory. If you encounter any permission errors, make sure your user account has sufficient privileges to install new packages.

```
Terminal
$ python3 -m pip install requests
Collecting requests
  Downloading requests-2.18.1-py2.py3-none-any.whl (88kB)
    100% |                              | 92kB 1.4MB/s
Collecting idna<2.6,>=2.5 (from requests)
  Downloading idna-2.5-py2.py3-none-any.whl (55kB)
    100% |                              | 61kB 2.5MB/s
Collecting urllib3<1.22,>=1.21.1 (from requests)
  Downloading urllib3-1.21.1-py2.py3-none-any.whl (131kB)
    100% |                              | 133kB 2.5MB/s
Collecting certifi>=2017.4.17 (from requests)
  Downloading certifi-2017.4.17-py2.py3-none-any.whl (375kB)
    100% |                              | 378kB 2.2MB/s
Collecting chardet<3.1.0,>=3.0.2 (from requests)
  Downloading chardet-3.0.4-py2.py3-none-any.whl (133kB)
    100% |                              | 143kB 4.1MB/s
Installing collected packages: idna, urllib3, certifi, chardet, requests
$
```

Here you can see pip retrieving the requests module, as well as related packages it depends on. Note this is the macOS X install, so your installation may look slightly different.

there are no Dumb Questions

Q: Why do you prefer the requests module over something built into Python? Wouldn't Python's built-in module always be the way to go?

A: The creators of the requests package created a library for making web requests that is arguably more straightforward and provides better functionality than what Python gives you out of the box, so much so that it is in everyday use by many online products and services. That said, there is nothing wrong with Python's built-in requests module (which, by the way, is called urllib, or is it urllib2? See, it's already confusing!), if you want to use that.

That's one great thing about being able to extend Python or most programming languages: developers are free to create their own extensions and share them with others.

Q: That's cool I can add new packages to Python. How do I find out all the packages I can add?

A: You can search for new packages right from the command line, like this:

```
python3 -m pip search hue
```

which will search for packages that match the 'hue' keyword. Another great way to find Python packages is to search for them with Google using search terms like "python3 request module" or "python3 hue lighting," as an example. Also, check out *http://pypi.org*, a repository of software for Python.

Q: I'm running Python 3, but it doesn't seem to support pip.

A: pip was added to Python with release 3.4; double-check your version number and upgrade to the latest version. Check with *https://www.python.org* for the latest release.

All we need now is a good Web API...

Now that you have the `requests` package installed, you're finally ready to make your first web request from Python. Of course to do that, you need an interesting Web API to make a request of. If you'll remember in the beginning of this chapter we promised to take you to outer space and back, and we're going to do that using a Web API that provides the current location of the International Space Station (ISS). You'll find it at *open-notify. org*. Let's take a look at what Open Notify offers:

Visit open-notify.org to check out more documentation for the ISS API. You'll find the highlights here.

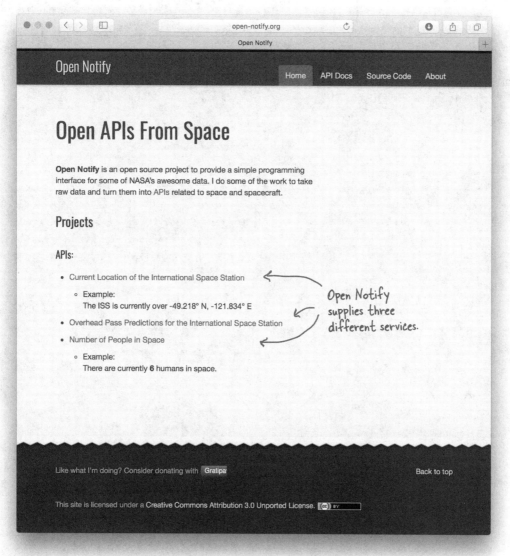

Open Notify supplies three different services.

A closer look at the API

As you can see on *open-notify.org*'s front page, there are three "Open APIs from space": an API for getting the ISS's current location, an API for making overpass projections, and an API for getting the number of people in space. We're going to start by looking at the current location API, which you can see more detail on by clicking on the "Current Location of..." link:

Here are the docs for the ISS Current Location API.

If you were paying attention earlier in the chapter, you've already seen that this API returns the current latitude and longitude of the International Space Station.

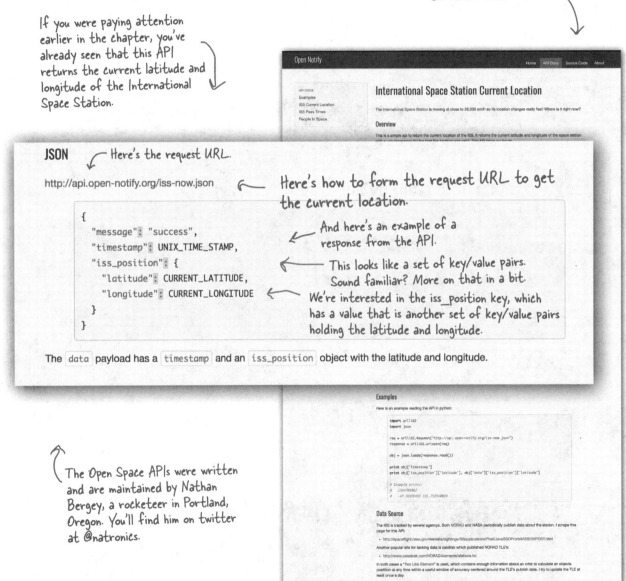

JSON — Here's the request URL.

http://api.open-notify.org/iss-now.json ← Here's how to form the request URL to get the current location.

```
{
  "message": "success",
  "timestamp": UNIX_TIME_STAMP,
  "iss_position": {
    "latitude": CURRENT_LATITUDE,
    "longitude": CURRENT_LONGITUDE
  }
}
```

And here's an example of a response from the API.

This looks like a set of key/value pairs. Sound familiar? More on that in a bit.

We're interested in the iss_position key, which has a value that is another set of key/value pairs holding the latitude and longitude.

The `data` payload has a `timestamp` and an `iss_position` object with the latitude and longitude.

The Open Space APIs were written and are maintained by Nathan Bergey, a rocketeer in Portland, Oregon. You'll find him on twitter at @natronics.

The data returned from the Open Notify Web API should look a bit familiar. Is there a Python data type it reminds you of?

Web APIs provide data using JSON

Pronounced Jason, usually with an emphasis on the "on."

Who's JSON, you say? JSON is actually an object notation that most Web APIs use to deliver their data. You're going to find this notation familiar, because it is syntactically quite similar to Python dictionaries.

There are other formats for exchanging data over the web, but you'll find JSON is the most popular.

Think of JSON as a set of key/value pairs specified as text. For example, say a weather Web API wants to send you the current conditions for London. It would create JSON that looks something like this and ship it your way:

Each pair consists of a string that acts as a key, and a value...

The JSON format wraps a set of key/value pairs in curly braces.

```
{
    "temperature": 67.2,
    "precip_prob": "40%",
    "location": {
        "city": "London",
        "country": "UK"
    }
}
```

...values can be strings or numbers.

All keys are strings in JSON.

Values can even be another, nested set of key/value pairs.

Note you can also specify lists, or, what JSON calls an array, with JSON.

When used with a Web API, this entire definition is placed into a text string and sent back as a response.

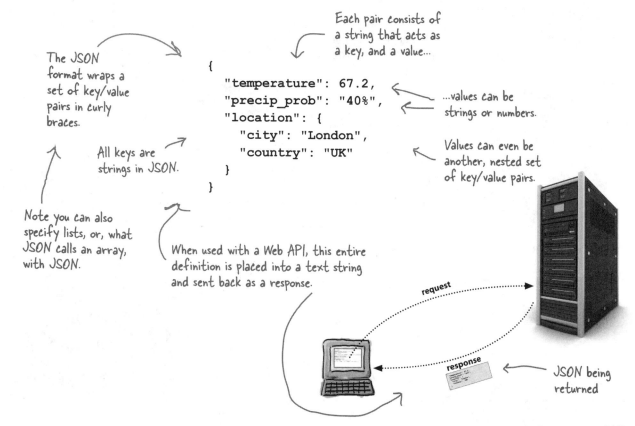

request

response

JSON being returned

there are no
Dumb Questions

Q: So are Python dictionaries and JSON the same thing?

A: It is easy to confuse the two given how much they look alike. Think of it like this: in Python when you specify code for a dictionary, at some point the interpreter reads that code and translates it to an internal data structure, which your code makes use of. But with JSON, we're specifying a set of key/value pairs that we can send over the network purely in a text format to another program or service. So JSON isn't Python; rather, it's meant to be a general-purpose format than can be read and interpreted by any language.

That said, it is rather nice the two are so much alike.

Q: So if I'm going to receive JSON as just text, how can my code use that?

A: Hang tight—you're asking the right question, and we'll get to that in just a bit.

Q: Why is it called JSON?

A: While JSON is meant to be a format independent of any programming language, it did grow out of one language in particular: JavaScript. So JSON stands for JavaScript Object Notation.

Q: I'm still confused. How do I know what Web APIs are out there and how I can use them?

A: You'll find clearinghouses for web-based APIs on sites such as *www.programmableweb.com*. Most companies with APIs also provide documentation, like *dev.twitter.com*, or *developer.spotify.com*, to name a couple.

Sharpen your pencil

Take the JSON on the previous page and convert it, by hand, into a Python dictionary in the space below. After you've done that, complete the code below. You'll need to look at the output to know what it does.

```
current =   _____
            _____
            _____
            _____
            _____
            _____
            _____
```

Soon you'll ask your code to do this for you.

```
loc = _____
print('In',
        loc['city'] + ', ' + _____,
        'it is',
                    _____, 'degrees')
```

```
Python 3.6.0 Shell

In London, UK it is 67.2 degrees
>>>
```

Now let's look at that request module again

To make a web request we're going to use the `requests` module's `get` function. Here's how it works:

1 **Use get to make the request.**

First we call the `requests` module's `get` function to make the actual request to the remote web server.

```
url = 'http://api.open-notify.org/iss-now.json'
```

Here's the URL we got from the Open Notify documentation.

```
response = requests.get(url)
```

We pass the URL to the get function, upon which the function contacts the remote web server.

When a response is received from the remote server, the function first packages it up in a nice response object, and then returns it.

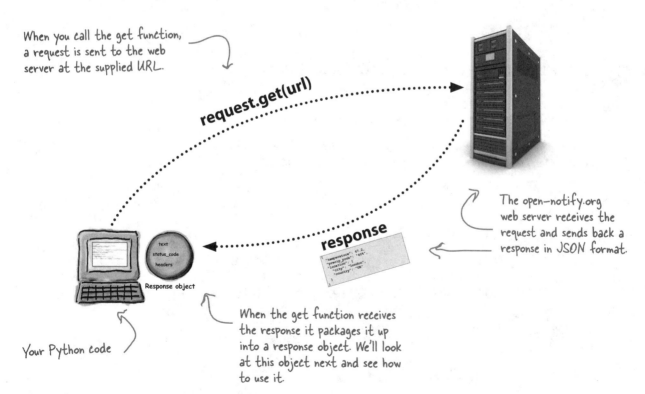

When you call the get function, a request is sent to the web server at the supplied URL.

request.get(url)

The open-notify.org web server receives the request and sends back a response in JSON format.

response

When the get function receives the response it packages it up into a response object. We'll look at this object next and see how to use it.

Your Python code

2 **Examine the response object.**

As we said, after the `get` function receives a response from the server it packages it up in a `response` object. Let's take a look:

Here are some of the more important attributes in the response object. For our purposes the text and status_code attributes are the ones to pay attention to.

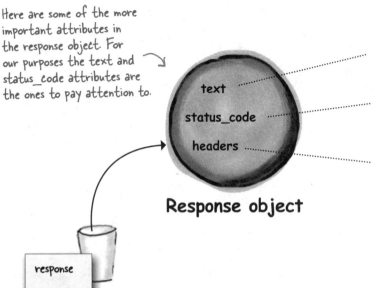

text

status_code

headers

Response object

response

The text property holds the real data of the response, typically in JSON format.

The status code holds a diagnostic code for the request. A code of 200 means the request was fulfilled without errors.

The headers are used to supply other information about the response, such as the content type of the response. For instance, the JSON encoding is called application/json.

3 **Check the status_code and grab the text data.**

When we get a response from the web server, we need to first check its status code. A code of 200 means that the request was satisfied. Of course other codes are possible as well, such as error codes. Assuming we get a 200 status code, we then use the `text` attribute to obtain the data returned from the Web API. Here's another little code fragment to do that. Check it out and we'll put it all together on the next page.

We're using the response object we got in ❶.

Let's check the status code and make sure we got a code of 200, for success.

```
if (response.status_code == 200):
    print(response.text)
else:
    print("Houston, we have a problem:", response.status_code)
```

If the status code was 200, we should have some data in the text attribute.

Otherwise, we've got an issue. For now we'll print the error. Remember, you can find a complete list of common status codes at https://en.wikipedia.org/wiki/List_of_HTTP_status_codes.

Putting it all together: making a request to Open Notify

Alright, we truly have all we need to make a request, so let's do that. You know how to call the `get` function with a URL to make an actual request to a Web API, and we know from the *open-notify.org* page what URL we need. You also know that the `response` object has a `status_code` you should check (and make sure we get a code of 200, meaning success) before you use the `response` object's text attribute.

So, let's now put it all together and reach out and touch the Open Notify Web API:

First, import the
requests module.

Let's set a variable url to the URL
address of the ISS web service.

```
import requests

url = 'http://api.open-notify.org/iss-now.json'

response = requests.get(url)

if (response.status_code == 200):
    print(response.text)
else:
    print("Houston, we have a problem:", response.status_code)
```

Here's the
response
object.

Then we use the get function, passing it
the URL we'd like to get data from.

Let's check the status code to make sure
everything was okay (that is, code 200).

And then let's print the
response to see what we got.
Remember, we're printing
the text property of the
response, which holds the
data sent back to us from
the Web API.

If the response code wasn't 200,
we've got some kind of issue, so let's
print out what it is. You can find a
full list of status code on Wikipedia:
https://en.wikipedia.org/wiki/List_
of_HTTP_status_codes.

Let's do a quick sanity check before proceeding...

At the time of writing, the ISS location service is a working, healthy service. Of course there are no guarantees in the future; so if for some reason the ISS location service is not operating as you're reading this book in 2036, we have a backup plan for you—check out the page http:// wickedlysmart.com/hflearntocode to see if you need to alter anything in the rest of this chapter; most likely you won't, but it never hurts to check first!

A Test ~~Drive~~ Flight

Get the code on the previous page into a file called *iss.py*, save your code, and choose the **Run > Run Module** menu item to make sure everything's good.

Here's what we got.

You need a live internet connection for this test drive!

Watch it!

Problems?

If you aren't seeing this output, first check to see if there is a status code other than 200 being reported (and look it up to see what it signifies). Not seeing a status code? Paste the URL into your browser to make sure you have connectivity and the service is up and running. Next, double-check your code, and double-check that the request package really got installed. Check any exceptions reported to the shell as well. If it appears as if something is wrong with the Open Notify service, then revisit the Watch it! on the previous page.

```
Python 3.6.0 Shell
{"iss_position": {"longitude": "-146.2862", "latitude":
"-51.0667"}, "message": "success", "timestamp": 1507904011}
>>>
```

Any idea where this location is?

How to use JSON in Python

So we've got our response from the ISS location service, and we're seeing JSON in the response, but right now *it's just a text string*, which isn't of much use, other than the fact we can print it. That's where Python's `json` module comes in; the `json` module gives us a function, `loads`, which takes a string containing JSON and translates it into a Python dictionary. How convenient is that? Here's an example of how the `json` module's `load` function works:

First we need to import the json module.

And here's a string containing JSON. Note, to Python, this is just a string with some text it.

```python
import json

json_string = '{"first": "Emmett", "last": "Brown", "prefix": "Dr."}'

name = json.loads(json_string)

print(name['prefix'], name['first'], name['last'])
```

So let's call json.loads on the string, and assign the resulting dictionary to the variable name.

And finally let's use the Python dictionary to access the first and last name attributes along with the prefix attribute.

Just a reminder: if you go testing this code, do not call it json.py (the same name as the module json). We discussed that issue in Chapter 7.

```
Python 3.6.0 Shell
Dr. Emmett Brown
>>>
```

Using the JSON module on our ISS data

With the `json` module now on our toolbelt, let's get it into our code and get access to the space station's latitude and longitude. Doing that is pretty straightforward: we already have the JSON from the Open Notify servers in our `response` object, so we just need to use the `loads` function from the `json` module to convert that to a Python dictionary.

> Add an import for the json module. We're separating module names by commas so we can put them on the same line.

```python
import requests, json

url = 'http://api.open-notify.org/iss-now.json'

response = requests.get(url)

if (response.status_code == 200):
    response_dictionary = json.loads(response.text)
    print(response.text)
    position = response_dictionary['iss_position']
    print('International Space Station at ' +
        position['latitude'] + ', ' + position['longitude'])
else:
    print("Houston, we have a problem:", response.status_code)
```

> Now let's use json.loads to take the JSON response, in string form, and convert it to a Python dictionary.

> Now let's grab the iss_position value, which is itself another dictionary.

And then print the lat and long values from the position dictionary.

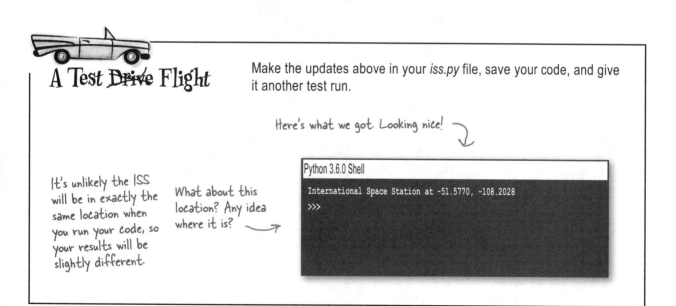

A Test ~~Drive~~ Flight

Make the updates above in your *iss.py* file, save your code, and give it another test run.

> Here's what we got. Looking nice!

```
Python 3.6.0 Shell
International Space Station at -51.5770, -108.2028
>>>
```

It's unlikely the ISS will be in exactly the same location when you run your code, so your results will be slightly different.

What about this location? Any idea where it is?

Let's add some graphics

Displaying the ISS location in text is, well, just not acceptable. After all, this is Chapter 10, so we should be displaying the ISS's location on a nice map, or something. Well, we have the technology—we're going to dust off our Python turtles and have a nice ISS display in no time. *We kid you not.*

"If I see one more Python Shell app, you're fired!"

Meet the screen object

Like we said, dust off those turtle skills. We're actually going to take those skills a little further by once again using the `screen` object we saw in Chapter 7. Recall that the `screen` object lets you change a few properties associated with the turtle window.

We still say "window" would have been a better name than screen for this object, but they didn't really ask for our opinion.

So let's add the `turtle` module to this code, and see how we're going to use the `screen` object. You can go ahead and make these additions to your *iss.py* file.

Add the turtle module.

```python
import requests, json, turtle
```
This first line just gets a reference to the turtle's screen object.

We're going to increase the size of the window to 1000 by 500 pixels, which matches the size of the image we're about to add.

```python
screen = turtle.Screen()
screen.setup(1000,500)
screen.bgpic('earth.gif')
screen.setworldcoordinates(-180, -90, 180, 90)
```
This sets the entire window's background to an image.

Get the "earth.gif" image from the book's source code ch10 folder.

```python
url = 'http://api.open-notify.org/iss-now.json'

response = requests.get(url)
```
This resets the coordinate system of the turtle window; we talk about this on the next page.

```python
if (response.status_code == 200):
    response_dictionary = json.loads(response.text)
    position = response_dictionary['iss_position']
    print('International Space Station at ' +
        position['latitude'] + ', ' + position['longitude'])
else:
    print("Houston, we have a problem:", response.status_code)


turtle.mainloop()
```

Just some housekeeping to display the turtle window, like in Chapter 7

You'll find this image in the book's ch10 folde; grab it and place it in your own folder.

earth.gif

Turtle Coordinates & Earth Coordinates

Let's take a closer look at the call to the `setworldcoordinates` method, which you'll see plays a big role in determining how we locate the ISS's position on our graphical map.

As you already know, the turtles live on a grid that is centered on the x and y-coordinate 0,0. We've set the grid to be 1000×500, so our grid ranges from −500,−250 in the bottom-left corner to 500,250 in the upper-right corner.

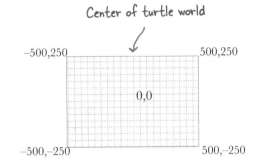

The Earth has its own grid system with latititude lines running west and east and longitude lines running north and south. Longitude runs from −180 to 180, with 0 being at the Prime Meridian. For latitude, the equator is at 0, running to 90 at the North Pole and −90 and at the south-most point.

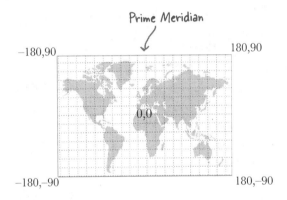

We can easily reset the grid system of the turtles, and have our turtle grid match the earth coordinates with the statement:

screen.setworldcoordinates(-180, -90, 180, 90)

which resets the turtle grid so the lower-left coordinate is −180, −90 and the upper-right coordinate is 180, 90. Our screen will retain its shape and size, but all turtle movement will be mapped using the new coordinate system.

This means we can now use common longitude and latitude coordinates to position the turtles on the screen.

Using the setworldcoordinates method we've set the coordinate system of the turtles to match that of the Earth.

Let's add a turtle to represent the ISS

Have you figured out how we're going to use a turtle to track the location of the ISS on the map? Well, let's add a turtle and find out. Make sure you add the code below to your *iss.py* file:

```python
import requests, json, turtle

screen = turtle.Screen()
screen.setup(1000,500)
screen.bgpic('earth.gif')
screen.setworldcoordinates(-180, -90, 180, 90)

iss = turtle.Turtle()
iss.shape('circle')
iss.color('red')

url = 'http://api.open-notify.org/iss-now.json'

response = requests.get(url)

if (response.status_code == 200):
    response_dictionary = json.loads(response.text)
    position = response_dictionary['iss_position']
    print('International Space Station at ' +
        position['latitude'] + ', ' + position['longitude'])
else:
    print("Houston, we have a problem:", response.status_code)

turtle.mainloop()
```

Let's instantiate a turtle, change its shape to a circle, and make its color red.

On the map, this circle is going to represent (for now) the location of the ISS over the earth.

A Test ~~Drive~~ Flight

Let's do a quick test before going further. Make the code additions from the past few pages, and then make sure you have the image *earth.gif* (again, you'll find it in the *ch10* folder in the book's source code) in the same directory as your code. Then give it a run.

If you see this, you're in business. All we're doing so far is changing the windows resolution, displaying a background image, changing the shape and color of the turtle, and changing the coordinate system.

Oh, is that all?

You should see a red circle, which is really a turtle, positioned at its default starting place at 0,0, only this time that's a longitude and latitude.

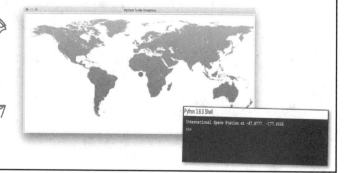

Turtles can look like space stations too

Although it isn't essential to building an app that uses a Web API, making our turtle look like a space station on screen certainly adds to the realism and fun. Here's a quick piece of code to do just that:

```
import requests, json, turtle

screen = turtle.Screen()
screen.setup(1000,500)
screen.bgpic('earth.gif')
screen.setworldcoordinates(-180, -90, 180, 90)

iss = turtle.Turtle()
turtle.register_shape("iss.gif")
iss.shape("iss.gif")
iss.shape('circle')
iss.color('red')

url = 'http://api.open-notify.org/iss-now.json'

response = requests.get(url)

if (response.status_code == 200):
    response_dictionary = json.loads(response.text)
    position = response_dictionary['iss_position']
    print('International Space Station at ' +
        position['latitude'] + ', ' + position['longitude'])
else:
    print("Houston, we have a problem:", response.status_code)

turtle.mainloop()
```

You'll find "iss.gif" also in the ch10 source code folder.

Let the turtle module know we want to use an image as a shape.

Then set the shape of the turtle to be the "iss.gif" image.

Note this step of registering a shape is an oddity of the turtle module. In other words, that's just the way it works. Many image-based libraries don't require a registration step like this.

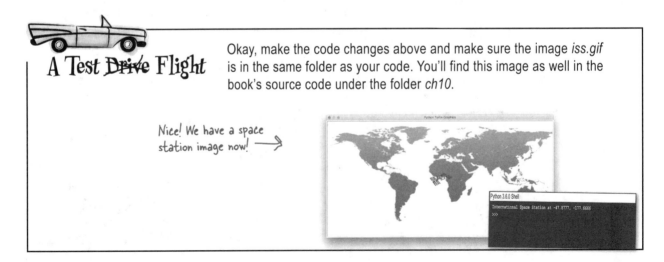

A Test Drive Flight

Okay, make the code changes above and make sure the image *iss.gif* is in the same folder as your code. You'll find this image as well in the book's source code under the folder *ch10*.

Nice! We have a space station image now! →

Forget the ISS—where are we?

We're close! We've got everything in place and we've got a location back from the Open Notify service, so all we need to do is put it all together. For starters we need to actually get the latitude and longitude assigned to variables so we can instruct our `iss` turtle where to move on the screen. One note, though: did you notice that in Open Notify's JSON those values are being represented by strings, not numeric values? We'll have to fix that. In fact, let's look at how to do that now:

Here's just a code fragment for now, the part of the code that checks the response and gets the latitude and longitude.

```python
if (response.status_code == 200):
    response_dictionary = json.loads(response.text)
    position = response_dictionary['iss_position']
    print('International Space Station at ' +
        position['latitude'] + ', ' + position['longitude'])
    lat = float(position['latitude'])
    long = float(position['longitude'])
else:
    print("Houston, we have a problem:", response.status_code)
```

Let's get the latitude and longitude from the position dictionary. Given they are both strings, we'll convert them to floats first.

You don't need to enter this code yet; we'll make all the changes at once in a couple pages.

The next step is moving the ISS on the screen. You're an old pro at this point with turtles. All we need to do here is write a simple function—let's call it `move_iss`—that takes a numeric latitude and longitude and moves the turtle. Let's make sure and lift up the pen before we move.

The move_iss function takes a latitude and longitude.

```python
def move_iss(lat, long):
    global iss

    iss.penup()
    iss.goto(long, lat)
    iss.pendown()
```

If we don't lift the pen, we're going to draw a line across the display.

Let's move to the right coordinate. Note that longitude is first, given the turtle takes its x-coordinate parameter first.

Now let's return the pen to its default down position and make the turtle visible.

Note we don't technically have to put the pen back down, but we're just being a good citizen given that is the default position of the pen. After all, another developer may be confused by this if they expect you to not change the pen in your function.

Finishing off the ISS code

Let's add the function `move_iss` to our code, as well as the code to get the latitude and longitude from the `position` dictionary, and then we'll call `move_iss` with those values:

```
import requests, json, turtle

def move_iss(lat, long):
    global iss

    iss.penup()
    iss.goto(long, lat)
    iss.pendown()

screen = turtle.Screen()
screen.setup(1000,500)
screen.bgpic('earth.gif')
screen.setworldcoordinates(-180, -90, 180, 90)

iss = turtle.Turtle()
turtle.register_shape("iss.gif")
iss.shape("iss.gif")

url = 'http://api.open-notify.org/iss-now.json'

response = requests.get(url)

if (response.status_code == 200):
    response_dictionary = json.loads(response.text)
    position = response_dictionary['iss_position']
    print('International Space Station at ' +
        position['latitude'] + ', ' + position['longitude'])
    lat = float(position['latitude'])
    long = float(position['longitude'])
    move_iss(lat, long)
else:
    print("Houston, we have a problem:", response.status_code)

turtle.mainloop()
```

We're just adding move_iss near the top of the file.

We no longer need a print statement for the location—we've got graphics now!

Let's take the latitude and longitude strings, convert them to floats, and pass them to move_iss along with our iss turtle.

A Test ~~Drive~~ Flight

Alright, make sure you've got your code all entered and cleaned up and then you should be ready to finally see the ISS location on your map. Give it a test run!

The ISS circles the earth every 92 minutes, so run your code a few times to see the position change.

The ISS is also traveling at 4.75 miles per second.

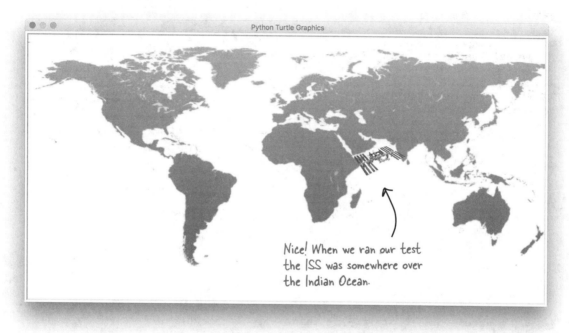

Python Turtle Graphics

Nice! When we ran our test the ISS was somewhere over the Indian Ocean.

Congrats! Mission accomplished!

Brain Building

Well, that was fanstastic: with a bit of code we've located the ISS and created a cool graphical display. But you know what would make this code even cooler is if it tracked the ISS *over time*, rather than just tracking it *one time*. Let's do that, but before we do, this code could really use some cleanup. After all, we aren't using all those great abstraction muscles we've been building. Here's our attempt to refactor this code a bit. See if it isn't a lot more readable (which you're going to want on the next page):

```python
import requests, json, turtle

iss = turtle.Turtle()

def setup(window):
    global iss

    window.setup(1000,500)
    window.bgpic('earth.gif')
    window.setworldcoordinates(-180, -90, 180, 90)
    turtle.register_shape("iss.gif")
    iss.shape("iss.gif")

def move_iss(lat, long):
    global iss

    iss.penup()
    iss.goto(long, lat)
    iss.pendown()


def track_iss():
    url = 'http://api.open-notify.org/iss-now.json'
    response = requests.get(url)
    if (response.status_code == 200):
        response_dictionary = json.loads(response.text)
        position = response_dictionary['iss_position']
        lat = float(position['latitude'])
        long = float(position['longitude'])
        move_iss(lat, long)
    else:
        print("Houston, we have a problem:", response.status_code)


def main():
    global iss
    screen = turtle.Screen()
    setup(screen)
    track_iss()

if __name__ == "__main__":
    main()
    turtle.mainloop()
```

Let's put all the window and turtle setup in a setup function.

Notice we used "window" as the parameter name here (which is technically going to be passed as a screen object). This might or might not have been a good variable naming idea, but we couldn't help ourselves. We should probably add a real code comment to alert others.

We didn't make any changes to the move_iss function.

We took the code that talks to the Web API and put it in a function called track_iss.

And finally we're being good coders by providing a main function.

Alright, here's the code to track the ISS in real time. With this code you'll see the location of the ISS change every 5 seconds. This being a Brain Building exercise, your job is to figure out how it works. Read the code and see if you can guess, and then in the next chapter we'll find out exactly how it does what it does.

```python
import requests, json, turtle

iss = turtle.Turtle()

def setup(window):
    global iss

    window.setup(1000,500)
    window.bgpic('earth.gif')
    window.setworldcoordinates(-180, -90, 180, 90)
    turtle.register_shape("iss.gif")
    iss.shape("iss.gif")

def move_iss(lat, long):
    global iss

    iss.hideturtle()
    iss.penup()
    iss.goto(long, lat)
    iss.pendown()
    iss.showturtle()

def track_iss():
    url = 'http://api.open-notify.org/iss-now.json'
    response = requests.get(url)
    if (response.status_code == 200):
        response_dictionary = json.loads(response.text)
        position = response_dictionary['iss_position']
        lat = float(position['latitude'])
        long = float(position['longitude'])
        move_iss(lat, long)
    else:
        print("Houston, we have a problem:", response.status_code)
    widget = turtle.getcanvas()
    widget.after(5000, track_iss)

def main():
    global iss
    screen = turtle.Screen()
    setup(screen)
    track_iss()

if __name__ == "__main__":
    main()
    turtle.mainloop()
```

We've added only two lines of code.

With this code you'll see the ISS location update every 5 seconds.

BULLET POINTS

- Using Python you can communicate with Web APIs and incorporate their data and services into your application.

- A Web API typically provides a documented Application Programming Interface (**API**) that describes the data it can provide and services it has available.

- Often you'll need to register and obtain a key or authorization token to use a Web API.

- To use a Web API from Python, you make a request to it using the web's **HTTP** protocol, just like your browser does.

- Web services respond to requests, sending data, often using the JSON notation.

- **JSON** stands for JavaScript Object Notation, and was created to provide a standard way of data exchange between any languages.

- JSON's syntax is very similar to Python dictionaries.

- The requests package is freely available and comes from an open source effort to make web requests in Python easier.

- A package is a collection of Python modules.

- You can install the requests package using the **pip** utility.

- **pip** stands for "**pip** installs packages"

- Using the requests library we issued a request using the **get** method.

- The **get** method returns a **response** object, which includes a status code, the text of the response (often in JSON), and the headers of the request.

- The status code is 200 when the request was satisfied.

- The built-in json module provides methods to take a JSON string and translate it to a Python dictionary or list.

- The screen object of the turtle library allows us to set a background image as well as reset the coordinate system of the turtle grid.

Coding Crossword

Welcome back to earth. Let's give your right brain something different to do.

As always, it's your standard crossword, but all of the solution words are from this chapter.

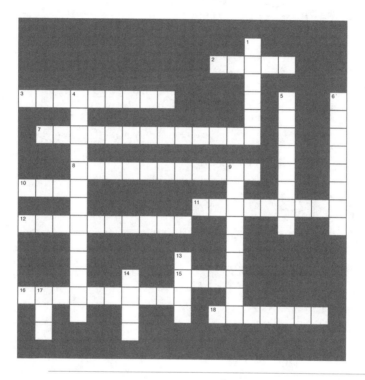

Across

2. We had to register one of these with the turtle module.
3. What you are when you get a 200 status code.
7. To access a Web API you may need this.
8. Our code needed this.
10. Format for data exchange.
11. Run north and south.
12. 200 is a good value.
15. Data attribute of the response object.
16. Language JSON was originally from.
18. What's in a package?

Down

1. He wrote the ISS location service.
4. Which space station?
5. Open source package.
6. What does pip install?
9. Minutes per orbit.
13. Protocol used for web requests.
14. Turtles live on this.
17. Documented functions of a Web AI

Exercise Solution

Enter the following URL in your browser. What do you get?

`http://api.open-notify.org/iss-now.json`

Very cool, we just got the current location of the space station. Note it contains a few keys and that the iss_position key holds another set of key/value pairs (the longitude and latitude).

Here's what we got. ————➔

```
{
    "message": "success",
    "timestamp": 1500664795,
    "iss_position":
        {
            "longitude": "-110.6066",
            "latitude": "-50.4185"
        }
}
```

The formatting will depend on your browser. Some browsers may even download this into a file, which you can then open as a text file.

Note that the longitude and latitude are being represented as strings. We'll have to convert them to floats when the time comes to use them.

Sharpen your pencil Solution

Take the JSON on the previous page and convert it, by hand, into a Python dictionary in the space below. After you've done that, complete the code below. If you need a hint, look at the output.

```python
current = {'temperature': 67.2,
           'precip_prob': '40%',
           'location': {
                   'city': 'London',
                   'country': 'UK'
               }
           }
loc = current['location']
print('In',
      loc['city'] + ', ' + loc['country'],
      'it is',
      current['temperature'],'degrees')
```

```
Python 3.6.0 Shell

In London, UK it is 67.2 degrees
```

Coding
Cross
Solution

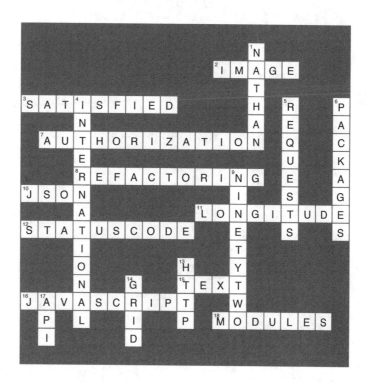

Getting Interactive

Pronounce GUI like "gooey." ➝

You've certainly written some graphical applications, but you haven't created a real user interface yet. That is, you haven't written anything that lets the user interact with a graphical user interface (otherwise known as a GUI). To do that you need to adopt a new way of thinking about how a program executes, one that is more **reactive**. Wait, did the user just click on that button? Your code better know how to react and what to do next. Coding for interfaces is quite different from the typical procedural method we've been using, and it requires a different way of thinking about the problem. In this chapter you're going to write your first real GUI, and no, we're not going to write a simple to-do list manager or height/weight calculator, we're going to do something far more interesting. We're going to write an artificial life simulator with emergent behavior. What does that mean? Well, turn the page to find out.

Enter the WONDERFUL WORLD of Amazing
ARTIFICIAL LIFE

Just ADD CODE—that's ALL! By using **our incredibly simple algorithm**, with only **four rules**, you'll be viewing real artificial life with **emergent behavior** in no time. Here's how it works:

Our artificial life consists of a set of cells that live on a grid.

At each square of the grid a cell can be alive or dead.

If a cell is alive, it is colored black.

We compute the next generation of cells according to four simple rules.

THE RULES

❶ **BIRTH**: a new cell is born if it is surrounded by exactly three live cells.

❷ **LIFE**: a cell lives on as long as it is surrounded by two or three live cells.

❸ **DEATH**: a cell dies of loneliness if it is surrounded by fewer than two live cells.

❹ A cell dies of overcrowding if it is surrounded by four or more live cells.

These simple rules are actually known as the *Game of Life*. To play the game, start by placing living cells on the grid and then start computing generations by following the rules. While the rules may seem quite simple, you're going to see that the only way to know how life is going to play out is *to play the game*. That's right; such interesting behavior emerges from these simple rules that we can't even tell you if the game will ever stop evolving without actually running the computation—more on that deep topic in a bit —but, for now, it sounds like if we're going to play, we're going to have to write our own Game of Life simulator. Let's do that!

The Game of Life was discovered by British mathematician John Conway. More at https://en.wikipedia.org/wiki/John_ Horton_Conway.

> Ever heard of sea monkeys?
> I think we've got a real business
> opportunity here, even better than
> Phrase-O-Matic!

A closer look at the Game of Life

Okay, you've seen the four simple rules, so let's step through the game in a little more detail so we understand how it works. You know that the Game of Life happens on a grid, and at each location on the grid we can have a cell that is either alive or dead. If it's alive, we color it so we can see it. If it's dead, it's just transparent.

Our Game of Life universe successively computes new generations of cells, and to do that it applies the four rules to every location in the grid, after which it updates all the cells at once, based on the outcome. It then does this over and over and over, computing new generations. Let's look at how the rules apply to a few cases.

Let focus on the center cell in each example.

For all cells we count the number of neighbors it has.

Note the center cell here is dead, unlike the other examples.

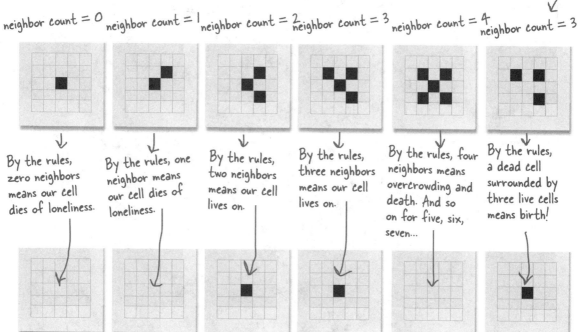

neighbor count = 0 neighbor count = 1 neighbor count = 2 neighbor count = 3 neighbor count = 4 neighbor count = 3

By the rules, zero neighbors means our cell dies of loneliness.

By the rules, one neighbor means our cell dies of loneliness.

By the rules, two neighbors means our cell lives on.

By the rules, three neighbors means our cell lives on.

By the rules, four neighbors means overcrowding and death. And so on for five, six, seven...

By the rules, a dead cell surrounded by three live cells means birth!

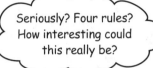

Seriously? Four rules? How interesting could this really be?

Oh, you'd be surprised...

The Game of Life is a **generative system**. A generative system has a predetermined, often simple, set of rules, but generates behavior that you could not have guessed, or would not have expected. Generative systems have been used for art, music, as the basis of philosophical arguments about the universe, and in fields like machine learning. And there is no better example of a generative system than Conway's Game of Life. From those four simple rules, here are a few behaviors you might see in the simulator you're about to build...

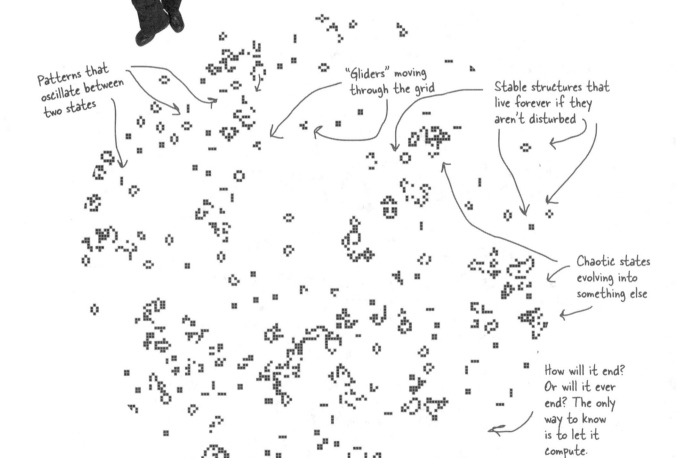

Patterns that oscillate between two states

"Gliders" moving through the grid

Stable structures that live forever if they aren't disturbed

Chaotic states evolving into something else

How will it end? Or will it ever end? The only way to know is to let it compute.

Sharpen your pencil

Before you get started coding, work through a few generations of the Game of Life. Use generation 1 as the starting point and then compute generations 2 through 6, by applying the Game of Life rules. Here are the rules again:

- If a dead cell has three living neighbors, it becomes alive in the next generation.

- If a live cell has two or three living neighbors, it lives on in the next generation.

- If a live cell has fewer than two living neighbors, it dies in the next generation.

- If a live cell has more than three neighbors, it dies in the next generation.

This is your starting point.

Don't forget to compute the dead cells around the lives ones: you may have a birth!

Generation 1

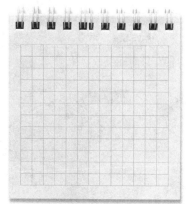

Generation 2

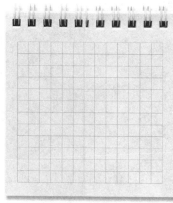

Generation 3

Apply the rules of the Game of Life, and mark the results in generation 2.

And then continue on applying the rules to generation 2 and so on.

Generation 4

Generation 5

Generation 6

What we're going to build

Well, as you can see from the graph paper exercise, it's a little hard to get a feel for how the Game of Life is a "generative system with emergent properties" without the help of a computer. So, what we're going to do now is build a Game of Life *simulator*. Our simulator will display the grid of cells, let users interact by clicking in the grid to enter cells, and provide a few buttons we can use to control the actions of the simulator. For starters we want to be able to start and stop the simulator. We also might want to clear the grid and start over, or even load it up with a few pre-configured patterns. So, we're talking about building a full-fledged user interface.

Now, a great thing to do when creating a user interface is to, literally, sketch it out on a napkin. We're not kidding; it's a great technique. Let's make a sketch:

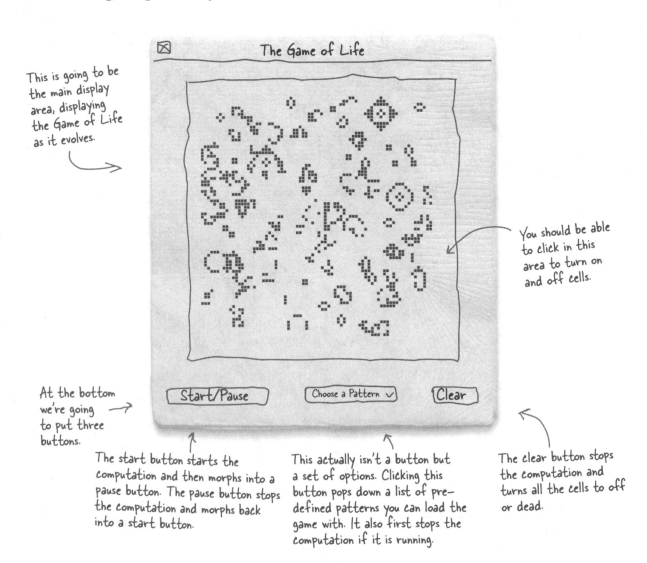

This is going to be the main display area, displaying the Game of Life as it evolves.

The Game of Life

You should be able to click in this area to turn on and off cells.

At the bottom we're going to put three buttons.

Start/Pause   Choose a Pattern ∨   Clear

The start button starts the computation and then morphs into a pause button. The pause button stops the computation and morphs back into a start button.

This actually isn't a button but a set of options. Clicking this button pops down a list of pre-defined patterns you can load the game with. It also first stops the computation if it is running.

The clear button stops the computation and turns all the cells to off or dead.

Do we have the right design?

Interface design and testing is an entire subfield in itself—there are people who spend their whole careers designing, testing, and perfecting interfaces. That said, there are simple and effective techniques you can use to improve your own interfaces, even if you don't have a six-figure usability budget. One of those is called *paper prototyping*. With paper prototyping, we mock up a user interface on paper (we've already done that), and then have candidate users go through a set of *use cases*, using the paper mockup as if it were a real interface. Doing so allows you to observe real users and the mistakes and misunderstandings about your design.

Usability testing entails testing products on actual users to see how well they work (or don't).

Think of use cases as a set of actions or scenarios the typical user would go through.

Usability gurus claim you can uncover about 85% of usability problems with this technique.

Exercise

It's time to do some paper protype testing. Photocopy this page, and the next one (or print a copy from *http://wickedlysmart.com/hflearntocode*), and cut out the pieces where indicated. Next, find a few friends, put the prototype down in front of them, and then ask them a few questions (we'll give you a little script of questions in two pages).

Cut this out, as it's going to be your paper interface.

Main Interface

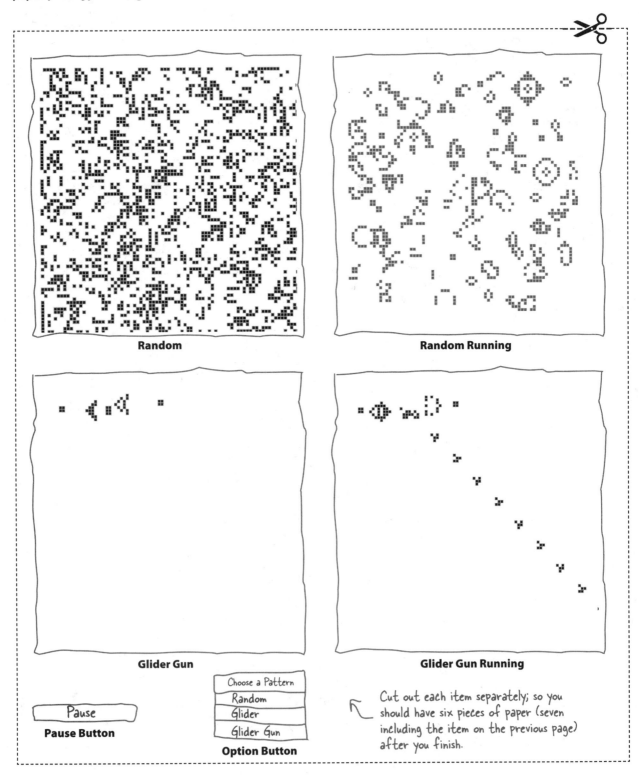

Random

Random Running

Glider Gun

Glider Gun Running

Pause

Pause Button

Choose a Pattern

Random

Glider

Glider Gun

Option Button

Cut out each item separately; so you should have six pieces of paper (seven including the item on the previous page) after you finish.

Exercise

Here's a script to take each user (your tester) through; ask your tester to say out loud what they are thinking as they go through the exercise. Make notes about the mistakes they make along with any interface misconceptions. Of course, you want to make note of the things that are working well too.

1. Place the **Main Interface** in front of your tester.

2. Give your tester a brief explanation of the Game of Life and what the simulator does.

3. Tell the tester an easy way to start is to load a random pattern into the grid. Ask them if they can figure out how to do that.

   When they say they are clicking on "Choose a Pattern," place the **Option Button** cutout on top of the "Choose a Pattern" button.

   When they say they are clicking on the "Random" option, place the **Random** cutout over the grid, and remove the **Option Button** cutout.

   Tell them they have now loaded the grid with a random selection of live cells.

4. Ask the tester if they can figure out how to start computing new generations.

   Wait for the tester to click on Start. If they don't, give your tester some hints. When Start is clicked, place the **Random Running** cutout over the grid; also place the **Pause Button** cutout over the start button. Explain to them that they are watching an evolving scene of living and dying cells.

5. Ask the tester if they can now clear the grid. If they can't find the clear button, then give them hints until they do. When they click on the clear button, remove the **Random Running** and the **Pause Button** cutouts.

6. Ask the tester to directly enter some live cells. If necessary help the tester until they click in the grid. Use a pen to drawn in points on the grid.

7. Ask the tester to generate some new generations of cells. Again, the tester should click the start button. When they do, place the **Random Running** cutout over the grid; also place the **Pause Button** cutout over the start button. Explain to them that they are watching an evolving scene of living and dying cells.

8. Ask the tester to pause the cell generation. They should find the pause button; when they do, remove the **Pause Button** cutout.

9. Ask them to now load the glider gun pattern. When they click "Choose a Pattern," place the **Option Button** cutout on top of the "Choose a Pattern" button. When they click on "glider gun," place the **Glider Gun** cutout on the grid and remove the **Option Button** cutout.

10. Ask them to start the simulator again. When they click the start button, place the **Glider Gun Running** cutout over the grid; also place the **Pause Button** cutout over the start button. Explain they are watching the simulator generate an endless stream of gliders crawling down the grid.

11. Tell the tester that concludes the test and thank them for participating.

 It never hurts to have a few cookies on hand as a thank you.

NOTE: If you find major problems in your testing, well, we'd like to stop and address them, but this is a book in print, so we unfortunately don't have that luxury. But keep those issues in mind as we proceed through the chapter and think about how you'd do things differently.

How we're going to build the simulator

Now that we've got the interface designed on paper and we've also done a bit of paper prototype testing, we can feel pretty good about moving forward on the implementation. We do need some idea of how we're going to tackle implementing all this, though.

To do that we're going to use a tried-and-true design that is used across the industry for building user interfaces, and it involves thinking about our code in three conceptual pieces: the underlying data *model*, the *view*, and the *controller*, otherwise known as MVC.

Now, separating things into a discrete model, view, and controller typically requires that we use object-oriented techniques—something we're not even going to talk about until the next chapter, but we are going to follow this design conceptually. In other words, we're not going to go crazy following the MVC pattern, but we are going to take some inspiration from it, while keeping things as simple as we can.

Here's how we're going to think about the design:

The View	**The Controller**	**The Model**

The **view** code is concerned with what is displayed on the interface. It does not care about the specifics of what is being computed other than knowing it has to display data on a grid.	The **controller** takes any user requests coming through the interface (like to start the game) and maps them to requests that need to be made of the model or the view.	The **model** code only cares about the data for the grid and cells, and how to compute new generations. It doesn't care or know about the view.

You'll often hear this design referred to as the MVC design pattern, or as model-view-controller.

An entire subfield of study called "software design patterns" concerns how these designs emerged over time and how they work.

So we have three distinct pieces to code: a view that only worries about how to display things; a model that only cares about computing a grid of cells and doesn't want to know anything about how it is being displayed; and a controller, which manages user interaction and relays commands to the view and model as necessary.

So why all the trouble? Why do we need MVC? Well, history has taught developers that apps built with user interfaces can all too quickly become a pile of unmanageable spaghetti code (yes, that is a technical term; Google it). MVC allows us to avoid that by keeping each piece focused on one responsibility (among other reasons).

At this point you don't need to fully understand MVC, but at least now you've had some exposure to the idea, and as you'll see, it's going to give us a good way to approach building our simulator. So, with that, let's get started!

Building the data model

Even though we just did all that interface design work, we're actually going to set it aside for a bit and work on the data model for the simulator. As we've discussed, by the model we mean that we need a way to represent all the cells on the grid, and then a way to compute each generation of the game on that grid. Let's dive right in.

Representing the grid

To represent the simulator grid we're going to store a grid of integer cell values, with a value of `0` meaning a dead cell and a value of `1` meaning a live one.

Now you've written plenty of code that uses a one-dimensional list of items, but a grid is 2D—it has a width and a height. So how do we create a 2D list? By using a technique of lists within lists. Here's how it works: say you want a grid that is three items high and four items wide. You can do it like this:

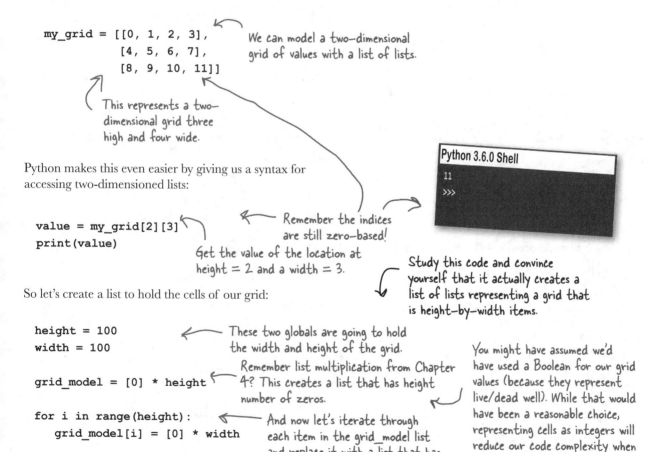

```python
my_grid = [[0, 1, 2, 3],
           [4, 5, 6, 7],
           [8, 9, 10, 11]]
```

We can model a two-dimensional grid of values with a list of lists.

This represents a two-dimensional grid three high and four wide.

Python makes this even easier by giving us a syntax for accessing two-dimensioned lists:

```python
value = my_grid[2][3]
print(value)
```

Remember the indices are still zero-based!

Get the value of the location at height = 2 and a width = 3.

Python 3.6.0 Shell
```
11
>>>
```

Study this code and convince yourself that it actually creates a list of lists representing a grid that is height-by-width items.

So let's create a list to hold the cells of our grid:

```python
height = 100
width = 100

grid_model = [0] * height

for i in range(height):
    grid_model[i] = [0] * width
```

These two globals are going to hold the width and height of the grid.

Remember list multiplication from Chapter 4? This creates a list that has height number of zeros.

And now let's iterate through each item in the grid_model list and replace it with a list that has width number of zeros.

You might have assumed we'd have used a Boolean for our grid values (because they represent live/dead well). While that would have been a reasonable choice, representing cells as integers will reduce our code complexity when we count a cell's live neighbors.

Computing a generation of the Game of Life

Now that we have a place to store our cells, we need some code to compute each generation of the Game of Life as it evolves. To do that we're going to have to examine every single cell and to figure out whether it lives, dies, or is born in the next round. Let's first just check out how to iterate through each cell in the list:

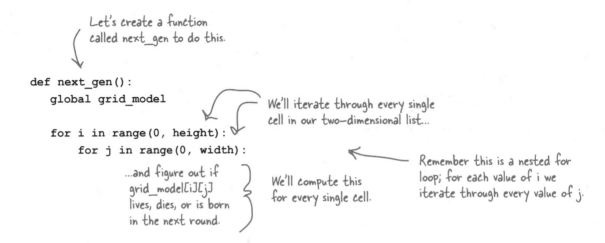

Let's create a function called next_gen to do this.

```python
def next_gen():
    global grid_model

    for i in range(0, height):
        for j in range(0, width):
```

We'll iterate through every single cell in our two-dimensional list...

...and figure out if grid_model[i][j] lives, dies, or is born in the next round.

We'll compute this for every single cell.

Remember this is a nested for loop; for each value of i we iterate through every value of j.

Computing each cell's fate

Each cell's fate is controlled by the Game of Life rules. Let's take another look:

- If a dead cell has three living neighbors, it becomes alive in the next generation.

- If a live cell has two or three living neighbors, it lives on in the next generation.

- If a live cell has fewer than two living neighbors, it dies in the next generation.

- If a live cell has more than three neighbors, it dies in the next generation.

So for each cell we iterate over we're going to have to apply these rules, and follow our logic here. If the cell is dead, then we need to check if it has three neighbors; if it does, it is born. If the cell is already alive, then it has to have either two or three neighbors to continue living. In all other cases, the cell is dead in the next round. So even though we have four rules, it really comes down to those two conditions to determine if the cell is alive or dead. We'll apply that logic in a bit. First, though, there's one crucial piece of information we need before we can begin computing any of this: the number of live neighbors each cell has. As you might imagine, to do that we're going to have to look at all the adjacent cells around any given cell to know how many neighors it has living.

Let's see how to do that.

Here's the `count_neighbors` function; it takes a grid and a row and column in the grid and returns the number of live neighbors for that location.

Ready Bake

```
def count_neighbors(grid, row, col):

    count = 0

    if row-1 >= 0:

        count = count + grid[row-1][col]

    if (row-1 >= 0) and (col-1 >= 0):

        count = count + grid[row-1][col-1]

    if (row-1 >= 0) and (col+1 < width):

        count = count + grid[row-1][col+1]

    if col-1 >= 0:

        count = count + grid[row][col-1]

    if col + 1 < width:

        count = count + grid[row][col+1]

    if row + 1 < height:

        count = count + grid[row+1][col]

    if (row + 1 < height) and (col-1 >= 0):

        count = count + grid[row+1][col-1]

    if (row + 1 < height) and (col+1 < width):

        count = count + grid[row+1][col+1]

    return count
```

This is Ready Bake code. All you need to do is type it in (or grab it out of the book's source code folder). While we think you're fully up to the task of writing this code (at this point, we know you have your conditionals down), going through this code in detail is not the real focus of this chapter.

That said, it is great exercise for your brain to go through this code and understand it. The difficulty of this code isn't so much that it has to check every neighbor, but it also has to take into account the edge conditions of cells near the edge of the grid. So at a minimum, take the time to understand this code. And if you want to take it further, when you've finished the chapter, come back and write a new `count_neighbors` function from scatch.

So here's our Ready Bake code just for you. Enjoy.

Conceptually, this code, for a given cell, adds the number of live cells to the neighbor count.

The code becomes more complex, though, because we have to check for edge conditions of the cells on the edge of the grid.

Here's how you access each neighbor around a cell.

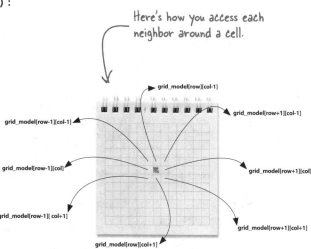

grid_model[row][col-1]
grid_model[row+1][col-1]
grid_model[row-1][col-1]
grid_model[row-1][col]
grid_model[row+1][col]
grid_model[row-1][col+1]
grid_model[row+1][col+1]
grid_model[row][col+1]

Code Magnets

Lucky you. While you were reading about Ready Bake code, we went ahead and wrote the `next_gen` function and put it on the refrigerator. But as is always the case in the *Head First* books, someone came along and messed it up. Can you help us get it back together? Careful, there are extra magnets you don't need.

THE RULES

BIRTH: a new cell is born if it is surrounded by three live cells.

LIFE: a cell lives on as long as it is surrounded by two or three live cells.

DEATH: a cell dies of loneliness if it is surrounded by fewer than two live cells.

A cell dies of overcrowding if it is surrounded by four or more live cells.

Here's the rules again.

We put these up for you already.

```
def next_gen():
```

```
global grid_model
```

```
for i in range(0, height):
        for j in range(0, width):
```

```
cell = 0
```

```
and
```
```
or
```
```
if count == 2 or count == 3:
```

```
cell = 1
```
```
else:
```
```
if count == 3:
```
```
elif grid_model[i][j] == 1:
```

```
count < 2:
```

```
cell = 1
```
```
if grid_model[i][j] == 0:
```
```
if count > 4
```

```
cell = 0
```

```
count = count_neighbors(grid_model, i, j)
```

A Test Drive

Before we get too far along, let's get this code organized and give it a test drive just to make sure we're on the same page. Copy the code below into a file called *model.py*. Make sure you include the Ready Bake code as well. Although this code won't do much (yet), go ahead and give it a test drive and fix any errors.

```python
height = 100
width = 100

grid_model = [0] * height
for i in range(height):
    grid_model[i] = [0] * width

def next_gen():
    global grid_model

    for i in range(0, height):
        for j in range(0, width):
            cell = 0
            print('Checking cell', i, j)
            count = count_neighbors(grid_model, i, j)

            if grid_model[i][j] == 0:
                if count == 3:
                    cell = 1
            elif grid_model[i][j] == 1:
                if count == 2 or count == 3:
                    cell = 1

def count_neighbors(grid, row, col):

if __name__ == '__main__':
    next_gen()
```

Let's pull together the code from the last few pages.

Here's what we got— not much yet, but it's a start.

Python 3.6.0 Shell

```
Checking cell 99 76
Checking cell 99 77
Checking cell 99 78
Checking cell 99 79
Checking cell 99 80
Checking cell 99 81
Checking cell 99 82
Checking cell 99 83
Checking cell 99 84
Checking cell 99 85
Checking cell 99 86
Checking cell 99 87
Checking cell 99 88
Checking cell 99 89
Checking cell 99 90
Checking cell 99 91
Checking cell 99 92
Checking cell 99 93
Checking cell 99 94
Checking cell 99 95
Checking cell 99 96
Checking cell 99 97
Checking cell 99 98
Checking cell 99 99
>>>
```

Don't miss this line that we put in just for testing.

Put the entire function body here from the Ready Bake code two pages back.

Ready Bake

If printing takes a while on your machine, you can always choose the Shell > Interrupt Execution menu item to stop the program.

You should see all the cells being checked if things are running correctly.

Completing the model code

We're not quite there yet. Oh, the logic of our code is just fine, but right now we're just *computing* the value of a cell in the next generation; we aren't actually *doing anything* with it. Here's the problem, though, if we were to store the next-generation cell values in the current grid (as we're computing them), we'd throw off all the `count_neighbor` calculations because we'd be computing with a mix of current and next-generation values at the same time. So, to solve this problem we're going to need *two grids*, one to hold the current values and one to hold the next generation. Then, when we've completely computed the next generation, we'll have to make it the current generation. Here's how we do that:

```python
grid_model = [0] * height
next_grid_model = [0] * height

for i in range(height):
    grid_model[i] = [0] * width
    next_grid_model[i] = [0] * width

def next_gen():
    global grid_model, next_grid_model

    for i in range(0, height):
        for j in range(0, width):
            cell = 0
            print('Checking cell', i, j)
            count = count_neighbors(grid_model, i, j)

            if grid_model[i][j] == 0:
                if count == 3:
                    cell = 1
            elif grid_model[i][j] == 1:
                if count == 2 or count == 3:
                    cell = 1
            next_grid_model[i][j] = cell

    temp = grid_model
    grid_model = next_grid_model
    next_grid_model = temp
```

Let's create a second grid, called next_grid_model.

Rather than show the entire file, we're only showing the code with changes; go ahead and make these additions to your code.

Add a global declaration.

After we've computed a cell, we'll store it in the correct position in next_grid_model.

Once next_grid_model is completely computed, we need to make it the grid_model. To do that we swap the two so that grid_model now points to the data in next_grid_model's grid, and vice versa.

there are no Dumb Questions

Q: Why do we have to swap grid_model and next_grid_model? Isn't it enough to assign next_grid_model to grid_model?

A: That will work fine until you start computing another generation, and then you'll have grid_model and next_grid_model assigned to the same list, which means you'll be counting cell neighbors and changing them in the same list. Not good. So, we go ahead and swap the two lists so that when we do compute the next generation, grid_model will be assigned to the current generation and next_grid_model will have the next-generation values written to it.

Sharpen your pencil

We're not really exercising the `next_gen` code if we're testing with a grid full of zeros. Write a function, `randomize`, which takes a grid, a width, and a height and places random ones and zeros at each cell location:

```python
import random

def randomize(grid, width, height):
```

Your code here

A Test Drive

Let's do another test run. While we have no way to view our model yet—that's the whole point of building a user interface—this is another good time to test things out. Just to be clear, here's all the code.

```python
import random
```
← *We'll be using the random module.*

```python
height = 100
width = 100

def randomize(grid, width, height):
    for i in range(0, height):
        for j in range(0, width):
            grid[i][j] = random.randint(0,1)
```
← *Add your randomize function at the top...*

```python
grid_model = [0] * height
next_grid_model = [0] * height
for i in range(height):
    grid_model[i] = [0] * width
    next_grid_model[i] = [0] * width

randomize(grid_model, width, height)
```
...and call it once the grid is created.

Continued on next page...

```
def next_gen():
    global grid_model, next_grid_model

    for i in range(0, height):
        for j in range(0, width):
            cell = 0
            print('Checking cell', i, j)
            count = count_neighbors(grid_model, i, j)

            if grid_model[i][j] == 0:
                if count == 3:
                    cell = 1
            elif grid_model[i][j] == 1:
                if count == 2 or count == 3:
                    cell = 1
            next_grid_model[i][j] = cell
            print('New value is', next_grid_model[i][j])
    temp = grid_model
    grid_model = next_grid_model
    next_grid_model = temp

def count_neighbors(grid, row, col):



if __name__ == '__main__':
    next_gen()
```

If printing takes a while on your machine, you can always choose the Shell > Interrupt Execution menu item to stop the program.

Here's what we got; your results will differ of course because the cell values are random.

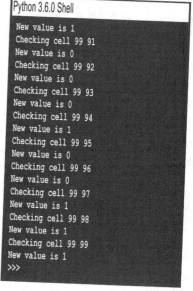

```
Python 3.6.0 Shell
New value is 1
Checking cell 99 91
New value is 0
Checking cell 99 92
New value is 0
Checking cell 99 93
New value is 0
Checking cell 99 94
New value is 1
Checking cell 99 95
New value is 0
Checking cell 99 96
New value is 0
Checking cell 99 97
New value is 1
Checking cell 99 98
New value is 1
Checking cell 99 99
New value is 1
>>>
```

Add another print statement just for testing.

 Ready Bake

Where are we?

Well, that was a nice chunk of code. For the most part, we've now completed the code representing the model of the simulator. And, while we can't visualize the grid in any way yet, we've built a way to store and compute each generation of our generative game.

Now we're going to treat *model.py* like a module and move on to code the user interface, which is going to visualize and control the model.

Let's get started.

Exercise

Before we move on, make sure you remove the two **print** statements from the **next_gen** function, as you'll no longer be needing them.

Make sure you do this!

Building the view

Ready to actually see something on the screen? Us too. This is where we start building the view, the onscreen representation of our simulator. To build the view we're going to use the built-in Python `Tkinter` module, which allows us to create GUIs using many of the common components you typically see in user interfaces, like buttons, text entry boxes, menus, and a canvas you can draw on programmatically. In `Tkinter` we call those components *widgets*. Here are some of the widgets we're going to use:

> While there doesn't seem to be a definitive pronunciation of Tkinter, most folks call it "Tea Kay inter" or "Tea Kin Ter."

The outer window is a widget that holds all the other widgets.

The simulator grid is a canvas widget, which allows you to draw geometric shapes (we'll be drawing lots of little squares to represent live cells).

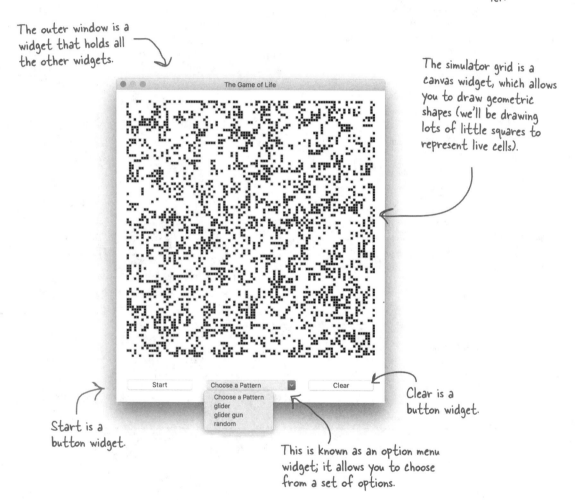

Start is a button widget.

Clear is a button widget.

This is known as an option menu widget; it allows you to choose from a set of options.

That's just a small sampling of the widgets available in `Tkinter`; if interested, you'll find a lot more information at *https://en.wikipedia.org/wiki/Tkinter*.

Creating your first widget

You have some idea of what a widget is going to look like on your screen, but what does a widget look like in code, and how does it relate to Python? From a coding perspective, widgets are just objects. Typically we instantiate a window widget first (which will appear on your screen as soon as you instantiate it), and then we instantiate and add other widgets to the window. So let's start by creating a new window widget and then we'll add a start button to it. One note, in Tkinter, the class that represents a window is called Tk.

Serious Coding

There's another way to import a module you haven't seen yet. When we use the `from` keyword, like:

from tkinter import *

We no longer have to prepend every function, variable, and class name with the module name. So, for instance, we can use `Tk()` rather than `tkinter.Tk()`.

Let's start by importing the tkinter module, only we'll do it in a slightly different way.

Don't forget to pay attention to case sensitivity; we have lowercase tkinter, Tk (uppercase T, lowercase k), and so on.

It's customary to call the top-level window the "root." So we named our variable root.

And then let's instantiate a new window; remember we do that with the Tk class.

```
from tkinter import *

root = Tk()
root.title('The Game of Life')
```

And let's set the title attribute, which will appear at the top of the window.

Notice that when we create a widget, we pass it the root window it's going to be part of.

```
start_button = Button(root, text='Start', width=12)

start_button.pack()

mainloop()
```

Next we instantiate a Button object, giving it a couple of arguments to control the text on the button and the width of the button (in characters) on the screen.

And finally, just like we did with our turtles, we need to turn over control to Tkinter and allow it to monitor the window for clicks and similar events.

This line tells the Tkinter module to place the button in the window wherever it can. This is called a layout manager, and we'll talk more about it in a bit. Basically, if you have a bunch of widgets in a window, you need a layout manager to help you position them.

This is a function from the Tkinter module, and again, we don't have to prepend the module name because of the way we imported Tkinter.

A Test Drive

Place the code above in a file named *view.py* and give it a test drive.

You should see a window on the screen similar to this one. However, depending on your operating system, operating system version, and so on, you may see something slightly different.

The Game of Life
Start

Click the button; what happens?

If you don't see the full title, you can manually resize the window a bit.

Adding the rest of the widgets

Let's add the rest of the widgets we need for the simulator. We've got a start button, but we still need a canvas, a clear button, and an option button (otherwise known as an OptionMenu). We're going to go ahead and add a few other things too and put it all in a `setup` function. Feel free to re-enter all this code from scratch in *view.py* if it's easier than editing the previous version.

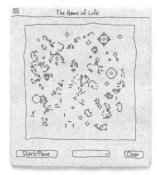

```python
from tkinter import *
import model
```
The view is going to need access to the model module (the one we wrote), so let's go ahead and import it.

```python
cell_size = 5
```
You'll see what this is used for in a bit. Our cells on the screen are going to be bigger than one pixel, so we need to adjust the screen size to accommodate this.

Here's our setup function. Let's get the global variables we need out of the way and get to the widgets.

```python
def setup():
    global root, grid_view, cell_size, start_button, clear_button, choice
```
And notice we're using keyword arguments. The tkinter module is full of them.

```python
    root = Tk()
    root.title('The Game of Life')
```
Here's the Tk top-level window as before.

```python
    grid_view = Canvas(root, width=model.width*cell_size,
                       height=model.height*cell_size,
                       borderwidth=0,
                       highlightthickness=0,
                       bg='white')
```
First up we need a canvas to draw all those cells on. You'll note we're supplying a fair number of arguments, like the width, height, border thickness, and background color.

```python
    start_button = Button(root, text='Start', width=12)
    clear_button = Button(root, text='Clear', width=12)
```
Here's our start button from before. We need a clear button too.

```python
    choice = StringVar(root)
    choice.set('Choose a Pattern')
    option = OptionMenu(root, choice, 'Choose a Pattern', 'glider', 'glider gun', 'random')
    option.config(width=20)
```
This works with the option menu; we'll come back to this shortly.

And this is the option menu widget, which we had in our original design. You'll see we instaniate an Option Menu object just like the other widgets, but this widget has a few other things we need to discuss as well. We'll come back to this.

```python
    grid_view.pack()
    start_button.pack()
    option.pack()
    clear_button.pack()
```
Remember we need a layout manager to place the widgets in the window. So let's call pack on each widget to make that happen.

```python
if __name__ == '__main__':
    setup()
    mainloop()
```
And let's not forget to call setup!

A Test Drive

Get all that new code on the previous page in *view.py* and give it a test drive.

Here's our output. Remember, yours may look different depending on your environment.

└ For comparison, here's our design.

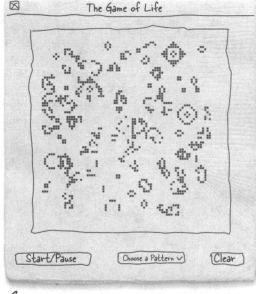

Do you see this? The layout manager isn't doing such a great job. We don't want these buttons to stack on top of each other.

We want our buttons like this. Note, we're not going to worry about the border around the canvas, as you'll see it looks fine without the border in the actual interface.

Correcting the layout

The `Tkinter` layout manager, which packs our widgets into the window as best it can, isn't giving us the layout we want. We could spend some time tweaking the pack layout manager, but, as it turns out, `Tkinter` has a few layout managers, and we're going to use another manager that is better suited for our layout: the *grid layout manager*. The name is coincidental, in that it has nothing to do with the simulator grid. Rather, the grid layout manager allows us to place our widgets into a grid structure within the main window. Doing that is pretty straightforward if we know where we want things placed.

Vertically stacked is not what we want.

Placing the widgets into a grid layout

Let's take our design and think about it as if it were being placed into a grid. Here's what it looks like:

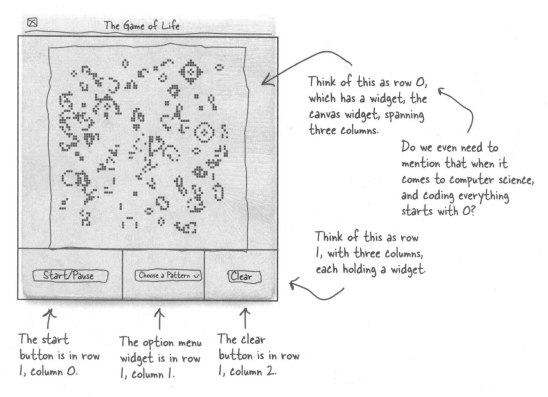

Think of this as row 0, which has a widget, the canvas widget, spanning three columns.

Do we even need to mention that when it comes to computer science, and coding everything starts with 0?

Think of this as row 1, with three columns, each holding a widget.

The start button is in row 1, column 0.

The option menu widget is in row 1, column 1.

The clear button is in row 1, column 2.

Translating the grid layout to code

Now that we know where each widget goes, here's how we tell the grid manager to place the widgets into the grid:

Put the grid_view canvas in a grid at row 0, spanning three columns. We also added some visual padding to make it look nicer.

```
grid_view.grid(row=0, columnspan=3, padx=20, pady=20)
start_button.grid(row=1, column=0, sticky=W, padx=20, pady=20)
option.grid(row=1, column=1, padx=20)
clear_button.grid(row=1, column=2, sticky=E, padx=20, pady=20)
```

Put the buttons and the option menu widget in row 1, in their respective columns, also with a little padding.

Note the sticky parameter tells the layout manager to keep the buttons, essentially, stuck to the west (left) and east (right) sides, instead of being centered. This just helps the buttons stay in a good position for different window sizes.

using a grid layout

A Test Drive

Open *view.py* and replace the existing layout manager code with our new grid-based code. After that give it a test drive and see if things look better. Also, if you haven't already, remove both `print` statements from your *model.py* file.

```
grid_view.pack()          ⟵  Find this code in view.py, and
start_button.pack()          replace it with this code. ↓
clear_button.pack()
option.pack()

grid_view.grid(row=0, columnspan=3, padx=20, pady=20)

start_button.grid(row=1, column=0, sticky=W, padx=20, pady=20)

option.grid(row=1, column=1, padx=20)

clear_button.grid(row=1, column=2, sticky=E, padx=20, pady=20)
```

Much better! Short of displaying cells, we've pretty much got the view looking like we want.

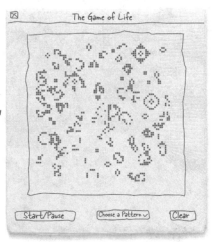

there are no
Dumb Questions

Q: Why is it customary to call the top-level window the "root"? Like the root of a tree?

A: It's a computer science term, and you're not too far off on the tree analogy. Think of a root system with the big thick root at the top branching off into smaller roots. In the same way, the big top window branches off into smaller components. For instance, an OptionMenu widget has a pop-up menu, and in that you'll find a number of options to choose, and each of

those has a string it displays, and so on, smaller and smaller, like roots. You'll find tree and root analogies all over computer science: the root of a file directory, the root of a complex data structure, and so on.

Q: How come our buttons don't do anything when we click them?

A: Because we haven't told them what to do yet. Hang on!

Moving on to the controller

We're getting there. We've got our model all ready to hold cells and compute new generations, and we've got a view that looks like our paper prototype. Now our job is to wire all this up and get this interface actually doing something—in other words, we need to start implementing the controller aspects of our simulator. To do that we're going to take your brain on another mind-bending trip into a slightly different way of thinking about computation—don't worry, this is nothing like the detour we took on recursive functions; it's much more straightforward, yet different than what you're used to.

First, though, let's quickly connect the view to the model. Doing that is our first real step toward having a functional simulator. After we've connected the two, we'll start writing our controller code and start incrementally implementing the functionality behind each component in our interface.

Adding an update function

To get the view and model connected, we're going to write a function, `update`, that we'll use over and over. The `update` function will be responsible for calling the model's `next_gen` function and then using the view to draw the model's cells on the screen, or more precisely, on the canvas we created in the interface.

Let's write a little pseudocode to understand the `update` function:

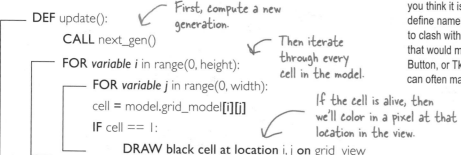

The only difference between this pseudocode and the code we're going to write is that on the canvas we'll draw small rectangles rather than individual pixels. Why? Small pixels are very hard to see, so we'll draw a 5×5 pixel square on the canvas instead. You might remember the global variable `cell_size`, which controls this. You'll see how this works in just a bit. Oh, one more thing: we're only going to draw cells that are living. So, to get rid of any cells that have died since the last generation, we'll need to erase the entire canvas first before redrawing any cells. Let's look at the code...

there are no Dumb Questions

Q: If I use tkinter import * won't it clash with my own variable, function, and class names?

A: The **from/import** statement imports a module such that all its variable, function, and class names are defined at your top level, meaning you don't have to prepend their module name when you use them. The advantage is that this saves you having to always use a module name. The disadvantage is that your own variable, function, and class names may accidentally clash with those in the imported module. So why risk it? Well, if you think it is unlikely that you're going to define names in your own code that are going to clash with the module (in the case of Tkinter that would mean clashing with names like Button, or Tk, or other widget names), then it can often make your code more readable.

BRAIN POWER

Why do you think we're only drawing live cells instead of live and dead cells?

```
def update():
    global grid_view

    grid_view.delete(ALL)
    model.next_gen()

    for i in range(0, model.height):
        for j in range(0, model.width):
            if model.grid_model[i][j] == 1:
                draw_cell(i, j, 'black')
```

Delete anything drawn on the canvas using the canvas object's delete method.

Compute the next generation of cells in the model.

Following the pseudocode...

If a cell at i, j is live, we then draw a small, black rectangle.

This is our function, not Tkinter's, so we will still need to write this function.

That implements all the logic of our update function, but we left one thing unimplemented: the function to draw a rectangle, draw_cell. Let's do that now:

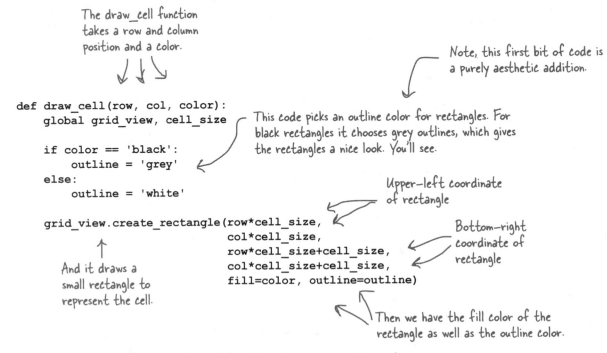

The draw_cell function takes a row and column position and a color.

Note, this first bit of code is a purely aesthetic addition.

```
def draw_cell(row, col, color):
    global grid_view, cell_size

    if color == 'black':
        outline = 'grey'
    else:
        outline = 'white'

    grid_view.create_rectangle(row*cell_size,
                               col*cell_size,
                               row*cell_size+cell_size,
                               col*cell_size+cell_size,
                               fill=color, outline=outline)
```

This code picks an outline color for rectangles. For black rectangles it chooses grey outlines, which gives the rectangles a nice look. You'll see.

Upper-left coordinate of rectangle

Bottom-right coordinate of rectangle

And it draws a small rectangle to represent the cell.

Then we have the fill color of the rectangle as well as the outline color.

Think of the draw_cell function as just a helper function that uses Tkinter's canvas method create_rectangle to draw a rectangle. This function "helps" by handling the arithmetic of figuring out the top-left and bottom-right coordinates of the rectangle we need given the value of cell_size.

A Test Drive

Things should start to get interesting. Open *view.py* and add the update and draw_cell functions. Also add a call to update to test things out. Give it a whirl.

```python
def update():
    global grid_view

    grid_view.delete(ALL)

    model.next_gen()
    for i in range(0, model.height):
        for j in range(0, model.width):
            if model.grid_model[i][j] == 1:
                draw_cell(i, j, 'black')


def draw_cell(row, col, color):
    global grid_view, cell_size

    if color == 'black':
        outline = 'grey'
    else:
        outline = 'white'

    grid_view.create_rectangle(row*cell_size,
                               col*cell_size,
                               row*cell_size+cell_size,
                               col*cell_size+cell_size,
                               fill=color, outline=outline)
```

← Place update below your setup function, just above the check for __main__

```python
if __name__ == '__main__':
    setup()
    update()
    mainloop()
```

↖ Let's put in our call to update.

Here's what we got. Now we're getting somewhere!

Ready for another new style of computation?

If you think about all the code you've written, you're in the driver's seat in that the computation is always proceeding according to your direction. At every point in the computation, you've got code that says what to do next. For a lot of code, though, this isn't the case. A lot of code follows a more *reactive* style of computation.

To understand what that means, imagine your start button just sitting there doing nothing. Suddenly a user comes along and clicks on it, and then what? Well, some piece of code is going to have to wake up and start doing something. In other words, you need code that *reacts to events* that occur in your app. Often those events will be a user clicking on a button, choosing a menu item, typing into a text box, and so on. But they could be other things too, like, say, a timer going off, data arriving over a network, and so on. Often we call this *event-based or event-driven programming*.

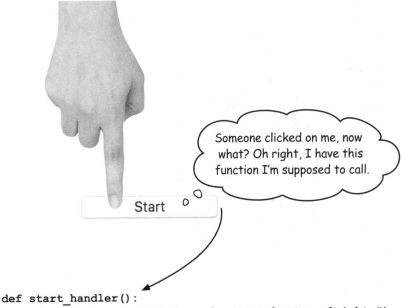

> Someone clicked on me, now what? Oh right, I have this function I'm supposed to call.

```python
def start_handler():
    print("Yup, you clicked on the start button alright.")
    print("Thanks for stopping by.")
```

The code that handles an event, like a button click, has different names in different languages: event handlers, observers, and callbacks, to name a few. We'll stick with *event handlers* because we're writing code that handles an event that occurs in our code. No matter what you call these bits of code, the way you construct them is similar: we tell the object that generates the event, like our button, the function we want it to call when the event occurs. One other thing to know: often event handlers are also passed a special event object when they are called. More on that in a bit. For now, let's see if we can get an event handler written and working.

Let's add a click handler

Our controller code isn't going to require writing all that much code, so we're just going to put the controller code in with the *view.py* file (instead of creating a new *controller.py* file). Go ahead and open *view.py* again. Add this line just below the line that instantiates the start button object:

```
start_button = Button(root, text='Start', width=12)
start_button.bind('<Button-1>', start_handler)
```

You can call bind on any widget to associate an event with a function to call when that event occurs.

The event we're interested in is a click from the left button of a mouse (which works on Mac or Windows machines, or just about any machine with a mouse, for that matter).

And we want to call the function start_handler whenever the button is clicked.

Now below your setup function and above the update function, add a new function, start_handler.

This is the function we told the start button to call when it gets clicked on.

Handlers get passed an event object that contains information about the event, like which button was clicked. Here we don't really need any of that information, but we'll be making use of it later in the chapter.

```
def start_handler(event):
    print("Yup, you clicked on the start button alright.")
    print("Thanks for stopping by.")
```

A Test Drive

Make those two updates to *view.py* and take the code for a test drive. Click on the start button and then check your Python Shell for any output.

We clicked the start button a few times.

Notice how each time you click the function start_hander is immediately called.

```
Python 3.6.0 Shell
Yup, you clicked on the start button
alright.
Thanks for stopping by.
Yup, you clicked on the start button
alright.
Thanks for stopping by.
```

So in this style of programming, my code is sitting around waiting to be called as different actions or events happen in the user interface?

That's right. Whether the user clicks on a button, chooses an option from a menu, clicks on the canvas to perhaps add a live cell (yes, we're going to do that), or some other event occurs, a common style of coding is to register functions that will be called (that's where the name *callback* came from) when the event occurs. As you get used to this style of coding, you'll find it is a natural way to program.

You might be wondering, though, if none of my code is executing and I'm just waiting for events, how come the program doesn't just end? And is there any code that is being executed as my code waits? That's where the `mainloop` function fits in. You'll notice in this code and in the turtle examples in the book we always call `mainloop` as the last thing our code does. When you do that, the code in `mainloop` takes over monitoring everything that is happening in the interface, and when it sees a user interaction it then calls out to your code. So, there is always code running, and in this case it is the code in `mainloop`.

Here's some code you've never seen before. What do you think it does? Hint: this code also calls a handler function when an event occurs.

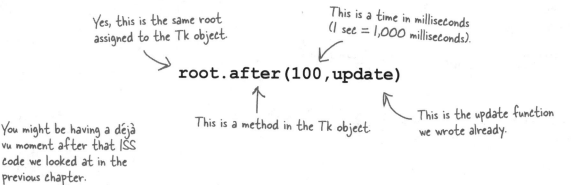

Yes, this is the same root assigned to the Tk object.

This is a time in milliseconds (1 sec = 1,000 milliseconds).

```
root.after(100, update)
```

This is a method in the Tk object.

This is the update function we wrote already.

You might be having a déjà vu moment after that ISS code we looked at in the previous chapter.

How the start/pause button is going to work

The start button is an important button because, when clicked, it needs to tell the simulator to start computing new generations. If you remember the paper prototype, it also needs to morph into a pause button. Let's work up a little *state diagram* showing how the start button works before we jump into code. In this diagram we're going to use new global variable, is_running, which is True if the start button has been clicked and the simulator is generating new generations. If the game hasn't started or is paused, then is_running is False.

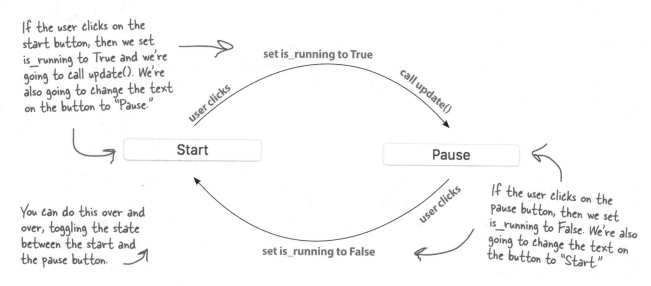

If the user clicks on the start button, then we set is_running to True and we're going to call update(). We're also going to change the text on the button to "Pause."

set is_running to True

call update()

user clicks

Start

Pause

user clicks

If the user clicks on the pause button, then we set is_running to False. We're also going to change the text on the button to "Start."

You can do this over and over, toggling the state between the start and the pause button.

set is_running to False

Implementing the start/pause button

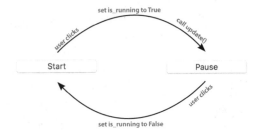

set is_running to True

user clicks

Start

Pause

call update()

user clicks

set is_running to False

First we need a global `is_running` variable. Let's add that to the top of the *view.py* file:

```
from tkinter import *
import model

cell_size = 5
is_running = False
```

← Let's add this global,
initially set to False.

Now we just need to follow the state diagram. Find the `start_handler` function you just wrote, and we're going to make some changes:

```
def start_handler(event):
    print("Yup, you clicked on the start button alright.")
    print("Thanks for stopping by.")
    global is_running, start_button

    if is_running:
        is_running = False
        start_button.configure(text='Start')
    else:
        is_running = True
        start_button.configure(text='Pause')
        update()
```

← Let's get rid of this
old code.

If we're already running (meaning the
button is in the paused state), then we set
is_running to False and change the button
name to "Start."

Otherwise, we set is_running to True, set
the button text to "Pause," and call update
to compute a generation.

A Test Drive

Make those two updates to *view.py* and take the code for a test drive. Try clicking on the start and pause buttons over and over. Do you see generations being computed?

Make sure the start
button toggles between
Start and Pause.

When you click the start/pause
button repeatedly, you should see
generations being computed!

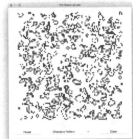

Another example of a
small bit of code making
a huge difference, but
there's an even bigger
moment coming.

Another kind of event

If you click fast enough, you can actually see generations of cells being computed by your `next_gen` function. That's not too bad, but your fingers are going to get tired, and these being computers, you'd probably like to compute them a little faster than you are capable of clicking. To make that happen, we're going to use another kind of event, one not based on what the user does (like clicking a button), but one based on time.

The Python `Tk` object provides an interesting method named `after`. Let's take a look at how it works:

You'll find similiar functionality in most programming languages.

You can call the after method on the root Tk object.

The first argument is a time in milliseconds.

There are 1,000 milliseconds in a second.

The second argument is a function to call after that time has elapsed.

`root.after(100, update)`

Okay, but what does it do exactly? Let's drop in on some code invoking the `after` method.

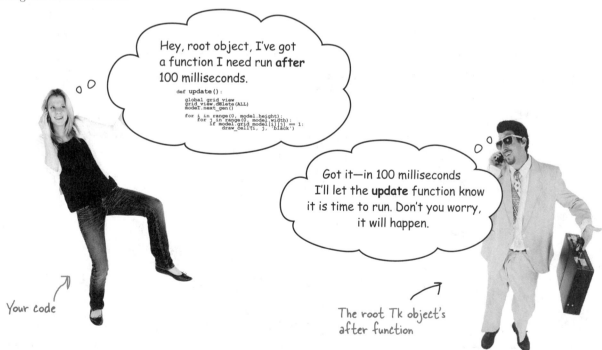

Hey, root object, I've got a function I need run **after** 100 milliseconds.

```
def update():
    global grid_view
    grid_view.delete(ALL)
    model.next_gen()

    for i in range(0, model.height):
        for j in range(0, model.width):
            if model.grid[i][j] == 1:
                draw_cell(i, j, 'black')
```

Got it—in 100 milliseconds I'll let the **update** function know it is time to run. Don't you worry, it will happen.

Your code

The root Tk object's after function

Hey, **update** function, it's been 100 milliseconds, so you're up: get running.

Perfect, it worked just as advertised. When 100 milliseconds had elapsed, my update function ran. Just what I wanted. Thanks, root!

Sharpen your pencil

Trace through this code; can you tell what it outputs? How does it work? Check your answer at the end of the chapter.

Brain Building

Do you think this qualifies as a recursive function?

```python
from tkinter import *

root = Tk()
count = 10

def countdown():
    global root, count

    if count > 0:
        print(count)
        count = count - 1
        root.after(1000, countdown)
    else:
        print('Blastoff')

countdown()
mainloop()
```

If only we had a way to call the update method over and over so that we'd see new generations of cells computed without all that clicking. That would be dreamy. But I know it's just a fantasy...

We have the technology: the after method

The `after` method is just what we need to get our simulator computing at regular intervals. In fact, we hope you spent a little time understanding that last Sharpen exercise because we're going to use a similar technique here in our `update` method:

```
def update():
    global grid_view, root, is_running

    grid_view.delete(ALL)
    model.next_gen()

    for i in range(0, model.height):
        for j in range(0, model.width):
            if model.grid_model[i][j] == 1:
                draw_cell(i, j, 'black')
    if (is_running):
        root.after(100, update)
```

We'll need to add the root and is_running globals, as we'll be using them.

Okay, now, when update is called, if is_running is True, then this call will schedule another call to update in 100 milliseconds (1/10 of a second).

A Test Drive

There are those times when *one line* of code makes all the difference. Guess what? This is one of those times. Get those last changes into *view.py* and get ready to see your app transformed into a Game of Life simulator.

(1) Click the start button and watch the simulator run.

(2) Click the pause button to temporarily suspend it.

(3) Repeat as often as you like and restart the simulator to get a new round of random starting cells.

This is starting to look like more than just a random selection of cells. →

Did you see any oscillating patterns? Gliders going across the screen? Areas of chaos that come and go? →

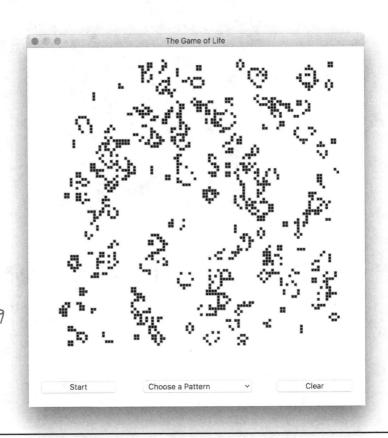

Are we there yet?

Well, we've certainly come a long way. In fact, we have all the big stuff working. We just need to finish up a few interface details. Up first, we have the clear button to implement—it's going to clear the screen and set all the cells to dead. With a clear screen we'll want the ability to click and add our own live cells to the canvas. And finally, we have our option menu, which is going to let us preload some patterns into the grid. We're going to tackle these one at a time, starting with the clear button.

Exercise

How about the clear button? It needs to set `is_running` to `False` and then set each cell's value to `0`. It also needs to set the start button's text to "Start" again. And, it should call `update` to update the display before ending (with every cell in the model set to `0`, the screen should clear).

Use the start button as an example and write the code for the clear button:

```
start_button.bind('<Button-1>', start_handler)

def start_handler(event):
    global is_running, start_button

    if is_running:
        is_running = False
        start_button.configure(text='Start')
    else:
        is_running = True
        start_button.configure(text='Pause')
        update()
```

You'll need to let the clear button know about your handler, just like we did with the start button.

And here's the start_handler again, which should serve as a good example.

Your code here!

If you're stumped on zeroing out the cells in the model, refresh your memory by looking at how the update function iterates over the cells.

When you've written the code, double-check it with ours at the end of the chapter and then get it in your *view.py* file. Give it a try.

How to enter and edit cells directly

Right now the game works by randomly choosing a bunch of live cells and then when we click the start button it begins computing new generations. What would be nice, though, is to be able to click and draw our own live cells on the grid before we click Start. To do that, we're going to use a technique similar to the one we used to handle button clicks. That is, when the user clicks on the canvas, we'll use an event handler (in other words, a function) that takes that click and translates it into a live cell onscreen and in the model.

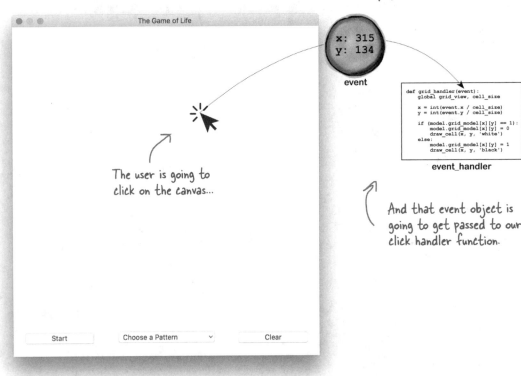

...which is going to generate an event and send along an event object with the x- and y-position of the click.

```
x:  315
y:  134
```
event

```
def grid_handler(event):
    global grid_view, cell_size

    x = int(event.x / cell_size)
    y = int(event.y / cell_size)

    if (model.grid_model[x][y] == 1):
        model.grid_model[x][y] = 0
        draw_cell(x, y, 'white')
    else:
        model.grid_model[x][y] = 1
        draw_cell(x, y, 'black')
```
event_handler

And that event object is going to get passed to our click handler function.

The user is going to click on the canvas...

We'll begin building this code by binding a left button click to the canvas just as we did with the start and clear buttons.

```
grid_view.bind('<Button-1>', grid_handler)
```

When the user clicks the left button on the grid_view canvas, call the grid_handler function.

Writing the grid_view handler

Let's think through how we want the `grid_handler` function to work. How about this: if the user clicks on a white (dead) cell in the grid, then we make it a live cell and turn it black. And, if the cell is black already, we'll change its state to dead and turn it back to white. Of course, the cell also needs to change visually in the view, and we need to update its value in the model.

Let's look at how to do this in code:

Remember the grid handler function takes an event as a argument.

We can get the x- and y-position of the click from the event object. You'll find there is an attribute for each.

```python
def grid_handler(event):
    global grid_view, cell_size

    x = int(event.x / cell_size)
    y = int(event.y / cell_size)

    if (model.grid_model[x][y] == 1):
        model.grid_model[x][y] = 0
        draw_cell(x, y, 'white')
    else:
        model.grid_model[x][y] = 1
        draw_cell(x, y, 'black')
```

Remember our grid is scaled by the cell size, so we need to find out the true x and y (row and column, if you like) in the grid model. To do this we divide by the cell size. We use the int function to make sure the result is an int and not a floating-point number.

If the current cell in the model is 1, we set it to 0 and call our draw_cell function to color in the cell white.

Otherwise, we set the model to 1 and call our draw_cell function to color in the cell black.

A Test Drive

Add the `grid_handler` function above to *view.py*, just below the `setup` function. And also remember to put the call to the `bind` method in your code (see below). *Finally, it's time to delete that call to randomize in* model.py; *that way you'll start with a clear grid.*

Don't miss this step.

```python
grid_view.grid(row=0, columnspan=3, padx=20, pady=20)
grid_view.bind('<Button-1>', grid_handler)
```

Place the call to bind just below where you set the grid for the grid_view.

Now, when you run the simulator you could see a nice blank screen. Click in the screen to add live cells before clicking the start button.

We recommend drawing a glider pattern and clicking Start. If you mess up, just click again to erase the cell.

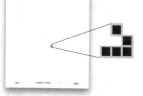

If clicks aren't working, make sure you're clicking in the middle of the window.

Now it's time to add some patterns

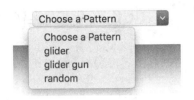

We're going to put one more bit of polish on this app by providing an option menu to allow users to choose from a list of preexisting patterns. Our design supplies three patterns, but you should feel free to add your own.

Remember that you've already instantiated an option menu in your code, but we purposely put off discussing that code because the option menu widget works a little differently than the button and canvas widgets. Let's look at the code we have so far to create the option menu:

> The Tkinter module provides an object that stores values. Here we're creating an object to hold a string and assigning it to the variable choice. You'll see how this is used in a sec.

> We then set the value of the choice object to 'Choose a Pattern,' which is the initial choice we want selected in the widget.

```
choice = StringVar(root)
choice.set('Choose a Pattern')
option = OptionMenu(root, choice, "Choose a Pattern",
                                  "glider",
                                  "glider gun",
                                  "random")

option.config(width=20)
```

> We then instantiate the option menu and pass it the root window (as is always the case with widgets), our variable for holding a string value, and a set of options that appear in the menu.

> To make things look better, we also widened the widget by giving it a width of 20.

As you can see in the interface this all looks great, but it doesn't do anything. As with the buttons and the canvas, we need to add an event binding to the option menu, but the way we do that is a little different than we're used to. Here's how we add a binding for the option menu:

> We add one more argument to the OptionMenu constructor, which is the command (think "handler") to invoke when a user chooses an option.

```
choice = StringVar(root)
choice.set('Choose a Pattern')
option = OptionMenu(root, choice, "Choose a Pattern",
                                  "glider",
                                  "glider gun",
                                  "random",
                    command=option_handler)
option.config(width=20)
```

Exercise

Add this small bit of code to your *view.py* file before we forget to do it!

Writing a handler for the OptionMenu

Writing an option menu handler is a bit different as well, because we aren't just reacting to a simple button click. Instead the user has chosen an option in the menu, and we need to figure out what that option is and then act on it.

As you might have figured out, the first item in our menu, "Choose a Pattern," is an instruction to the user; it isn't meant to do anything. For the rest of the options, let's write some code to see how we're going to handle them:

This handler gets an event too, although we won't need to make use of it.

We're going to be using the Tkinter StringVar object we saw earlier.

```python
def option_handler(event):
    global is_running, start_button, choice

    is_running = False
    start_button.configure(text='Start')

    selection = choice.get()
    if selection == 'glider':
        model.load_pattern(model.glider_pattern, 10, 10)

    elif selection == 'glider gun':
        model.load_pattern(model.glider_gun_pattern, 10, 10)

    elif selection == 'random':
        model.randomize(model.grid_model, model.width, model.height)

    update()
```

Let's stop the simulator from running and reset the start button.

The choice variable holds a StringVar object with the value the user selected in the option menu. A StringVar provides a get method to get the value it holds.

Once we have the user's selection we can test to see which option it was, and either load a pattern or call randomize.

Note that we need to write the load_pattern function as well as define what the patterns look like.

After we change the model, we need to update the display for the user.

If the user chooses random, we conveniently have already written a randomize function, so we just need to call it!

Exercise

Go ahead and place this code into your *view.py* file above your `start_handler` function. We can't run it yet, because we haven't written the model's `load_pattern` method or defined the patterns. We'll do that next, and then come back and give it all a test drive.

Okay, you threw me with that StringVar object. So, it's an object that holds the choice we made with the option menu? Is it like a special object that acts like a variable? Given we have variables already, why do we need it?

It *is* a little confusing. After all, we're happily coding along, using everyday Python variables, and out of nowhere `Tkinter` throws in its own variables in the form of an object. Why? There are a couple reasons we need to use `Tkinter` variables here. The first is that the Tk graphics library (which `Tkinter` is built on) is actually a *cross-platform* library (meaning it works with lots of languages, not just Python). As you gain experience with `Tkinter`, you'll see a few things that don't feel Python-like because `Tkinter` was not designed specifically for Python.

The other reason is that the `StringVar` class allows you to do a bit more than just store and retrieve values; using a `StringVar` you can track the changes to a variable's value. For instance, say you're building a weather monitor and you want to update your display anytime the temperature changes. Well, with a `StringVar` you can use its `trace` method to be notified anytime its value changes, like this:

```
temperature = StringVar()
temperature.trace("w", my_handler)
```

Anytime temperature is changed (written to in Tk terminology), our my_handler gets called.

We won't be making use of this additional functionality of `StringVar` in our code, but it's handy to know about for future reference, and is a great example of another form of event-based programming.

How to define your patterns

Let's define our patterns in the form of a two-dimensional list, like our grid model. So a pattern for a glider would look like this:

```
glider_pattern = [[0, 0, 0, 0, 0],
                  [0, 0, 1, 0, 0],
                  [0, 0, 0, 1, 0],
                  [0, 1, 1, 1, 0],
                  [0, 0, 0, 0, 0]]
```

Can you see the resemblance?

And the glider gun is a little more complicated:

```
glider_gun_pattern =  [[0, 0, 0, 0, 0, 0, 0, 0, 0, 0, 0, 0, 0, 0, 0, 0, 0, 0, 0, 0, 0, 0, 0, 0, 0, 0, 0, 0, 0, 0, 0, 0, 0, 0, 0, 0],
                      [0, 0, 0, 0, 0, 0, 0, 0, 0, 0, 0, 0, 0, 0, 0, 0, 0, 0, 0, 0, 0, 0, 0, 0, 1, 0, 0, 0, 0, 0, 0, 0, 0, 0, 0, 0],
                      [0, 0, 0, 0, 0, 0, 0, 0, 0, 0, 0, 0, 0, 0, 0, 0, 0, 0, 0, 0, 0, 0, 1, 0, 1, 0, 0, 0, 0, 0, 0, 0, 0, 0, 0, 0],
                      [0, 0, 0, 0, 0, 0, 0, 0, 0, 0, 0, 0, 1, 1, 0, 0, 0, 0, 0, 0, 1, 1, 0, 0, 0, 0, 0, 0, 0, 0, 0, 0, 1, 1, 0],
                      [0, 0, 0, 0, 0, 0, 0, 0, 0, 0, 0, 1, 0, 0, 0, 1, 0, 0, 0, 0, 1, 1, 0, 0, 0, 0, 0, 0, 0, 0, 0, 0, 1, 1, 0],
                      [0, 1, 1, 0, 0, 0, 0, 0, 0, 0, 0, 1, 0, 0, 0, 0, 1, 0, 0, 0, 1, 1, 0, 0, 0, 0, 0, 0, 0, 0, 0, 0, 0, 0, 0],
                      [0, 1, 1, 0, 0, 0, 0, 0, 0, 0, 0, 1, 0, 0, 0, 1, 0, 1, 1, 0, 0, 0, 0, 1, 0, 1, 0, 0, 0, 0, 0, 0, 0, 0, 0],
                      [0, 0, 0, 0, 0, 0, 0, 0, 0, 0, 0, 1, 0, 0, 0, 0, 1, 0, 0, 0, 0, 0, 0, 1, 0, 0, 0, 0, 0, 0, 0, 0, 0, 0, 0],
                      [0, 0, 0, 0, 0, 0, 0, 0, 0, 0, 0, 1, 0, 0, 0, 1, 0, 0, 0, 0, 0, 0, 0, 0, 0, 0, 0, 0, 0, 0, 0, 0, 0, 0, 0],
                      [0, 0, 0, 0, 0, 0, 0, 0, 0, 0, 0, 0, 1, 1, 0, 0, 0, 0, 0, 0, 0, 0, 0, 0, 0, 0, 0, 0, 0, 0, 0, 0, 0, 0, 0],
                      [0, 0, 0, 0, 0, 0, 0, 0, 0, 0, 0, 0, 0, 0, 0, 0, 0, 0, 0, 0, 0, 0, 0, 0, 0, 0, 0, 0, 0, 0, 0, 0, 0, 0, 0]]
```

Can you see the resemblance here too?

Exercise

You don't need to type these in. Just look in your Chapter 11 source code and you'll find *glider.py* and *glider_gun.py*. Open them and copy these two assignment statements to the bottom of your *model.py* file (just below the `count_neighbors` function). No need to test yet, other than making sure you don't have any syntax errors.

Writing the pattern loader

Now we need to write the code to load a pattern into the grid mode. All the pattern loader needs to do is take a list and copy its ones and zeros into the grid model. Actually, before it does that, it should clear out the grid model and write zeros into all its cells.

We're going to load our patterns by copying them into the grid_model.

We'll also support an optional x- and y-offset for the pattern.

We should also allow the pattern to be offset on the grid, so it can be placed, say, in the middle of the grid. We'll do that by taking an x-offset and a y-offset as arguments, and rather than copying the pattern starting at the top of the grid (location 0, 0), we'll place the pattern at the offset location. Here's the code:

Our function takes a pattern (like glider or glider_gun) in the form of a two-dimensional list.

It also takes two other arguments, an x- and y-position to locate the top-left cell of the pattern on the grid.

You'll remember of course parameter defaults from Chapter 5.

Alert: there's duplicated code here (look at the clear_handler); there's an opportunity for refactoring this code later (a homework assignment).

And zero out all the cells.

```python
def load_pattern(pattern, x_offset=0, y_offset=0):
    global grid_model

    for i in range(0, height):
        for j in range(0, width):
            grid_model[i][j] = 0

    j = y_offset

    for row in pattern:
        i = x_offset
        for value in row:
            grid_model[i][j] = value
            i = i + 1
        j = j + 1
```

Let's set i and j to the offsets.

Now we just iterate through each value in the pattern and assign it to the corresponding point on the grid_model.

A Test Drive

Add the `load_pattern` function from the previous page to your *model.py* file, just below your patterns, and you should be all ready for an exhaustive test of the Game of Life simulator! Given all the code and code changes in this chapter, you'll find the complete source code for the simulator over the next several pages.

model.py

```python
import random

height = 100
width = 100

def randomize(grid, width, height):
    for i in range(0, height):
        for j in range(0, width):
            grid[i][j] = random.randint(0,1)


grid_model = [0] * height
next_grid_model = [0] * height
for i in range(height):
    grid_model[i] = [0] * width
    next_grid_model[i] = [1] * width

def next_gen():
    global grid_model, next_grid_model

    for i in range(0, height):
        for j in range(0, width):
            cell = 0
            count = count_neighbors(grid_model, i, j)

            if grid_model[i][j] == 0:
                if count == 3:
                    cell = 1
            elif grid_model[i][j] == 1:
                if count == 2 or count == 3:
                    cell = 1
            next_grid_model[i][j] = cell

    temp = grid_model
    grid_model = next_grid_model
    next_grid_model = temp
```

```
def count_neighbors(grid, row, col):

    count = 0
    if row-1 >= 0:
        count = count + grid[row-1][col]
    if (row-1 >= 0) and (col-1 >= 0):
        count = count + grid[row-1][col-1]
    if (row-1 >= 0) and (col+1 < width):
        count = count + grid[row-1][col+1]
    if col-1 >= 0:
        count = count + grid[row][col-1]
    if col + 1 < width:
        count = count + grid[row][col+1]
    if row + 1 < height:
        count = count + grid[row+1][col]
    if (row + 1 < height) and (col-1 >= 0):
        count = count + grid[row+1][col-1]
    if (row + 1 < height) and (col+1 < width):
        count = count + grid[row+1][col+1]
    return count

glider_pattern = [[0, 0, 0, 0, 0],
                  [0, 0, 1, 0, 0],
                  [0, 0, 0, 1, 0],
                  [0, 1, 1, 1, 0],
                  [0, 0, 0, 0, 0]]

glider_gun_pattern = [[0, 0, 0, 0, 0, 0, 0, 0, 0, 0, 0, 0, 0, 0, 0, 0, 0, 0, 0, 0, 0, 0, 0, 0,
0, 0, 0, 0, 0, 0, 0, 0, 0, 0, 0, 0],
               [0, 0, 0, 0, 0, 0, 0, 0, 0, 0, 0, 0, 0, 0, 0, 0, 0, 0, 0, 0, 0, 0, 0, 0, 1, 0, 0,
0, 0, 0, 0, 0, 0, 0, 0, 0],
               [0, 0, 0, 0, 0, 0, 0, 0, 0, 0, 0, 0, 0, 0, 0, 0, 0, 0, 0, 0, 0, 0, 1, 0, 1, 0, 0,
0, 0, 0, 0, 0, 0, 0, 0, 0],
               [0, 0, 0, 0, 0, 0, 0, 0, 0, 0, 0, 0, 1, 1, 0, 0, 0, 0, 0, 0, 1, 1, 0, 0, 0, 0, 0,
0, 0, 0, 0, 0, 1, 1, 0],
               [0, 0, 0, 0, 0, 0, 0, 0, 0, 0, 0, 0, 1, 0, 0, 0, 1, 0, 0, 0, 0, 1, 1, 0, 0, 0, 0, 0,
0, 0, 0, 0, 0, 1, 1, 0],
               [0, 1, 1, 0, 0, 0, 0, 0, 0, 0, 0, 1, 0, 0, 0, 0, 0, 1, 0, 0, 0, 1, 1, 0, 0, 0, 0, 0,
0, 0, 0, 0, 0, 0, 0, 0],
               [0, 1, 1, 0, 0, 0, 0, 0, 0, 0, 0, 1, 0, 0, 0, 1, 0, 1, 1, 0, 0, 0, 0, 1, 0, 1, 0, 0,
0, 0, 0, 0, 0, 0, 0, 0],
               [0, 0, 0, 0, 0, 0, 0, 0, 0, 0, 0, 1, 0, 0, 0, 0, 0, 1, 0, 0, 0, 0, 0, 0, 0, 1, 0, 0,
0, 0, 0, 0, 0, 0, 0, 0],
               [0, 0, 0, 0, 0, 0, 0, 0, 0, 0, 0, 0, 1, 0, 0, 0, 1, 0, 0, 0, 0, 0, 0, 0, 0, 0, 0, 0,
0, 0, 0, 0, 0, 0, 0, 0],
               [0, 0, 0, 0, 0, 0, 0, 0, 0, 0, 0, 0, 0, 1, 1, 0, 0, 0, 0, 0, 0, 0, 0, 0, 0, 0, 0, 0,
0, 0, 0, 0, 0, 0, 0, 0],
               [0, 0, 0, 0, 0, 0, 0, 0, 0, 0, 0, 0, 0, 0, 0, 0, 0, 0, 0, 0, 0, 0, 0, 0, 0, 0, 0, 0,
0, 0, 0, 0, 0, 0, 0, 0]]
```

```
def load_pattern(pattern, x_offset=0, y_offset=0):
    global grid_model

    for i in range(0, height):
        for j in range(0, width):
            grid_model[i][j] = 0

    j = y_offset

    for row in pattern:
        i = x_offset
        for value in row:
            grid_model[i][j] = value
            i = i + 1
        j = j + 1

if __name__ == '__main__':
    next_gen()
```

view.py

```
from tkinter import *
import model

cell_size = 5
is_running = False


def setup():
    global root, grid_view, cell_size, start_button, clear_button, choice

    root = Tk()
    root.title('The Game of Life')

    grid_view = Canvas(root, width=model.width*cell_size,
                             height=model.height*cell_size,
                             borderwidth=0,
                             highlightthickness=0,
                             bg='white')

    start_button = Button(root, text='Start', width=12)
    clear_button = Button(root, text='Clear', width=12)

    choice = StringVar(root)
    choice.set('Choose a Pattern')
    option = OptionMenu(root, choice, 'Choose a Pattern', 'glider', 'glider gun', 'random',
                        command=option_handler)
    option.config(width=20)
```

```
  grid_view.grid(row=0, columnspan=3, padx=20, pady=20)
    grid_view.bind('<Button-1>', grid_handler)
    start_button.grid(row=1, column=0, sticky=W,padx=20, pady=20)
    start_button.bind('<Button-1>', start_handler)
    option.grid(row=1, column=1, padx=20)
    clear_button.grid(row=1, column=2, sticky=E, padx=20, pady=20)
    clear_button.bind('<Button-1>', clear_handler)

def option_handler(event):
    global is_running, start_button, choice

    is_running = False
    start_button.configure(text='Start')

    selection = choice.get()

    if selection == 'glider':
        model.load_pattern(model.glider_pattern, 10, 10)

    elif selection == 'glider gun':
        model.load_pattern(model.glider_gun_pattern, 10, 10)

    elif selection == 'random':
        model.randomize(model.grid_model, model.width, model.height)

    update()

def start_handler(event):
    global is_running, start_button

    if is_running:
        is_running = False
        start_button.configure(text='Start')
    else:
        is_running = True
        start_button.configure(text='Pause')
        update()

def clear_handler(event):
    global is_running, start_button

    is_running = False
    for i in range(0, model.height):
        for j in range(0, model.width):
            model.grid_model[i][j] = 0

    start_button.configure(text='Start')
    update()

def grid_handler(event):
    global grid_view, cell_size

    x = int(event.x / cell_size)
    y = int(event.y / cell_size)

    if (model.grid_model[x][y] == 1):
        model.grid_model[x][y] = 0
        draw_cell(x, y, 'white')
    else:
        model.grid_model[x][y] = 1
        draw_cell(x, y, 'black')
```

```
def update():
    global grid_view, root, is_running

    grid_view.delete(ALL)

    model.next_gen()
    for i in range(0, model.height):
        for j in range(0, model.width):
            if model.grid_model[i][j] == 1:
                draw_cell(i, j, 'black')
    if (is_running):
        root.after(100,update)

def draw_cell(row, col, color):
    global grid_view, cell_size

    if color == 'black':
        outline = 'grey'
    else:
        outline = 'white'

    grid_view.create_rectangle(row*cell_size,
                               col*cell_size,
                               row*cell_size+cell_size,
                               col*cell_size+cell_size,
                               fill=color, outline=outline)

if __name__ == '__main__':
    setup()
    update()
    mainloop()
```

Nice! Here's what we got playing with the ever-fascinating glider gun.

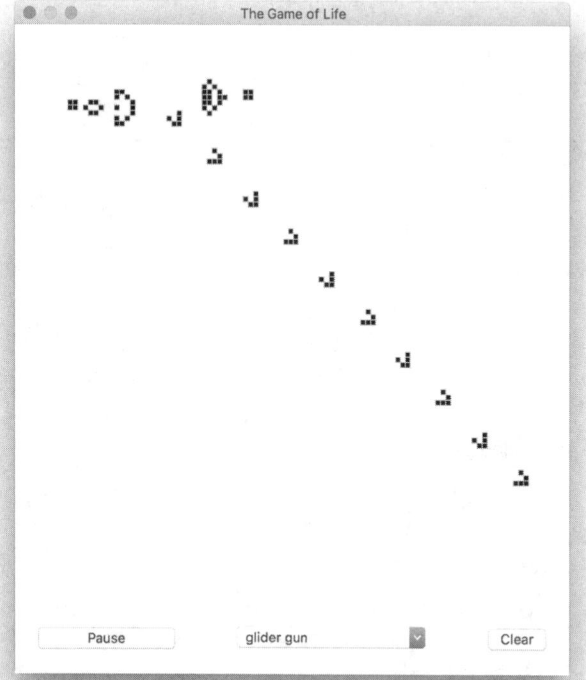

To replicate this, choose the "glider gun" option and click the start button.

The Game of Life

Pause   glider gun   Clear

> Nice job! The Game of Life
> simulator is spectacular! Let me know
> when you want to discuss marketing this.
> I'm thinking comic book classified ads.

BULLET POINTS

- Generative code produces output you could not have guessed by looking at the code.

- The Game of Life was discovered by mathematician John Conway.

- GUIs are graphical user interfaces.

- Paper prototyping is a method of testing a GUI before coding it.

- We designed our app by separating code into model, view, and controller responsibilities.

- Tkinter is a Python module for building user interfaces.

- Tkinter provides widgets that are presented in code as objects and onscreen as common user interface components.

- The Tk object represents a main window.

- Tkinter provides several layout managers, which organize widgets within a window.

- We used the grid layout manager to place our widgets.

- A reactive or event-based style of computation is often used when creating user interfaces.

- In this model we supply handlers in the form of functions that are called when certain events occur.

- We use the bind method on Tkinter widgets to register a function to handle an event.

- Most handlers are passed an event object, which contains more information about an event.

- Most programming languages also provide a method of registering a handler to be called after a duration of time has elapsed.

- Tkinter provides the after method on the Tk object to schedule code to be executed at a later time.

- The OptionMenu keeps the user's selection in a StringVar object.

- The Tkinter mainloop monitors the interface for user interaction.

Taking your Game of Life Simulator
EVEN FURTHER!

You've built a great little simulator! And it's just the beginning because there's so much more you can do with it. In lieu of a crossword, here are some ideas to consider.

LEARN MORE

- Start by learning more: *http://web.stanford. edu/~cdebs/GameOfLife/*

- Google "Game of Life" along with "Maze," "Night/Day," "Walled City," or "Reverse," to see some other examples of interesting alternative rules.

- Research Cellular Automata to find out more about the Game of Life and its mathematical basis: *https://en.wikipedia. org/wiki/Cellular_automaton*

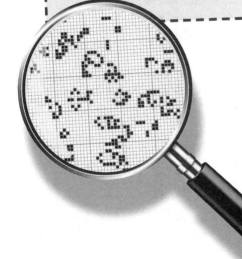

CODE MORE

- Tweak the rules. Here's another set of rules:

  1. If a cell is alive, it stays alive in the next generation.

  2. If a dead cell has two live cells adjacent to it, the dead cell changes state to live.

- Write code to save and load your patterns from a file.

- Implement a torus: our implementation uses a rectangle that ends at the borders. Change your code so that the lefthand side wraps around to the right, and the top to the bottom so the entire grid is one continuous surface (it's not that hard with a little thought).

- Add color: how about basing the color on how long a cell lives?

- Add "ghosting": if a cell has been alive, give it a light grey color. Have it fade over time.

- Find ways to optimize the code and make it super fast.

Sharpen your pencil Solution

Before you get started coding, work through a few generations of the Game of Life. Use generation 1 as the starting point and then compute generations 2 through 6, by applying the Game of Life rules. Here are the rules again:

- If a dead cell has three living neighbors, it becomes alive in the next generation.
- If a live cell has two or three living neighbors, it lives on in the next generation.
- If a live cell has fewer than two living neighbors, it dies in the next generation.
- If a live cell has more than three neighbors, it dies in the next generation.

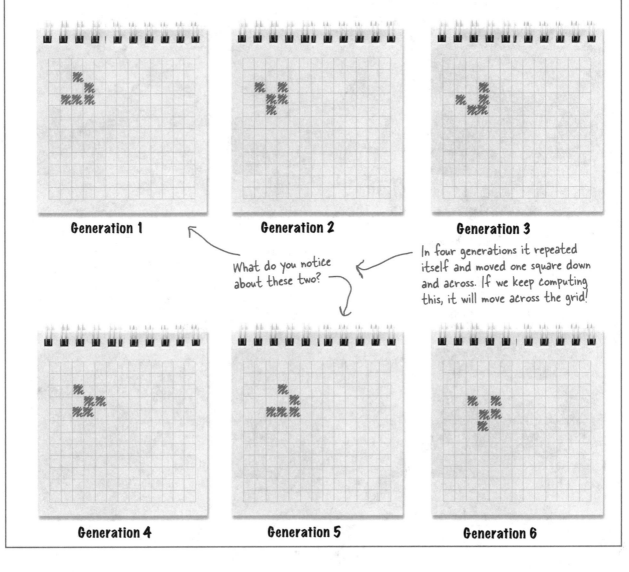

Generation 1

Generation 2

Generation 3

What do you notice about these two?

In four generations it repeated itself and moved one square down and across. If we keep computing this, it will move across the grid!

Generation 4

Generation 5

Generation 6

Code Magnets Solution

Lucky you. While you were reading about Ready Bake code, we went ahead and wrote the `next_gen` function and put it on the refrigerator. But as is always the case in the *Head First* books, someone came along and messed it up. Can you help us get it back together? Careful, there are extra magnets you don't need.

```python
def next_gen():

    global grid_model

    for i in range(0, height):
        for j in range(0, width):

            cell = 0

            count = count_neighbors(grid_model, i, j)

            if grid_model[i][j] == 0:

                if count == 3:

                    cell = 1

            elif grid_model[i][j] == 1:

                if count == 2 or count == 3:

                    cell = 1
```

Most cases result in the cell being dead in the next gen, so we'll just set it to that.

This implements the BIRTH rule.

This implements the LIFE rule.

We didn't need all these.

```
if cou    and
cell =
count < 2       :
         or
```

Sharpen your pencil
Solution

We're not really exercising this code if we're testing with a grid of all zeros. Write a function, `randomize`, which takes a grid, a width, and a height and places random ones and zeros at each cell location:

```
import random

def randomize(grid, width, height):
    for i in range(0, height):
        for j in range(0, width):
            grid[i][j] = random.randint(0,1)
```

Iterate over the grid, and assign a random int to each location.

Sharpen your pencil
Solution

Trace through this code; can you tell what it outputs? How does it work?

Brain Building
Do you think this qualifies as a recursive function?

Technically the function countdown never calls itself; instead, it is asking the root Tk object to call it at some point in the future (1 second in this case). But it certainly has a recursive feel!

```
from tkinter import *

root = Tk()
count = 10

def countdown():
    global root, count

    if count > 0:
        print(count)
        count = count - 1
        root.after(1000, countdown)
    else:
        print('Blastoff')

countdown()
mainloop()
```

We explicitly call countdown the first time, which schedules the first "after" call of countdown. Each time countdown is then called, it keeps scheduling more invocations of countdown 1 second later—that is, until count == 0, when the function ends without scheduling another call.

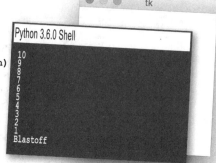

Because you're instantiating a Tk widget, you'll see a new window pop up when you run this code.

**Exercise
Solution**

How about the clear button? It needs to set `is_running` to `False` and then set each cell's value to `0`. It also needs to set the start button's text to "Start" again. And it should call `update` to update the display before ending (with every cell in the model set to `0`, the screen should clear).

Use the start button as an example and write the code for the clear button:

```
start_button.bind('<Button-1>', start_handler)

def start_handler(event):
    global is_running, start_button

    if is_running:
        is_running = False
        start_button.configure(text='Start')
    else:
        is_running = True
        start_button.configure(text='Pause')
        update()
```

You'll need to let the clear button know about your handler, just like we did with the start button.

And here's the start_handler again, which should serve as a good example.

```
clear_button.bind('<Button-1>', clear_handler)

def clear_handler(event):
    global is_running, start_button

    is_running = False
    for i in range(0, model.height):
        for j in range(0, model.width):
            model.grid_model[i][j] = 0

    start_button.configure(text='Start')
    update()
```

Here's the code to add the clear_handler.

First we set is_running to False.

Then we zero out the cells in the model.

Now reset the button text to 'Start'.

Finally, update the display.

When you've written the code, double-check it with ours at the end of the chapter and then get it in your *view.py* file. Give it a try.

Clear's working great! But, boy, we really need a way to click and add our own cells.

12 object-oriented programming

A Trip to Objectville

In this book you've used functions to abstract your code.

And you've approached coding in a **procedural manner** using simple statements, conditionals, and `for`/`while` loops with functions—none of this is exactly **object-oriented**. In fact, it's not object-oriented *at all!* We have looked at objects and how to use them in our code, but you haven't created any objects of your own yet, and you haven't really approached designing your code in an object-oriented way. So, the time has come to leave this boring procedural town behind. In this chapter, you're going to find out why using objects is going to make your life so much better—well, better in a **programming sense** (we can't really help you with other areas of your life *and* your coding skills, all in one book). Just a warning: once you've discovered objects you'll never want to come back. Send us a postcard when you get there.

Breaking it down, a different way

Remember back in Chapter 1 when we said there were two skills that you needed to learn to code? The first was breaking a problem into a small set of actions, and the second was learning a programming language so that you can describe those actions to a computer. At this point, you've learned a good deal of both those skills.

And that's good, because those skills are the foundation of any coding you (or anyone) will ever do. However, there is another perspective on breaking problems down, one that almost every modern language encourages and one that most professional programmers favor: it's known as *object-oriented programming*, with which we had our first encounter in Chapter 7.

With object-oriented programming, rather than writing an algorithm using the techniques we've learned for abstraction, conditional logic, and so on, we instead model a set of objects and how they interact. In some ways object-oriented programming is an advanced technique that is full of its own jargon, techniques, and best practices. But in other ways it's often an intuitive way to break problems down, as you'll soon see.

Now object-oriented programming (otherwise known as OOP), is a topic that could (and has) filled many books. In this chapter we're going to try to get the gist of OOP down so you're in a good position to read and understand code written in object-oriented style. We're also going to get you to the point where you can use object-oriented techniques in your own code, which includes creating your own classes. And, after this chapter, you'll also be in a great position to continue your object-oriented studies.

Remember classes from Chapter 7?

What's the point of object-oriented programming, anyway?

OOP allows you to design your code at a higher level. It allows you to focus on the big picture.

You've heard that before—remember when you learned how to take a piece of code and abstract it into a function? That freed you to start thinking of your code as a set of functions that could be called to solve your problem rather than having to mentally track the spaghetti code of low-level `if`s, `elif`s, `for/in`s, and assignments. OOP takes all that to the next level—with OOP you model real (or virtual) objects, including their state and behavior, and we let them interact to solve problems.

For example, take the difference between having to:

1. Create a heating coil out of wire,
2. Hook it to electricity,
3. Turn the electricity on,   ← *Procedural way to think about toasting bread*
4. Get a piece of bread,
5. Hold it 2 cm from the coil,
6. Keep holding bread until done,
7. Remove bread,
8. Turn off electricity.

and just using some objects:

1. Place **toast** in **toaster**.   ← *Object-oriented way to think about toasting bread*
2. Push **toast_button** on **toaster**.
3. Remove **toast** when **toaster** finished.

The first way is procedural, while the second way is object-oriented: you have a set of objects (bread, a toaster, and a toaster button), so you're thinking at the level of the problem (my bread's in the toaster, so now I just need to push the toast button), not down in the nitty-gritty of every step that needs to occur (while the heating coil is at 240 degrees and toast is 2 cm away and the toasting time hasn't elapsed).

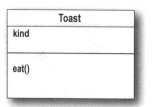

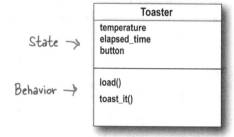

State →

Behavior →

Button
is_pressed

push()

Remember from Chapter 7 all objects are instantiated from classes and have attributes (state) and methods (behavior).

BRAIN POWER

Say you were implementing a classic ping-pong–style video arcade game. What would you choose as objects? What state and behavior do you think they'd have?

Pong!

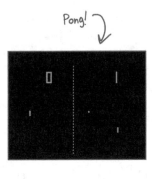

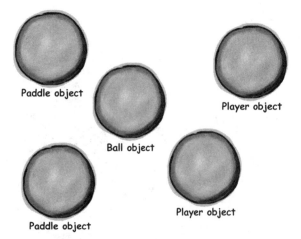

Paddle object

Player object

Ball object

Paddle object

Player object

What do you like about object-oriented languages?

"It's easier to understand how to use an object than a random bunch of functions and data in a module."

—Joy, 27, software architect

"I like that the data and the functions that operate on that data are together in one object."

—Brad, 19, coder

"It helps me code in a more natural way. My coding feels closer to the real problem."

—Chris, 39, project manager

"I can't believe Chris just said that. He hasn't written a line of code in five years."

—Daryl, 44, works for Chris

"Other than turtles?"

—Avary, 7, junior coder

Designing your first class

In Chapter 7 you saw how to use classes to instantiate objects, and since that chapter you've seen quite a few objects: the built-in types (string, floats, and so on), turtles, widgets, and the HTTP `requests` object, to name a few. But you've never created a class of your own. We're going to do that now.

Like using pseudocode to plan out your procedural code, it helps to plan out your objects (or more specifically the classes that create them) before jumping into code. Let's start simple and plan out a `Dog` class:

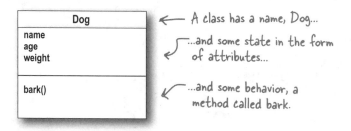

← A class has a name, Dog...

...and some state in the form of attributes...

...and some behavior, a method called bark.

Before we write the code for this class, let's think about how it is going to be used. Here's some code that uses our yet-to-be-implemented `Dog` class:

There's no need to type in or run this code yet.

```
codie = Dog('Codie', 12, 38)
jackson = Dog('Jackson', 9, 12)
codie.bark()
jackson.bark()
```

Remember this is called calling the constructor.

First we instantiate two dogs with different attributes.

Then we make use of the bark method to have each dog make a sound.*

Here's the output.

```
Python 3.6.0 Shell
Codie says "WOOF WOOF"
Jackson says "woof woof"
>>>
```

Now you're going to objectify me?

Remember Codie?

* Did you notice each dog has a different bark? Hmm, how'd that happen?

Based on this code example, we need to have a constructor in the `Dog` class that takes a name, age, and weight and then creates a new dog object for us. We also have a `bark` method that differs in its output based on some aspect of the dog—if we had to guess, we'd say big dogs say "WOOF WOOF" and smaller dogs say "woof woof." Sound familiar? Let's write some code to do this.

Writing your first class

We're going to start with what we've been referring to as the constructor; in other words, we're going to write the code that initializes our dog objects. After that we'll implement the `bark` method.

So study this code, and then let's talk about it:

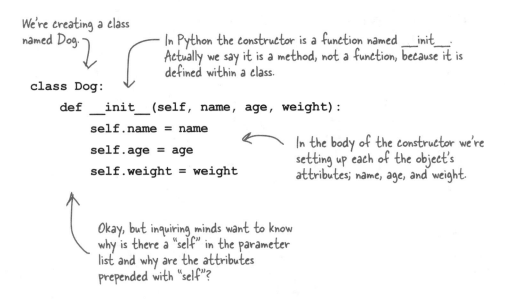

We're creating a class named Dog.

In Python the constructor is a function named __init__. Actually we say it is a method, not a function, because it is defined within a class.

```python
class Dog:

    def __init__(self, name, age, weight):
        self.name = name
        self.age = age
        self.weight = weight
```

In the body of the constructor we're setting up each of the object's attributes; name, age, and weight.

Okay, but inquiring minds want to know why is there a "self" in the parameter list and why are the attributes prepended with "self"?

How the constructor works

The key to understanding how the constructor (and other methods) works is understanding the role of the `self` parameter. Let's walk through what happens when the constructor is called. Pay close attention; if you blink you'll miss it.

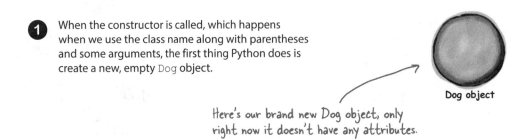

```python
codie = Dog('Codie', 12, 38)
```

1 When the constructor is called, which happens when we use the class name along with parentheses and some arguments, the first thing Python does is create a new, empty Dog object.

Here's our brand new Dog object, only right now it doesn't have any attributes.

Dog object

2 Next, your arguments are passed along to the `__init__` function. Something else happens too: Python takes the newly created object and passes it as the first argument, which we named `self`.

...and the newly created object is passed as the first argument.

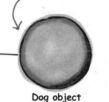

Dog object

After step 2 the newly created Dog object is assigned to the parameter self.

Next, the class's constructor is invoked with the supplied arguments, and one addition...

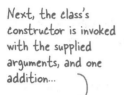

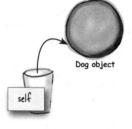

Dog object

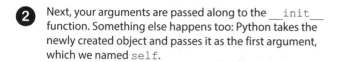

```
__init__(      , 'Codie', 12, 38)
```

```
def __init__(self, name, age, weight):
```

self

---

3 The body of the constructor is then executed. We assign each parameter (`name`, `age`, and `weight`) to an attribute of the same name in the instance of the `Dog` object using dot notation.

After step 3, all the arguments we passed to the constructor have been assigned to attributes in the Dog object.

Again, our brand new Dog object is passed as the first argument.
↓

```
def __init__(self, name, age, weight):
    self.name = name       ←——— Because self is the new Dog
    self.age = age               object, we're assigning the
    self.weight = weight         values name, age, and weight
                                 to attributes in the Dog
                                 object.
```

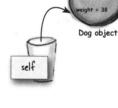

name = 'Codie'
age = 12
weight = 38

Dog object

self

---

4 When the constructor completes, Python takes the `Dog` object and returns it as a result of calling the constructor. In this case, when the `Dog` object is returned, it is assigned to the variable `codie`.

After step 4, the new Dog object, complete with the attributes name, age and weight, is assigned to the variable codie.

```
codie = Dog('Codie', 12, 38)
```

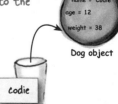

name = 'Codie'
age = 12
weight = 38

Dog object

codie

there are no
Dumb Questions

Q: How does __init__ get away without returning a value, yet one is returned from calling the constructor?

A: There are all kinds of things happening behind the scenes with constructors. When you call the constructor it first creates a new object for you, then it takes care of passing that object as the first argument to __init__, and finally it handles returning that object for you. In other words, it's all built into the way Python works.

Q: Is there something special about the name "self"?

A: No, anytime a constructor is called it passes a copy of the new object as the first argument to the __init__ method. By convention we name this parameter *self*. But we don't have to. That said, this is such a widely adopted convention that if you don't call the first parameter *self* you'll get strange looks from your fellow developers.

You'll find many object-oriented languages have a concept like self with a different name, like "this" for instance.

Also avoid using *self* as the name of a local or global variable, as it will cause mass confusion.

Q: So object attributes are just variables that hold normal Python values?

A: Pretty much. An attribute can be assigned any valid Python value, just like a variable. And, before you ask, methods are just like Python functions, only they are defined within an object instead of globally. There actually is one other difference too: methods also have a self parameter, which we'll look at shortly.

A Test Drive

We haven't written the `bark` method yet, but let's test what we have. Copy the code below into **dog.py** and then give it a test drive.

Here's our new class...

```
class Dog:
    def __init__(self, name, age, weight):
        self.name = name
        self.age = age
        self.weight = weight
```

...and a function for printing dogs.

```
def print_dog(dog):
    print(dog.name + "'s", 'age is', dog.age,
                         'and weight is', dog.weight)
```

This isn't a very object-oriented way to print our dogs, but we'll see how to improve it in a few pages.

Let's create two instances of Dog objects and pass them to print_dog.

```
codie = Dog('Codie', 12, 38)
jackson = Dog('Jackson', 9, 12)
print_dog(codie)
print_dog(jackson)
```

Notice as long as we pass our print_dog function a dog, things work as expected!

```
Python 3.6.0 Shell
Codie's age is 12 and weight is 38
Jackson's age is 9 and weight is 12
>>>
```

Writing the bark method

Before we actually write the bark method, let's talk about the difference between a method and a function. Sure, methods are defined in a class, but there's more to it than that. Think about how a method is called: it is always invoked with respect to *an object*. Like this:

← Remember when we call a method, we often say we "invoke" it.

```
codie.bark()
```

Or:

↖ Objects

```
jackson.bark()
```

And, as you'll see, methods typically operate on the attributes of that specific object. Given that, methods are always passed the object they are being invoked on as their first argument.

← Similar to how __init__ is passed the object as its first argument.

Let's write the bark method now and you'll see how this works:

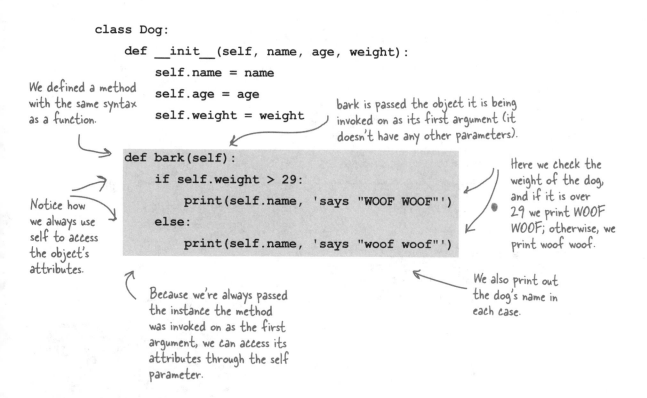

```
class Dog:
    def __init__(self, name, age, weight):
        self.name = name
        self.age = age
        self.weight = weight

    def bark(self):
        if self.weight > 29:
            print(self.name, 'says "WOOF WOOF"')
        else:
            print(self.name, 'says "woof woof"')
```

We defined a method with the same syntax as a function.

bark is passed the object it is being invoked on as its first argument (it doesn't have any other parameters).

Notice how we always use self to access the object's attributes.

Here we check the weight of the dog, and if it is over 29 we print WOOF WOOF; otherwise, we print woof woof.

Because we're always passed the instance the method was invoked on as the first argument, we can access its attributes through the self parameter.

We also print out the dog's name in each case.

How methods work

Let's walk through how the method invocation works to make sure we understand it.

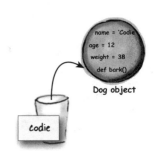

name = 'Codie'
age = 12
weight = 38
def bark()

Dog object

← *Let's see how the bark* →
method works when it is
invoked on the Codie object.

```
codie.bark()
```

1 When we call a method on an object, in this case the `codie` object, Python takes that object and passes it to the method as the first argument, along with any other arguments you supply (`bark` obviously doesn't have any others).

When the bark method is
invoked on the Codie object,
Python passes that object
as the first argument,
which gets bound to the
parameter self.

name = 'Codie'
age = 12
weight = 38
def bark()

Dog object

codie

self

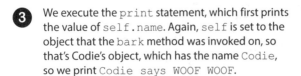

```
def bark(self):
    if self.weight > 29:
        print(self.name, 'says "WOOF WOOF"')
    else:
        print(self.name, 'says "woof woof"')
```

self is set to Codie's
object, so self.weight
is 38 and greater
than 29. So we invoke
the first clause.

2 Next we evaluate the body of the method. The first line compares `self.weight` to 29. In this case the object assigned to self is Codie's `Dog` object, and the value of `self.weight` is 38, so this condition is `True` and the first clause is executed.

```
print(self.name, 'says "WOOF WOOF"')
```

← *The print statement first*
prints the name attribute of
the object assigned to self.

3 We execute the `print` statement, which first prints the value of `self.name`. Again, `self` is set to the object that the `bark` method was invoked on, so that's Codie's object, which has the name `Codie`, so we print `Codie says WOOF WOOF`.

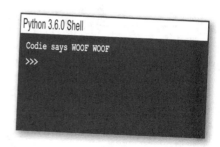

Python 3.6.0 Shell

Codie says WOOF WOOF
>>>

4 With that, the method completes. As we coded it the `bark` method doesn't return a value, although, like a function, it could have.

Sharpen your pencil

In Chapter 2 we wrote some code to compute a dog's age in human years. Add a method to our Dog's class to compute its age in human years. You can call the method `human_years`; it takes no arguments and returns the result as an integer.

```
dog_name = input("What is your dog's name? ")
dog_age = input("What is your dog's age? ")
human_age = int(dog_age) * 7
print('Your dog',
      dog_name,
      'is',
      human_age,
      'years old in human years')
```

Here's our code from way back in Chapter 2. Oh, the memories...

Here's our code so far. Add a method, human_years, that returns the dog's age in human years.

```
class Dog:
    def __init__(self, name, age, weight):
        self.name = name
        self.age = age
        self.weight = weight

    def bark(self):
        if self.weight > 29:
            print(self.name, 'says "WOOF WOOF"')
        else:
            print(self.name, 'says "woof woof"')




def print_dog(dog):
    print(dog.name + "'s", 'age is', dog.age,
                    'and weight is', dog.weight)


codie = Dog('Codie', 12, 38)
jackson = Dog('Jackson', 9, 12)
print(codie.name + "'s age in human years is ", codie.human_years())
print(jackson.name + "'s age in human years is ", jackson.human_years())
```

Add the new method here.

Adding some inheritance

Let's say we have the need for a new kind of dog in our code: a service dog, those trusty companions who have been well trained to help those needing assistance. They're dogs, but they're dogs with skills. So, do we need to start over and define a totally new class `ServiceDog` from scratch? That would be a shame because we've put a fair bit of time into our existing `Dog` class (work with us here), and it would be great if we could reuse that work. Well, we can.

You'll find almost every modern programming language provides the ability for classes to inherit attributes and behavior from another class. We call this capablity *inheritance* and it is a cornerstone of object-oriented programming.

Returning to our service dog, we can define the `ServiceDog` class so that it inherits the attributes (a name, age, and weight) and the ability to bark from our original `Dog` class. But going further, our `ServiceDog` class can add new attributes, like a handler (the person the dog is assisting, not to be confused with a event handler in the last chapter) and, say, a `walk` method to help their handler with walking.

Let's see how to define the `ServiceDog` class...

This is how we draw a class diagram showing ServiceDog inheriting from the Dog class.

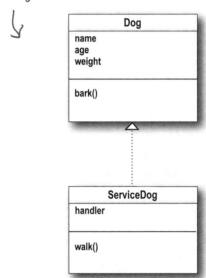

BRAIN POWER

What other dogs can you imagine inheriting from the `Dog` class? What new attributes might they have? What new methods?

Implementing the ServiceDog class

Let's implement the `ServiceDog` class and walk through its syntax and semantics:

Remember, syntax is all about how we can type it in, and semantics is all about what it means.

This syntax says we're declaring a new class ServiceDog that inherits from the Dog class.

Our new class name

The class we're inheriting from

Here's the ServiceDog constructor.

```
class ServiceDog(Dog):
    def __init__(self, name, age, weight, handler):
        Dog.__init__(self, name, age, weight)
        self.handler = handler

    def walk(self):
        print(self.name,'is helping its handler', self.handler, 'walk')
```

Notice it has the same parameters as the Dog class, but also has a new, extra parameter.

The ServiceDog constructor also expects to receive an extra handler argument.

This line calls the constructor of the Dog class and passes it all the arguments it needs, including self.

This adds a new attribute, handler, to self.

We also have a new method, walk.

The walk method uses attributes from the Dog and the ServiceDog classes.

Alright, that's a mouthful, so let's see how this code works.

Let's create a ServiceDog object with a handler named 'Joseph'.

```
rody = ServiceDog('Rody', 8, 38, 'Joseph')
print("This dog's name is", rody.name)
print("This dog's handler is", rody.handler)
print_dog(rody)
rody.bark()
rody.walk()
```

We can access inherited attributes, like name...

...or attributes from ServiceDog, like handler.

A ServiceDog is a type of Dog, so we can still call print_dog and have it work fine.

We can also call inherited methods, like bark.

...or methods just ServiceDogs can do, like walk...

Uh oh, service dogs should not be barking loudly...

Rody, a service dog

```
Python 3.6.0 Shell

This dog's name is Rody
This dog's handler is Joseph
Rody's age is 8 and weight is 38
Rody says "WOOF WOOF"
Rody is helping its handler Joseph walk
>>>
```

A closer look at subclassing

When we create a class that inherits from another class, we say that class is a *subclass* of the other. We also commonly use subclass in the form of a verb and say that we're *subclassing* another class. In this case when we defined the ServiceDog class, we were subclassing the Dog class.

But let's take a closer look at the syntax and semantics we used creating the ServiceDog subclass, starting with the class statement:

When you define a new class you can either define it from scratch, or you can supply a class in the parentheses that you want to subclass.

More terminology: often Dog is called the base class, because it is the base of all the classes that derive from it (right now we just have one, ServiceDog, but we'll make some more).

```
class ServiceDog(Dog):
```

It's also common to call this class the superclass. So here Dog is the superclass of ServiceDog.

We told you OOP had a lot of terminology!

Now let's look at the constructor method, __init__:

The declaration of the parameters is nothing out of the ordinary, just notice that we've added additional parameters (well, one in this case, handler, but you could add as many as you want).

```
def __init__(self, name, age, weight, handler):
    Dog.__init__(self, name, age, weight)
    self.handler = handler
```

And the last line is assigning the handler parameter to the attribute of the same name.

Note that only ServiceDogs will have this attribute because only ServiceDogs will execute this _init_ method.

Typically this should be the very first thing you do in a constructor when subclassing.

This next line may look a little different. Here we're calling the constructor of the Dog class. This sets up all attributes that are common to all dogs. If we didn't do this, then the name, age, and weight would not be set up in the object we're instantiating.

Finally we have the new method, walk:

In a subclass you can define a method just as you would in a base class. Notice that this method is available only in objects instantiated from the ServiceDog, not any old Dog.

```
def walk(self):
    print(self.name,'is helping its handler', self.handler, 'walk')
```

A ServiceDog IS-A Dog

When we have an inheritance relationship between two classes we say we have an IS-A relationship—a ServiceDog IS-A Dog. The concept doesn't just apply to direct descendants: for example, below you'll see that SeeingEyeDog inherits from ServiceDog, which, again, inherits from Dog, so a SeeingEyeDog IS-A ServiceDog, but a SeeingEyeDog IS-A Dog as well. On the other hand, while ServiceDog IS-A Dog, it's not a SeeingEyeDog (because SeeingEyeDog inherits from ServiceDog and can do things that ServiceDog doesn't know how to do).

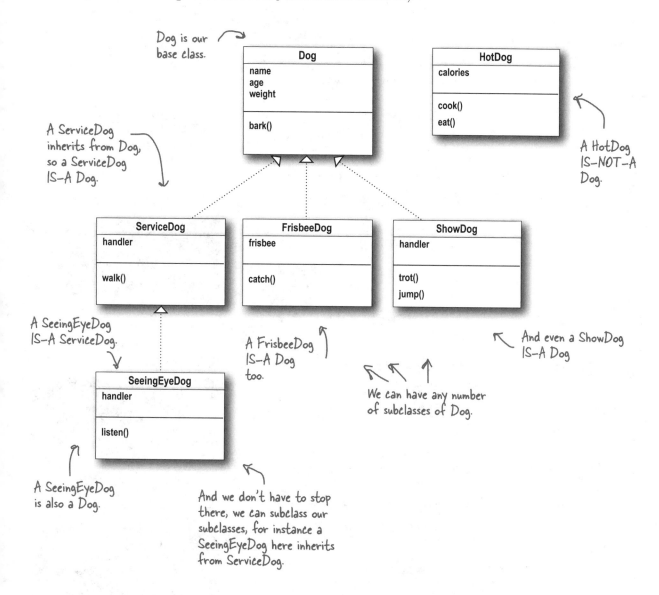

Dog is our base class.

A ServiceDog inherits from Dog, so a ServiceDog IS-A Dog.

A HotDog IS-NOT-A Dog.

A SeeingEyeDog IS-A ServiceDog.

A FrisbeeDog IS-A Dog too.

And even a ShowDog IS-A Dog

We can have any number of subclasses of Dog.

A SeeingEyeDog is also a Dog.

And we don't have to stop there, we can subclass our subclasses, for instance a SeeingEyeDog here inherits from ServiceDog.

Testing IS-A in code

If we have an arbitary object, can we tell if it IS-A certain class? For instance, let's say someone instantiates this object:

```python
mystery_dog = ServiceDog('Mystery', 5, 13, 'Helen')
```

They then hand you the object. Is it a `Dog`? `ServiceDog`? Something else? How can we tell?

That's where the `isinstance` built-in function comes in. Here's how it works:

isinstance takes an object and a class as arguments.

In this example isinstance evaluates to True because mystery_dog is a ServiceDog.

```python
if isinstance(mystery_dog, ServiceDog):
    print("Yup, it's a ServiceDog")
else:
    print('That is no ServiceDog')
```

isinstance is True if the object is the same class, or inherits from the class—in other words, if the object IS-A class.

Python 3.6.0 Shell

```
Yup, it's a ServiceDog
>>>
```

Let's try another:

In this example isinstance is still True because mystery_dog inherits from Dog.

```python
if isinstance(mystery_dog, Dog):
    print("Yup, it's a Dog")
else:
    print('That is no Dog')
```

Now isinstance is True if the object IS-A Dog.

Python 3.6.0 Shell

```
Yup, it's a Dog
>>>
```

And one more:

Now isinstance is True if the object IS-A SeeingEyeDog.

Not this time: isinstance evaluates to False because our ServiceDog is not a SeeingEyeDog.

```python
if isinstance(mystery_dog, SeeingEyeDog):
    print("Yup, it's a SeeingEyeDog")
else:
    print('That is no SeeingEyeDog')
```

Python 3.6.0 Shell

```
That is no SeeingEyeDog
>>>
```

Sharpen your pencil

Given the class diagram on the left, fill in the values that `isinstance`
evaluates to on the right. Remember `isinstance` always evaluates to
`True` or `False`. We did the first one for you.

**Your answer,
True or False**

↓

```
simple_cake = Cake()
chocolate_cake = FrostedCake()
bills_birthday_cake = BirthdayCake()
```

__False__	`isinstance(simple_cake, BirthdayCake)`
_____	`isinstance(simple_cake, FrostedCake)`
_____	`isinstance(simple_cake, Cake)`
_____	`isinstance(chocolate_cake, Cake)`
_____	`isinstance(chocolate_cake, FrostedCake)`
_____	`isinstance(chocolate_cake, BirthdayCake)`
_____	`isinstance(bills_birthday_cake, FrostedCake)`
_____	`isinstance(bills_birthday_cake, Cake)`
_____	`isinstance(bills_birthday_cake, BirthdayCake)`

Cake

flavor

bake()
cut()
eat()

△

FrostedCake

frosting

frost()

△

BirthdayCake

name_on_cake

add_name()
add_candles()

Exercise

Subclasses aren't just for your own classes; you can subclass Python's built-in classes too. How about we subclass the Python string class (otherwise known as the `str` class)? We're going to create a subclass called `PalindromeString`, which includes the method `is_palindrome`. Study the code below and then give it a try. Can you think of another method you'd like to add to `str`? There's no solution at the end of the chapter; everything is on this page:

We're going to create a new class PalindromeString, which is a subclass of Python's built-in str class (otherwise known as string).

```python
class PalindromeString(str):

    def is_palindrome(self):
        i = 0
        j = len(self) - 1
        while i < j:
            if self[i] != self[j]:
                return False
            i = i + 1
            j = j - 1
        return True
```

We're just going to add a new method to our subclass, so we don't need to implement a constructor.

If you don't supply a constructor, then when this class is instantiated the superclass's constructor is used (which is str's constructor).

Here's our new method. Remember the iterative version of is_palindrome?

Notice the use of self throughout. In this case, self is the str object itself, so we can do anything with it we'd do with a string.

Now let's put our subclass to the test. Remember a PalindromeString IS-A str, so we can do anything with it we do with a string, and it inherits a lot of functionality from str.

```python
word = PalindromeString('radar')
word2 = PalindromeString('rader')
print(word, 'length is', len(word), 'and uppercase is', word.upper())
print(word, word.is_palindrome())
print(word2, 'length is', len(word2), 'and uppercase is', word2.upper())
print(word2, word2.is_palindrome())
```

Here's the output. Can you think of other ways you could use your new ability to subclass the str class?

By the way, do you remember in Chapter 9 we were looking for a way to match Verb, VERB, VeRB, verb, and so on? You can use the upper (or lower) method to convert it to all uppercase (or lowercase) before the comparison.

```
Python 3.6.0 Shell

radar length is 5 and uppercase is RADAR
radar True
rader length is 5 and uppercase is RADER
rader False
>>>
```

How would you describe yourself?

How would you describe yourself? Using the __str__ method, of course! It's time to replace that print_dog function with something more object-oriented. Here's a quick Python convention: if you add a method to your class named __str__ and in that method return a description in the form of a string, then when you print out any object from that class, print will use your description.

```python
class Dog:
    def __init__(self, name, age, weight):
        self.name = name
        self.age = age
        self.weight = weight

    def bark(self):
        if self.weight > 29:
            print(self.name, 'says "WOOF WOOF"')
        else:
            print(self.name, 'says "woof woof"')

    def human_years(self):
        human_age = self.age * 7
        return human_age

    def __str__(self):
        return "I'm a dog named " + self.name
```

Add a __str__ method to the Dog class to craft a custom string for print to use.

Let's test this out by calling print on a few objects.

```python
codie = Dog('Codie', 12, 38)
jackson = Dog('Jackson', 9, 12)
rody = ServiceDog('Rody', 8, 38, 'Joseph')
print(codie)
print(jackson)
print(rody)
```

Note we're in no way changing how print works; we're just changing how any instance of the Dog class prints.

Q: So when I have a class like ServiceDog and I create a ServiceDog object, behind the scenes are there actually two objects, one with the Dog attributes and methods and one with the ServiceDog attributes and methods?

A: No, there's just one object with all the attributes. For methods, the objects refer to their definitions in the classes, so they don't really live in the objects. But conceptually, just think of an object you instantiate as a single ServiceDog object.

Q: I heard Python has something called multiple inheritance?

A: Yes, that's where you don't inherit from just one class, but more than one. Like a flying car might inherit from both an automobile and an airplane class. It's good you know multiple inheritance exists, but not all experts agree that it's a good idea. Some languages consider multiple inheritance such a horrible, error-prone practice they forbid it. Put it on your list of things to look into as you become more experienced in OOP, but remember, there are often better ways to approach your object-oriented designs.

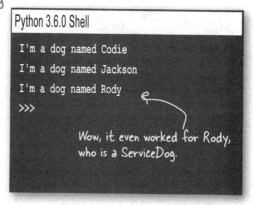

```
Python 3.6.0 Shell
I'm a dog named Codie
I'm a dog named Jackson
I'm a dog named Rody
>>>
```

Wow, it even worked for Rody, who is a ServiceDog.

Overriding and extending behavior

A few pages back, did you notice that Rody barked a big "WOOF WOOF"? That behavior would probably be frowned upon while Rody is working as a service dog. If you look at the Dog class, that's how the behavior is implemented for dogs over 29 lbs. So, are service dogs stuck with that behavior for good? Actually, no, we can always override and extend the behavior of classes we inherit from. Here's how:

```python
class Dog:
    def __init__(self, name, age, weight):
        self.name = name
        self.age = age
        self.weight = weight

    def bark(self):
        if self.weight > 29:
            print(self.name, 'says "WOOF WOOF"')
        else:
            print(self.name, 'says "woof woof"')

    def human_years(self):
        human_age = self.age * 7
        return human_age

    def __str__(self):
        return "I'm a dog named " + self.name


class ServiceDog(Dog):
    def __init__(self, name, age, weight, handler):
        Dog.__init__(self, name, age, weight)
        self.handler = handler
        self.is_working = False

    def walk(self):
        print(self.name,'is helping its handler', self.handler, 'walk')

    def bark(self):
        if self.is_working:
            print(self.name, 'says, "I can\'t bark, I\'m working"')
        else:
            Dog.bark(self)
```

Note that you can add any attributes you want to a class in the __init__ method. The __init__ method is your chance to set up any attributes needed to model the internal stage of your object. Attributes don't have to mirror the parameters of the method.

Let's add a new attribute to the ServiceDog, a Boolean attribute named is_working that's initially set to False.

Notice in this string we need both double and single quotes. So we escape the single quotes.

Now we're going to redefine the bark method in ServiceDog. Whenever we call bark on a dog of type ServiceDog, this method will be executed rather than the one in Dog. We say we're overriding the bark method.

If is_working is True, then the dog says that it is working and it can't bark. Otherwise, we call the bark method in the Dog class, passing it self. In this latter case, the bark method will end up doing what it normally does (barking).

A Test Drive

Let's give this code a try. Replace the contents of your file *dog.py* with the code on the previous page. Then add the code below at the bottom to test it out.

⌐ Create our dog Rody.

```python
rody = ServiceDog('Rody', 8, 38, 'Joseph')

rody.bark()                    ← Have him bark
                                 (remember is_working
                                  is initialized to False).

rody.is_working = True  ←
rody.bark()
```

Now set is_working to
True and try again.

We haven't seen a lot
of this, but remember
to change an object's
attribute value you just
assign it as you would a
variable to another value.

The ServiceDog has now
extended the behavior of
Dog, yet when is_working
is False it still has the
same behavior as Dog.

```
Python 3.6.0 Shell

Rody says "WOOF WOOF"
Rody says "I can't bark, I'm working"
>>>
```

Welcome to Jargon City

Remember we mentioned OOP has a lot of jargon?
Let's cover some of that jargon before we get too far
down the road. Welcome to Jargon City.

Classes can have **attributes** and **methods**.

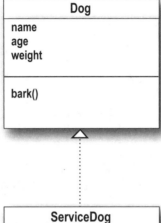

We say that Dog is the **superclass** of ServiceDog. We also often call Dog a **base** class.

Both Dog and Service Dog are **classes**.

We say that ServiceDog **inherits** from Dog.

We say that ServiceDog is the **subclass** of Dog. We also call it a **derived** class, because it is based on Dog.

We say that ServiceDog **overrides** the bark method in Dog.

We can **instantiate** Dog or ServiceDog **objects** by calling their **constructors**.

True or false? All ServiceDogs are Dogs but not all Dogs are ServiceDogs.

Answer: *True.*

Sharpen your pencil

Take a look at the class definitions on the left, which contain a few overridden methods. Execute the code below (in your head) and write down the output here. As always, you'll find the solution at the end of the chapter.

```python
class Car():
    def __init__(self):
        self.speed = 0
        self.running = False

    def start(self):
        self.running = True

    def drive(self):
        if self.running:
            print('Car is moving')
        else:
            print('Start the car first')

class Taxi(Car):
    def __init__(self):
        Car.__init__(self)
        self.passenger = None
        self.balance = 0.0

    def drive(self):
        print('Honk honk, out of the way')
        Car.drive(self)

    def hire(self, passenger):
        print('Hired by', passenger)
        self.passenger = passenger

    def pay(self, amount):
        print('Paid', amount)
        self.balance = self.balance + amount
        self.passenger = None

class Limo(Taxi):
    def __init__(self):
        Taxi.__init__(self)
        self.sunroof = 'closed'

    def drive(self):
        print('Limo driving in luxury')
        Car.drive(self)

    def pay(self, amount, big_tip):
        print('Paid', amount, 'Tip', big_tip)
        Taxi.pay(self, amount + big_tip)

    def pour_drink(self):
        print('Pouring drink')

    def open_sunroof(self):
        print('Opening sunroof')
        self.sunroof = 'open'

    def close_sunroof(self):
        print('Closing sunroof')
        self.sunroof = 'closed'
```

Trace through this code in your head, writing the output you expect below.

```python
car = Car()
taxi = Taxi()
limo = Limo()

car.start()
car.drive()

taxi.start()
taxi.hire('Kim')
taxi.drive()
taxi.pay(5.0)

limo.start()
limo.hire('Jenn')
taxi.drive()          ← Careful, this one
limo.pour_drink()        is a little
limo.pay(10.0, 5.0)      tricky.
```

Your output here ↘

Python 3.6.0 Shell

Object can HAS-Another object

Object attributes aren't limited to just simple types like numbers and strings, they can be assigned to lists and dictionaries as well. They can even be assigned to other objects. When an attribute is set to another object, we say there is a HAS-A relationship. If we have a class named `House` and its objects have an attribute set to a `Kitchen` object, for example, we say the `House` HAS-A `Kitchen`.

When there is a HAS-A relationship between objects, we say that one object is composed with another object (a `House` is composed with a `Kitchen`). Object-oriented experts get even more precise as to whether both objects can stand on their own or not (a kitchen doesn't make much sense without a house, but a person, who owns a house, makes sense without the house) and they have specific terms for those. We'll let you explore these relationships as you gain experience.

But you're probably wondering, what's the big deal? So what? An object can have another object as an attribute—that's sort of what I'd expect, so why the big production?

You've seen that an object can inherit behavior—for instance, a `ServiceDog` gets its `human_years` behavior, as well as some of its `bark` behavior, from the `Dog` class. Well, another common way to give an object additional behavior is to compose it with another object. Think about that `House` object—when you use *composition*, or compose the `House` object with a `Kitchen` object, all of a sudden you have the new ability to cook.

Let's look at how to compose objects and then we'll see how we can add new behavior (and even delegate some responsibility) to another object.

How many $5 words can you find in this chapter?

How would you define a set of classes to build a object-oriented house?

Exercise

Your turn to create a new class. How about a frisbee-catching dog? We've already created a Frisbee class for you:

```python
class Frisbee:
    def __init__(self, color):
        self.color = color

    def __str__(self):
        return "I'm a " + self.color + ' frisbee'
```

A Frisbee can't do much; it just has a color and a __str__ method so it prints well.

Your job is to help us finish the FrisbeeDog. It needs to catch a frisbee and give it back. It should have a __str__ method as well. Oh, and the dog can't bark if it has a frisbee in its mouth, so you'd better override the bark method.

This is a challenging exercise. Give yourself the time to work through it. Use the solution at the end of the chapter to the extent you need to. Be patient with yourself.

```python
class FrisbeeDog(Dog):
    def __init__(self, name, age, weight):
        Dog.__init__(self, name, age, weight)
        self.frisbee = None

    def bark(self):



    def catch(self, frisbee):




    def give(self):




    def __str__(self):
```

You'll want the FrisbeeDog to bark like other dogs, unless it has a frisbee in its mouth, in which case say "I can't bark, I have a frisbee in my mouth".

If catch gets called, take the frisbee passed to you and store it in the frisbee attribute.

When give is called, set the attribute to None and return the frisbee.

If the dog has a frisbee, then return the string "I'm a dog named <name here> and I have a frisbee"; otherwise, return what all Dogs return.

A Test Drive

Double-checking your answer to the previous exercise with our solution, add your new code to the **dog.py** file. Remove the previous test code and add the test code below to the bottom of your file.

```python
def test_code():
    dude =  FrisbeeDog('Dude', 5, 20)
    blue_frisbee = Frisbee('blue')

    print(dude)
    dude.bark()
    dude.catch(blue_frisbee)
    dude.bark()
    print(dude)
    frisbee = dude.give()
    print(frisbee)
    print(dude)

test_code()
```

Create a frisbeeDog and a Frisbee.

Print the dog and make it bark, and then have it catch the frisbee again. Then have it bark with the frisbee in its mouth.

Print the dog (now that it has the frisbee) and then have it give back the frisbee.

Notice how this code is looking a lot more object-oriented than procedural?

And then print the frisbee that was given back by the dog, and print the dog again (now that it's given up the frisbee).

Here's the output we got.

```
Python 3.6.0 Shell

I'm a dog named Dude
Dude says "woof woof"
Dude caught a blue frisbee
Dude says, "I can't bark, I have a frisbee
in my mouth"
I'm a dog named Dude and I have a frisbee
Dude gives back blue frisbee
I'm a blue frisbee
I'm a dog named Dude
>>>
```

Dude, a frisbee-catching dog.

Designing a Doggie Hotel

As you know we're never one to pass up a good business opportunity, and we hear dog boarding is a real growth industry. All we need to do is keep a few dogs, allow them to be checked in and checked out, and of course give them all a chance to bark every once in a while. Let's create some code to do that. Let's do some planning for the hotel by creating a class diagram for it.

Every hotel has a name attribute, to hold a name like "Doggie Hotel" or "Doggie Ranch" or "Puppy Playground".

A Hotel also has two attributes that are parallel lists. The lists hold the names of the dogs along with a corresponding dog object.

And we have two methods...

The check_in method takes a name and a dog, and checks the dog into the hotel.

The check_out method takes a name and returns the dog if the dog is staying at the hotel.

We can say our Hotel is composed with a set of Dog objects, the ones stored in the dogs attribute list.

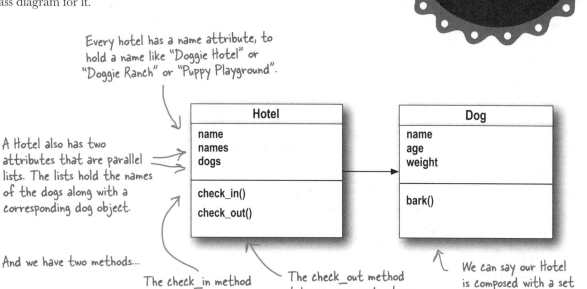

When it comes to writing some code for the Hotel class, there are a few things to consider. First, we should only check objects into the hotel if they are truly dogs. To be a dog an object should either be an instance of the Dog class, or a subclass of Dog. And we can only check dogs out of the hotel if they were checked in, so we need to check that condition as well.

Can you think of a better way to store dogs in the hotel than using two parallel lists?

Implementing the Doggie Hotel

Now that we've created a diagram for the `Hotel` class, let's work through implementing it. We'll start by implementing the constructor and then work through implementing the two methods, `check_in` and `check_out`.

> When we instantiate the Hotel class, we give it a name, like "Doggie Hotel".

```
class Hotel:
    def __init__(self, name):
        self.name = name
        self.kennel_names = []
        self.kennel_dogs = []
```

> And we'll use two lists, one to hold the dog names and another to hold the corresponding Dog objects.

> We've got a method to check dogs into the hotel. The method takes a Dog object.

```
    def check_in(self, dog):
        if isinstance(dog, Dog):
            self.kennel_names.append(dog.name)
            self.kennel_dogs.append(dog)
            print(dog.name, 'is checked into', self.name)
        else:
            print('Sorry only Dogs are allowed in', self.name)
```

> First make sure this is a Dog; no Cats or other objects allowed.

> When we check in, add the dog's name and the Dog object to the respective lists...

> ...and just a little output for testing.

> If the value passed to check_in isn't a Dog, we don't check it in. Sorry, cats.

> To check a dog out of the hotel, we just need to supply its name.

```
    def check_out(self, name):
        for i in range(0, len(self.kennel_names)):
            if name == self.kennel_names[i]:
                dog = self.kennel_dogs[i]
                del self.kennel_names[i]
                del self.kennel_dogs[i]
                print(dog.name, 'is checked out of', self.name)
                return dog
        print('Sorry,', name, 'is not boarding at', self.name)
        return None
```

> First check to make sure the dog is in the kennel...

> ...and if it is, get the Dog object from the list and then delete the name and object from the kennel lists.

> We also return the Dog object at the end of checkout. After all, you should get your dog back, right?

> If the dog isn't in the kennel, we let the user know this is the wrong kennel and return None.

A Test Drive

Add the `Hotel` class on the previous page to your *dog.py* file. Remove the previous test code and add the test code below to the bottom of your file. Oh, and don't forget the `Cat` class too.

```python
class Cat():
    def __init__(self, name):          Check out our
        self.name = name               new Cat class!

    def meow(self):
        print(self.name, 'Says, "Meow"')

def test_code():
    codie = Dog('Codie', 12, 38)       Let's create a bunch of Dogs, and dogs of
    jackson = Dog('Jackson', 9, 12)    different types, like ServiceDogs and FrisbeeDogs.
    sparky =  Dog('Sparky', 2, 14)
    rody = ServiceDog('Rody', 8, 38, 'Joseph')
    dude =  FrisbeeDog('Dude', 5, 20)
    kitty = Cat('Kitty')               We'll try a Cat too—you never know!

    hotel = Hotel('Doggie Hotel')
    hotel.check_in(codie)
    hotel.check_in(jackson)            Create a hotel and get all
    hotel.check_in(rody)               these pets checked in.
    hotel.check_in(dude)
    hotel.check_in(kitty)              Now let's check them all out
                                       and make sure they're giving
                                       us back the right dog.
    dog = hotel.check_out(codie.name)
    print('Checked out', dog.name, 'who is', dog.age, 'and', dog.weight, 'lbs')
    dog = hotel.check_out(jackson.name)
    print('Checked out', dog.name, 'who is', dog.age, 'and', dog.weight, 'lbs')
    dog = hotel.check_out(rody.name)
    print('Checked out', dog.name, 'who is', dog.age, 'and', dog.weight, 'lbs')
    dog = hotel.check_out(dude.name)
    print('Checked out', dog.name, 'who is', dog.age, 'and', dog.weight, 'lbs')
    dog = hotel.check_out(sparky.name)

test_code()                    And let's keep the Doggie Hotel on        Output on the
                               their toes—we never checked in Sparky.     next page.
```

Here's the output!

Everyone got checked in...
    ...except the cat.

And the Doggie Hotel gave us all the right dogs back.

And they figured out we didn't drop off Sparky.

Fine, be that way.

```
Python 3.6.0 Shell

Codie is checked into Doggie Hotel
Jackson is checked into Doggie Hotel
Rody is checked into Doggie Hotel
Dude is checked into Doggie Hotel
Sorry only Dogs are allowed in Doggie Hotel
Codie is checked out of Doggie Hotel
Checked out Codie who is 12 and 38 lbs
Jackson is checked out of Doggie Hotel
Checked out Jackson who is 9 and 12 lbs
Rody is checked out of Doggie Hotel
Checked out Rody who is 8 and 38 lbs
Dude is checked out of Doggie Hotel
Checked out Dude who is 5 and 20 lbs
Sorry, Sparky is not boarding at Doggie Hotel
>>>
```

Using lists seems very clunky in the hotel. After all that work understanding dictionaries, that would seem a better way to implement the kennel, right?

Good call. You beat us to it—we were thinking the same thing. Of course a natural reservation is that once we start changing lists to dictionaries, those changes are going to propagate into the rest of the code, and then next thing you know we'll be changing everything.

Ah, but not so! After all, this is object-oriented programming and one of the benefits is **encapsulation**. Think about encapsulation like this: our objects are keeping internal state and behavior together, and as long as from the outside everything works as expected, the method we use to implement the inside of that object is our business. It shouldn't have any effect on the code using our object.

Let's fix the hotel and you'll see what we mean.

Renovating the Doggie Hotel

Get out the jackhammer; it's time to rework this hotel. Let's just rework `check_in` and `check_out` from scratch without showing each change; in this case, it's easy to look at:

When we instantiate the Hotel class, we give it a name, like "Doggie Hotel".

```
class Hotel:
    def __init__(self, name):
        self.name = name
        self.kennel_names = []
        self.kennel_dogs = []
        self.kennel = {}
```

And we're now going to use a dictionary to hold the dogs; let's call it kennel.

We've still got a method to check dogs into the hotel. The method takes a Dog object.

First make sure this is a Dog; no Cats or other objects allowed.

When we check in, we add the dog to the dictionary, using the dog's name as the key...

```
    def check_in(self, dog):
        if isinstance(dog, Dog):
            self.kennel[dog.name] = dog
            print(dog.name, 'is checked into', self.name)
        else:
            print('Sorry only Dogs are allowed in', self.name)
```

...and just a little output for testing.

To check a dog out of the hotel, we just need to supply its name.

First check to make sure the dog is in the kennel...

...and if it is, get the Dog object from the dictionary and then delete the dog from the dictionary.

```
    def check_out(self, name):
        if name in self.kennel:
            dog = self.kennel[name]
            print(dog.name, 'is checked out of', self.name)
            del self.kennel[dog.name]
            return dog
        else:
            print('Sorry,', name, 'is not boarding at', self.name)
            return None
```

We also return the Dog object at the end of checkout. After all, you should get your dog back, right?

Nice! Much clearer code!

If the dog isn't in the kennel, we let the user know this is the wrong kennel.

Remember from Chapter 8 that dictionaries are more efficient than lists when we need to find an item.

A Test Drive

Replace your `check_in` and `check_out` methods in *dog.py* file. And give it another test drive.

Notice we didn't change any other code! And we totally changed the way our dogs are stored and accessed. That's encapsulation at work; your other code doesn't need to know or care how you implemented the dogs, as long as you're providing the same object interface (in other words, the methods you can call on a Dog).

→

```
Python 3.6.0 Shell

Codie is checked into Doggie Hotel
Jackson is checked into Doggie Hotel
Rody is checked into Doggie Hotel
Dude is checked into Doggie Hotel
Sorry only Dogs are allowed in Doggie Hotel
Codie is checked out of Doggie Hotel
Checked out Codie who is 12 and 38 lbs
Jackson is checked out of Doggie Hotel
Checked out Jackson who is 9 and 12 lbs
Rody is checked out of Doggie Hotel
Checked out Rody who is 8 and 38 lbs
Dude is checked out of Doggie Hotel
Checked out Dude who is 5 and 20 lbs
Sorry, Sparky is not boarding at Doggie Hotel
>>>
```

Adding some hotel activities

Any guess what the favorite dog activity is at a dog hotel? Barking, of course. Let's add a `barktime` method to the hotel and let all the dogs get a chance to bark.

```python
def barktime(self):
    for dog_name in self.kennel:
        dog = self.kennel[dog_name]
        dog.bark()
```

Go through each dog name in the kennel and use it as a key to grab the Dog object.

And let the dog bark.

A Test Drive

Add the `barktime` method to your *dog.py* file. Remove the previous test code and add the test code below to the bottom of your file. Give it a spin.

```python
def test_code():
    codie = Dog('Codie', 12, 38)
    jackson = Dog('Jackson', 9, 12)
    rody = ServiceDog('Rody', 8, 38, 'Joseph')
    frisbee = Frisbee('red')
    dude =  FrisbeeDog('Dude', 5, 20)
    dude.catch(frisbee)

    hotel = Hotel('Doggie Hotel')
    hotel.check_in(codie)
    hotel.check_in(jackson)
    hotel.check_in(rody)
    hotel.check_in(dude)

    hotel.barktime()

test_code()
```

Looks like all the dogs are barking.

```
Python 3.6.0 Shell

Dude caught a red frisbee
Codie is checked into Doggie Hotel
Jackson is checked into Doggie Hotel
Rody is checked into Doggie Hotel
Dude is checked into Doggie Hotel
Codie says "WOOF WOOF"
Jackson says "woof woof"
Rody says "WOOF WOOF"
Dude says, "I can't bark, I have a frisbee in my mouth"
>>>
```

I can do anything you can, or Polymorphism

Relax

This is a chapter with a lot of new concepts. Take breaks, get sleep, give your brain time to absorb the material. You might want to take a break now.

Let's take a look at the output from our `barktime` test again:

```
Codie says "WOOF WOOF"          ← Codie is a Dog.
Jackson says "woof woof"        ← Jackson is a Dog too.
Rody says "WOOF WOOF"           ← Rody is a ServiceDog.
Dude says, "I can't bark, I have a frisbee in my mouth"
                                ← And Dude is a FrisbeeDog.
```

Technically, all the dogs were different types (with the exception of Codie and Jackson, who are both `Dogs`). Yet, we were able to write code that iterated over all of them, treat them uniformly, and call the `bark` method.

```
for dog_name in self.kennel:
    dog = self.kennel[dog_name]          No matter what kind of dog it is,
    dog.bark()                       ←   we can call bark, guaranteed.
```

What if `ServiceDog` or `FrisbeeDog` doesn't have a `bark` method? Ah, we know they are guaranteed to have a `bark` method because they are subclasses of `Dog` (said another way, they inherit from the `Dog` class), and the `Dog` class has a `bark` method. Now, in our case, `ServiceDogs` and `FrisbeeDogs` override the `bark` method, but it doesn't matter—one way or another, they have a `bark` method.

Why is this a big deal? Because we can count on this quality in our objects, we can write code that operates without worrying about how those objects do what they do, even if down the road we change how those objects work, or we create totally new dog types we never anticipated (like a `ShowDog` or a `PoliceDog`). In fact, all `Dog` types, current and future, can participate in the Doggie Hotel's `barktime` without any changes to the Doggie Hotel code.

The more experienced you become with coding, the more you're going to see this last bit as a huge advantage.

This quality we're discussing has a technical name: **polymorphism**. It's another one of those $5 words from the object-oriented crowd. Polymorphism means that you can have different objects with different underlying implementations (like a `FrisbeeDog` and a `ServiceDog`) that present the same programming interface (that is, they both have a `bark` method). This quality plays out in several ways in object-oriented programming and is a deep topic to explore that is related to inheritance. For now, just remember it is possible to write code that can be applied to many different objects as long as they have the set of methods you're expecting.

It's about time we teach the other dogs to walk

The only dogs in our implementation that know how to walk are service dogs. That's not right; all dogs walk. We've got the main `Dog` class and we have the `FrisbeeDog` class, which inherits from `Dog`, and both need to be able to walk. Do we need to add a `walk` method to both? Well, as we saw with the `__str__` method, given that `FrisbeeDog` inherits from `Dog`, if we add a `walk` method to `Dog`, then `FrisbeeDog`s will inherit that behavior. Given that, let's do a little reworking of the code to take advantage of that. We can even improve the `ServiceDog` in the process. Let's see how.

```python
class Dog:
    def __init__(self, name, age, weight):
        self.name = name
        self.age = age
        self.weight = weight

    def bark(self):
        if self.weight > 29:
            print(self.name, 'says "WOOF WOOF"')
        else:
            print(self.name, 'says "woof woof"')

    def human_years(self):
        human_age = self.age * 7
        return human_age

    def walk(self):
        print(self.name, 'is walking')

    def __str__(self):
        return "I'm a dog named " + self.name

class ServiceDog(Dog):
    def __init__(self, name, age, weight, handler):
        Dog.__init__(self, name, age, weight)
        self.handler = handler
        self.is_working = False

    def walk(self):
        if self.is_working:
            print(self.name,'is helping its handler',
                    self.handler, 'walk')
        else:
            Dog.walk(self)

    def bark(self):
        if self.is_working:
            print(self.name, 'says, "I can\'t bark, I\'m working"')
        else:
            Dog.bark(self)
```

We're showing only the classes that changed.

Let's add a simple walk method to Dog.

And for the ServiceDog, if it's working, we'll show a special message. Otherwise, we'll just do what all other dogs do.

A Test Drive

Add the `walk` code additions and changes from the previous page to your *dog.py* file. Remove the previous test code and add the test code below to the bottom of your file. Then take this code for a walk.

```python
def test_code():
    codie = Dog('Codie', 12, 38)
    jackson = Dog('Jackson', 9, 12)
    rody = ServiceDog('Rody', 8, 38, 'Joseph')
    frisbee = Frisbee('red')
    dude =  FrisbeeDog('Dude', 5, 20)
    dude.catch(frisbee)

    codie.walk()
    jackson.walk()
    rody.walk()
    dude.walk()

test_code()
```

⌐ Looks like all the dogs are walking.

```
Python 3.6.0 Shell

Dude caught a red frisbee
Codie is walking
Jackson is walking
Rody is walking
Dude is walking
>>>
```

Exercise

Override the `FrisbeeDog`'s `walk` method so that if a dog has a frisbee he says, "I can't walk, I'm playing Frisbee!" Otherwise `FrisbeeDog` acts like a normal `Dog`. Go ahead and add the code to your *dog.py* file. Use the same test code as the last Test Drive.

```python
class FrisbeeDog(Dog):
    def __init__(self, name, age, weight):
        Dog.__init__(self, name, age, weight)
        self.frisbee = None

    def bark(self):
        if self.frisbee != None:
            print(self.name,
                    'says, "I can\'t bark, I have a frisbee in my mouth"')
        else:
            Dog.bark(self)

    def walk():                                            ⟵ Override walk here.



    def catch(self, frisbee):
        self.frisbee = frisbee
        print(self.name, 'caught a', frisbee.color, 'frisbee')
```

⟵ The rest of the FrisbeeDog class goes here.

and responsibility

The power of inheritance

All we had to do is add a new method, `walk`, to the `Dog` base class and magically our dogs (the `ServiceDog` and the `FrisbeeDog`) that didn't walk before began walking. That's the power of inheritance. We can add, change, and extend the behavior of a whole set of classes by simply changing a class they inherit from. Now, in general that is a powerful tool in your hands, but as with any tool, it can be misused if you aren't careful. With inheritance we can also cause unintended consequences when we add new behaviors—what if we added a `chase_squirrel` method to the `Dog` class without thinking about the consequences for our `ServiceDog`?

You can also overuse inheritance to extend the functionality of your classes. There are other ways too, and we've mentioned one of them: composition. By putting classes together—or *composing* them—we often come up with object-oriented designs that are more flexible than using inheritance alone.

Using inheritance properly and not overusing it requires good object-oriented design and analysis skills (something you'll learn as you continue to develop your OOP skills). Now we're talking about some subtle aspects of OOP and object-oriented design, but it's good to be aware of these concepts in the beginning—too many coders get far into their coding careers before they become aware of topics like the power of composing classes.

So, again, these are subtleties you'll learn as you gain experience with OOP. For now let's take our hotel just a little further, and maybe we'll use composition in the process.

You know how to draw inheritance with a class diagram. Here a Kitchen is inheriting from a Room class, or, as we say, a Kitchen IS-A Room.

Room
entrance
width
height
enter()
leave()

House
kitchen
lock()
unlock()
sell()

Kitchen
description
cook()
clean()

Here's how you draw composition. Here a House HAS-A Kitchen. HAS-A means composition.

BRAIN POWER

There is still an issue with our new dictionary-based implementation of the Hotel class. For example, what if two dogs are checked in with the same name? What happens? How would you fix this issue?

Creating a Doggie Hotel walking service

The Doggie Hotel is looking for extra revenue opportunities, so what about providing a dog walking service to the dogs staying in the kennel? Sounds like a winner to us. Let's implement that:

```python
class Hotel:
    def __init__(self, name):
        self.name = name
        self.kennel = {}

    def check_in(self, dog):
        if isinstance(dog, Dog):
            self.kennel[dog.name] = dog
            print(dog.name, 'is checked into', self.name)
        else:
            print('Sorry only Dogs are allowed in', self.name)

    def check_out(self, name):
        if name in self.kennel:
            dog = self.kennel[name]
            print(dog.name, 'is checked out of', self.name)
            del self.kennel[dog.name]
            return dog
        else:
            print('Sorry,', name, 'is not boarding at', self.name)
            return None

    def barktime(self):
        for dog_name in self.kennel:
            dog = self.kennel[dog_name]
            dog.bark()

    def walking_service(self):
        for dog_name in self.kennel:
            dog = self.kennel[dog_name]
            dog.walk()
```

Adding a walking service is pretty straightforward; in fact, it looks almost exactly like our hotel barktime method, except the dogs walk instead of bark.

Iterate through every dog in the kennel and call each dog's walk method.

Okay, that was easy enough, but let's say we don't have time to walk a zillion dogs; after all, we're busy running this hotel! What we'd love to do is *delegate* the responsibility to someone else.

How are we going to hire a person to walk our dogs if we don't even have people objects?

Serious Coding

In OOP, when an object asks another object to perform a task, it's called **delegation**. Delegation is a way to give an object extra behavior without having to inherit it or implement it directly.

Good point. Let's fix that. How about we create a simple `Person` class, and then create a subclass called `DogWalker` who knows how to walk dogs?

Otherwise known as "subclassing"

```python
class Person:
    def __init__(self, name):
        self.name = name

    def __str__(self):
        return "I'm a person and my name is " + self.name
```

Just a simple Person class with a name. We could also add more later.

```python
class DogWalker(Person):
    def __init__(self, name):
        Person.__init__(self, name)

    def walk_the_dogs(self, dogs):
        for dog_name in dogs:
            dogs[dog_name].walk()
```

A DogWalker is just a Person, but it has a walk_the_dogs method.

This method just iterates through the dogs and calls each dog's walk method.

Great, now let's rework the `Hotel` class so that we can hire a `DogWalker` and then delegate the dog walking through the `walking_service` method:

These methods go in the Hotel class.

In our hire_walker method we make sure the object is a DogWalker, and if so hire them by adding them as an attribute.

```python
    def hire_walker(self, walker):
        if isinstance(walker, DogWalker):
            self.walker = walker
        else:
            print('Sorry,', walker.name, ' is not a Dog Walker')

    def walking_service(self):
        if self.walker != None:
            self.walker.walk_the_dogs(self.kennel)
```

Now in walking_service, if there is a walker attribute, then we ask the walker to walk the dogs.

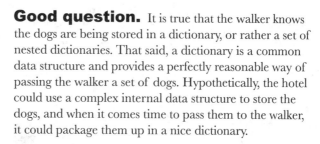

If you look at the DogWalker class, it knows that the Dogs are stored in a dictionary. If we change the code back to lists, then DogWalker will break. With encapsulation I thought we weren't supposed to know how things in an object were implemented?

Good question. It is true that the walker knows the dogs are being stored in a dictionary, or rather a set of nested dictionaries. That said, a dictionary is a common data structure and provides a perfectly reasonable way of passing the walker a set of dogs. Hypothetically, the hotel could use a complex internal data structure to store the dogs, and when it comes time to pass them to the walker, it could package them up in a nice dictionary.

You are right, though: if we do change our existing internal implementation of the hotel, we will have to keep in mind that walkers are expecting to get a dictionary of dogs. So we haven't fully encapsulated this aspect of the hotel.

All that said, if you really wanted to encapsulate this aspect of the hotel, and further separate the hotel and the walker (so that the walker doesn't have or rely on knowledge of the hotel's implementation), you could improve the implementation with the iterable pattern that we mentioned much earlier in the book. This pattern allows you to iterate over sequences of values without knowing anything about how they are implemented.

Doing so is a bit beyond the scope of this book, but, again, it's a great question and something to continue to exploring in your own designs.

A Test Drive

At this point you want to add the `Person` and `DogWalker` classes from two pages back, as well as add the `hire_walker` and `walking_service` methods to the `Hotel` class. Then use the test code below (replace your existing test code):

```python
def test_code():
    codie = Dog('Codie', 12, 38)
    jackson = Dog('Jackson', 9, 12)
    sparky =  Dog('Sparky', 2, 14)
    rody = ServiceDog('Rody', 8, 38, 'Joseph')
    rody.is_working = True
    dude =  FrisbeeDog('Dude', 5, 20)

    hotel = Hotel('Doggie Hotel')
    hotel.check_in(codie)
    hotel.check_in(jackson)
    hotel.check_in(rody)
    hotel.check_in(dude)

    joe = DogWalker('joe')
    hotel.hire_walker(joe)

    hotel.walking_service()

test_code()
```

← Rody wouldn't be working at the hotel, but let's try it out anyway.

← Let's create and hire our walker...

← ...and delegate the responsibility to Joe.

Looks like delegating the dog walking is off to a flying start!

```
Python 3.6.0 Shell

Codie is checked into Doggie Hotel
Jackson is checked into Doggie Hotel
Rody is checked into Doggie Hotel
Dude is checked into Doggie Hotel
Codie is walking
Jackson is walking
Rody is helping its handler Joseph walk
Dude is walking
>>>
```

Meanwhile, back at the turtle races...

Remember back in Chapter 7 when something went awry with the green turtle? If you'll recall the green turtle was mysteriously winning by large margins. The police are still stumped. With your new OOP knowledge, can you take another look and see what is going on?

```python
import turtle
import random

turtles = []

class SuperTurtle(turtle.Turtle):
    def forward(self, distance):
        cheat_distance = distance + 5
        turtle.Turtle.forward(self, cheat_distance)

def setup():
    global turtles
    startline = -620
    screen = turtle.Screen()
    screen.setup(1290,720)
    screen.bgpic('pavement.gif')

    turtle_ycor = [-40, -20, 0, 20, 40]
    turtle_color = ['blue', 'red', 'purple', 'brown', 'green']

    for i in range(0, len(turtle_ycor)):
        if i == 4:
            new_turtle = SuperTurtle()
        else:
            new_turtle = turtle.Turtle()
        new_turtle.shape('turtle')
        new_turtle.penup()
        new_turtle.setpos(startline, turtle_ycor[i])
        new_turtle.color(turtle_color[i])
        new_turtle.pendown()
        turtles.append(new_turtle)

def race():
    global turtles
    winner = False
    finishline = 560

    while not winner:
        for current_turtle in turtles:
            move = random.randint(0,2)
            current_turtle.forward(move)

            xcor = current_turtle.xcor()
            if (xcor >= finishline):
                winner = True
                winner_color = current_turtle.color()
                print('The winner is', winner_color[0])

setup()
race()

turtle.mainloop()
```

Study the code again carefully; it definitely looks like someone has hacked the program and added some new code. What does the new code do? What object-oriented concepts does the hack depend on?

↑ You'll find the solution in two pages!

CRIME SCENE DO NOT ENTER   CRIME SCENE DO NOT ENTER   CRIME SCENE DO NOT ENTER

Welcome to Objectville

A guide for better living through objects.

Welcome, new Objectville resident! Please accept our handy guide with tips & tricks for better living in Objectville. We hope you enjoy your stay.

☞ Get yourself acquainted. Take the time to explore the objects (and classes) around you. Look at other object-oriented Python code to get a feel for how it's been constructed and how objects are being used.

☞ Don't be shy about extending Python's built-in classes, which you can do just as with your own classes.

☞ Know up front that learning your way around Objectville is a life-long pursuit.

☞ Continue learning. You know the basics; now you need the experience. The only way to gain experience is to study and to practice deliberately, otherwise known as "build stuff!"

☞ Spend more time on the object-oriented basics, like inheritance and making use of polymorphism in your designs.

☞ Keep your objects simple and focused, and work your way up to complex object designs; practice building small houses before you design skyscrapers.

☞ Learn more about building with composition and using delegation in your code. You'll find this may make your design more flexible.

☞ Don't stop. You've got the momentum going, so keep learning.

The turtle races case SOLVED

Did you figure out what went awry? It looks like our sneaky hacker has used his subclassing skills to create a **subclass** of Turtle called SuperTurtle. Then in SuperTurtle he **overrode** the forward method so that 5 units get added onto the distance parameter before the call is made to the **base class's** (Turtle, in this case) forward method. The hacker obviously has a good knowledge of **polymorphism** because he knew that the game's race method would call forward on any kind of object, as long as it IS-A Turtle. See, a little OOP knowledge CAN be a dangerous thing!

Nice job!
You got him!

The hacker has created a subclass of Turtle that overrides the forward method and adds 5 more units anytime forward is called.

```python
import turtle
import random

turtles = []

class SuperTurtle(turtle.Turtle):
    def forward(self, distance):
        cheat_distance = distance + 5
        turtle.Turtle.forward(self, cheat_distance)

def setup():
    global turtles
    startline = -620
    screen = turtle.Screen()
    screen.setup(1290,720)
    screen.bgpic('pavement.gif')

    turtle_ycor = [-40, -20, 0, 20, 40]
    turtle_color = ['blue', 'red', 'purple', 'brown', 'green']

    for i in range(0, len(turtle_ycor)):
        if i == 4:
            new_turtle = SuperTurtle()
        else:
            new_turtle = turtle.Turtle()
        new_turtle.shape('turtle')
        new_turtle.penup()
        new_turtle.setpos(startline, turtle_ycor[i])
        new_turtle.color(turtle_color[i])
        new_turtle.pendown()
        turtles.append(new_turtle)

def race():
    global turtles
    winner = False
    finishline = 560

    while not winner:
        for current_turtle in turtles:
            move = random.randint(0,2)
            current_turtle.forward(move)

            xcor = current_turtle.xcor()
            if (xcor >= finishline):
                winner = True
                winner_color = current_turtle.color()
                print('The winner is', winner_color[0])

setup()
race()

turtle.mainloop()
```

A subclass of Turtle is defined!

A SuperTurtle object is being instantiated every time for turtle #4, the green turtle.

Polymorphism at work: this code calls forward on any object that IS-A Turtle, even if it is a SuperTurtle.

CRIME SCENE DO NOT ENTER   CRIME SCENE DO NOT ENTER   CRIME SCENE DO NOT ENTER

Got through the entire book? Including the OOP part? Well, I think we may have found our candidate.

Have you considered a career in coding?

If you're reading this page, assuming you didn't just skip to the end, congratulations! And you should really ask yourself how far you could take this! In case you haven't noticed, you've covered a huge distance in this book. The exciting and daunting thing is that this book just scratches the surface of software development. If nothing else, we hope you'll consider our suggestion, as you clearly have the right stuff to take this even further.

Here are a few suggestions for what's next:

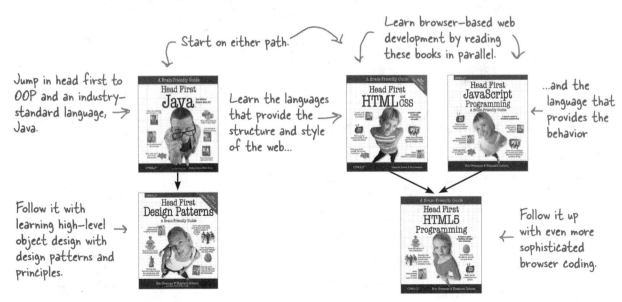

Start on either path.

Learn browser-based web development by reading these books in parallel.

Jump in head first to OOP and an industry-standard language, Java.

Learn the languages that provide the structure and style of the web...

...and the language that provides the behavior

Follow it with learning high-level object design with design patterns and principles.

Follow it up with even more sophisticated browser coding.

BULLET POINTS

- Object-oriented programming (OOP for short) focuses on solving problems by modeling real (or virtual) objects.

- Objects have state and behavior.

- Objects are created from classes, which act as blueprints.

- When we create a new object, we say we instantiate it.

- A constructor is a method that initializes a class.

- In Python the constructor is named __init__.

- The constructor is passed the object being created as the first argument.

- By convention we call the first parameter of a constructor **self**.

- Attributes are like variables within an object and can be assigned to any Python value.

- Methods are like functions, except they are passed the self argument.

- We can inherit the attributes and methods of another class by subclassing.

- The class we're subclassing is often called the superclass or supertype.

- We can override the methods of a superclass by defining methods of the same name in the subclass.

- We say we have an IS-A relationship when we subclass.

- We can test for IS-A relationships with the **isinstance** function in Python.

- The **isinstance** method returns True if an object is an instance of a class (or any of its superclasses).

- Override the **str** method to return the string you'd like displayed when your object is printed by **print**.

- When we write code that works for objects that expose the same interface we're taking advantage of polymorphism.

- We think of an object's interface as the methods we can call on an object.

- We compose objects by assigning another object to the attribute of an object.

- Composition is a common technique to extend a class's behavior.

- When we rely on another class to do work, we're delegating work to that class.

- Multiple inheritance occurs when you inherit behavior and state from more than one class.

Coding Crossword

This is it, the final crossword, and it's object oriented. Well, at least all the words are.

Across

4. Creates an object and initializes it.
6. Built-in function to check IS-A.
10. Dog that helps humans.
12. Code that works over objects with the same interface.
14. Convention for the first parameter of a method.
17. Holds state of object.
18. Has a lot of jargon.

Down

1. Not allowed in the hotel.
2. Type of inheritence that inherits from two or more classes.
3. Class from which others are subclassed or derived.
5. IS-A relationship.
7. Hiding implementation details.
8. Redefining the behavior of a method in a subclass.
9. HAS-A relationship.
11. Asking another object to do the work.

Sharpen your pencil
Solution

In Chapter 2 we wrote some code to compute a dog's age in human years. Add a method to our `Dog`'s class to compute its age in human years. You can call the method `human_years`; it takes no arguments and returns the result as an integer.

Here's our code so far. Add a method, human_years, that returns the dog's age in human years.

```python
class Dog:
    def __init__(self, name, age, weight):
        self.name = name
        self.age = age
        self.weight = weight

    def print_dog(dog):
        print(dog.name + "'s", 'age is', dog.age,
                        'and weight is', dog.weight)

    def bark(self):
        if self.weight > 29:
            print(self.name, 'says "WOOF WOOF"')
        else:
            print(self.name, 'says "woof woof"')

    def human_years(self):
        years = self.age * 7
        return years

codie = Dog('Codie', 12, 38)
jackson = Dog('Jackson', 9, 12)
print(codie.name + "'s age in human years is ", codie.human_years())
print(jackson.name + "'s age in human years is ", jackson.human_years())
```

To compute the dog's age in human years we use the dog's age attribute, multiply it by 7, and return it.

Here's the output.

Python 3.6.0 Shell

```
Codie's age in human years is  84
Jackson's age in human years is  63
>>>
```

Sharpen your pencil
Solution

Given the class diagram on the left, fill in the values that `isinstance` evaluates to on the right. Remember `isinstance` always evaluates to True or False.

Your answer, True or False
↓

```
simple_cake = Cake()
chocolate_cake = FrostedCake()
bills_birthday_cake = BirthdayCake()
```

Cake
flavor
bake() cut() eat()

_____**False**_____   `isinstance(simple_cake, BirthdayCake)`

_____**False**_____   `isinstance(simple_cake, FrostedCake)`

_____**True**_____   `isinstance(simple_cake, Cake)`

FrostedCake
frosting
frost()

_____**True**_____   `isinstance(chocolate_cake, Cake)`

_____**True**_____   `isinstance(chocolate_cake, FrostedCake)`

_____**False**_____   `isinstance(chocolate_cake, BirthdayCake)`

BirthdayCake
name_on_cake
add_name() add_candles()

_____**True**_____   `isinstance(bills_birthday_cake, FrostedCake)`

_____**True**_____   `isinstance(bills_birthday_cake, Cake)`

_____**True**_____   `isinstance(bills_birthday_cake, BirthdayCake)`

Sharpen your pencil
Solution

Take a look at the class definitions on the left, which contain a few overridden methods. Execute the code below (in your head) and write the output here.

```python
class Car():
    def __init__(self):
        self.speed = 0
        self.running = False

    def start(self):
        self.running = True

    def drive(self):
        if self.running:
            print('Car is moving')
        else:
            print('Start the car first')

class Taxi(Car):
    def __init__(self):
        Car.__init__(self)
        self.passenger = None
        self.balance = 0.0

    def drive(self):
        print('Honk honk, out of the way')
        Car.drive(self)

    def hire(self, passenger):
        print('Hired by', passenger)
        self.passenger = passenger

    def pay(self, amount):
        print('Paid', amount)
        self.balance = self.balance + amount
        self.passenger = None

class Limo(Taxi):
    def __init__(self):
        Taxi.__init__(self)
        self.sunroof = 'closed'

    def drive(self):
        print('Limo driving in luxury')
        Car.drive(self)

    def pay(self, amount, big_tip):
        print('Paid', amount, 'Tip', big_tip)
        Taxi.pay(self, amount + big_tip)

    def pour_drink(self):
        print('Pouring drink')

    def open_sunroof(self):
        print('Opening sunroof')
        self.sunroof = 'open'

    def close_sunroof(self):
        print('Closing sunroof')
        self.sunroof = 'closed'
```

Trace through this code in your head, writing the output you expect below.

```python
car = Car()
taxi = Taxi()
limo = Limo()

car.start()
car.drive()

taxi.start()
taxi.hire('Kim')
taxi.drive()
taxi.pay(5.0)

limo.start()
limo.hire('Jenn')
taxi.drive()  ←—  Careful, this one
limo.pour_drink()        is a little
limo.pay(10.0, 5.0)      tricky.
```

Your output here ↴

```
Python 3.6.0 Shell

Car is moving

Hired by Kim

Honk honk, out of the way

Car is moving

Paid 5.0

Hired by Jenn

Honk honk, out of the way

Car is moving

Pouring drink

Paid 10.0 Tip 5.0

Paid 15.0

>>>
```

Exercise
Solution

Your turn to create a new class. How about a frisbee-catching dog? We've already created a `Frisbee` class for you:

```python
class Frisbee:
    def __init__(self, color):
        self.color = color

    def __str__(self):
        return "I'm a " + self.color + ' frisbee'
```

A Frisbee can't do much; it just has a color and a __str__ method so it prints well.

Your job is to help us finish the `FrisbeeDog`. It needs to catch a frisbee and give it back. It should have a `__str__` method as well.

```python
class FrisbeeDog(Dog):
    def __init__(self, name, age, weight):
        Dog.__init__(self, name, age, weight)
        self.frisbee = None

    def bark(self):
        if self.frisbee != None:
            print(self.name,
                  'says, "I can\'t bark, I have a frisbee in my mouth"')
        else:
            Dog.bark(self)

    def catch(self, frisbee):
        self.frisbee = frisbee
        print(self.name, 'caught a', frisbee.color, 'frisbee')

    def give(self):
        if self.frisbee != None:
            frisbee = self.frisbee
            self.frisbee = None
            print(self.name, 'gives back', frisbee.color, 'frisbee')
            return frisbee
        else:
            print(self.name, "doesn't have a frisbee")
            return None

    def __str__(self):
        str = "I'm a dog named " + self.name
        if self.frisbee != None:
            str = str + ' and I have a frisbee'
        return str
```

We have a simple constructor; it just sets a frisbee attribute. Notice frisbee here is another object, so some composition going on.

We're overriding the bark method. If the frisbee dog currently has a frisbee, then it can't bark; otherwise, it barks like any other dog.

The catch method takes a frisbee and assigns it to the object's frisbee attribute.

The give method sets the frisbee attribute to None, and then returns the frisbee.

And here's the str method, which conditionally prints based on whether the dog has a frisbee or not.

Exercise Solution

Override the `FrisbeeDog`'s `walk` method so that if a dog has a frisbee he says, "I can't walk, I'm playing Frisbee!" Otherwise, `FrisbeeDog` acts like a normal `Dog`. Go ahead and add the code to your ***dog.py*** file. Use the same test code as the last Test Drive.

```python
class FrisbeeDog(Dog):
    def __init__(self, name, age, weight):
        Dog.__init__(self, name, age, weight)
        self.frisbee = None

    def bark(self):
        if self.frisbee != None:
            print(self.name,
                    'says, "I can\'t bark, I have a frisbee in my mouth"')
        else:
            Dog.bark(self)

    def walk(self):
        if self.frisbee != None:
            print(self.name, 'says, "I can\'t walk, I\'m playing Frisbee!"')
        else:
            Dog.walk(self)

    def catch(self, frisbee):
        self.frisbee = frisbee
        print(self.name, 'caught a', frisbee.color, 'frisbee')

    def give(self):
        if self.frisbee != None:
            frisbee = self.frisbee
            self.frisbee = None
            print(self.name, 'gives back', frisbee.color, 'frisbee')
            return frisbee
        else:
            print(self.name, "doesn't have a frisbee")
            return None

    def __str__(self):
        str = "I'm a dog named " + self.name
        if self.frisbee != None:
            str = str + ' and I have a frisbee'
        return str
```

← Dog has a frisbee if self.frisbee is not equal to None.

← If the dog has a frisbee, then output that the dog is playing. Otherwise, do what all Dogs do by calling the superclass's walk method.

```
Python 3.6.0 Shell

Dude caught a red frisbee
Codie is walking
Jackson is walking
Rody is walking
Dude says, "I can't walk, I'm playing Frisbee!"
>>>
```

Coding Cross Solution

✳ *The Top Ten Topics* ✳ *(We Didn't Cover)*

We've covered a lot of ground, and you're almost finished with this book. We'll miss you, but before we let you go, we wouldn't feel right about sending you out into the world without a little more preparation. We can't possibly fit everything you'll need to know into this relatively small chapter. Actually, we *did* originally include everything you need to know about Python programming (not already covered by the other chapters), by reducing the type point size to .00004. It all fit, but nobody could read it. So we threw most of it away, and kept the best bits for this Top Ten appendix.

This really *is* the end of the book. Except for the index, of course (a must-read!).

#1 List comprehensions

You've seen how we can create a list of numbers using the `range` function in Python, but there is an even more powerful way to construct lists that is similar to the way mathematicians construct sets of numbers. We call them *list comprehensions* and they can construct lists of any type. Let's first look at an example with numbers:

```
[x + x for x in range(10)]
```

↑ Doubles every number in the range from 0 to 9

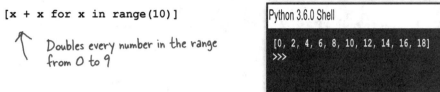

```
Python 3.6.0 Shell
[0, 2, 4, 6, 8, 10, 12, 14, 16, 18]
>>>
```

Or, how about an example with strings:

```
lyric = ['I', 'saw', 'heard', 'on', 'you', 'the', 'wireless', 'back', 'in', '52']
[s[0] for s in lyric]
```

Grabs the first letter of each word in the list lyric

```
Python 3.6.0 Shell
['I', 's', 'h', 'o', 'y', 't', 'w', 'b', 'i', '5']
>>>
```

Okay, but how does this actually work? Well, essentially a list comprehension creates a list from another list. To see how this works, let's look at the format of a list comprehension:

← Revisit the examples above with this formula in mind.

The first part is an expression that uses a variable that represents each item in the existing list.

We then have a for expression with the variable and the old list.

And finally, we have a conditional; we haven't seen one of these yet

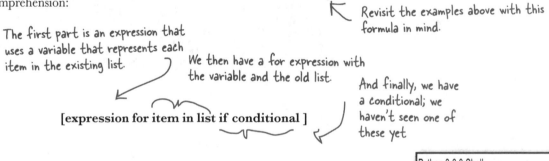

```
[expression for item in list if conditional ]
```

Here's how we can add a conditional to our example:

```
[s[0] for s in lyric if s[0] > 'm']
```

Only add the item to the list if it is a character greater than 'm'.

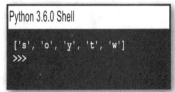

```
Python 3.6.0 Shell
['s', 'o', 'y', 't', 'w']
>>>
```

As with many things in this appendix, this will take some study to master, but you can see it is a powerful way to create new lists.

#2 Dates and times

Dates and times are an important part of many computations. You can import the Python `datetime` module like so:

```python
import datetime
```

Then you can create a `date` object by instantiating it with any date up until the year 9999 (or going to back to year 1):

Year, then month, then day

```python
my_date = datetime.date(2015, 10, 21)
```

Or you can create a `time` object by instantiating it with any time, providing hours, minutes, and seconds:

```python
my_time = datetime.time(7, 28, 1)
```
Hour, minutes, and seconds

Or combine them together with the `datetime` object:

Or combine them all together.

```python
my_datetime = datetime.datetime(2015, 10, 21, 7, 28, 1)
```

Let's print them all:

We can print each date and time object to see what it holds.

```python
print(my_date)
print(my_time)
print(my_datetime)
print(my_date.year, my_date.month, my_date.day)
print(my_time.hour, my_time.minute, my_time.second)
```

```
Python 3.6.0 Shell

2015-10-21
07:28:01
2015-10-21 07:28:01
2015 10 21
7 28 1
>>>
```

You can also get the current time with:

Notice you can get the current time down to microseconds.

```python
now = datetime.datetime.today()
print(now)
```

```
Python 3.6.0 Shell

2017-07-27 19:12:07.785931
```

Or use `datetime`'s formatting facilities:

```python
output = '{:%A, %B %d, %Y}'
print(output.format(my_date))
```
The date object supports a rich formatting language.

```
Python 3.6.0 Shell

Wednesday, October 21, 2015
```

That's just a start—in any language there's a lot to know about handling dates and times; check out the `datetime` and related modules in Python to dig deeper into this topic.

#3 Regular expressions

'ac*\dc?'

Remember all the trouble we had matching text that contained words and punctuation? We could have solved that problem using regular expressions. A *regular expression* is, formally, a grammar for describing patterns in text. For instance, using a regular expression (regex for short), you can write an expression that matches all text that starts with *t* and ends with *e*, with at least one *a* and no more than two *us* in between.

Regular expressions can get complex fast. In fact, they can seem like an alien language when you first encounter them. But you can get started with simple regular expressions fairly quickly, and if you like them, become a true expert.

You'll find regular expressions supported by most modern languages. Python is no exception. Here's how you use Python regular expressions:

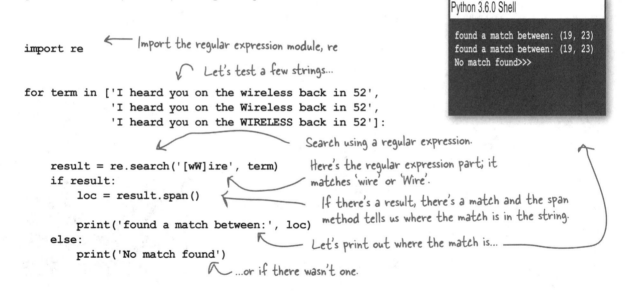

```
import re        ←── Import the regular expression module, re

                    ↙ Let's test a few strings...
for term in ['I heard you on the wireless back in 52',
             'I heard you on the Wireless back in 52',
             'I heard you on the WIRELESS back in 52']:

                              Search using a regular expression.
    result = re.search('[wW]ire', term)     Here's the regular expression part; it
    if result:                              matches 'wire' or 'Wire'.
        loc = result.span()                 If there's a result, there's a match and the span
                                            method tells us where the match is in the string.
        print('found a match between:', loc)
    else:                           Let's print out where the match is... ─────
        print('No match found')
                          ↖ ...or if there wasn't one.
```

Python 3.6.0 Shell

```
found a match between: (19, 23)
found a match between: (19, 23)
No match found>>>
```

In this example we used a very simple regular expression, but regular expressions are capable of matching sophisticated patterns—for example, valid usernames, passwords, and URLs. So, the next time you're about to write code to verify a valid username or something similar, pull out the regular expressions instead—a couple lines of regex could save you a lot of code.

Search is just one method provided by Python for matching strings with an expression. Python also has a sophisticated regex compiler in the `re` module you'll want to check out for intensive pattern matching applications.

The real key to understanding and using regular expressions is learning how to read and create patterns. To do that you'll want to study the general subject of regular expressions, and more specifically, the notation that Python uses for regular expressions.

#4 Other data types: tuples

Python lists have a sister data type we never told you about: tuples. Syntactically the two are almost identical. Check this out:

```
my_list = ['Back to the Future', 'TRON', 'Buckaroo Bonzai']
```

A Python list of movies—well, of strings, actually

```
my_tuple = ('Back to the Future', 'TRON', 'Buckaroo Bonzai')
```

A Python tuple of strings

So, what's the difference? Well, syntactically one uses square brackets and one use parentheses.

You also already know how to use them, for instance, in iteration:

```
for movie in my_list:
    print(movie)
for movie in my_tuple:
    print(movie)
```

Same output!

Python 3.6.0 Shell

```
Back to the Future
TRON
Buckaroo Bonzai
Back to the Future
TRON
Buckaroo Bonzai
```

And of course you can refer to the items in a tuple with an index too, like `my_tuple[2]`, which evaluates to `'Buckaroo Bonzai'`. Tuples even support most of the same methods as lists, so what's the difference? *Tuples are immutable*—meaning you can't change them like you can lists. Once you make a tuple, that's it, you're done—you can access its items, but you can't change them.

So why would you use them? Why do they exist? Because of what we call *time* and *space*; in other words, tuples take up less memory and you can operate on them faster than you can with lists. If you've got collections of items that are very large and/or you are computing lots of operations on them, then you may want to consider tuples, which can significantly improve both memory use as well as execution time.

It can also be computationally safer to work on data structures that can't change!

You'll also want to take a look at a few things you can do syntactically with tuples you can't do with lists:

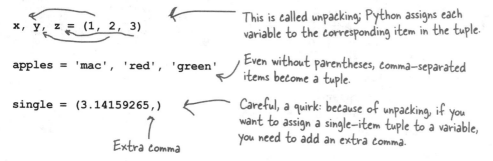

```
x, y, z = (1, 2, 3)
```

This is called unpacking; Python assigns each variable to the corresponding item in the tuple.

```
apples = 'mac', 'red', 'green'
```

Even without parentheses, comma-separated items become a tuple.

```
single = (3.14159265,)
```

Extra comma

Careful, a quirk: because of unpacking, if you want to assign a single-item tuple to a variable, you need to add an extra comma.

#5 Other data types: sets

There's another common data type we haven't discussed: sets. Do you remember sets from algebra class? You might recall sets have only one of each element value, and they have no order. You might also remember that common operations on sets include taking the union and intersection of one set with another. Well, Python has sets too; let's see what Python provides:

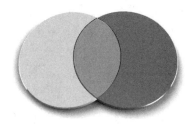

Sets are represented by comma-separated values enclosed in curly braces.

```python
set = {1, 3.14159264, False, 77}
```

Dictionaries have key/value pairs within curly braces, while sets have just values.

Sets can hold practically any Python type, but the values need to be unique.

Like lists, and unlike tuples, sets are mutable, meaning we can change them and add values to them:

```python
set.add(99)
```

Or remove them:

```python
set.remove(1)
```

And of course they provide more interesting methods we can use:

Python represents the empty list (having no items) as set().

```python
even = {2, 4, 6, 8, 10}
odd = {1, 3, 5, 7, 9}
prime = {1, 3, 5, 7}

even_and_prime = even.intersection(prime)
print(even_and_prime)

odd_and_prime = odd.intersection(prime)
print(odd_and_prime)

even_or_prime = even.union(prime)
print(even_or_prime)
```

```
Python 3.6.0 Shell

set()
{1, 3, 5, 7}
{1, 2, 3, 4, 5, 6, 7, 8, 10}
>>>
```

You can also check to see if a value is in a set with the familiar `if x in set` syntax. Check out the Python set documentation for even more interesting methods like set differences, symmetric differences, and supersets.

#6 Server-side coding

Many applications run as web services, providing services like Google search, social neworks, and ecommerce. These applications are powered by many different languages, including Python.

Learning server-side coding often requires familiarity with technologies such as the hypertext transport procotol (HTTP), HTML (a page markup language), and JSON (as we've seen, for data exchange), to name just a few. In addition, depending on the language you're working with, you'll most likely want to use a web framework or package. These packages provide functionality that takes care of many of the low-level details of serving web pages and data.

If you are working with Python, two of the more popular frameworks are Flask and Django.

Server-side code executes on a server on the internet.

request

Client-side code executes on the client—that is, on your computer.

```
@app.route("/")
def hello():
    return "Hello, Web!"
```

Here's a quick Flask example. With Flask we can route web traffic from the "root" (think home page) of a website to the function hello. Hello simply outputs a simple string.

Typically you'd output HTML or JSON here.

Flask is a small, more minimal framework aimed at smaller projects you want to get up and running quickly. Django is a much heavier-weight framework aimed at larger projects. As such, Django takes more time to learn but will do a lot more for you. Django provides page templating, forms, authentication, and a means to adminster databases. Because we'd guess you're just getting started in web development, so we'd recommend Flask as a place to start, and then upgrading to Django as your skills and needs increase.

Learning HTML and CSS is also a vital part of creating web pages. After Head First Learn to Code you're more than qualified to take on this book, and perhaps even Head First JavaScript Programming at the same time—JavaScript is the de facto standard for programming in the browser.

#7 Lazy evaluation

Say you wanted to write some code like this:

```
def nth_prime(n):
    count = 0
    for prime in list_of_primes():
        count = count + 1
        if count == n:
            return prime

def list_of_primes():
    primes = []
    next = 1
    while True:
        next_prime = get_prime(next)
        next = next + 1
        primes.append(next_prime)
    return primes
```

This code returns the nth prime number...

...from a list of primes.

We could generate an upper limit, say the first 1,000, but that could be very inefficient as well.

Clearly we can't really do this, because creating an infinite list of primes takes, literally, forever.

We'll leave this function as a homework assignment (or a quick Google search).

We can fix this code using a technique called *lazy evaluation* or *calculation on demand*, and in Python this is supported by something called a generator. Here's how we alter our code to create a generator:

```
def list_of_primes():
    next = 1
    while True:
        next_prime = get_prime(next)
        next = next + 1
        yield next_prime
```

We no longer need our primes array, so we've removed it.

Now each time we generate a new prime, we use the yield statement.

So what does `yield` do? A bit of magic. Think about it like this: in the `nth_prime` function we iterating over all the primes. When the `for` statement first calls `list_of_primes` and the `yield` statement is used, a generator is created (otherwise known as an iterator in many languages). The generator is an object that has one method, `next`, which can be called (behind the scenes in the case of the `for` statement) to get the next value. Each time `next` is called, the `list_of_primes` magically picks up computation where it last left off (computing the next prime) and as soon as the `yield` statement is invoked, it returns another value. This repeats as long as there are values being generated.

Lazy evaluation is a fascinating and powerful form of computation worth looking into more deeply.

#8 Decorators

Decorators come from an object-oriented design practice called design patterns. Python loosely implements the decorator pattern by allowing you to "decorate" functions with other functions. For instance, if you have a function that just returns some text, you could create a set of decorators that add things to that text, like HTML formatting. Say we wanted to easily add HTML paragraph tags to a piece of text. We could use decorators like this:

To make text a paragraph in HTML, we just start it with a <p> and end it with a </p>.

```python
def paragraph(func):
    def add_markup():
        return '<p>' + func() + '</p>'
    return add_markup


@paragraph
def get_text():
    return 'hello head first reader'


print(get_text())
```

We need to use our higher-order function knowledge here. First we're going to be passed a function, func, and then we'll create and return another function that surrounds whatever func returns, when called, with <p> and </p>.

Then we use the @ syntax to decorate another function, like get_text.

Now when get_text is called, it will be called within the decorator code, which causes the <p> and </p> tags to be added to whatever the get_text function returns.

As you can see, this can be a little mind-altering and probably gives you some indication that higher-order functions are worth studying.

Decorators are a powerful feature and can be used far beyond decorating text. In fact, you can add one or more decorators to any type of function that you'd like to give additional behavior to, without altering the original function.

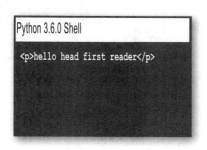

```
Python 3.6.0 Shell

<p>hello head first reader</p>
```

#9 Higher-order and first-class functions

You've come a long way in your understanding and use of functions. We've talked about functions as a way to abstract code, but there is so much further you can take them. In fact, you can do anything with a function that you can with other data types: you can assign a function to a variable, pass a function to another function, and even return a function from a function. When we can treat a function like any other object or data we call it *first class*, and when we either pass or return a function from another function, we call that a *higher-order* function. But what does it even mean to pass or return a function from a function?

Understanding higher-order functions is a topic worthy of some lengthy study; for now, whet your appetite with some code that demonstrates using functions in a higher-order manner.

```python
def pluralize(str):
    def helper(word):
        return word + "s"
    return helper(str)

val = pluralize('girl')
print(val)
```

Did you know you can declare a function within another function?

The helper function is only available within the pluralize function; no other code can call it.

The pluralize function uses helper to add an "s" onto a string.

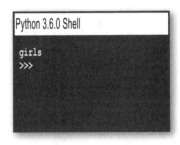

Okay, that's new, but let's make this truly *higher order*. Hang on to your hat:

```python
def addition_maker(n):
    def maker(x):
        return n + x
    return maker

add_two = addition_maker(2)

val = add_two(1)
print(val)
```

The function addition_maker takes a number n...

...and defines a function that takes another number, x, and adds n to it.

And then, it returns that function as the result of calling addition_maker.

So if we pass addition_maker the number 2, it returns a function, which here we assign to the variable add_two...

...that, when called, adds two to whatever it is passed, in this case the number 1.

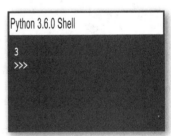

If that's a little hard to wrap your head around, welcome to the club. But, like recursion, with a little study and work, thinking in higher-order functions becomes second nature.

#10 A lot of libraries

We've seen a few Python libraries throughout this book, but there are many more built-in and third-party Python packages waiting for you. Here are a few to take a look at:

requests
This third-party package is worth mentioning again. If you need to make HTTP requests from your application, this is the package for you.

Flask, Django
You've seen these frameworks in passing as well. If you need to build server-side Python code, be sure to check out both. Flask tends to be for small-scale projects and Django for large applications, but both should serve you well.

sched
Need to execute code at specific times or on a schedule? The `sched` module is a standard Python module that allows you to create schedules and invoke code on that schedule.

logging
An upgrade from putting simple `print` statements in your code, the `logging` module is a built-in module that gives you a way to output informational warning or error messages. Even better, you can configure the type of messages that are output based on the type of execution (say, testing versus a production run of your code).

Pygame
Pygame is a library for writing video games. Pygame provides modules for dealing with game graphics as well as sound. If you're just starting to write games, this can be a great place to start.

Beautiful Soup
Data on the web isn't always available in JSON, and often you'll just need to grab a web page and sort through the HTML to find what you need. Unfortunately, many web pages contain poorly written HTML. The Beautiful Soup library tries to make all that easier and gives you a nice—no, beautiful—interface to web pages from Python.

Pillow
Pillow is an image library, with everything you need to read, write, and process many common image file formats. Pillow also provides support for displaying files and converting images to other formats.

You'll find a lot more at ***https://wiki.python.org/moin/UsefulModules***

I can't believe the book is almost over. Before you go, you really should read the index. It's great stuff. And after that you've always got the website. So I'm sure we'll see you again soon...

Don't worry, this isn't goodbye.

Nor is it the end. Now that you've got an amazingly solid foundation in learning to code, it's time to become a master. Point your browser to *http://wickedlysmart.com* to explore what's next!

What's next? So much more!

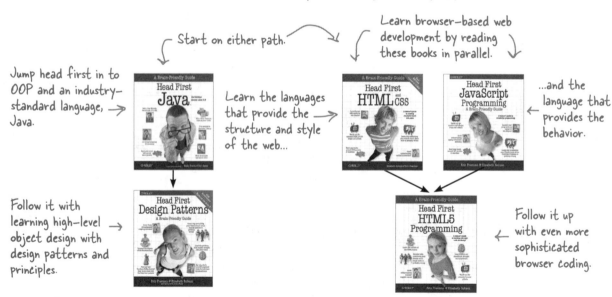

Start on either path.

Learn browser-based web development by reading these books in parallel.

Jump head first in to OOP and an industry-standard language, Java.

Learn the languages that provide the structure and style of the web...

...and the language that provides the behavior.

Follow it with learning high-level object design with design patterns and principles.

Follow it up with even more sophisticated browser coding.

Index

G

O